Inside Hitler's High Command

MODERN WAR STUDIES

Theodore A. Wilson
General Editor

Raymond A. Callahan
J. Gary Clifford
Jacob W. Kipp
Jay Luvaas
Allan R. Millett
Dennis Showalter
Series Editors

Inside Hitler's High Command

Geoffrey P. Megargee

Foreword by Williamson Murray

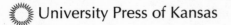 University Press of Kansas

Published by the University Press of Kansas (Lawrence, Kansas 66049), which was organized by the Kansas Board of Regents and is operated and funded by Emporia State University, Fort Hays State University, Kansas State University, Pittsburg State University, the University of Kansas, and Wichita State University.

Library of Congress Cataloging-in-Publication Data

Megargee, Geoffrey P., 1959–
   Inside Hitler's High Command / Geoffrey P. Megargee; foreword by Williamson
      Murray.
      p. cm. — (Modern war studies)
   Includes bibliographical references and index.
   ISBN 0-7006-1015-4 (alk. paper)
   1. Oberkommando der Wehrmacht. 2. World War, 1939–1945—Campaigns—Ger-
many. 3. Command of troops—Germany—History—20th century. 4. Germany—
Armed Forces—History—World War, 1939–1945. 5. Generals—Germany—
History—20th century. I. Title. II. Series.

   D757 .G339 2000
   940.54'213—dc21
                                                                    99-056340

British Library Cataloguing in Publication Data is available.

Printed in the United States of America
10 9 8 7 6 5 4 3 2 1

The paper used in this publication meets the minimum requirements of the American National Standard for Permanence of Paper for Printed Library Materials Z39.48-1984.

To

Ann Mohan Megargee
1922–91

Dr. Charles Burdick
1927–98

Contents

Foreword

Williamson Murray

The past two decades have seen a flood of works praising German military effectiveness on the battlefield. There is indeed a grain of truth behind such works, but in their claims that the German way of war is worthy of emulation they miss two important points. The first is that German military effectiveness depended to a great extent on the ideological commitment of troops and leaders. This factor played a significant role not only on the eastern front in the latter stages of the war, as Omar Bartov has demonstrated, but also in the Wehrmacht's early victories against Poland, Scandinavia, the Low Countries, and France. Thus, arguments about the efficacy of German tactical and operational virtuosity must also contain a recognition that German soldiers were willing to take extremely high casualties to accomplish their mission. For example, the lead companies in the crossing of the Meuse on 14 May 1940, which spearheaded the breakthrough by the 7th Panzer Division and XIX Panzer Corps, suffered upward of 70 percent casualties *but remained in the battle all the way south to Stonne* three days later. Such ideological commitment represented an important and incalculable factor in the German victories.

There is another and even more important point to be made about German military effectiveness, however. That has to do with the fact that when they unleashed a second great conflict in 1939, the Germans managed to repeat almost every major mistake that they had made in the First World War. How does one explain the mind-set of the high command and the strategic framework within which the Germans lost the war? How did the high command reach and implement its decisions? No one has answered these questions systematically before. This extraordinary book by Geoff Megargee fills that gap in the historical literature of the Second World War. Megargee not only examines the personalities involved in directing the war from the German side but also examines the intellectual framework within which the senior leaders calculated the military possibilities, as well as the structure and functioning of the organizations within which they operated.

It is a fascinating story, not least because it helps to dispel some long-held but inaccurate popular beliefs. When the war was over, not surprisingly since he was no longer around to defend his record, Hitler received virtually all the blame for Nazi Germany's catastrophic defeat. The generals and admirals enthusiastically blamed the Führer for the Reich's egregious strategic mistakes (and most of the operational mistakes as well). Yet, German strategic myopia was more than a matter of the pretensions of a former corporal who thought he was Napoleon.

After all, to cite perhaps the most obvious example, the decision to invade the Soviet Union in June 1941 occasioned no objections from the army and the Luftwaffe. In the latter case, there was considerable enthusiasm for the new adventure after the frustrations of the Battle of Britain and the night Blitz. The army's leadership delightedly threw itself into the problems associated with planning and then conducting a great land campaign. *Grossadmiral* Erich Raeder, commander of the Kriegsmarine, did come up with an alternative, the so-called Mediterranean strategy, which appeared late in the game and was never seriously considered. Moreover, one suspects that Raeder proposed his alternative to Operation *Barbarossa* more due to interservice politics than to any real strategic sense.

Six months after their invasion of the USSR, the Germans made their second and even greater strategic mistake. Hitler's declaration of war on the United States followed hard on the heels of the Japanese attack on Pearl Harbor. The German declaration received the enthusiastic support of the navy, which had been arguing strongly over the previous four months for such a course. Meanwhile, the army and the Luftwaffe, which were deeply enmeshed in the difficulties of the looming catastrophe on the eastern front, remained entirely disinterested in the matter. And to sum up the general strategic obliviousness of the German high command, none of the senior commanders or staff officers in Hitler's headquarters in East Prussia could point out where Pearl Harbor was, when the Führer inquired about its location.

Not surprisingly, the Germans also proved incapable of working with their allies in a fashion that contributed to the larger common good. To the German military leaders, allies were a nuisance that, at best, one could expect to do one's bidding without any concern for their own interests. The contrast with the Axis' opponents, particularly the Anglo-American alliance, could not be more graphic. This was a disadvantage that grew worse as the war proceeded.

The roots of such strategic blunders and command problems ran deep. On the one hand the Germans remained thorough prisoners of their own military culture, as well as being subject to the limitations of Central Europeans in understanding the wider world. They worshiped at the altar of operational maneuver to the exclusion of wider strategy. They seemed to believe that everything would fall into place if they could just win enough battles, but they failed to recognize the economic, political, or geographic limits on their ability to do so. Megargee's work provides both a background for these intellectual tendencies and a detailed description of their repercussions during the war itself.

In examining the German mentality, this work also lays out a clear explanation of the factors that contributed to the German failures in intelligence, personnel, and logistics. In the first case, works on the Allies' intelligence efforts have provided detailed accounts of the success of their code breaking (the Ultra factor) that contributed so significantly in the operational successes against the U-boats, in targeting the weak points in the German economy, and in identifying German operational intentions on the ground. Similarly, on the eastern front from Stalingrad on, the Soviets so successfully employed deception *(maskirovka)* that they virtually blinded German military intelligence, with catastrophic results for the Wehrmacht's conduct of operations. The Germans' systems—if such is the correct word—for personnel management and logistics showed similar flaws. Their manuever plans were often brilliant, but they suffered consistently from a lack of manpower and resources with which to bring those plans to a successful conclusion.

The less well known fact is that these German failures flowed from a general contempt for the supporting staff functions. The mentality of the German general staff and the officer corps, which reflected their deeply held values, placed intelligence, personnel management, and logistics at the bottom of the Wehrmacht's priorities. For a conflict in Central or Western Europe, this did not matter greatly, as the battles in 1939 and 1940 indicated. But when the war spread into a great continental struggle from the North Cape to the Mediterranean and from the Caribbean to Stalingrad, in which the Third Reich pitted itself against powers with global resource bases and vast industrial capabilities, the German military leadership was quite literally at sea.

Admittedly, one can argue that had the German generals considered these matters more coherently and intelligently, they would not have lasted for long in Adolf Hitler's government. But the crucial point here is that the German military leaders were a major part of the problem. Virtually never, whatever their disagreements with Hitler at the operational level, did the senior officers of the Wehrmacht disagree with the Führer's strategic assessments or show any understanding of the limits of their capabilities.

Another great flaw in the German high command was that the Germans fabricated a command structure that reflected and exacerbated their intellectual vulnerabilities. At the highest level, the structure made it impossible to weigh the wider strategic, political, and military factors that, in the end, determined the outcome of the Second World War. There were rarely any joint elements in which the services could evaluate the wider strategic issues. Instead, the so-called armed forces high command became a parallel operational entity to the army's headquarters, with its own theaters to manage and no authority over the navy, the Luftwaffe, the SS, or the Nazi Party organs within its sphere. In part this sad state of affairs was undoubtedly the result of the Führer's predilections. But the German senior military leaders, in their constant infighting and their obdurate opposition to any significant joint cooperation among the services at the highest level, deserve an equal portion of the blame.

In every respect Megargee has written an outstanding book about a topic that deserves careful attention. He has laid out for our examination the details of how the Germans ran the war. And the results of their direction, it is worth remembering, were a catastrophe not only for Germany but for Europe as well, and came perilously close to destroying Western civilization.

Preface

In December 1941, Major Claus Schenk Graf von Stauffenberg, a German General Staff officer who would later attempt to assassinate Adolf Hitler, told a class of new General Staff candidates, "Our high command organization in the Second World War is more idiotic than the most capable General Staff officer could invent, if he received the task to create the most senseless wartime high command structure he could."[1] Stauffenberg's remark highlights one of the fundamental contradictions in the history of the Third Reich: Germany conquered most of the European continent in two years and held off its enemies for more than another three, despite the fact that its high command was a chaotic mixture of competing agencies and personalities with a megalomaniac at its head. The problems within the command system were, in fact, much more widespread and serious than many people realize.

According to the popular view that emerged after the war, Adolf Hitler and a few men in his immediate circle led Germany to ruin, despite the superiority of its army and against consistent opposition from the General Staff. That latter organization has gone down in history as a monolithic, highly professional, and anti-Nazi entity that planned campaigns with machinelike efficiency even while it abhorred the regime it served. Like most myths, this one contains a kernel of truth. However, the situation that existed within the high command was much more complicated than the myth shows. True, Hitler was in complete control of strategy before the war even began, and his influence over operations grew as the war went on until his generals had little freedom of action. The departure of myth from reality is visible, though, in some widespread assertions and assumptions: that Hitler was always wrong and his generals right; that they opposed him consistently and correctly; and that the war would have gone in Germany's favor had the generals been in charge. The fact is that the German military leaders found themselves in a mess that was largely of their own making, and then, after Germany's defeat, the survivors used Hitler and his close associates as a body of entirely plausible scapegoats.

A particular set of historiographical circumstances made this myth possible. To begin with, the source material that touches on the topic is vast and complex. After the war, millions of pages of primary material came into the hands of historians: speeches, memorandums, private and official diaries, records, and orders. Scholars needed time to make sense of this material, and only a limited number of them had access to it; clear, accurate answers to even the simplest questions would only emerge over decades. The role that the surviving German military leaders played in the historical investigations exacerbated the problem. Their postwar memoirs, letters, interviews, and studies added to the sheer quantity of available material. Naturally, the answers they provided were often clearer and more comprehensive than those that the records provided, at least initially. Historians were understandably thrilled to have such a resource at their disposal; many secondary works relied heavily on the survivors' contributions. Those secondary works, as well as the survivors' memoirs, in turn found a large public, and so they gained the high ground for the historical debates that followed.

The problem in this series of developments was that the survivors' stories were flawed in many ways. The men who wrote them were not scholars and often did not have access to many of the original records. In many cases they also had much to hide. So, for reasons both innocent and insidious, their accounts constitute a mix of truth, half-truth, omission, and outright falsehood that is difficult to untangle. The task of separating fact from fiction involves careful comparison of the German leaders' accounts with each other and with the wartime documents. The process has been slow and painstaking.[2]

Thus the layperson who has wanted to form conclusions about the German high command has faced an almost impossible challenge. There has been no single, authoritative work on the subject, the memoirs are unreliable, and the other sources are often of questionable relevance or accuracy. Some of the general histories of the war, such as Gerhard Weinberg's *A World at Arms* and the series *Germany and the Second World War,* are as good as such works can be, but because of their scope they can only touch on our topic peripherally.[3] Some of the narrower works on specific military institutions, campaigns, or other themes are more relevant. The quality can be extremely spotty, however, and many of the best works are available only in German. The same is true of biographies. Some, such as Christian Hartmann's *Halder: Generalstabschef Hitlers 1938–1942,*[4] are scholarly works of high quality; others are little more than exercises in hero worship. In short, every source requires careful criticism, and any work that relies more on postwar accounts than on contemporary records is of little worth.[5] Few people have the time or skills necessary to make a balanced judgment.

The goal of this book is to correct that situation by examining the evolution and workings of the high command in detail. The topic is a complicated one. It comprises a multitude of factors that interacted synergistically over the course of years, with roots that go back for centuries. Thus in order to answer the study's basic question—how did the system work?—one has to look at a number of overlapping questions:

What was the balance of political power within the high command? What struggles went on, and how did they affect the command's structure and its ability to function?

What role did individual personalities play in the effectiveness of the command and in its organizational development?

What were the Germans' fundamental ideas regarding war, strategy, and command? How did these ideas affect the structure and functioning of the command system? How did they interact with National Socialist ideology?

What was the day-to-day routine within the high command? How did information flow? How did the key players reach and implement decisions? How did their physical environment and the demands of their work affect their perceptions and abilities?

How did the logistics, personnel management, and military intelligence systems fit into the planning process?

What structural changes did the command undergo, and what were their effects? What forces drove those changes, and how did the changes come about?

How did the command react to the changing circumstances of the war?

As a framework within which to answer those questions, this book will focus on strategic and operational decision making, for two reasons. First, the sources and analysis are richest in those areas and thus offer the most complete picture. Second, the strategic and operational decisions were arguably the most important that the command made. Some explanation of those terms is a prerequisite.[6] Strategy is the realm of thought and action that is concerned with war in its broadest context. In other words, strategy is the way in which the nation uses military force to achieve its political goals. Strategic planning defines the timing, targets, and purposes of war. The decision to invade Poland in September 1939 was strategic, for example. Such a decision involves calculation of the risks involved, of society's ability to support military action, and of the military's capability to execute the strategy successfully.

Operational planning steps in where that last element of strategic planning leaves off. At the operational level, military leaders plan campaigns to achieve strategic goals. They must take into account the nature of those strategic goals; their own force structure and military doctrines; the strengths, weaknesses, and plans of the enemy; and the geographic and climatic factors in the area where they will be operating. Military intelligence, logistical planning, and personnel management play important roles at this level. The campaign by which the Germans conquered Poland, which entailed deep penetration of the enemy lines at chosen points by mobile forces with air support, with the object of disrupting the enemy's command system and surrounding and destroying his combat elements, fell within the realm of operations.

Although these two levels of warfare are different, they do interact, and not just in the planning phase of a war or campaign. Certainly strategic goals, which themselves have their roots in political, economic, and even social considerations, help to determine operational plans, but operations also affect strategy. Hitler pressed for a campaign against the west in the autumn of 1939, immediately after Poland fell, because he believed that, with time, the Allies would grow stronger and Germany weaker. His generals, on the other hand, believed that an early attack would fail because the army was not ready. Both sides in the debate knew that the outcome of the campaign would have serious strategic consequences. Success would allow Germany to turn east for the next strategic step. Failure might doom the nation to a war of attrition that Germany was ill equipped to fight. Thus operational capability affects the calculations upon which a nation bases its strategy; the progress of a campaign can change those calculations, and thus the nation's strategy, in the middle of the conflict.

In order to answer the questions I have posed as fully as possible within the strategic and operational realms and still keep the length of the work within reasonable bounds, I have had to make several compromises in terms of scope. First and foremost, for the purposes of this work I am defining the term "high command" to include the following elements: Hitler and his immediate circle of advisers; the Armed Forces High Command (Oberkommando der Wehrmacht, or OKW) with its principal military planning element, the Armed Forces Command Staff (Wehrmachtführungsstab); and the Army High Command (Oberkommando des Heeres, or OKH), with its core group, the Army General Staff (Generalstab des Heeres). Problems of space and time precluded an examination of the Luftwaffe's and the navy's command structures in similar detail. Likewise, I have had to make some harsh judgments regarding those headquarters elements that did not play a direct role in strategy or operations. There was no space to investigate many areas such as armaments planning or the weapons inspectorates, for example.

Even within these limits, however, the subject remains enormously complex, and, as with all but the most basic historical investigations, the effort to present a seamless, readable, and complete narrative introduces distortion. The reality was not neat. The people in the high command made many of their decisions on a day-to-day basis, without complete information, and often under stress. End results came about because of simultaneous action on the part of many individuals, combined with a plethora of outside factors, over a lengthy period. Historians simultaneously benefit from hindsight and suffer from incomplete knowledge, but they must nonetheless place everything in a coherent package to make the whole understandable; thus they cannot mirror reality exactly. With all that said, however, the only possibility is to plunge ahead while bearing the problems in mind. There is still plenty of room for valid insights, after all.

The chapter organization reflects what I hope will be an acceptable balance between chronological and topical approaches. The work begins with an introduction to the major trends in the development of the German command system up to 1933. The next two chapters deal with the prewar Nazi era, in which the armed forces and Hitler laid the foundation for aggressive war. Chapters 4 and 5 address the first two years of that war, with emphasis on the crucial strategic decisions that all but determined the course of the conflict thereafter. Chapters 6 and 7 use the planning for Operation *Barbarossa,* the invasion of the Soviet Union, as a frame within which to examine the support functions—intelligence, logistics, and personnel—that were the Germans' Achilles' heel in the operational realm. Chapter 8 is a detailed account of one week in the life of the high command, a glimpse into the work patterns and decision-making processes of the two main headquarters. The following three chapters cover the rest of the war, but their focus is different from that in the earlier chapters. Strategic and even operational decisions became less and less important as the war went on, and so the emphasis in the closing chapters is on other factors that illustrate the growing problems in the high command, especially the internecine battles for resources and the increasing influence of the Nazi Party.

I see this project as essentially synthetic in nature. Those who specialize in studying the German armed forces will, I suspect, find few major surprises in these pages. Certainly, I offer no radically new interpretation of the war as a whole. The primary value of the work lies in the fact that it draws together information that has been scattered throughout a large number of sources, many of them in German, up until now. My goal is to present the reader with the most up-to-date information and thus correct some of the myths and errors that have sprung up in the last fifty-odd years. The result is, I hope, a picture of the German high command that is both more accurate and subtly more complete than that which a reader could acquire by studying the sources individually, even if he or she had the time and expertise. The whole was more than the sum of the parts, and one must examine it accordingly. To the extent that I have done so in a form that the average educated person will find clear, readable, and informative, I have achieved my objective.

This study could quite simply never have reached completion without the help of a great many people. Pride of place must go to the late Charles Burdick, who suggested the topic for a master's thesis, guided my first stumbling efforts, and continued to be a source of advice and encouragement until his death. My adviser at Ohio State University, Williamson Murray, encouraged me to turn the thesis into a dissertation, honed my analytical skills, helped me to improve my writing, and provided a wealth of good advice on sources and interpretations. I am also especially grateful to Jürgen Förster of the Militärgeschichtliches Forschungsamt in Potsdam for the invaluable help he has given me over the years, as well as for the hospitality and friendship he has extended to me during my trips to Germany. The same is true for Professor Bernd Martin of the Albert-Ludwigs-Universität Freiburg, who sponsored me during my Fulbright grant, allowed me to attend his weekly colloquium for graduate students, and tolerated my halting attempts at academic German. I would also like to thank the many colleagues and friends who have provided valuable suggestions at various points in the work's genesis: Alan Beyerchen, Wilhelm Deist, Robert Doyle, Oliver Griffin, Mark Grimsley, John Guilmartin, Russell Hart, Christian Hartmann, Timothy Hogan, Kelly McFall, Richard Megargee, Manfred Messerschmidt, Allan R. Millett, Heinrich Schwendemann, Dennis Showalter, Gerhard Weinberg, and David Zabecki.

My sincere thanks also to the Fulbright-Kommission in Bonn and the United State Information Agency for the Fulbright grant that supported my research in Germany. The staff at the Bundesarchiv-Militärarchiv in Freiburg was of immense help during my time there; they truly establish a standard by which we should measure all such institutions. Thanks as well to Rolf-Dieter Müller and Hans-Erich Volkmann of the Militärgeschichtliches Forschungsamt, who invited me to a conference on the Wehrmacht in September 1997 at which I picked up many valuable insights. The staff of The Ohio State University Libraries has always been courteous, helpful, and knowledgeable. I would also like to thank the Department of History at The Ohio State University, both for the graduate associateship that made my studies possible and for the Ruth Higgins Research Fellowship that facilitated the completion of my dissertation in the summer of 1998.

Special thanks go to General a.D. Johann Adolf Graf Kielmansegg and General a.D. Ulrich de Maizière for taking the time to meet with me and answer questions about their service with the General Staff before and during the Second World War. Both men provided invaluable background material that was available nowhere else.

A host of others have helped in innumerable ways, often without even knowing. To my friends in Germany and the United States, thank you.

Last, but really most, my thanks go to my father, Anthony Scherer Megargee, who, in addition to providing much-needed material support, inspired the twin loves of history and language that have brought me this far.

These people deserve a great deal of the credit for whatever is good in this work. The errors are mine alone.

Abbreviations

The reader should be aware that in practice some abbreviations varied from document to document, for example, WFA might be W.F.A., gK.Chefs might be gK.Ch. or g.Kdos. Chefs., and so on.

Abt.	*Abteilung:* branch (also used for "battalion" and "unit" in other contexts outside of this book)
Abt. L	Abteilung Landesverteidigung: National Defense Branch
a. D.	*ausser Dienst:* retired
ADAP	*Akten zur deutschen auswärtigen Politik* (see bibliography)
Ausb.-Abt.	Ausbildungsabteilung: Training Branch
BA-MA	*Bundesarchiv-Militärarchiv* Freiburg
Bd.	*Band:* volume (i.e., of a book or journal)
Betr.	*Betreffend:* regarding
DRZW	*Das Deutsche Reich und der Zweite Weltkrieg* (see bibliography)
FHO	Fremde Heere Ost: Foreign Armies East
FHq	*Führerhauptquartier:* Hitler's headquarters
FHW	Fremde Heere West: Foreign Armies West
GAHC	*The German Army High Command, 1939–1945* (see bibliography)
geh.	*geheim:* secret
Gen d Inf	*General der Infanterie* (or *Artillerie,* etc.)
GenQu	*Generalquartiermeister:* the chief supply officer in the General Staff
GenLt	*Generalleutnant*
GenMaj	*Generalmajor*
GenStdH	Generalstab des Heeres: General Staff of the Army
GFM	*Generalfeldmarschall*

gK.Chefs	*geheime Kommandosachen-Chefsachen:* (the highest routine security classification)
GMS	*German Military Studies* (see bibliography)
GZ	Generalstab-Zentralabteilung: the General Staff's Central Branch
H.Dv.	*Heeresdienstvorschrift:* army regulation
HGr	*Heeresgruppe:* army group
HQu	*Hauptquartier:* headquarters
Ia	An operations officer in an army group or lower headquarters, or assistant chief of a branch of the General Staff, OKH
I.A.	*"im Auftrag":* by order of
Ib	A supply officer
Ic	An intelligence officer
i.G.	*"im Generalstabsdienst":* in General Staff service; denotes a member of the General Staff
IM	Staff I, group *"Mitte"* in the Operations Branch of the General Staff; handled affairs for Army Group Center; similarly, IS *(Süd)* and IN *(Nord).*
KTB	*Kriegstagebuch:* war diary
L	(See Abt.L)
LdsBef	Abteilung Landesbefestigungen: Fortifications Branch
MGFA	Militärgeschichtliches Forschungsamt: Research Institute for Military History, Potsdam, Germany
N	*Nachlass:* personal papers
NAMP	National Archives Microfilm Publication
Nr.	*Nummer:* number
NS	*Nationalsozialistisch*
ObdH	Oberbefehlshaber des Heeres: commander in chief of the army
ObdW	Oberbefehlshaber der Wehrmacht
o.D.	*ohne Datum:* no date
OKH	Oberkommando des Heeres: Army High Command
OKL	Oberkommando der Luftwaffe
OKM	Oberkommando der Marine
OKW	Oberkommando der Wehrmacht
OpAbt	*Operationsabteilung*
OQu	*Oberquartiermeister:* assistant chief of staff
OrgAbt	*Organisationsabteilung*
Qu	*Quartiermeister:* supply
PA	Personalamt: Personnel Office (sometimes HPA for Heerespersonalamt)
RH	(designates army records in BA-MA)
RL	(designates air force records in BA-MA)
RM	(designates navy records in BA-MA)
RW	(designates OKW records in BA-MA)

SA	Sturmabteilung
SD	Sicherheitsdienst
Skl	*Seekriegsleitung:* the navy's topmost operational planning element
SS	Schutzstaffen
T	*Truppenamt* (usually followed by a branch number)
WA	Wehrmachtamt: Armed Forces Office
WB	*Wehrmachtbefehlshaber:* armed forces (joint) commander
WFA	Wehrmachtführungsamt: Armed Forces Command Office
WFSt	Wehrmachtführungsstab: Armed Forces Command Staff
WNV	Abt.Wehrmachtnachrichtenverbindung: Armed Forces Communications Branch
WPr	*Wehrmachtpropaganda Abteilung*
WZ	Wehrmachtzentralabteilung: Armed Forces Central Branch

1

The Roots of the German
Command System

The German high command did not simply appear out of a vacuum in 1933, of course. Hitler inherited the product of an evolutionary process that had been going on in the military for over a century. That product included structural, cultural, and intellectual elements, some understanding of which is essential in order to make sense of later developments. The structural element comprised a military bureaucracy that the Prussians had created in order to plan and direct military operations more effectively. The culture was that of the General Staff, which had emerged as a powerful institution in the nineteenth century and had come to dominate the army in the years after the First World War. Its patterns of behavior, its collective needs and ambitions, and its beliefs regarding war, authority, and staff work would shape the military's capabilities and intentions. Finally, the Germans arrived at their own unique ideas about military policy, strategy, and operations, ideas that would help to determine the nature and course of the Second World War. Together, the structures, culture, and ideas offered strengths and weaknesses, advantages and disadvantages. They inform the themes that dominate this work, for the simple reason that they largely explain the Third Reich's initial successes and ultimate defeat.

THE STRUCTURE

In the last quarter of the nineteenth century, some wag coined an aphorism that has proved irresistible to historians. As the saying went, Europe contained five perfect institutions: the Roman curia, the British Parliament, the Russian ballet, the French opera, and the Prussian General Staff. For all its hyperbolic catchiness, its significance actually comes from the kernel of truth it contains. In the case of the General Staff, this was the first bureaucratic body in history that developed military plans in peacetime and saw to their execution in war, and it had just played a critical role in the original unification of the German Reich.[1] Another point worth noting is that, of the five institutions, the General Staff was by far the newest. The Prussians created it against the background of the political, industrial, and military revolutions that had been sweeping Europe since the 1790s, and its structure reflected other organizational models that emerged as the nineteenth century progressed. It would eventually become the dominant force in the German command structure, but only after a long and difficult series of bureaucratic battles. Thus two parallel structural trends emerged in the first century of the staff's history: the evolution of its internal organization and that of the larger Prusso-German command apparatus.[2]

The origins of these trends go back at least to a series of memorandums that a Prussian officer, Christian von Massenbach, wrote as the eighteenth century drew to a close. He suggested that the state ministries of foreign affairs, war, and commerce consult with one another regarding means and objectives for war. A General Staff would draft war plans ahead of time, using the ministries' guidance, information on potential enemies and theaters of war, and expertise built up through systematic exercises and the study of military history. Some staff officers, meanwhile, would serve with troop units in order to gain practical experience and to advise their commanders. Massenbach's ideas gained some credibility during the wars against Napoleon, and by 1824 the General Staff had grown to twenty-nine officers in three sections, each of which had a different geographic area of focus.

The staff gained little in terms of authority or capabilities over the next thirty peaceful years, but changes began with the rise of Helmuth von Moltke to the position of chief in 1857.[3] Among other things, he incorporated the telegraph and railroad into Prussian mobilization planning. His and the staff's performance in the Wars of Unification (against Denmark in 1864, Austria in 1866, and France in 1870–71) confirmed the utility of the bureaucratic system for planning and directing campaigns. The organization's size and authority grew steadily over the following decades. By 1914 the Great General Staff, as it was then known, comprised twenty-one branches, manned by over three hundred officers. Standardized working procedures regulated its activities and those of the staffs below it. Its officers had become a world-renowned military elite.

The bureaucratic order within the General Staff found no counterpart, however, at the policy and strategy levels above it, where ill-defined spheres of authority and bureaucratic competition were the norm. Until 1914 the competition centered on the person of the kaiser. Chancellors, war ministers, heads of military cabinets, chiefs of the General Staff, and other high-ranking officers of all sorts vied for the ruler's ear and for whatever independence they could create for themselves and their organizations. Under Wilhelm II, no fewer than forty army and eight naval officers had the right of immediate access to him. Administrative authority, including recruiting, armaments planning, and budgets, remained separate from command authority, which dealt with the military's organization, doctrine, and employment. There was no unified high command or system of committees that would allow policy makers and military strategists to consider the relevant issues within a structured environment. This organizational chaos was one of the root causes behind Germany's entry into war in 1914 and its subsequent defeat.[4]

In the First World War the General Staff reached the peak of its power. Its wartime authority gave it control of operations and strategy from the start. Then in 1916, in the aftermath of massive losses that the Germans had suffered at Verdun and the Somme, Field Marshal Paul von Hindenburg and Lieutenant General Erich Ludendorff took over command and launched ambitious plans to centralize control of the German economy in the War Ministry and the General Staff, both of which they controlled. Thus began the so-called era of war socialism. The General Staff, which until this point had remained largely isolated from society, now had to somehow direct that society in order to obtain the men, equipment, weapons, and munitions it needed to prosecute the war. Soon the staff was involved with such diverse matters as industrial and food production, raw materials allocation, politico-military affairs, the press, films, and propaganda. In addition, Ludendorff had schemes in mind that would have involved the staff in every facet of German society, including education, housing, and even birth rates and the control of venereal disease.[5] In the end, though, these plans came to naught; the war's problems did not prove amenable to organizational solutions.

The Versailles treaty of 1919 dictated that Germany abolish the General Staff, which the Allies saw as a font of Prussian militarism as well as a formidable planning organ. On paper this was a severe blow to the German command system. The reality was not quite what it appeared to be, however. The Germans kept the core of the General Staff, including planning, organization, and intelligence elements, in the guise of the so-called Truppenamt, or Troops Office, within the Defense Ministry's Army Directorate (Heeresleitung). Other elements, such as the military history branch, split off but remained in being under other agencies. With these organizations in place, the Germans could continue to carry out the same functions that the General Staff had performed before the war.

There was no denying the fact that, even in its disguised form, the General Staff had lost some of its former political power. The new republic's president, a civilian, was the commander in chief of the armed forces. A defense minister watched over the Army and Navy Directorates; he had to answer to both the president and the federal parliament, the Reichstag. The Army Directorate had its own chief (Chef der Heeresleitung), who supervised five

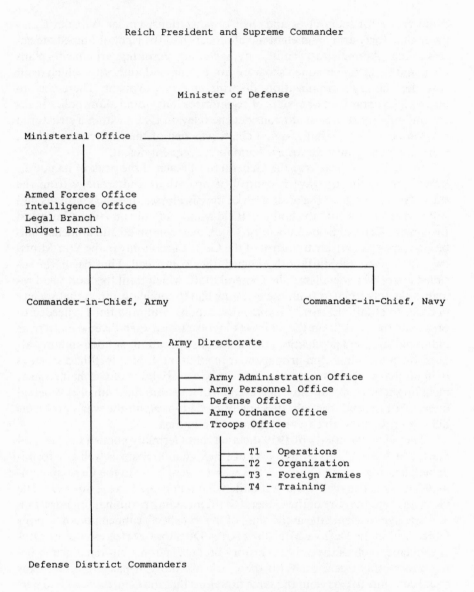

Figure 1. The German high command, 1920–1935.

offices, including the Truppenamt. So, from being a military dictator in all but name during the war, the chief of the General Staff had fallen to a position four links down in the chain of command—but, here again, the change was not so drastic as it appeared. For one thing, the republican government depended upon the army to maintain order; the General Staff, in the person of

Lieutenant General Wilhelm Groener, had struck a bargain to that effect with the regime in the first hours after the latter's birth. And Hans von Seeckt, the chief of the Truppenamt from July 4, 1919, was able to oversee the transition to the post-Versailles era and ensure that the General Staff's influence, if less than in 1917, would still be greater than it had ever been before the war. Not only did he direct the General Staff's transition into the Truppenamt, but he also saw to it that General Staff officers would dominate the Reichsheer's officer corps.[6]

Seeckt's influence increased when he became chief of the Army Directorate in 1920, and the extent of that influence signaled that the state's problems with its military command structure had not disappeared, even if that structure appeared more rational. Seeckt insisted that the Reichswehr remain outside of party politics, but he pursued his own policy initiatives and achieved surreptitiously what he could not gain through more legitimate means. He stubbornly resisted any form of political control, and he pushed the defense minister to the margins of policy formulation. After Seeckt left office in 1926, the balance of power swung back toward the Defense Ministry, but the basic fact of competition between the ministry and the Army Directorate had not changed.[7] Not even the rise of a former General Staff officer—Groener—to the position of defense minister in 1928 eliminated the competition. The Germans had still not succeeded in parceling out authority in such a way that the government and the army could speak with one voice. In part this was an indication that structural changes are of only limited utility in eliminating discord within a bureaucratic system. Only a change in the culture of the General Staff could have improved the situation to any significant degree, and no such change was forthcoming.

THE CULTURE

Seeckt's success at giving the General Staff a dominant position within the small, exclusive Reichsheer officer corps meant that the staff's own particular culture, which was already a foundation stone of German officer identity, would continue to shape the army during the Reichswehr era and under the Nazi regime. That culture remained fundamentally unchanged from the 1890s onward, just when the later Wehrmacht's most influential members were entering service. It comprised a set of values and practices that gave the German army some of its greatest strengths and most telling weaknesses.

In the German army, and especially in the General Staff, officers were a functional elite. The system selected them on the basis of demonstrated qualities, which it then further refined: a balance of intellectual prowess and strength of personality. They learned to plan carefully, issue clear orders, delegate authority, and use initiative.[8] The process by which the General

Staff selected and educated its member officers was central in maintaining the staff's cultural continuity. An examination of that process reveals, first of all, a conflict between two fundamentally different approaches.

Since the process of professionalization began in the Prussian officer corps in the nineteenth century, a debate had been going on between those who believed that officers should develop their intellects and those who believed that moral factors were more important.[9] By the second half of the century, the former group was clearly winning. Candidates for the officer corps faced stringent educational requirements, and those for the General Staff were even tougher. Gerhard Johann von Scharnhorst, the great military reformer of the Napoleonic era, had provided the initial impetus for this idea, but his educational reforms had not lasted.[10] Moltke the Elder instituted a more rigorous, and long-lived, educational system in the late 1850s. Candidates had to attend the War Academy (the Kriegsakademie, which the General Staff controlled after 1872), perform acceptably during two years of probationary duty with the staff, and then participate in a staff exercise under the chief himself; only a select few passed all the hurdles.

Since Moltke's time, in keeping with their emphasis on professional education, the Germans had concentrated more and more on an intellectual, "scientific" approach to war. The social composition of the General Staff reflected this approach. The staff was a meritocracy in which the traditional source of officers—the nobility—steadily lost ground. By 1913 fully half of the General Staff's officers came from the middle classes.[11] However, the traditional Prussian aristocratic values, which had dominated the officer corps for more than two centuries, did not die out, even in the minds of most "intellectual" officers. In keeping with those values, the army emphasized the need for "character" in its leaders. This was an ill-defined but important quality that would allow an officer to function effectively in battle, and it remained a consideration up through the Second World War. "Character" included such attributes as endurance, decisiveness, levelheadedness, drive, discipline, obedience, and loyalty.[12]

A strong link existed between the debate over the relative importance of intellect and character, on the one hand, and the German understanding of warfare, on the other. In many respects that understanding essentially mirrored the ideas of the great military theorist Carl von Clausewitz, even though few officers had read his works.[13] In Clausewitz's view, war is an inherently chaotic but not entirely random phenomenon, a "messy mix of order and unpredictability."[14] That is, both laws and chance govern war, and "only those general principles and attitudes that result from clear and deep understanding can provide a *comprehensive* guide to action."[15] Part of that understanding would have to come from study, Clausewitz knew; he was one of the original proponents of officer education. He also saw, however, that no amount of study could prepare an officer for combat completely. There are no hard-and-fast rules that can reduce war to a mechanical exercise, and so would remain an essential qualification for an officer.

Thus the outcome of the debate over the relative merits of intellect and character represented a working compromise in which both remained important. In other words, the Germans believed that both intellect and character informed the "general principles and attitudes" that Clausewitz said could provide a guide to action. They eventually brought those principles and attitudes together under the heading *"Kriegführung"*: the conduct of war. The manual *Truppenführung (Troop Command)* characterized that symbiosis when it defined *Kriegführung* as "an art, a free, creative activity based upon scientific principles. 'The lessons of *Kriegführung* . . . cannot be treated exhaustively in a manual. The principles, such as they are, must be usable in light of the circumstances.'"[16] An officer needed both intellect and instinct; he needed to be able to think *and* act. The manual explained, "The worth of the man remains, despite technology, decisive; his significance has grown with the dispersion of combat. The emptiness of the battlefield demands independently thinking and acting combatants who think over, then decisively and boldly take advantage of every situation, infused with the conviction that success depends upon them."[17] The 1939 edition of the *Handbook for General Staff Duty in War* expanded upon the concept:

> The General Staff officer should possess strength of character and a sense of tact in the highest measure.
>
> Clear, creative thinking and logically consistent action; calm consideration; determined vigor; untiring capacity for work; firmness with himself; and physical health: these things must distinguish him. A comradely closeness with the troops and a never-resting concern for their needs belong to his foremost duties.
>
> He must feel the pulse of the troops in order to properly evaluate their capabilities when he advises his commander. His esteem among the troops is an unmistakable measure of his effectiveness.
>
> Foresighted vision in the uncertainty of war and the unbendable will to deny the initiative to the enemy should govern his thinking and his advice.[18]

Perhaps Moltke summed up the concept best, however, when he wrote, "Great successes presuppose bold risk-taking. But careful thought must precede the taking of risks."[19]

Obviously the Germans expected a lot of their officers. Intellect and character are difficult to find, all the more so in combination. The General Staff did its best to screen for both as part of the selection process. Each applicant to the War Academy had to take an examination and also submit a letter from his commanding officer that would attest to the strength of his personality. For the successful applicants, the training and education at the War Academy attempted to develop their intellectual and behavioral attributes further. (The development of General Staff officers depended upon both education, that is, the imparting of specialized knowledge, and training, that is, the development of skills, habits, and attitudes.) The training aimed to instill common habits of mind, the ability to communicate clearly, and creativity within the framework of a standardized decision-making process. The goal was to develop a way of thinking, a *Gedankengang,* rather than a patterned response to a given situation. Some exercises specifically required officers to deviate from their orders, so that they would develop a sense of initiative.[20] Following their time at the War Academy, the candidates entered into a probationary period with the General Staff, one of the goals of which was to see how well they could stand up to the stress of staff work—an essential element of "character."[21] This double emphasis, on intellect and character, continued to mark General Staff selection, education, and training right though the Weimar era.[22]

Several key principles and practices helped to define the culture of the Prusso-German officer corps and especially the General Staff. One of these was the practice of "command by directive," that is, the encouragement of initiative within a defined set of mission parameters. In the early nineteenth century, Scharnhorst and his co-reformer, August Neidhardt von Gneisenau, recognized that a senior commander could no longer be completely familiar with the situation that each of his subordinates faced, and so they promoted the idea that orders should indicate objectives while leaving subordinates the widest possible latitude in deciding how to achieve them. At the same time, they began training lower-ranking officers to exercise initiative in fulfilling the commander's intent, all the while maintaining close coordination with adjoining units and higher headquarters.[23] Moltke made the practice standard during his tenure, and at one point he recorded some advice that later military leaders would have done well to heed: "The advantage that a commander believes he can achieve through continued intervention is usually only an apparent one. By doing so he takes over an activity that other people are meant to carry out, more or less destroys their effectiveness as well, and multiplies his own tasks to such an extent that he can no longer fulfill them completely."[24]

In the First World War the Germans extended the "command by directive" principle by granting exceptional powers to relatively junior officers because of their demonstrated ability or knowledge of a particular situation. The wartime careers of two officers, Georg Bruchmüller and Fritz von Lossberg, illustrate how this principle worked. Bruchmüller, who began his war career as a major on temporary active duty and never rose above brevet colonel, nonetheless attracted the attention of a succession of superiors with his artillery tactics. By spring 1918 he had de facto control of all the artillery in Crown Prince Wilhelm's army group—a position that usually merited the rank of lieutenant general.[25] Colonel Lossberg was similarly junior, but he was one of Germany's foremost experts on defensive warfare. He eventually became a sort of one-man fire brigade; the Supreme Army Command placed him as a corps or army chief of staff in whatever sector was in the greatest danger. Once there, he enjoyed a uniquely German kind of command authority: *Vollmacht,* the right to issue directives in a superior's name.[26] Moreover, Lossberg stipulated that a commander on the scene of an enemy attack would have control of a reinforcing unit, no matter what the rank of that unit's commander. That innovation eventually became doctrine throughout the army.[27]

Another uniquely German principle of command grew out of the practice of assigning staff officers to field commanders.[28] The practice began in the early nineteenth century, with two goals in mind. One was to give staff officers a better understanding of warfare at the lower levels, so that their orders would not become unrealistic. The other was to use those officers, who shared a common outlook and education, to give the army command structure a degree of doctrinal uniformity that would not otherwise exist. In support of that second goal, the Prussians created the so-called principle of joint responsibility, which held that a chief of staff was equally responsible, along with the commander, for all command decisions. Therefore, a staff officer had a duty—not just an option—to voice any disagreement he had with his commander's plans and to record his objections in writing. This principle dovetailed with an informal staff network that paralleled the formal chain of command.[29] If a staff officer was not satisfied with his commander's actions, he had the right to report his objections to the next higher chief of staff and, if necessary, all the way up to the chief of the General Staff himself. If the more senior staff officer agreed with the objection, he could enlist the aid of his commander to bring the subordinate commander into line. This system took on the name *Generalstabsdienstweg* (General Staff channel). Its goal was to "ensure the spiritual unity of the General Staff and enable it to assert its will against difficult or reluctant army commanders."[30]

The principle of joint responsibility was a boon to both the Prusso-German army and the General Staff well into the twentieth century. The principle did not eliminate a staff officer's duty to obey his commander, who had the ultimate power of decision. In fact, historians who have addressed this issue agree that staff officers rarely recorded their objections or appealed up through the staff channels. The model for the relationship between a commander and his chief of staff was a marriage; they might not always agree, but they usually worked out their disagreements quietly and privately.[31] However, the principle of joint responsibility did create a mechanism whereby the commander and his chief of staff could work out disagreements in an orderly fashion, and it helped ensure that commanders—many of whom were noblemen without extensive military training—would have access to alternative ideas, as well as reason to take them seriously. For their part, staff officers knew that their advice had to be sound, since they shared responsibility for the results. The principle also helped to bolster the power and independence of the General Staff as an institution by giving it a voice of its own within the army.[32]

As the General Staff's values and practices informed those of the officer corps as a whole during the Wilhelmine era, the Prusso-German army gained some important strengths that carried over into the Reichswehr period and beyond. The dual emphasis on intellect and character provided the army with officers who were arguably better prepared for modern warfare at the tactical and operational levels than their counterparts in other states. Command by directive, *Vollmacht,* and the principle of joint responsibility made the Prusso-German army more flexible and proactive. No military culture is perfect, however; each has weaknesses to match its strengths. For the Germans, a certain narrowness of vision, a generous dose of hubris, and an overweening faith in the power of will combined to handicap them. They came to believe that their control over events was greater than it really was, that they could manage a war as they could a railroad timetable, and that they could overcome any obstacle through sheer force of character.

As was true for the Germans' strengths, their officer training and education system mirrored and promoted their weaknesses, especially the narrowness of their vision. As the General Staff evolved, the debate over intellect and character existed in parallel with another debate over the nature of the education that officers should receive. Originally that education was broad in scope. At the War Academy, for example, the course load in the 1860s and 1870s included a number of elective nonmilitary subjects such as literature, philosophy, general history, and the natural sciences. By the end of the century, however, the Germans had opted for a narrower selection of practical, technical studies; tactics, staff duties, and military history dominated the curriculum. Even the course terminology reflected the change in the school's mission: the term "art of war" *(Kriegskunst)* disappeared and "science of war" *(Kriegswissenschaft)* took its place. By the end of the nineteenth century the school's goal was to turn out technical specialists.[33]

Military history played a fundamental role in restricting the officers' intellectual scope.[34] At first glance it appears to have been only one subject among several in the War Academy curriculum, but its influence was pervasive. It provided the basis for the tactical classes that the officers took and was even the foundation for actual war plans. Its importance grew apace as officers with combat experience left the service in the decades after 1871. Moreover, the General Staff's historiographical methods were problematic. The staff contained a separate branch that specialized in historical studies. Its members were not trained historians but considered themselves qualified on the basis of their status as officers. Their version of history was narrowly technical; they focused almost exclusively on infantry tactics and commanders' actions while omitting any broader context. They also forced the wars about which they wrote into an artificial framework that emphasized the superiority of the attack over the defense and of moral over material factors.

In fairness to the Germans, no army developed a culture in the late nineteenth century that prepared it completely for the industrial mass warfare of the twentieth.[35] And the German system did have advantages in flexibility and tactical proficiency that many others did not. Still, the German approach contained the seeds for truly cataclysmic errors. The Schlieffen Plan, with which Germany entered the First World War, is the classic case in point. Count Alfred von Schlieffen served as chief of the General Staff from 1891 to 1905. He was a narrow technical specialist whose plan attempted to remove any opportunity for flexibility or initiative. He rejected Clausewitz's emphasis on the unpredictability of war, as well as Moltke's dictum that "no plan of operations can look with any certainty beyond the first meeting with the major forces of the enemy."[36] His conviction was that modern, mass armies could be—indeed, *had* to be—controlled centrally. In a perversion of "command by directive," Schlieffen defined exact objectives and strict timetables for all the armies in the attack. When the Germans attempted to implement the plan in August and September 1914, all of the potential problems with such control became real.[37] After the resulting debacle, the Germans returned to a more flexible command system—but their overall approach to war continued to be narrowly mechanistic, and they still tended to rely upon force of will to make up for any material problems. These attitudes would color the political, strategic, and operational debates that would take place within the Reichswehr.

THE IDEAS

In the Reichswehr era, the General Staff's institutional culture and intellectual background interacted with Germany's strategic situation and the experiences of the First World War to produce a vision of the future. Naturally, there was not a consensus on every point, and debates on some issues never died down completely. In general, however, German officers shared a common intellectual framework, and so they tended to differ only on less important subjects. They retained a desire to see Germany become a world power, and they regarded the army as a key to fulfilling that desire, even if they sometimes disagreed on how the army would carry out its role. The intellectual climate they created proved to be the perfect environment for National Socialism and for the outbreak of a second great conflagration.

Two points found ready acceptance among most General Staff officers in the interwar period. The first of these was that, in any future conflict, the General Staff would be the only body qualified to make decisions on military strategy and operations. As such it would have the dominant voice in any decision for war or peace, and, once war was declared, it would run the war as it saw fit, without civilian interference. The roots of these views went back at least as far as Moltke the Elder. Clausewitz had written that politics must exert a constant influence upon the conduct of war, since the latter had to serve the former's purpose.[38] Moltke, on the other hand, insisted that politics would come into play before and after a war, but that the requirements of military operations must determine the army's actions while the conflict is in progress.[39] Moltke and Bismarck fought bitterly over this idea during the war with France in 1870–71, and only Wilhelm I's personal intervention settled the dispute—in Bismarck's favor.[40] After 1890 that triumverate was gone, and with it the ability to properly balance military and civilian spheres. Chancellors after Bismarck studiously avoided involving themselves in the General Staff's plans, even when those plans had clear strategic implications, and Wilhelm II was unwilling or unable to insist on a coordinated planning process. Thus, for example, no fewer than three chancellors knew of Schlieffen's plan of campaign for the west, but none of them believed he had the right to question its strategic assumptions.[41] After the war, the Weimar regime proved much more willing to take an active role in strategic affairs, but powerful elements within the Reichsheer did all they could to bypass the government's prescriptions.

The other idea that General Staff officers held dear was that another war was inevitable; indeed, that it would be the only way in which Germany could revise the Versailles treaty and regain its rightful place in Europe. A Defense Ministry document of April 1923 stated that Germany could win its freedom, national independence, and economic and cultural rejuvenation only through war. Lieutenant Colonel Kurt von Schleicher, chief of the Political Department in the Truppenamt at the time, backed that up in December by detailing the military leadership's goals: "1. Strengthen state authority; 2. rehabilitate the economy; 3. rebuild a military capability; all are prerequisites for a foreign policy that has the goal of creating a Greater Germany." In May 1925 another ministry document stated bluntly: "That Germany will in the future have to fight a war for its continued existence as a people and state is certain."[42] A Truppenamt memo of March 1926 was more specific. It defined the following goals of German policy: the reoccupation of the Rhineland; the return of the Saar, the Polish corridor, and Upper Silesia; and the elimination of the demilitarized zone. The struggle to achieve these goals would, the Truppenamt predicted, lead to conflict with France, Belgium, Poland, Czechoslovakia, and perhaps Italy. The eventual goal was to reestablish Germany as a continental power first and then to claim a position as a world power.[43]

The General Staff's easy acceptance of war as a tool with which to alter the strategic balance in Europe demonstrates that Germany was suffering from a dearth of capable strategic thinkers. The German military clung to the idea that it could achieve strategic goals through operational victory in short, intense wars, much like the Wars of Unification. In so doing, the planners showed little understanding of their adversaries' capabilities or motives. Their ideas reflected a "continental view" that equated strategy with operations and did not take proper account of global power relationships. These intellectual trends were hardly new. Schlieffen had based his entire plan upon them, as his breezy dismissal of Britain's potential showed. The General Staff went on to implement Schlieffen's plan, in spite of clear evidence that the war would be exactly the kind of long affair that Germany could not afford.[44] The Verdun offensive of 1916, the decision to launch unrestricted submarine warfare in 1917, and the complete strategic bankruptcy of the 1918 spring offensive all add weight to the argument that Germany's leaders had lost touch with the strategic realities of the modern world.[45]

Defeat is sometimes enough to spark fundamental reform within a military system; this had been the case in Prussia after its loss to Napoleon in 1806. The First World War, for all its horrific impact, did not create a like effect in Germany. This was true because the General Staff developed a set of explanations for the defeat that missed the most important issues. The military's leaders did not examine the strategic assumptions that Germany had made before the war began, nor did they question the wisdom of Germany's strategic direction after the war settled down into stalemate. Instead, most General Staff officers came to believe that Germany had lost the war because of a combination of other factors: operational mistakes, mostly connected with the battles at the Marne and Verdun; failed domestic policies; conflict between the army and the home front; and the lack of a strong centralized command.[46]

The key element in that belief structure was the myth of the "stab in the back"; in this version of events, the government (and particularly the Jews) had failed the fighting men, first by not unifying German society behind the war effort and then by concluding a treasonous truce when the army was still capable of fighting. The myth fulfilled two functions. First, it kept the General Staff's hands clean when people began looking for a scapegoat. This was the goal of Groener's policies in the closing days of the war; he made sure that the General Staff maintained a safe distance from the armistice negotiations.[47] Second, the myth allowed the General Staff to avoid facing up to the consequences of its actions. Here the motive was unconscious but no less real. The General Staff was simply not prepared to question its own strategic assumptions.[48]

Thus Germany's military leaders missed the opportunity to learn the true lessons of the Great War, lessons that might have saved their nation untold misery in the decades ahead. They gained no understanding of global strategy or the relation of ends to means. Instead, the military embraced war as the sole solution and set about finding ways to do it better next time. In doing so, the army focused on three areas. The first, predictably, was the interplay of new weapons, tactics, and operational concepts that might break the stalemate of trench warfare. The second was psychological warfare and its application in maintaining public morale. The third was the organization of society for war. "Total war" became the General Staff's model. Future wars would target all the sources of enemy strength, not just military forces. There would be no difference between combatants and noncombatants. All the resources of the nation would therefore have to be linked in a fight for survival. The effort would require an authoritarian government, but one that would accept the General Staff's primacy in military matters.[49] The keys to success in the next war would be total mobilization, central direction, and rapid operational victory.

In setting these grand goals, however, the German military faced something of a problem. The Treaty of Versailles had left Germany with such a small army that it would have trouble fighting Poland, never mind France, as the Truppenamt's own exercises demonstrated.[50] Therefore, the planning and theorizing went forward on two levels. On one level, the military assumed that Germany would one day rearm, and so some planning went forward based on that eventuality. In the meantime, the search began for a military policy, a force structure, and a strategy that would allow Germany some measure of security in the short term. Both of these lines of thought recombined, in turn, in a debate over the shape of any future war.[51] Everyone agreed that Germany could not win a war of attrition. The question was, what alternative remained? Opinions varied widely, but in the end the military chose a course that deepened its strategic troubles as well as placing it in a dangerous political position.

Seeckt, who served as chief of the Army Directorate from 1920 to 1926, believed that the answer to Germany's strategic dilemma lay in a small, highly professional, highly mobile force. He drew on his experiences on the eastern front in the First World War, where smaller but more effective German forces had defeated larger Russian armies. He maintained that a smaller force could overcome the limitations of positional warfare through rapid, surprise attacks. In his scheme, the human spirit, plus technology, would prevail over greater numbers. The old mass army was immobile, Seeckt maintained; it could only crush its enemies by sheer weight. His force would strike quickly and decisively to disable the enemy's mass of men. Seeckt's ideas fell partly into the realm of fantasy, however, in that they required a military force that Germany could not build while the Versailles treaty was still in effect. When the French put his notions to the test by occupying the Ruhr in 1923, the Germans were helpless.[52] And in the meantime, other, differing schools of thought were appearing.

Some officers, especially Werner von Blomberg and Joachim von Stülpnagel of the Truppenamt, considered Seeckt's ideas to be hopelessly out of date. They argued for a strategy that would focus on a nationalist war of liberation of the kind Germany had used against Napoleon. In their vision, armed citizens would carry out a guerrilla war against any invading army. This "people's war" would leave much of the country in ruins, but, in theory, the invader would be vulnerable to a counterstroke by even a small force. After Seeckt's departure in

1926, Blomberg and Stülpnagel tried to implement their ideas, but they ran into insurmountable problems. Their plans depended upon two preconditions: the ability to prepare the country for war ahead of time, especially in a psychological sense, and the formation of a counterstroke force with a strong armored component. Both these prerequisites proved impossible to fulfill because of the Versailles treaty's restrictions and a lack of political will and financial resources within Germany. Moreover, a 1930 study established that a "people's war" was unlikely to succeed, given the nation's circumstances.[53]

Groener, who served as defense minister from 1928 to 1932, and his deputy, Schleicher, both opposed Seeckt's ideas as well; their proposals—starting from a different premise entirely—were the most reasonable that anyone put forward in the interwar period. Seeckt had insisted that a military buildup had to be the first priority, since no country could hope to rebuild its economy if it lacked power on the international scene. Schleicher countered that the economy had to come first, since that would provide the basis for rearmament. Both he and Groener agreed on a more internationalist approach than Seeckt had in mind. When Groener became defense minister, he took the first steps to put German military planning on a realistic footing; he insisted that political goals had to match military means if Germany was to consider military action. He stipulated that there were some situations in which Germany could not hope to defend itself, and therefore in those cases the only answer was to avoid conflict. According to his view, war between France and Germany was unlikely, since both depended upon American financial assistance. Support from the United States could be used in the meantime to finance rearmament, without the need for budgetary redistribution within Germany. In the event of an invasion by Poland—which Groener considered a possibility, since Poland was not tied into the international system to the same extent as France—German forces would conduct a fighting retreat and prepare a counterstroke that would prompt intervention by other powers and force a peace. Germany would come out on top in the negotiations that would follow, he said, because it was more important economically than Poland.[54]

Most members of the officer corps wanted no part of such plans. Because their military culture lacked a strong appreciation for the subtleties of strategy, they could not properly evaluate international power relationships and, hence, German opportunities. At the same time, they still believed that they and only they should direct the nation in its preparations for, and conduct of, war. They had defended that principle for generations, and they were not going to give it up now. They looked upon war as inevitable, especially given the aggressive goals that they—and much of the civilian leadership—wanted to pursue. They saw that the status quo, in the form of the hundred-thousand-man army, would never allow them to win that struggle, or even to defend German territory. International cooperation, as Groener and his supporters pursued it, seemed to have hit a dead end by 1930. That conclusion led the military leaders to promote rapid rearmament, followed by a war they would direct, a war that would bring together all the nation's resources in support of a series of lightning-fast operational victories. That was the only solution they could see.[55]

Having reached this conclusion, however, the military faced a major problem: it constituted a "secondary system" within German politics and society, that is, it could support policy but not dictate it.[56] As long as a republican government ruled Germany, the military's choices were severely limited. That situation changed after the world economic crisis and attendant political collapse struck Germany at the end of the 1920s, thus destroying Groener's efforts and helping to bring Hitler into power. The officer corps had long favored the rise of an authoritarian regime that would preserve the military's power and provide the requirements for modern, total war; now, it seemed, they had what they wanted.[57] From Hitler's statements in *Mein Kampf,* the services could assume that he would strive for dominance on the Continent. In a meeting with the leading generals on February 3, 1933, and in his other statements, Hitler called for rearmament, the reinstitution of the draft, withdrawal from the international security system, and the revision of the Versailles treaty. Certainly, these statements gave the military no grounds for complaint. In fact, most officers favored an alliance with the Nazis in 1933.[58]

This, then, was the situation when the Nazis seized power. In the course of the previous century the Germans had created a bureaucratic structure—the General Staff—that could plan, organize, and direct military operations in a consistent, uniform way. At the higher levels, however, bureaucratic competition and confusion had been the norm; in the recent past, competition between the General Staff and the War Ministry had contributed to problems in policy and strategy formulation. That competition would continue. Behind the strife in the upper levels and the efficiency at the lower levels lay the intellectual and cultural norms of the General Staff. The members of that organization considered themselves to be the only people who were qualified to make decisions on military affairs; but their views of politics, strategy, and the nature of modern warfare itself were seriously flawed. Moreover, they were about to put themselves at the disposal of a man who, they believed, would give them the resources and independence they needed to make Germany a dominant power on the Continent. That was exactly what Adolf Hitler wanted them to believe.

2

Expansion and Debate, January 1933 to November 1937

On January 30, 1933, Adolf Hitler became chancellor of Germany. Eventually he would turn the military's world on its head, but for the first five years after he took power the generals could maintain the illusion that their position was secure. Hitler needed their support while he focused on the process of *Gleichschaltung,* through which all the disparate elements of German society came firmly under Nazi domination.[1] Moreover, he and the generals had no great cause for disagreement at first. For a time the new chancellor would give the military's leaders what they wanted and otherwise leave them alone; in turn, they would prove quite willing to overlook the less pleasant aspects of his personality and program. A massive rearmament program, debates over the structure of the high command, foreign policy developments, and increasingly concrete war plans would occupy most of the generals' time and attention, while Hitler consolidated his power base.

Almost from the day he assumed power, Hitler promised the generals what they wanted most. At a dinner on February 3 at the home of the chief of the Army Directorate, Lieutenant General Kurt von Hammerstein-Equord, Hitler pledged to rebuild a standing army. He also promised to bring an end to the parliamentary politics that had caused the army so much trouble, and he said that his government would not tolerate Marxism or pacifism. At the same time, he assured the assembled generals that he would never use the Reichswehr to quell internal unrest, nor would he allow its amalgamation with his political army, the Sturmabteilung, or SA. His overall policy goal would be to regain a position of power for Germany through the abrogation of the Treaty of Versailles. He did not want to predict exactly how Germany would use that power, but the best course, he said, would be to conquer more living space in the east.[2] He repeated his assurances in a speech to the Reichswehr's commanders at the Defense Ministry on February 7.[3] All of this was good news to

Gerd von Rundstedt, Werner von Fritsch, Werner von Blomberg. (Courtesy Bundesarchiv, photo no. 73/23/7)

the military; Hitler's remarks drew a cautiously optimistic response from most of his listeners. In the months that followed he reinforced that optimism at every opportunity. He wanted the army to believe that it would remain one of the foundations of the German state, just as it had for nearly three centuries.

Hitler had the good fortune to find an ally in the man President Hindenburg had chosen to be the new defense minister: Lieutenant General Werner von Blomberg. Hindenburg had wanted someone who would promise to maintain the Reichswehr as the nation's apolitical instrument and to protect it against any outside interference.[4] He and Blomberg were on good terms, and Blomberg was really the only acceptable candidate at the time, but his outlook was anything but apolitical. He had already demonstrated a positive attitude toward National Socialism by working with Hitler in order to use the SA as an auxiliary defense force in East Prussia.[5] In fact, he and Hitler shared many of the same broad goals, and Blomberg wanted to bring the army closer to the Nazi Party. On the same day that Hitler addressed the military's leaders for the first time, Blomberg told a group of senior army commanders that the current government represented "a broad national desire and the realization of that toward which many of the best have been striving for years."[6] Thus Hitler had good reason to be pleased with Hindenburg's choice.

Walter von Reichenau. (Courtesy National Archives, photo no. 242-GAP-102-R-1)

Blomberg has been the target of vicious criticism from many quarters for the role he played as defense minister. Some of this criticism was exaggerated, but there is no question that Blomberg was a fateful choice for Germany. He had had a mostly successful career to this point: he entered the Kriegsakademie in 1904, served on the General Staff from 1908 to 1911, held a number of staff positions during the First World War, and by 1927 had risen to that most exalted of positions, chief of the General Staff (known then as the Truppenamt).[7] Later, however, he became embroiled in a debate with Defense Minister Groener over military policy and strategy, and in September 1929 Groener arranged for Blomberg's transfer to the defense district command in East Prussia.[8] Personally he was intense, keen, and energetic, open and honest, often impulsive. Lieutenant General Freiherr Werner von Fritsch, who served under Blomberg twice, said of him that he was a difficult man to work for because he was too inclined toward romantic fantasy, tended to vacillate, always sought novelties, and was too vulnerable to outside influence. Certainly Hitler found him easy to dominate. Soon a pair of nicknames for Blomberg began to circulate: "Hitler-Junge Quex," after a film character who idolized Hitler, and "Gummi-Löwe" or "Rubber Lion."[9]

Blomberg brought his chief of staff with him to his new position, as was customary in the German army: he placed Colonel Walther von Reichenau in charge of the Ministerial Office, which Groener had created in 1929 to help him defend his interests against those of the services.[10] Here was another stroke of good fortune for the new chancellor, for Reichenau was even more enthusiastic about the National Socialists than his superior was. His consuming interest in politics had already set him aside from many of his compatriots. He was a broadly educated man who should have seen the weaknesses in the National Socialist movement, but he also considered the Nazis an excellent vehicle for Germany's return to the world stage. He was therefore one of the first German officers to come out openly in favor of Nazi leadership, and now he was in a position to influence relations between the armed forces and the Party.[11]

The military's first priority was to accelerate the rearmament program that it had begun in 1928. In this Hitler let the armed forces take charge; he did not concern himself with the overall issue of rearmament until 1936.[12] Now Blomberg's ideas on military policy and strategy took on real significance. Like most of his compatriots, Blomberg saw defense policy issues in purely military terms, and so he promoted rapid, unilateral rearmament so that Germany could pursue its goals by force. The idea that such a policy might align other nations more strongly against Germany did not upset him. "In that case, the more enemies, the more honor!" he said to one of his compatriots.[13] His new course took on concrete form right away, as he and Foreign Minister Konstantin von Neurath tried to obstruct the international disarmament conference in Geneva; Hitler had to overrule them to prevent Germany's early isolation.[14]

Ludwig Beck. (Courtesy Bundesarchiv, photo no. 102/17587)

Planning the details of the army's rearmament program fell to the Truppenamt, which now found that its grandest dreams seemed within reach. The army had gained unprecedented autonomy, Hitler was providing the funds it needed to accelerate rearmament, and the Truppenamt had control of the planning process. Now the General Staff could create the force structure it had wanted since the last war.[15] Two men in the army's command hierarchy would play especially important roles in army rearmament over the next five years: the chief of the Army Directorate, Lieutenant General Fritsch, and the chief of the Truppenamt, Major General Ludwig Beck.

Fritsch, who took over command of the army on February 1, 1934, was a General Staff officer who had served as chief of the Operations Branch in the Truppenamt under Blomberg. He was extremely energetic and disciplined, strongly religious, highly intelligent, and capable but also modest. He was not an easy man to get to know, but most of his subordinates liked and respected him nonetheless. He had no interest in politics or politicians and harbored no great personal affection for the Nazis; they and their leader offended his aristocratic sensibilities. Only the intercession of his old comrade Seeckt persuaded him to take up command of the army at all. He agreed with many of Hitler's goals and was just as interested in rearmament as Blomberg, but he was far less interested in inculcating the army with National Socialist principles.[16]

Ludwig Beck took up his post as chief of the General Staff on October 1, 1933. His tenure there took on special significance later on because of his opposition to Hitler's aggressive plans in 1937–38 and because of his participation in the coup attempt of July 1944. Opinions of the man vary tremendously. The fashion in the first decades after the war, and one that has persisted, was to see him as a military and political visionary who saw where Nazism was leading Germany and who would have stopped Hitler if his comrades had supported him. More recent analyses have been more critical.[17] We do know that Beck was a man of no small intellectual gifts who tended to take a broader view of affairs than many of his contemporaries. Nevertheless, and in part despite himself, he helped set the stage for the conflict whose inception he would oppose.

Beck and Fritsch shared many of the same views on military affairs. The two men were friends of long standing, and they had worked together in 1931 and 1932 on the manual *Truppenführung,* which provided not just tactical doctrine but also a philosophical foundation on the nature of war and an officer's role.[18] They shared a belief in the primacy of the General Staff in all military policy decisions, and they were committed to its exclusive right to command in war.[19] Beck combined these fundamental views with a sophisticated understanding both of European politics and of Germany's position on the Continent. The lesson he took from the First World War was that a strategist could no longer think in purely military terms, as Schlieffen had, but must think politically in the broadest possible sense. He believed that a future war in Europe was likely to be a war of long duration on several fronts. In that light, Germany's situation offered definite opportunities but also significant dangers. Military leaders needed to see operations in the context of the entire conflict if Germany were to do more than win a few battles.[20]

Therein lay the inescapable dilemma for any German strategist, however. The government's goals precluded acceptance of the status quo. The effort to realize those goals would likely involve war against several other powers, as the army had long recognized. Here was the same problem that had plagued German planners for decades: How could Germany defeat a superior coalition? Beck believed that Germany could win a war only by military means; the nation could not depend on economic warfare or on some combination of limited war with diplomacy. A war of attrition was not an option, moreover; victory had to come through rapid, decisive, offensive military operations.[21] So, despite Beck's attention to the broader aspects of European warfare, he arrived at the same strategic conclusion as had Schlieffen before him. He knew that the next war would tend to be a long one against several foes, but he also knew that Germany's only hope lay in a short, decisive conflict, and so he set about to create the military prerequisites for such a war. His vision, like Schlieffen's, was of an operational solution to Germany's strategic dilemma.

But here Beck, along with Fritsch and Blomberg, ran into another, more practical obstacle: the Treaty of Versailles had left Germany in such a position of military inferiority that years of intense effort would be necessary to catch up. Rapid, unilateral rearmament was their answer. In mid-December 1933 Beck signed the authorization to form a three-hundred-thousand-man peacetime army, and before the end of the year orders had gone out to start the buildup in April 1934.[22] This new rearmament program aimed to create a twenty-one-division army (a threefold increase) in four years. In May 1934, however, Hitler expressed his desire to see this new force ready by April 1, 1935. Fritsch, Beck, and the Truppenamt resisted the idea, but only on purely military grounds; they feared that such a rapid expansion would compromise the quality of the new force, since there would not be enough time for training.[23] They did not bring diplomatic or material considerations into their argument, despite the problems that were emerging. As far as matériel was concerned, Major General Liese of the Army Ordnance Office pointed out in May 1934 that the army did not have stocks of munitions or fuel to last more than six weeks in combat.[24] On the diplomatic side, relations with France and Britain began to deteriorate that same spring because of Germany's aggressive moves. The military reacted by digging in its heels, considering alliances in southeastern Europe, and *accelerating* rearmament. In the process it also let financial considerations fall by the wayside.[25]

While rearmament was getting under way, the senior officers of the Reichsheer and the Defense Ministry were also thinking about the structure of the future high command. Blomberg, Reichenau, Fritsch, and Beck were largely in agreement regarding the need for a centralized command. The Nazi regime offered them the political support they needed to focus Germany's energies on military affairs; all that was lacking was the structure to direct those energies in peace and in war.[26] Opinion was divided, though, on the nature of that structure, and along familiar lines at that. The old rivalry of ministry and general staff was reemerging.

Blomberg and Reichenau believed that the Defense Ministry should be the core of the wartime command system. In their view, the three services should be on an equal footing, with a central headquarters above them. The two men appeared to be in a good position to implement their plan. Blomberg was the first active-duty officer to serve as defense minister in the history of the Republic. In April 1933 he became the chancellor's permanent representative to the new Reich Defense Council, which included the ministers of foreign affairs, interior, economics, finance, and propaganda. At the end of the month Hindenburg named him—if not publicly—Reich defense minister and commander in chief of the armed forces. The second part of the title represented a real break with tradition; never before had a serving general possessed so much authority to coordinate the nation's war effort, even nominally.[27] Meanwhile, both Blomberg and Reichenau had begun acting behind the scenes to undermine the authority of the chief of the Army Directorate, Hammerstein. The latter, whose criticism of the Nazis had placed him in a weak position politically, did nothing to stop the intrusions into his sphere.[28]

Blomberg wanted to formalize a command structure that would take his new authority into account, and so on October 17, 1933, he ordered the services to prepare studies on the issue.[29] Beck saw an opportunity; he and others on his staff were concerned about "the exertion of influence by the Ministerial Office, a political organ, upon purely military matters." Beck had the Truppenamt's Army Organization Branch work up a draft plan that proposed the following structure. A Reich Defense Council, to include the chancellor and the defense minister, would be responsible for planning and organizing the nation's war effort. A Working Committee would perform many of the council's routine tasks; the committee's membership would include experts from the Defense Ministry and the three armed services. The defense minister would be commander in chief of the armed forces (Chef der Wehrmacht). To assist him in the preparation and execution of directives, the defense minister would have an Armed Forces Staff consisting of two army, one navy, one air, and one economics staff officer. The chief of each armed service directorate would then act according to the minister's directives in planning and conducting military operations. The draft also suggested, almost as an afterthought, that the chief of the General Staff might be the head of the Reich Defense Council's Working Committee, and that the role of the Armed Forces Staff could be handled by the General Staff.[30] The idea was to exclude the defense minister from the military command process and guarantee the army commander a say in policy making.

Using this and other drafts as his basis, Beck prepared a memorandum that he submitted to the Defense Ministry on January 15, 1934. In it, as a rationale for his proposal, he presented the ideas that would be the core of the army's argument for the next four years and more. Bringing the three services together under one commander in chief was a necessity, he said, "not just caused by the person of the present minister of defense." Naturally, the commander in chief would need a staff to work out his orders, as well as other offices to handle the ministerial tasks such as directing the economy and the propaganda effort. However, that Wehrmacht staff would have no influence over operations. Furthermore, the army was and would remain the decisive arm, given Germany's continental aspirations; thus the chief of the Army Directorate would be deputy to the commander in chief of the Wehrmacht, while also bearing full responsibility for directing the army's operations. By implication, in Beck's plan the army would hold considerable, if informal, authority over the other services.[31]

By this time Fritsch was on the scene, preparing to assume command of the army on February 1. No doubt the alliance between Fritsch and Beck gained strength because of the threat from the defense ministry; they were both interested in maintaining the army's independence and in making it the core of the new command, against the wishes of Blomberg and Reichenau. Fritsch had acted quickly to counteract the inroads that the defense minister and his assistant had made into the Army Directorate under Hammerstein: he forbade his subordinates to report directly to the ministry on military matters, and he demanded that he receive copies of all political reports going from army agencies to the ministry.[32]

In the meantime, Blomberg and Reichenau had not been idle. Perhaps in reaction to the plan Beck submitted in January, or perhaps of their own accord, they redesignated the Ministerial Office as the Wehrmachtamt, or Armed Forces Office, on February 12. The redesignation was important in a symbolic sense: it highlighted the two men's goal of creating an organization that would allow Blomberg greater control of the services and more say in military planning. Within the new office, which included elements to handle legal matters, counterintelligence, and budgeting, there was also a so-called National Defense Branch (Abteilung Landesverteidigung, or Abt. L). This last was to be Blomberg's military planning staff; in Reichenau's vision it would grow to become a Wehrmacht General Staff, with authority over all three services. In May 1934 Reichenau actually proposed such an arrangement; the army countered in July by saying again that the services would do their own operational planning and that they must remain directly subordinate to the Wehrmacht commander in chief, not to his staff, which could only be a working group.[33] There is no indication that the army's argument had any effect on Blomberg, who encouraged Reichenau to grab more power. That autumn the latter officer took over control of the Reich Defense Council's Working Committee from Beck, and on November 1 the Armed Forces Office added a new Defense Economy and Weapons Branch to try to coordinate the services' armaments programs.[34]

What fueled this continuing dispute? Several factors acted together. Certainly, the protagonists were in agreement on the need for a centralized command. Also, each figure in the dispute placed the army's interests above those of the other services. The army expressed this idea more openly than did the Defense Ministry, but the fact is that the key players on each side were all army officers. None of them suggested, or ever would suggest, that an officer from the navy, the emerging Luftwaffe, or Hitler's political army, the SA, should take over direction of the armed forces. Thus they did not disagree over ends but only over means, and the debate remained largely internal to the army.

The balance of objective and subjective factors in the debate is difficult to judge. On the one hand, many of the organizational arguments were valid. Each man believed that he was backing the best solution to the problem of Germany's future command structure. This was not an argument that anyone could easily settle on objective terms; each side's proposal had merit. That fact allowed each of the protagonists to justify his continued—some would say stubborn—support of a particular solution. On the other hand, ego and ambition certainly played a role in the debate; that was why it centered on operational command. The leaders had been steeped in the traditions and history of the General Staff. Although they understood the importance of matters such as economic management and armaments production, they attached far more importance to command; that was where the glory was.[35] After all, Moltke the Elder had not made his reputation by debating force structure with the Reichstag. And although the General Staff tradition also emphasized selfless, anonymous service, one would be foolish indeed to pretend that these men had no ambition. As Colonel Alfred Jodl later said to Brigadier General Erich von Manstein, "The whole shame is that the stronger personalities sit in the OKH. If Fritsch, Beck, and you were in the OKW, you would think differently." Manstein admitted the truth in Jodl's remark; he said that they (he, Fritsch, and Beck) would surely take charge if that were the case, that they would never permit a perfect juxtaposition of the army and armed forces commands, and that they would never allow themselves to be burdened with the tasks of the Reich defense minister.[36] The fact was that each of the protagonists believed himself qualified to exercise operational command and to give advice, or perhaps even direction, at the strategy and policy levels. Given each man's faith in himself and his organization, the fact that his particular solution would put him in a position of power is hardly surprising.

Finally, personal animosity and politics added to the mix of motivations. Fritsch, Beck, and many other senior army officers regarded Blomberg and Reichenau with some suspicion. The efforts of both men to force the army into a more National Socialist mold struck many officers as far too radical.

Reichenau in particular suffered from his reputation as a "Nazi general." Moreover, he behaved in ways that many senior officers found socially unacceptable, and his caustic comments toward people with whom he disagreed made him many enemies.[37] His brother officers' hostility should not be confused with anti-Nazi feelings. Both Beck and Fritsch were early supporters of National Socialism in a broad sense; that is, they saw the Nazi movement as a positive development for Germany. Beck had testified in 1930—as had Hitler—on behalf of three young officers under his command who stood accused of high treason for spreading Nazi propaganda. His support of their views, as opposed to their character, nearly led to his dismissal.[38] Both he and Fritsch drew the line, however, as did many of their senior comrades, at any intrusion by the Party into army affairs. They wanted the army to remain independent.[39] For their part, Blomberg and Reichenau, along with a growing circle of officers—especially young ones—considered the senior members of the Army Directorate to be hopelessly old-fashioned, out of step with the times, and perhaps even dangerous to the political survival of the army as an institution.

However complex its sources, the real significance of the conflict lay in its fruitlessness and the energy it absorbed. By engaging in these continuous internal disputes, the leaders of both the Army Directorate and the Ministry of Defense deprived the army of unity at a crucial moment in Germany's political and military development. Opposition to Hitler was not the issue; none of the military leaders was so inclined at this point. However, there was still a chance that, by acting in concert, they could decide on a unified command structure that would work effectively. Instead, because they were expending so much energy arguing among themselves, they could neither work together on military policy nor resist the political maneuvers on the part of the organizations they were determined to dominate: the navy and the Luftwaffe. As Blomberg attempted to exert his authority as commander in chief of the Wehrmacht, the leaders of these organizations—Erich Raeder and Hermann Göring, respectively—did their best to keep him from succeeding. They were also not about to subordinate themselves to Fritsch and Beck.

Admiral Raeder was impressed with Hitler. Raeder admired the chancellor's political skills, his command over people, and his drive and intelligence. He believed that Hitler had sound ideas regarding the navy's role. "I may state with pleasure and satisfaction," he told a group of his officers in 1933, "that the Reich chancellor . . . is deeply convinced of the great political significance of a navy."[40] The two men quickly formed a strong rapport, and Blomberg found himself at a disadvantage when trying to have a say in naval affairs, for Raeder was not prepared to hand over control of the navy to an army officer.[41]

Hermann Göring, minister of aviation and, after March 1935, commander in chief of the Luftwaffe, presented an even more difficult problem. He was skilled at political intrigue, ambitious, brutal, and utterly without scruples. He lacked experience as a senior commander, but he nevertheless grasped at all the military power he could. And he had one great advantage that Blomberg lacked: he was Hitler's political crony. As of early 1934 he had little formal authority; in fact he was, at least officially, Blomberg's subordinate. In practice he was impossible to control. He had succeeded, over opposition from the army and navy, in centralizing control of Germany's fledgling air force in the Air Ministry in May 1933. Blomberg did his best to undermine Göring's position, but to no effect. Göring bypassed Blomberg at every opportunity, and because of him the Luftwaffe would land firmly outside of the Wehrmacht commander in chief's span of control. Before long Göring would even try to take Blomberg's place.[42]

Troublesome though they were, neither the nascent Luftwaffe nor the navy was as serious a threat to the army as the SA, led by Ernst Röhm. Röhm had been Hitler's close ally since the earliest days of the Nazi movement. He was a soldier at heart, or so he claimed, but he combined his militarism with the "socialist" element in National Socialism and with the rootlessness, opportunism, and love of violence shared by so many disillusioned veterans of the First World War. He was also one of those "front officers" whom Seeckt had eliminated from the Reichsheer, and he never forgave the army, or especially the General Staff, for that snub. Röhm's greatest wish was to turn his SA into a new "people's army" and incorporate the old army within it.[43] Röhm's pretensions frightened the generals, whose support Hitler could ill afford to lose while he was still consolidating his power. By 1934 Röhm was starting to express his dissatisfaction with Hitler's leadership and with the course of the National Socialist "revolution" to that point. The SA began to stockpile arms and set up guard detachments around its various headquarters. Hitler did his best to settle Röhm down and create an understanding between the SA and the army, but without success. When Röhm continued to resist, Hitler had him and the other SA leaders arrested and summarily shot on June 30, 1934.[44]

The political implications of this act were as serious as they were complex. The generals, although they were heavily involved in the background of the purge, were caught off guard by its brutality. They had counted on something more restrained, something that would at least appear legal. And they had definitely not expected the concurrent murder of several of Hitler's old enemies, including Schleicher and several other high-ranking officers. General Fritsch spoke with Blomberg about an investigation, but the Wehrmacht commander rejected the idea.[45] For their part, Blomberg and Reichenau— like most officers—were satisfied to put the whole affair behind them. They were happy with the fate of the SA and did not want to rock the boat. These senior officers' acquiescence in their comrades' brutal murder sent ripples throughout the officer corps. The message was clear: the army's leaders would stand behind the National Socialists, even when the latter took steps against members of the officer corps themselves. Moreover, the fall of the SA opened the door for the Schutzstaffel or SS, Hitler's personal bodyguard, to evolve into an even more dangerous rival.[46]

By eliminating the SA, Hitler demonstrated his loyalty (however temporary) to the military; soon the military would have a chance to reciprocate. On August 2, 1934, President Hindenburg died. Hitler immediately combined the offices of president and chancellor, naming himself Führer (Leader) of the German Reich and supreme commander of the Wehrmacht. The military was quick to affirm its support. Under the Weimar regime, members of the military had sworn an oath to defend the constitution. Now Blomberg and Reichenau, on their own initiative, had the members of the Reichswehr swear a new oath of loyalty: "I swear by God this holy oath, that I will render to Adolf Hitler, Leader of the German nation and people, Supreme Commander of the Armed Forces, unconditional obedience, and I am ready as a brave soldier to risk my life at any time for this oath."[47]

Very few officers had the opportunity to consider the consequences that might come from such an oath, since Blomberg and Reichenau appended it to the memorial services for Hindenburg at the last minute. Beck later described the day as the darkest of his life, and Fritsch was barely able to dissuade him from resigning.[48] Fritsch himself questioned the measure's legality to Blomberg. Most officers, however, were not greatly troubled. Perhaps the Führer's reaction helped to sooth their nerves. Hitler, naturally enough, was very pleased with the Reichswehr's display of loyalty. He wrote a public letter of thanks to Blomberg, in which he said: "Just as the officers and soldiers of the Wehrmacht bind themselves to the new state in my person, so shall I always regard it as my highest duty to defend the existence and inviolability of the Wehrmacht in fulfillment of the testament of the late field marshal and, faithful to my own will, to anchor the army in the nation as the sole bearer of arms." This seemed to be the effect that Reichenau may have wanted from the oath all along: to bind the Führer to the Wehrmacht just as much as the reverse.[49] Eighteen months had passed since Hitler took office, and the mass of his officers still fundamentally misunderstood the man's nature.[50]

For the next three years the generals continued to have little cause for complaint, and in any case they were extremely busy. Work on the December 1933 rearmament program went forward into 1935, at which point the pace of events picked up even more, as Hitler publicly abrogated the arms limitations contained in the Versailles treaty. On March 5 he announced the formation of the Luftwaffe out of the Air Ministry.[51] He followed that on March 16 with the announcement that Germany was rearming and reintroducing conscription; two months later, on May 21, he signed a secret Reich Defense Law, under which the small, professional army became a national service army. The Reichswehr of the Weimar Republic became the Wehrmacht (although the latter term had been in widespread use for some time, as in

Blomberg's title, for example). The Reich defense minister received the new title of Reich war minister and exercised command of the Wehrmacht as the commander in chief, subordinate only to the Führer and supreme commander. The army and navy directorates became the high commands of the army and navy (Oberkommando des Heeres [OKH] and Oberkommando der Marine [OKM]), and the chiefs of those directorates became commanders in chief.[52]

For the most part the name changes did not translate into any significant reorganization; the General Staff began to expand and reorganize itself internally, but most of the other top structures did not change. The big changes were taking place at the lower levels, where rearmament was having its greatest effect. In 1935 and 1936 the goals of that program expanded steadily. By the summer of 1936, the army was planning to have a wartime force ready within four years. According to the plan, that force, including reserves, would number 102 divisions, a total of 2.6 million men—half a million more than in 1914. The General Staff already considered the army ready for a defensive war, and it expected to be ready to pursue Germany's aggressive aims by 1940. The Führer backed that goal up with his Four-Year Plan, in which he called for rearmament to be an industrial priority, regardless of the economic consequences.[53]

The army was not going to have everything its own way, however. Problems with the rearmament program were already appearing. In fact, the term "program" might be too strong. Germany did not plan or execute its rearmament effort in a coherent way. Hitler identified neither clear goals nor a time frame within which he expected to act, and so the three services came up with their own, uncoordinated plans and fought with one another for resources. Above them, no fewer than three agencies competed to direct the overall effort: the Defense Economy and Weapons Branch in the War Ministry's Armed Forces Office, the Plenipotentiary General for the War Economy, and the Plenipotentiary General for the Four-Year Plan. Göring took over the last and newest organization in October 1936, and he spent a good deal of his time trying to cut the other two out of the process, while they in turn tried to block him.[54] The outcome was a rearmament effort that was largely unplanned, uncoordinated, and uncontrolled. Each service simply strove to get as much as it could, without much regard for the real limits that Germany faced and the damage that rapid rearmament was doing.

One problem concerned the supply of officers. In October 1933 there were about 3,800 active officers in the army; in the next year that number rose by over 72 percent, to 6,553.[55] The officer corps as a whole—and especially the General Staff Corps—could maintain that pace of expansion only by loosening entrance requirements and cutting training time. And at that, the Germans were still not making up the shortfall. A memorandum released by the Organizational Branch of the General Staff on July 24, 1936, stated that the peacetime army would be short over 13,000 officers in 1941, and that under normal circumstances the army could not make up that shortfall until 1950![56] The Army Personnel Office also alerted the General Staff to the problem; it had planned in 1933 for an officer strength equaling 7 percent of the total army, but by 1935 the real figure had already sunk to a little over 1 percent, and the army's effectiveness was bound to suffer if the trend continued.[57]

The influx of new officers also had political repercussions. As the number of officers increased, the army had to accept many who were already dedicated Nazis. Nazism had been creeping into the officer corps for some time, actually, but now the issue took on an entirely new dimension. Blomberg and Reichenau believed this was a positive development. In fact, the minister of war was already calling on the services to ensure that officer candidates demonstrated the right attitude toward National Socialism. In a memo of July 22, 1935, to the service commanders, for example, he began by saying that "it is self-evident that the Wehrmacht should declare its support for the National Socialist state concept."[58] In a speech in April 1937 he went farther still by accepting Hitler's idea that the army drop all educational prerequisites for acceptance into the officer ranks. He believed this measure to be one of "the most important demands of the new German socialism" and one that would strengthen the moral structure of the army.[59]

As the number of Nazi officers grew, the unity of the officer corps, which was vital to good discipline and efficiency as well as to political stability, slipped away. The army became increasingly polarized between those few older officers who, like Fritsch and Beck, wanted to keep the Party at arm's length and a growing number of younger officers who wanted the army to become a thoroughly National Socialist institution. Thus the political element of the debate exacerbated the normal generational conflict that occurs in large organizations everywhere. At the same time, the vastly greater number of opportunities that the army's expansion offered, together with the opportunistic atmosphere engendered by National Socialism, brought out crass motivations that had not had much room to grow in the Reichsheer. Petty jealousies, ambition, and the use of influence to gain promotion became more and more the rule rather than the exception. The army's leaders tried hard after 1935 to create a new sense of community within the officer corps, based on the Nazi principles they thought useful in combination with older army traditions. These efforts were not successful. The officer corps was a long way from dissolution, but neither was it the spiritually unified structure it had been in the 1920s.[60]

In the short term, the officer corps' growing pains were a minor issue, compared with rearmament's economic effects. There simply were not enough financial or material resources to meet the services' demands. Hjalmar Schacht, president of the Reichsbank, warned that the rearmament program would break the German economy. Colonel Georg Thomas of the Defense Economy and Weapons Branch said that the current "armament in breadth," with its emphasis on the rapid buildup of the armed forces without much concern for reserves, would hinder the "armament in depth" that the armed forces really needed. And in August 1936, Brigadier General Friedrich Fromm, in a study Fritsch initiated, pointed out that the army's latest plan presented serious difficulties in terms of the availability of ammunition, equipment, raw materials, industrial plant, and skilled workers. He went on to say that the army could meet the plan if the required funds and foreign exchange were available, but he doubted that such would be the case. In his conclusion, Fromm stated that Germany would either have to use the Wehrmacht at the end of the rearmament period or scale back rearmament. Fromm received no reply to his study, but his raw data appeared in a document Fritsch used to explain the costs of the program that he intended to pursue in any case![61]

The military leaders' options were narrowing, but they could not or would not come to grips with that fact. If they continued with their current rearmament program, the economy would collapse, the diplomatic situation would worsen, and their adversaries would begin to direct their greater resource bases toward their own arms programs. To draw back from rearmament would mean, for all practical purposes, giving up on the goals that both the military and Hitler held so dear, especially because the leaders had long since discarded any other means of achieving them. That was not something anyone at the top of the command structure was prepared to do: as late as 1936, Beck categorically rejected any slowing of rearmament—precisely because of the tense international situation and Germany's isolation! The only remaining alternative was to use the Wehrmacht prematurely, but the generals were not prepared to do that either.[62]

Fortunately—from the army's standpoint—Hitler's foreign policy seemed to show the right mix of boldness and restraint in the years leading up to 1937. He concluded a nonaggression treaty with Poland in 1934 and a naval pact with Great Britain the following year; the latter, though meaningless over the long term, helped to soothe foreign governments that were upset with Germany's rearmament program. His attempt in 1934 to overthrow the Austrian government backfired, but since then he had strengthened ties with Italy—which had effectively opposed the Austrian move—and with Japan. The reoccupation of the Rhineland in March 1936 had seemed the riskiest move yet, but the Führer had managed to carry it off.[63] Hitler's successes could hardly have failed to impress most of his military leaders. He had abrogated the hated Versailles treaty and given Germany back its sovereignty and its pride, all without prompting a forceful reaction from any of the other European powers. Likewise, his support for Franco in the Spanish civil war kept the other powers distracted from Germany's arms buildup and gave the Wehrmacht a chance to try out some new doctrines.[64]

That is not to say that every policy initiative met with a positive response. On May 2, 1935, Blomberg ordered Fritsch to start planning for an invasion of Czechoslovakia (code name *Schulung* or *Training*).[65] Beck responded with a memo to Fritsch the next day, in which he condemned the higher military leadership for even proposing such a plan; he maintained that an invasion of Czechoslovakia would be folly, given the present state of Germany's army and the certainty that an attack would bring in other European powers. Such an act of desperation, he wrote, would lead to a situation in which the military leadership would lose the trust of the country and the soldiers, and both contemporaries and history would damn the men who led it. In a cover letter to Fritsch, he added that he would submit his resignation if Blomberg intended to go ahead with practical war preparations.[66]

Beck's memo is absolutely clear on one point: Beck was not protesting against the foreign policy goals inherent in *Schulung*. Neither he nor Fritsch had any objections to Hitler's long-term plans. Beck's argument was not that an attack on Czechoslovakia would be wrong, just that Germany's army was not yet ready.[67] Nothing much came of *Schulung* for the moment; Beck did not have to carry out his threat to resign. Nor, however, was there any halt in deployment planning; it went forward steadily as Germany's military strength grew. As Michael Geyer points out, the General Staff assumed that the army would act aggressively as soon as rearmament was complete.[68] As rearmament progressed, its plans became more and more concrete. By the middle of 1936, the military was clearly preparing for aggressive war, with Czechoslovakia as the first target.[69] The contradictions in the military's thinking carried over into its designs, however. There was no way to bring Germany's goals into sync with its industrial and economic capacity, and the planners never came to grips with that fact. Their plans were full of assumptions that would have to be met before Germany could launch a war, assumptions that were often at odds with the diplomatic and economic situations that rapid rearmament was creating.[70]

Beck's and Fritsch's dispute with the War Ministry still had as much to do with the continuing fight over authority and structure in the evolving high command system at this point as they did with political and strategic matters. Blomberg's order of May 2, 1935, stated that "the overall leadership of *Schulung* lies, because it will be a joint operation of all three armed services, in the hands of the Reich Defense Minister."[71] Beck objected to the purely instrumental role that Blomberg clearly wanted the General Staff to play in the planning process. Blomberg's directive did not ask for a feasibility study or any advice on the politico-strategic level; it simply demanded an operational plan. Beck and Fritsch both believed that they should have a say in the basic question of peace versus war, and they fought for a high command structure that would give them that say.

In the second half of 1935, the War Ministry and the OKH each tried a variety of indirect maneuvers in an effort to gain additional leverage. On August 24, for example, Blomberg addressed a memo to the services, in which he asked them to forward information to the Armed Forces Office on all basic decisions, that is, those concerning organizational, operational, mobilization, or budget questions, so that he could prepare for his consultations with the service commanders. Apparently, however, this memo met with some resistance, for Blomberg felt compelled to send out another on October 31, in which he said, "I have reason to emphasize the need to strictly execute my order to keep the Armed Forces Office informed."[72] These memos may have been partly a reaction to an order that Beck sent to his staff subordinates, to the effect that he would not permit them to deal with the Wehrmacht commander or the Armed Forces Office directly.[73]

For its part, the army tried to use its control of personnel assignments to affect the balance of power. Fritsch and Beck believed they could torpedo the War Ministry's ambitions by filling key positions with officers who would defend the army's point of view. For example, in the late summer of 1935 Beck went to the chief of the Army Personnel Office, Lieutenant General Viktor von Schwedler, and said that he needed an officer to be Reichenau's replacement as head of the Armed Forces Office. The officer should be a good administrator, Beck added, but not too bright, and someone who would not sell the army out. Schwedler said he could only think of one man: Brigadier General Wilhelm Keitel. Beck took the suggestion to Fritsch, who nominated Keitel to Blomberg. Blomberg accepted, and Keitel took up his post on October 1. However, Keitel soon demonstrated that he believed just as firmly in the principle of centralized Wehrmacht command as Reichenau had, and he outdid Reichenau in loyalty to Hitler.[74]

Keitel was in good company, for all of Beck's nominees to fill slots in the War Ministry switched allegiances, thus nullifying his attempts to gain additional influence. Colonel Alfred Jodl was one especially significant case. Beck had sent him to the ministry in July 1935 to take over as head of the National Defense Branch, Blomberg's embryonic military planning staff. Jodl, like Keitel, was a veteran of the General Staff, but his service there did not translate into loyalty. He set right to work to turn the branch into a proper planning staff. Other, younger General Staff officers, such as Lieutenant Colonel Bernhard von Lossberg, Lieutenant Colonel Kurt Zeitzler, and Colonel Walter Warlimont, followed Jodl's lead.[75]

In October 1935 the War Ministry took a step to strengthen its position as a central command over all the services: it set up a Wehrmachtakademie, or Armed Forces Academy. The school's goal was to provide training to a select few officers of middle rank—lieutenant colonels and colonels—on higher strategy, military economics, and interservice coordination, so that they could go on to joint staff duty. The mission harkened back to the so-called Reinhardt Courses of the late 1920s and early 1930s, when selected officers would study economics and politics at the University of Berlin after completing their General Staff training. The school also looked to the British Imperial Defense College as a model. Its first commander was General Wilhelm Adam, formerly chief of the General Staff and a good friend of Beck, so a conflict existed from the start between General Staff and War Ministry thinking over the school's proper function. Opposition from the Luftwaffe and the navy was more serious, however, and in the end the school closed after running only two courses.[76]

In December 1935 the memo war between the OKH and the War Ministry began to heat up again. The Armed Forces Office had produced a study on a two-front war against France and Czechoslovakia, and Beck took this opportunity to fight for his vision of the best command organization. Again he made the argument that this would of necessity be a land campaign, and that the army would therefore be the decisive arm. He went on to propose that the army's commander in chief should have a say in all major decisions, including those of a political nature. Further, the army commander should be the sole adviser to the Wehrmacht commander on all matters pertaining to land warfare, and he should have complete independence of command in wartime. The Army General Staff should be the primary advisory body within the command system, since it had assets that the Wehrmacht staff did not.[77]

Beck's arguments fell on deaf ears in the War Ministry. Blomberg, Keitel, and Jodl remained determined to enlarge the scope of their authority. They were convinced that the army could never reclaim the power it had held in the last war; the nature of modern warfare and the National Socialist state both militated against such an outcome. One development in the spring of 1936 did seem to augur well for the army: on his birthday, April 20, Hitler promoted Fritsch to the rank of full general and accorded him ministerial rank. Now, although Blomberg (who also received a promotion, to field marshal) was still Fritsch's superior as commander in chief of the Wehrmacht, Fritsch had a place in the cabinet. For the first time, an army spokesman had access to the Führer equal to Blomberg's, at least nominally.[78] Fritsch's pleasure at this change cannot have lasted long, however. Cabinet meetings were few and far between, since Hitler had no great use for that body.

The next major blowup over the command system occurred in the summer of 1937, in connection with a "Directive on Unified War Preparation of the Wehrmacht" that Blomberg wanted to issue. Keitel met with Beck several times to discuss drafts of the document, but the two never could agree on the fundamental question of command authority. Blomberg finally issued the directive anyway on June 24; it provided an overview of Germany's strategic situation and then directed the services to prepare plans for two eventualities: a surprise attack by France (the so-called *Case Red*) or a surprise attack by Germany against Czechoslovakia (*Case Green*). Potential problems in Austria and Spain also received some attention. The memo elicited howls of protest from the army, which simply was not prepared to allow the War Ministry to give it direction on strategy.[79]

Fritsch countered with his own long memorandum in August. He did not attempt to deal with the strategic issues but instead concentrated on structure.

He explained—once again—that the army was the most important of the armed services and stated that "a strategic Armed Forces high command independent of an Army Command is unthinkable."[80] He went on to suggest that the best solution to the problem of unifying the commands would be to form an Armed Forces Operations Group out of the Armed Forces Office; this group would be attached to the Army General Staff. The General Staff would actually run the war, using the Operations Group to coordinate with the other services. In his reply Blomberg turned down Fritsch's proposals, saying only that he would "do the natural thing: that is to include him, the Army Commander, in my [Blomberg's] command and operational procedure by referring to him and not going over his head."[81] Fritsch threatened to resign if Blomberg did not pass his memo on to Hitler; Blomberg threatened his resignation if Fritsch forced the issue. In the end Fritsch gave in.[82]

In an effort to strengthen his argument for a united command, Blomberg ordered joint Wehrmacht maneuvers for September 20 to 26, 1937. Blomberg believed that such maneuvers would demonstrate that a central organization should direct operations as well as handling administration, in contrast to the army's position. But the attempt backfired. Blomberg soon had to recognize that his own staff, the National Defense Branch, was far too small to plan and conduct large-scale maneuvers: the Wehrmacht commander finally had to give the mission to the General Staff, much to its satisfaction.[83]

While Blomberg and the army fought one another over command authority, Jodl and Keitel had been taking their own steps to reorganize and expand their sphere. Jodl's diary for 1937 documents several meetings and memorandums regarding the structure of the command. In October Keitel began to plan a partial reorganization of the Armed Forces Office. The staff had grown because of the additional demands with which it had to deal, so part of the reorganization amounted to name changes, such as "branch" to "office," that would reflect the subdivisions' expanded responsibilities. Other changes would be more fundamental: Keitel wanted to separate the command functions from the ministerial tasks within the office, so that Blomberg would have two clearly defined spheres in which to work.[84]

Keitel and Jodl would have to wait some months before they would get the chance to implement their design, but that chance would indeed come. It would be the outgrowth not of the debate over the command structure but of a combination of elements: tensions between the army and the SS, continuing problems with the pace of rearmament, Hitler's distrust of his senior military officers, and one of those instances in which a key figure's personal life takes on seemingly disproportionate significance. These factors would all contribute to a crisis in the German command system in the first months of 1938, at the end of which Blomberg and Fritsch would be gone and the high command would have assumed the shape it would keep, with only minor variations, right through the first two years of the Second World War.

3
Converging Trends, November 1937 to March 1939

The year 1938 would be a fateful one for Germany and for the world. In that year Hitler's foreign policy brought together all the debates and problems of the previous five years. The Führer needed to push ahead with rearmament in order to pursue his territorial goals, but economic problems hindered him. At the same time Germany's economic weaknesses created pressure to use the military in order to gain resources. The balance of military and economic strength with long-term foreign policy goals shaped strategy, while the debates over strategy also involved the question of authority and thus the issue of the high command's structure. And, of course, internal political rivalries were part and parcel of any conflict over authority as well. Through a combination of political and diplomatic savvy on Hitler's part, weakness and miscalculation on the part of his foreign and domestic opponents, and a series of fortuitous events, Germany and the Nazi Party would gain considerable strength in 1938, while the German army would take on an almost entirely instrumental role and a cataclysmic war would become all but inevitable.

THE ORGANIZATIONAL AND POLICY DEBATES CONTINUE

A meeting that took place on the afternoon of November 5, 1937, illustrated the position of power that Hitler had already reached; it also marked, if not a turning point, then an event that amplified and accelerated certain trends. Blomberg had asked for a meeting in order to discuss raw materials allocation. The services were competing for scarce resources, and in this area as in so many others, Hitler had become the sole arbiter. The Führer decided to expand on the meeting's theme by discussing his foreign policy goals. For that purpose (in addition to Blomberg's), he called together a small but important

37

group: Neurath, Blomberg, Fritsch, Göring, and Raeder were the principals. Colonel Friedrich Hossbach, Hitler's Wehrmacht adjutant, also attended; his notes, which he expanded into a summary five days later, are our only record of the event.[1]

As he frequently did, on this occasion Hitler went on at great length about the general situation. He spoke of the need to acquire more living space for Germany, since autarky was impossible and participation in the world economy did not offer a solution to the nation's economic problems. The nation would have to settle the issue of Lebensraum by 1943 to 1945 at the latest, he said, after which point the other European powers would catch up in armaments and the Party leadership would be growing old. Austria and Czechoslovakia would be the first targets, and the chance might come up to strike at them sooner without risking intervention by France or Britain. The addition of those countries would give Germany valuable human and material resources, especially after the forced emigration of three million of their citizens. Thus the military had to be ready to strike as soon as the opportunity offered itself. To Hitler the question of timing was paramount. Rearmament was encountering—and creating—economic difficulties that he could not ignore; their importance shows up in the fact that they took up the entire second half of the meeting.[2]

No doubt Hitler was counting on support from his advisers. Their response must have been a shock and a disappointment. In the discussion that followed the Führer's monologue, Blomberg and Fritsch raised serious objections to his plans. These were not moral objections. Neither of the generals was put off, apparently, by talk of the violent overthrow of two independent states and the ejection of millions of their people. In any case, Blomberg and Fritsch had demonstrated their full agreement with Hitler's long-term goals many times over.[3] What disturbed the generals was the possibility that Germany might become embroiled in a war with France and Britain before the Wehrmacht was ready. They disagreed with many specific points of Hitler's analysis, and they cautioned him against moving too quickly.

Of the military leaders, Fritsch and Beck (the latter learned of the meeting from his superior, as well as from Hossbach) took Hitler's statements most seriously. There is some indication that Fritsch spoke with Hitler about the issues again on November 9, just before the former departed for two months' leave in Egypt. If he did, there is no evidence that his effort did more than annoy the Führer.[4] Beck could take no direct action for the moment, but he did put his objections in writing. In a set of remarks dated November 12, he laid out a point-by-point rebuttal of Hitler's analysis. He rejected the idea that Germany could adjust its borders without serious and unforeseen consequences. He objected to the fact that Hitler made his analysis without consulting his military experts. He dismissed Hitler's predictions regarding France as "wishful thinking." And he summed up by stating that the problems of Austria and

Czechoslovakia needed much more careful thought.[5] On December 14 he followed that up with a memorandum to Blomberg, in which he stated that the army would not be ready before 1942 or 1943.[6]

Blomberg tried a less direct way to moderate Hitler's plans. He and Jodl, with help from Beck and the General Staff, drafted a revision to the "Directive on the Unified War Preparation of the Wehrmacht" of June 24; the new plan for *Case Green,* the invasion of Czechoslovakia, came out on December 21. The plan cannot have struck Hitler as a particularly enthusiastic endorsement. It called for an attack after Germany had reached full readiness for war, a prerequisite that was open to interpretation. Here again the Germans' strategic dilemma stood out. They could not attack until they were ready, but they had to attack if they wanted to escape the economic trap in which they had placed themselves.[7] In the face of such a problem, the senior generals wanted to hold back. Hitler, on the other hand, saw more danger in waiting than in pressing forward.

This disagreement over foreign policy contributed to Hitler's growing distrust of his senior army officers. He had never been comfortable with the more aristocratic Prussian members of that corps, men who admired his political skills but looked upon him personally with the particular disdain that northern Germans so often reserve for their southern neighbors, and who also dismissed his pretensions as a strategist. The resistance that he encountered from Blomberg, Fritsch, and Beck gave him a focus for his dissatisfaction. He may not have been actively seeking a way to rid himself of that triad after the November 5 meeting, but he was certainly becoming impatient with them.[8] Not only did the generals oppose his foreign policy plans, but Hitler may also have blamed them for the slow pace—as he saw it—of rearmament.[9]

Hitler's relations with the generals also suffered because of the efforts of various figures within the dictator's inner circle. Göring and Blomberg had been at odds for years, and eventually the Luftwaffe commander decided that he wanted the position of war minister.[10] Meanwhile, Heinrich Himmler had taken up where Röhm had left off; he wanted his SS to become an independent armed force. Both men, but especially the latter, launched a deliberate smear campaign against Fritsch, Blomberg, and other senior army officers, with the help of Himmler's assistant, Reinhard Heydrich, and the SD (Sicherheitsdienst, or Security Service, a neutral bureaucratic name for the heinous core of the SS).[11] The fact that Hitler allowed the smear campaign to go on says a great deal about his attitude toward the generals. He did not believe everything that Himmler and the others told him, but he did not quash their efforts, either.

Then, in late January 1938, Hitler received word that Blomberg's new bride, one Eva Gruhn, had posed for pornographic pictures. In an army in which every officer had to obtain permission before marrying, this was a major scandal; Hitler and the army's leaders were of one mind in demanding

Wilhelm Keitel. (Courtesy Bundesarchiv, photo no. 183/H 30 220)

Blomberg's resignation from his post and the service. At the same time, and at the Führer's instigation, Himmler resubmitted a dossier on Fritsch that Hitler had rejected earlier, in which the general stood accused of homosexual practices. The charge was a lie, as both Himmler and Hitler knew, but they used it to force Fritsch from office as well.[12]

With Blomberg and Fritsch on their way out, Hitler had to decide on their replacements. He discussed nominees for commander in chief of the Wehrmacht with Blomberg at meetings on January 26 and 27.[13] Blomberg eventually offered a fateful suggestion: Why shouldn't the Führer take the post himself? After all, he was already the commander in the ultimate sense. Hitler had not considered this option before, and he remained outwardly non-committal, although the suggestion certainly got his attention. He did say that, should he take the post, he would need an assistant to handle all the staff work that would be required. He asked, "Who is that general you have had at your side up to now?" "Oh, Keitel," Blomberg replied, "he would not come into consideration. He is nothing more than my *chef de bureau* [office manager]." "That is exactly the kind of man I am looking for," said Hitler, and ordered that Keitel report to him. Keitel met with Hitler that afternoon and again the next day. Hitler's first thought was to discuss a possible successor for Blomberg. Göring had enlisted Keitel, like several others, to put his name forward, but Hitler was adamantly opposed; he considered Göring ill suited for the post. He had decided, he told Keitel, to take over command of the Wehrmacht personally, and he wanted Keitel to be his chief of staff. He assured Keitel that he was "indispensable."[14]

Thus began Keitel's direct service to the Führer; it would last more than seven years. For Hitler, Keitel was indeed the perfect choice. From others he earned almost universal opprobrium for his role. Franz Halder, later chief of the General Staff, described him as a conciliator:

> It was given to him to build bridges, to alleviate sources of friction, to reconcile enemies or at least to bring them closer. . . . He was, and this was something that one always had to admire later, a person of extreme diligence, literally a workaholic, of the highest conscientiousness in his field—but always in a way that kept his personality out of it, so that he himself never stood out in a leading way. . . . Soft and accommodating, he increasingly adapted himself to avoid any conflict with Hitler at all.[15]

This is perhaps the most generous possible interpretation of Keitel's role. One must note that he quickly became convinced of Hitler's genius as a political and military leader. "At the bottom of my heart I was a loyal shield-bearer for Adolf Hitler," he told Allied interrogators after the war; "my political conviction would have been National Socialist." Moreover, he fell completely under the spell of Hitler's personality, and his way of avoiding conflict was to agree loudly with everything the Führer suggested. Eventually he acquired the nickname—used only behind his back, of course—of "Lakeitel," a play on *Lakei,* or lackey.[16]

Keitel and Hitler also discussed a replacement for Fritsch. Hitler suggested Reichenau. Keitel, who knew the army would never accept Reichenau, proposed Lieutenant General Walther von Brauchitsch. Hitler did not want to drop his candidate, but he agreed with Keitel for the moment.[17] The negotiations over Brauchitsch were complicated, however. Hitler communicated three conditions to the new candidate through Keitel: he would have to bring the army closer to the state and its ideology, to replace the chief of the General Staff if necessary, and to recognize the current command organization.[18] Moreover, as Brauchitsch learned over the course of the next few days, Hitler intended to relieve or reassign a number of senior officers. Brauchitsch had no objection to the first of the conditions, but he wanted to reserve judgment about the command structure and personnel changes. Additionally, he was uneasy (as was Hitler) about his personal life: he was in the process of trying to divorce his wife so that he could marry another, already twice-married woman, and his wife was holding out for a sizable financial settlement.

In the end the various parties resolved the difficulties so that Brauchitsch could take up his new post, which he did on February 4, 1938. The deal that opened the way also created problems for both him and the army. The facts are these: the first Frau Brauchitsch did receive a large financial settlement, some of which came from Hitler; the divorce and Brauchitsch's remarriage followed soon after. Brauchitsch did not fire Beck, but he did oversee the dismissal of several other high-ranking officers, and a new command structure emerged that was not to the army's liking. Brauchitsch was also a firm admirer of Hitler; he cooperated in bringing National Socialist ideas into the army. These facts soon led to rumors within the officer corps to the effect that Brauchitsch had sold out to Hitler.[19] That was probably too harsh a judgment, but certainly Brauchitsch was grateful to the Führer for his position—and aware that he could lose it as easily as he had gained it. In any case, no matter what the truth of the matter, the rumors themselves were enough to detract from the new commander's effectiveness. They added to the resentment that many officers felt toward Brauchitsch because he had taken up Fritsch's post when the latter's guilt was still in question, and without consulting other army leaders.

External factors aside, Brauchitsch's character was hardly suited to his new position. He did not have the force of personality to stand up to Hitler on those occasions when the two men disagreed. His physical condition may have contributed to that problem: he had a heart problem that left him chronically tired and weak, and he was prone to fainting spells, headaches, and feelings of oppression. His public manner was hesitant, even timid; he often seemed aloof, impersonal, stiff, and arrogant. Hitler frequently found his bearing infuriating, but the Führer rarely had any trouble cowing him. In that

Walther von Brauchitsch. (Courtesy Bundesarchiv, photo no. 183/E 780)

sense Brauchitsch was another good match from Hitler's standpoint, since the latter did not want to see a strong personality in charge of the army.[20]

The effect of the Blomberg-Fritsch affair on the development of the high command structure was immediate and significant. Blomberg's dismissal raised fears in Keitel's mind for the centralized command concept that the two of them had been working on. When Hitler took over command instead, Keitel and Jodl were overjoyed. Jodl recorded the news, and Keitel's intentions, in his diary:

> Gen. K[eitel] says to me: the unity of the Wehrmacht is saved. Because I cannot burden the Führer with all the decisions I need stronger powers. I must also be able to remove myself more from day-to-day affairs. To this end it will be necessary to have the planned reorganization of the Armed Forces Office take effect in part on April 1 or even March 1. You cannot let me down on this. We can put Warlimont in charge [of the National Defense Branch] right away and you can take over the Command Group.[21]

Keitel and Jodl set to work immediately, together with the secretary of state in the Reich Chancellery, Hans Heinrich Lammers, to prepare a directive for Hitler's signature that would give the Wehrmacht command the authority they wanted.[22]

While all this furious activity was going on in the War Ministry, Beck prepared and submitted a memorandum on January 28, in another effort to shape the command system as he wanted and protect the army's interests. This time he proposed a twofold division in the command. A "state secretary for Reich defense" would coordinate the nation's war effort; he meant this post as a sop for Keitel. On the military side, the army's commander in chief would act as a sort of "Reich general staff chief," with authority over the other services. Beck justified that suggestion by arguing, again, that the army would be the decisive arm in war. Finally, the National Defense Branch would be attached to the Army General Staff as a coordinating agency.[23]

Beck and the rest of the army's generals must have been shocked when, a week later, Hitler released the decree upon which Lammers, Keitel, and Jodl had been working so diligently. The provisions of the Führer Decree of February 4, 1938, on the leadership of the Wehrmacht were as follows:

> From now on I will directly exercise command authority over the entire Wehrmacht personally. The former Armed Forces Office in the Reich War Ministry, with its functions, now becomes the Armed Forces High Command (Oberkommando der Wehrmacht or OKW) and my military staff, directly under my command. At the head of the staff of the Armed Forces High Command stands the former Chief of the Armed Forces

Office as "Chief of the Armed Forces High Command." He holds the rank of a Reich Minister. The Armed Forces High Command will handle, at the same time, the affairs of the Reich War Ministry; the Chief of the Armed Forces High Command exercises, on my behalf, the authority formerly held by the Reich War Minister. The Armed Forces High Command is responsible for the unified preparations for the defense of the Reich in peacetime, in accordance with my directives.[24]

This development was a severe blow to Beck's hopes for a leading role in the command structure. Nowhere in the army's calculations to this point had there been any thought that the head of state might take over personal command of the Wehrmacht. And that was not the only shock the army was to suffer on February 4. In an address to the leaders of the Wehrmacht at the War Ministry, Hitler revealed the scandals involving Blomberg and Fritsch— taking care to put them in the worst possible light. Most of his listeners had never before heard the allegations, and they were stunned. Hitler made a real show of his indignation and convinced his audience that he had lost a great deal of faith in the army's leadership. The address left the attending officers thoroughly intimidated. The embarrassment that the Führer had suffered, they believed, would at least partially justify whatever might follow.[25]

Actually, the danger still existed that the army would rally to the defense of Fritsch, for whom a court of honor would soon convene. Within Party circles there was even fear that the army would launch a coup. A coup of another sort, however, this one in the realm of foreign policy, allowed Hitler to distract the army and the nation from Fritsch's case and the other changes he was making in the military. By February 1938 tensions in Austria were reaching a crisis stage, and Hitler conspired with the Austrian Nazis to pressure the chancellor, Kurt von Schuschnigg, into accepting Nazi participation in the government. Schuschnigg agreed to Hitler's demands at a meeting at Hitler's retreat in Berchtesgaden on February 12 but then returned to Vienna and, on March 9, called for a plebiscite. Hitler was furious. On March 10 he called in Keitel and demanded that the army be ready to enter Austria within two days.[26]

Hitler's order caught the army flat-footed; it had no plans ready for such an operation. Beck and his assistant chief of staff for operations (Oberquartiermeister I), Erich von Manstein, conferred with Keitel that afternoon and then returned to the OKH to draft the necessary orders over the course of the evening. Mobilization began while they were at their task, and despite some significant problems, the incursion took place as planned on March 12. Within days the annexation of Austria was a fact. Hitler had pulled off another foreign policy victory, flouted the demands of the Western powers yet again, and in the process had interrupted Fritsch's trial. The trial resumed on March 17 and soon found Fritsch innocent, but by that time Hitler's position was unassailable.[27]

The Führer also took steps domestically, both to limit any damage from the Blomberg-Fritsch crisis and to draw the maximum benefit from it. On February 4 he had ended his railings against the army leadership with these comments: "After such sorrowful experiences I must consider anyone capable of anything. The 100,000-man army has failed to produce any great leaders. From now on I shall concern myself with personnel matters and make the right appointments."[28] In fact he had already made his first moves in this arena, in part with a view toward disguising the reason for Fritsch's removal, in part out of personal or Party antipathy. On February 3 Brauchitsch had gone to see Schwedler to give him the names of a collection of officers who would have to leave their posts. Schwedler himself was on the list, along with two of his top assistants; they would be sent away from Berlin to troop commands. (Keitel had already suggested his brother Bodewin as a replacement for Schwedler, and Hitler had accepted.) Beck's assistant Manstein suffered the same fate, although Beck himself kept his position for the moment. All in all, a total of fourteen generals had to leave active duty, and forty-six officers were reassigned.[29]

Hitler made one other important personnel decision during the crisis. His Wehrmacht adjutant, Colonel Friedrich Hossbach, had aroused his ire by telling Fritsch of the allegations against him, in direct contravention of Hitler's order, and so the Führer told Keitel to get rid of him. Hossbach, a General Staff officer, had been firmly in Fritsch's and Beck's camp and had been a valuable source of information and some influence. He also held a dual position: in addition to being the Wehrmacht adjutant, he was chief of the Central Branch of the Army General Staff, which handled General Staff officer assignments and records, among other things. As Hossbach's replacement, Keitel suggested an old comrade of his, Major Rudolf Schmundt, and Hitler agreed.[30]

Schmundt was a likable and obliging man and a capable General Staff officer. He idolized Beck, who had been his teacher at the War Academy. His disappointment therefore must have been so much the greater when, in accordance with normal practice, he reported to Beck before taking up his new post, and the General Staff chief gave him the cold shoulder. Hossbach received him in a similar vein and even refused at first to turn over the office's paperwork. Such was their hostility over Schmundt's appointment, which normally would have been Beck's responsibility. At any rate, Schmundt rapidly switched his allegiance to the OKW camp and became a devout follower of the Führer. Soon he acquired a nickname within the General Staff: "His Master's Voice." The link between the adjutant's office and the General Staff's Central Branch now became a liability rather than an asset for the army, and the appointment of a separate *army* adjutant, Captain Gerhard Engel, did little to improve the situation.[31]

With the OKW now in existence, the issue of the command structure appeared to have been settled. However, the army noted that Hitler's decree of

Rudolf Schmundt. (Courtesy Bundesarchiv, photo no. J 27 812)

February 4 had only given the OKW responsibility for *peacetime* planning and coordination. Here was a loophole: the question of *wartime* command was still open. The army wanted to establish just how much authority it would have within its own strictly military, that is, operational, sphere, and also how much influence it might be able to wield over strategy. Beck and Brauchitsch now tried to turn the other service commanders against the OKW, using Beck's last suggestion (the one that included the position of "Reich general staff chief") as a basis. Raeder was willing to go along to an extent, but he wanted his influence to equal that of the army commander within the proposed system. Göring rejected the entire idea, preferring Keitel's purely nominal leadership to that of some Reich General Staff dominated by the army.[32]

With that plan on the rocks, the army's leaders now went ahead again on their own initiative to push for an alternative system. In a memorandum dated March 1, 1938, they proposed a definition of the army commander in chief's authority that would result, according to Jodl, in "a complete demotion of the OKW."[33] The OKW responded by stating that Hitler would certainly support the army's plan if the army could get the other services to go along with it. Since that was impossible, Brauchitsch tried sending another memorandum on March 7 that was merely a reworked version of Fritsch's August 1937 memo and that of March 1. The fundamental argument remained the same: the command of the Wehrmacht must be unified in its most important arm: the army. A Reich secretary of war would be responsible for organizing the nation's war effort. The commander in chief of the army would be adviser to the secretary of war as Reich chief of staff simultaneously; he would have complete control of army operations and would work through an Operations Branch to give broad direction to the other services.[34]

Keitel and Jodl worked hard with the army's latest suggestion. They set the contrasting arguments—theirs and the army's—alongside one another in a note of March 22, 1938, and gave the army the chance to clarify certain points. Then they created a memorandum entitled "Command in War as a Problem of Organization," which went out on April 19 under Keitel's signature. Keitel started out by saying that one could not separate the conduct of operations from economic and psychological warfare and from the organization of the nation's war effort, as the army had suggested: "The war of the future does not allow for a purely military strategy."[35] He went on to say that, while the army would undoubtedly play a decisive role in any war, circumstances might require that the needs of the navy or the air force be given primacy. Therefore the army could not have a dominant position; as in the last war, its decisions would not give proper consideration to the needs of the other services. Citing Clausewitz, Keitel maintained that the organization set up under the Führer Decree of February 4 represented the best possible way to bring the political and military sides of war into agreement. He reassured the army, however, that "a unified command of the armed forces in wartime would in no way interfere with the individual commands of the three branches of the service and it would be the policy of the high command to issue only standing orders and not day-to-day directives." Thus, in his opinion, "the present armed forces administration is the best and most logical for an authoritarian state."[36]

Hitler almost certainly approved the April 19 memorandum before Keitel sent it to Brauchitsch. In the weeks following February 4, he had intervened several times to try to quell the continuing controversy, with which he was becoming increasingly frustrated. On February 25 he gave Brauchitsch the rank of Reich minister, and then on March 2 he transferred some selected powers from Keitel to the service commanders. These measures had not satisfied the army, and Hitler had begun to perceive the army's memorandums as personal attacks that Brauchitsch should have stopped. He now assured the army that Keitel would never become the chief of a Wehrmacht General Staff, but he also said that he wanted to think the matter over.[37]

Soon the question of the command structure again overlapped with matters of foreign policy. With Austria out of the way, Hitler once more turned his attention to Czechoslovakia.[38] On April 21, 1938, he told Keitel to begin planning for an eventual military confrontation. Hitler did not intend to start a war right away, but he wanted to be ready to act quickly if the opportunity presented itself. Keitel, with Jodl's help, prepared a directive for the operation, but he held it back from the army at first, along with any indication of Hitler's intentions, because he feared the opposition it would arouse. Such was the degree of mistrust now present between the OKW and the OKH, that one withheld information of vital political and strategic importance from the other.[39]

Very soon thereafter, Beck presented Brauchitsch with another memorandum on Germany's political and strategic situation. Whether he had somehow gotten word of the preparations in the OKW remains unclear, but the intent of his May 5 memo certainly was not. Beck warned, as he had in November of the previous year, against any moves that could spark a general European war. He sent the memo to Brauchitsch, who was loath to face the Führer again on this issue. Brauchitsch took the memo to Keitel, and the two of them watered it down by removing the sections dealing with political and strategic matters and leaving in just those concerning narrow military issues. Hitler still rejected it in the harshest terms.[40]

The debate became more strident as tensions with Czechoslovakia increased in the second half of May. The Czechs carried out a partial mobilization on May 21 in reaction to reports of German troop concentrations on the border; the mobilization caused diplomatic tensions and a loss of prestige that enraged Hitler.[41] On May 28 he told a gathering of state, Party, and military leaders that he intended to destroy Czechoslovakia as soon as possible, despite the risk of war with the west. The announcement prompted an even stronger memo from Beck, dated May 29, in which he again combined structural with strategic and operational concerns:

> Regular, informed advice to the supreme commander of the armed forces in questions of warfare and above all of military operations must be called for in the same measure as a clear delimitation of and respect for responsibilities. If measures are not taken soon to change the current relationships, which have become unbearable, and if the present anarchy remains the dominant condition over the long term, the further fate of the armed forces in peace and war, as well as the fate of Germany in a future war, can be seen in only the blackest terms.[42]

But on May 30, even as Brauchitsch was mulling over Beck's most recent complaints, Hitler released his latest version of the order for *Case Green,* which reflected his anger toward Germany's neighbors to the southeast and his determination to destroy them. The May 30 version began: "It is my unalterable decision to crush Czechoslovakia through military action in the foreseeable future."[43]

On the same day, Hitler also addressed the structural debate by modifying the decree of February 4 along exactly the lines that Keitel and Jodl wanted. The new directive further defined Keitel's sphere of authority to include the supervision of unified defense preparations in accordance with Hitler's directives, the handling of questions regarding the Wehrmacht as a whole, and all ministerial matters. It went on to say that in questions concerning the entire Wehrmacht, those offices within the services' commands that carried out the actual work were subject to the OKW chief's directions. It also called upon the services to keep Keitel informed on all fundamental questions.[44]

Beck was still not ready to give up. In another memo, this one dated June 3, he directly questioned the OKW's ability to give sound advice regarding operations against Czechoslovakia. He wrote that he recognized the need for an attack, and that the General Staff had been working on plans for it for some time. But, he said, the OKW was not familiar with those plans and so was unqualified to advise the supreme commander.[45] Then, after conducting staff exercises that predicted a European war if Germany went forward with *Case Green,* Beck prepared an even stronger memo on July 16. On the same day he briefed Brauchitsch on the measures he believed would be necessary to avoid a military conflict: the leading generals should sign a petition to the Führer; if that did not work, they should resign en masse. On July 19 Beck repeated his warnings, and on August 4 he explained them to an assembly of the army's senior generals. But Brauchitsch refused to back him up, and the generals rejected his plea. While they agreed that a European war would be disastrous for Germany, they did not see that a war with Czechoslovakia would spread.[46]

At the end of July, Manstein, then a division commander, provided Beck with some unsolicited—and illuminating—advice. In his view, the problems Beck was experiencing were the result of a faulty command organization. "It seems completely unavoidable to me, that the fact alone that the Führer is receiving advice on military questions from two sides must in the end shake his confidence in that advice," he wrote. "Also, diverging views or the entrance also of lesser figures from the OKW could be used to discredit the military leadership."[47] He went on to suggest that in wartime, Hitler should have command of both the armed forces *and the army;* that would eliminate the internal conflicts (which the army had been losing) and place great power in the hands of the chief of the General Staff. As far as an attack on Czechoslovakia was concerned, Manstein considered this a political decision that Hitler should make, and for which he would have to accept responsibility. Finally, Manstein argued that if only the commander in chief of the army and the chief of the General Staff could form a closer personal bond with Hitler, they could win his trust and overcome the bad advice coming from the OKW.

Manstein's letter underscores the futility of Beck's efforts to inspire resistance against Hitler's plans. In fact, Manstein managed to encapsulate, in just a few pages, the main problems with the officers of the high command: their inclination to deal with operational and organizational details instead of broader issues of "politics"; their unwillingness to let go of personal power for the sake of unified leadership; and their complete obliviousness to the dangers of Germany's strategic position.[48] Beck was neither a saint nor a genius. He sympathized with Hitler's goals and exhibited many of the General Staff's traditional intellectual weaknesses. But he did rise above Manstein's level, and that of most other officers, if only too late.

The August 4 meeting did not help the relationship between Beck and Brauchitsch, which had been troubled from the start. Beck had resented the manner in which Brauchitsch had negotiated for his office without letting the chief of the General Staff play his accustomed role. Since then, Beck's constant warnings and admonishments had begun to get on Brauchitsch's nerves. The commander in chief turned more and more often to Lieutenant General Franz Halder, Beck's new assistant chief of staff for operations, instead of dealing with Beck directly. For his part, Brauchitsch was increasingly isolated. His willingness to take Fritsch's office, and his refusal to push for that officer's rehabilitation after his acquittal by court-martial, had won him many enemies in the senior officer corps. He certainly could not get support from the OKW; he was at odds with Jodl, Schmundt, and both the Keitel brothers. And his attempts to bring the army's objections to Hitler, however weakly pursued, earned him streams of abuse.[49]

Beck made one final attempt that summer to alter the course of Hitler's foreign policy. He insisted that Brauchitsch present his memorandums to the Führer, which Brauchitsch did at the beginning of August. A heated exchange followed, according to Brauchitsch's testimony after the war, but the debate's only effect on Hitler was to make him more determined than ever to wipe out any resistance the General Staff might offer to his plans. On August 10, 13, and 15, he addressed groups of officers to try to win them to his way of thinking—with mixed success. The officer corps was not ready to follow Beck's call to resist, but they were not completely acquiescent either.[50] At any rate, Beck had had enough. On August 18 he asked for permission to resign, and Hitler granted it, with the caveat that, "for foreign policy reasons," the change not be made public just yet.[51] Beck gave up his position at the end of August 1938 and, on October 31, retired from the army. Before leaving his post, however, he added a final note to the internal records of the General Staff: "In order to make our position clear to historians in the future and to keep the reputation of the high command clean, I wish, as Chief of the General Staff, to make it a matter of record that I have refused to approve any kind of National Socialist adventure. A final German victory is impossible."[52]

Opinions on Beck's replacement, Franz Halder, have covered the gamut from sincere approbation to bitter criticism.[53] The range of opinion reflects a complex, even contradictory, nature that in some ways embodied the typical General Staff officer. On the one hand Halder was an above-average military technician, but his understanding of global strategy and of Germany's position in the world was correspondingly weak. He believed in the moral element of command, the indefinable quality of "character" that every officer needs. "Time and time again," he told an interviewer after the war, "so history teaches us, the spirit has overcome technology, mastered it, shown it new ways."[54] Personally he demonstrated his "character" through remarkable endurance and self-discipline. Even at the beginning of Halder's career—and he entered the General Staff early—his superiors noted his extreme diligence and correctly perceived the ambition and pride that lay behind it. He was religious and conservative, with a strong sense of duty. His public manner was often stiff and almost ritualistically correct, sometimes pedantic, sober, often prosaic. He reminded many people of a teacher: either a university professor or a high school teacher, depending on the observer's attitude toward him. That outward appearance covered up, perhaps deliberately, an extremely sensitive nature and a tendency to let the mood or the circumstances of the moment overwhelm him. Many of his colleagues remarked on his tendency to break into tears on occasion, and he held onto both his friendships and his enmities with equal devotion.

Halder's relationship with Hitler was as complex as his personality. His outward manner stimulated the dictator's insecurity and thus heightened his suspicion and anger. Additionally, Halder had spent his entire career in staff positions, whereas Hitler boasted frequently of his frontline experience and maintained a combat soldier's distrust of staff officers. Halder valued technical expertise and logical processes; he could hardly be impressed with Hitler's instinctive, dilettantish approach to command. He apparently shared Beck's

Franz Halder. (Courtesy Bundesarchiv, photo no. 70/52/8)

concerns regarding the foreign policy line that the Führer was taking. He did not, however, use direct confrontation, as Beck had; he preferred to avoid open conflict, perhaps because he wanted to maintain control of his own emotional nature, perhaps because he saw that direct opposition was futile. Instead he engaged in various kinds of obstructionist behavior. He would express disapproval with brief, grim remarks or a sour expression, which only served to annoy the Führer. He would also work behind the scenes to modify, avoid, or hinder Hitler's orders; that approach worked at times but was counterproductive in the long run, as Hitler recognized the tactic and took steps to defeat it. And finally, early in his tenure, Halder took part in plans for a coup, in the hope that a chance to depose the dictator might come along.

The developing crisis over Czechoslovakia seemed to offer just such an opportunity. Halder believed that Hitler's policies would lead to a larger war, but he knew that most senior officers, as well as the public at large, did not share that opinion. That was the sticking point for him. Although he initiated contacts with other conspirators and was serious in his intentions, he would not commit himself to act until war was imminent. He also faced the obstacle that, as a staff officer, he did not command any troops, and Brauchitsch's attitude remained uncertain enough that no one wanted to bring him into the conspiracy. Support from some other key commanders seemed certain, however, and plans went forward as the diplomatic crisis approached its peak in September 1938. The conspirators had nearly reached the point of launching the coup when, on September 29, Britain and France surrendered to Hitler's demands and signed the Munich Agreement. Hitler had pulled off yet another diplomatic triumph, his greatest so far. Plans for a coup collapsed immediately, and Halder suffered a near breakdown from the stress. From that point forward, Halder accepted a purely instrumental role for himself and the army, in his actions if perhaps not always in his heart.[55]

The Munich Agreement was not the only unpleasant surprise that the crisis forced Halder to confront. He also discovered, in the course of preparing the plan for the invasion, that Hitler would not restrict himself to issuing political and strategic guidance. After Hitler first heard the plan that Halder and his staff had prepared, he decided that the operational concept was flawed. His wish to have Brauchitsch and Halder change the plans, which he made known to them through Keitel, met with a flat rejection at first. Finally Hitler ordered them to report to him. He tried to explain the error of their ways, but when they still refused to abandon their point of view he abruptly ordered them to change the dispositions; then he dismissed them. Halder was badly shaken. The OKH, which had long since lost any say in strategy, could no longer pretend even to have sole control of operations.[56]

German troops entered the Sudetenland peacefully on October 1, in accordance with the Munich Agreement. Hitler's operational plan had not been put to the test, but neither had his generals' dire warnings come true. His success gave the Führer the confidence to hold another housecleaning in the officer corps. Beck's retirement became public at this point, and Hitler also had dismissed several other generals, men who had demonstrated some measure of opposition to the regime. Brauchitsch's reaction was to make ever greater protestations of loyalty, as in his order to the army of December 18, 1938, in which he referred to Hitler as "our leader of genius" and admonished the officer corps that it "must not be surpassed by anybody in the purity and genuineness of its National-Socialist outlook."[57] If this impressed the Führer, there was little sign of it; his skepticism toward and distrust of the General Staff and the senior officer corps remained. He also knew that his power was secure, that there was little the army could or would do to stop him.

Hitler made no secret of the fact that he considered Munich a defeat. He had wanted to destroy Czechoslovakia, but the Western powers had robbed him of the chance. Germany's economic problems remained significant, and control of the rest of Czechoslovakia would help considerably. However, the Munich Agreement had left that country militarily defenseless, and Hitler immediately started planning to complete what he had begun. In March 1939 the Germans took over the rest of Czechoslovakia, and within a few days thereafter Hitler told Brauchitsch to begin planning for operations against Poland.[58] The Germans did not know it, but they had just crossed a threshold. The takeover of Czechoslovakia hardened Western opinion against them. When next they threatened war, they would have to follow through. This is a useful place at which to break off the narrative and examine, first, the command structure as it existed just prior to the war and, second, the significance of the changes that had taken place since the end of 1937.

THE ORGANIZATION OF THE HIGH COMMAND, SPRING 1939

Every bureaucratic system includes both formal and informal structures and processes. That is, a bureaucracy is set up to function in a certain way, and often it does. At the same time, though, as anyone who has worked in a bureaucracy knows, the organizational chart is only part of the story. Personal relationships and power struggles distort formal hierarchies, people bend or break the rules, spheres of authority overlap, and inefficiencies and miscommunications bedevil the best-laid plans. With the changes that went into place in early 1938, the German command system assumed the formal structure that it would keep, with minor modifications, right through the first two years of the Second World War. An examination of the system's formal structure at this point can yield two sets of results. First, such an overview will begin to identify some of the structure's objective strengths and weaknesses, in isolation from the informal processes. And second, those informal processes will stand out more clearly against a picture of the system's formal elements.

As commander in chief of the Wehrmacht, Hitler occupied the top of the German command hierarchy. The Oberkommando der Wehrmacht, as his military planning staff, was his main source of information and, to the extent that he wanted it, advice. As Keitel envisioned it in 1938, the OKW's military mission was to issue broad directives to the services that would provide strategic and operational guidance for large-scale undertakings.[59] Because that mission was so limited in scope, the OKW devoted a much smaller portion of its assets to actual military planning than did the OKH. The OKW's major elements were four so-called Office Groups.[60] One was the Defense Economy Staff (Amtsgruppe Wehrwirtschaftsstab) under Thomas. Another was the Office Group for General Armed Forces Affairs (Amtsgruppe Allgemeine Wehrmachtangelegenheiten) under Colonel Hermann Reineke, with branches handling supply and internal affairs such as discipline and administration, as these applied to the armed forces as a whole. The third was the Office Group for Foreign and Counter-Intelligence (Amtsgruppe Auslandnachrichten und Abwehr) under Admiral Wilhelm Canaris. The last element was the Amtsgruppe Führungsstab, the Command Staff, which was responsible for advising the Wehrmacht commander in chief on all problems relating to the conduct of military operations. This element operated under the direction of Major General Max von Viebahn until he suffered a breakdown during the Sudeten Crisis and Keitel relieved him; Jodl then took over as acting chief, followed later by Colonel Walter Warlimont. The staff soon became known as "Jodl's working staff" or "Warlimont's staff."[61]

Even within the Command Staff, however, only a portion of the assets worked on strictly military tasks. The staff contained three branches: Armed Forces Propaganda, Armed Forces Communications, and National Defense (Abteilung Landesverteidigung). The last was the Führer's military planning staff; it dealt with all problems connected with war in the field. Its basic directive charged it with the elaboration of all the Führer's directives and with the task of keeping Hitler and the chief of the OKW informed. In no sense was it generously manned. It comprised small planning elements from the army, navy, and air force, plus a supply group, a communications group, an administrative section, and several liaison officers: in all, fewer than thirty officers and civilian officials, plus two to three times that number of clerks, typists, communications specialists, and other support staff.[62]

Since the National Defense Branch had not developed into the Wehrmacht General Staff that Jodl had envisioned, operational planning for land warfare, as well as many other responsibilities relating to the army, remained the responsibility of the OKH. When Hitler came to power in 1933, the army's command structure had not changed significantly from what it was in 1920, but since 1933 it had expanded right along with the army. The T2, or Organization Branch, of the Truppenamt had been responsible for creating the new system, with the peacetime structure as its first priority.[63] The structure that evolved would have been

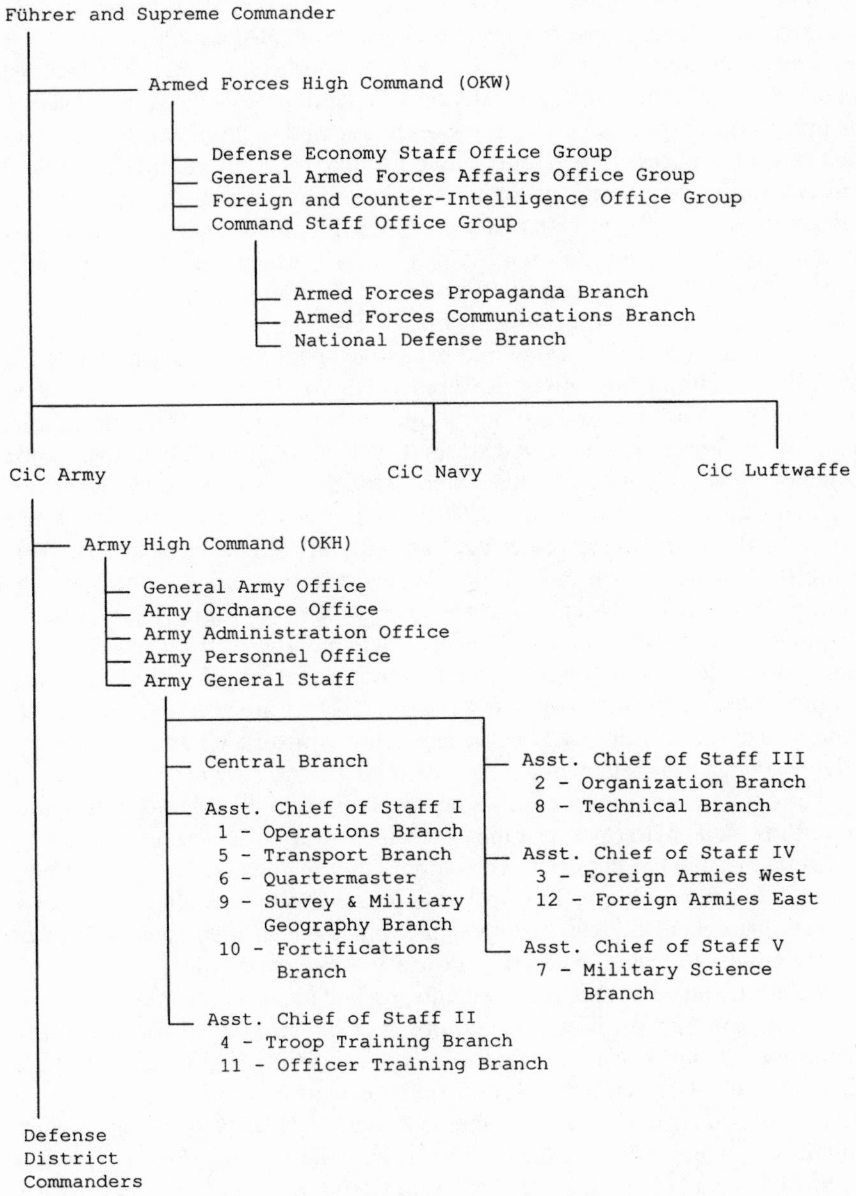

Führer and Supreme Commander

├──────── Armed Forces High Command (OKW)
│   │
│   ├─ Defense Economy Staff Office Group
│   ├─ General Armed Forces Affairs Office Group
│   ├─ Foreign and Counter-Intelligence Office Group
│   └─ Command Staff Office Group
│   │
│   ├─ Armed Forces Propaganda Branch
│   ├─ Armed Forces Communications Branch
│   └─ National Defense Branch
│
├───────────────────────────────────┬───────────────────────────┐
│   │   │
CiC Army   CiC Navy   CiC Luftwaffe

│
├─── Army High Command (OKH)
│   │
│   ├─ General Army Office
│   ├─ Army Ordnance Office
│   ├─ Army Administration Office
│   ├─ Army Personnel Office
│   └─ Army General Staff
│   │
│   ├─ Central Branch   ├─ Asst. Chief of Staff III
│   │   │   2 - Organization Branch
│   ├─ Asst. Chief of Staff I   │   8 - Technical Branch
│   │   1 - Operations Branch   │
│   │   5 - Transport Branch   ├─ Asst. Chief of Staff IV
│   │   6 - Quartermaster   │   3 - Foreign Armies West
│   │   9 - Survey & Military   │   12 - Foreign Armies East
│   │   Geography Branch   │
│   │   10 - Fortifications   └─ Asst. Chief of Staff V
│   │   Branch   7 - Military Science
│   │   Branch
│   └─ Asst. Chief of Staff II
│   4 - Troop Training Branch
│   11 - Officer Training Branch
│
Defense
District
Commanders

Figure 2. The German high command, January 1, 1939, showing the changes of Spring 1935 and February 1938.

recognizable to a General Staff officer of a generation before; its designers rein-troduced old organizational models that had worked satisfactorily.

The commander in chief of the army (Oberbefehlshaber des Heeres) headed the army command hierarchy. His duties in peacetime were to oversee the army's training, to promote good discipline and morale, and to maintain the army's readiness. In wartime he would take over command of the field army while also overseeing the administrative apparatus that supported it. He was responsible to the minister of war until Hitler effectively abolished that position; thereafter, he reported directly to the Führer. His direct subordi-nates were the Defense District (Wehrkreis) commanders in peacetime, the commanders of army groups in wartime.[64]

The OKH was the planning and executive agency for the commander in chief. Its most important missions were to organize and command the army, to train the troops and their officers, and to procure everything needed to maintain the army at its required strength.[65] The OKH contained five major elements, each with its own chief. The General Army Office (Allgemeines Heeresamt), the Army Ordnance Office (Heereswaffenamt), and the Army Administration Office (Heeresverwaltungsamt) all handled various aspects of administration and procurement. The Army Personnel Office (Heerespersonalamt) dealt with officer matters: recruitment, training, evaluations, promotions, and assignments. The last element, the Army General Staff (Generalstab des Heeres), existed to plan, prepare for, and direct military op-erations. Because the German army considered this function to be the com-mand's most important task, the General Staff coordinated and directed the activities of the other elements of the OKH to a large extent.[66]

The chief of the General Staff's position reflected his organization's spe-cial authority. The first paragraph of the chief's duty instructions stated that he was the permanent deputy of the commander in chief of the army and his primary adviser on all questions relating to the conduct of land operations. Further, his sphere of responsibility encompassed all questions connected with the conduct of war; he had the authority to determine the army's person-nel, material, and economic requirements, as well as the guidelines for the or-ganization, training, arming, and equipping of the army. He had the right to express his opinion before any decision could be made that would affect his sphere. The chief of the General Staff thus stood as first-among-equals in re-lation to the chiefs of the other elements in the OKH; they were not his sub-ordinates, but his opinions held more weight than theirs. Finally, he was responsible for all General Staff officers, in Berlin or with troop units. He ap-proved their selection, training, evaluation, promotion, and assignment.[67]

As a staff officer, even the most senior, the chief of the General Staff did not have the authority to issue orders of a fundamental nature on his own. In peace and war, he would receive those basic orders from the commander in chief and then see to their execution. This is a fine point but an important one. In practice, the chief of the General Staff frequently issued instructions to subordinate head-quarters, especially in wartime. This only occurred, however, after the commander in chief had approved those operations in concept. The chief of the General Staff would sign orders under the initials "I.A." for *"Im Auftrag"*: "by order of" the commander in chief. The chief of the General Staff thus had considerable freedom of action, while the commander in chief bore ultimate responsibility.[68]

The Army General Staff helped the chief to fulfill his duties, much as the OKH as a whole assisted the commander in chief of the army. The expansion of the army after 1933 vastly increased the amount of work that the staff had to undertake, and so it expanded as well. The first important change took place in June 1935, after the secret Reich Defense Law of May 21 dictated the changeover from Truppenamt to General Staff. At that point the number of branches *(Abteilungen)* doubled to eight. Further gradual changes followed over the course of the next three years; then General Halder oversaw a major reorganization after he took over as chief in the autumn of 1938.[69] In each of these cases, the changes resulted in the reapportionment of old responsibilities more than the creation of new ones.

By 1938 there were fourteen branches in the General Staff, each with its own chief, who was responsible for the organization and functioning of the branch. The branches carried out their tasks independently, in accordance with the service regulations and the guidelines laid down by the chief of the General Staff. The branch chiefs reported directly to the chief of the General Staff or, when circumstances so dictated, to the commander in chief directly, in which case they would inform the former of any important developments later on. Each branch would coordinate with other branches, with other army offices outside the General Staff, or with agencies outside the OKH, as required to complete the project at hand.[70]

Just as the General Staff was the key element in the OKH, the First Branch (Operations) occupied a central position within the General Staff.[71] This branch planned and directed the army's campaigns. Its chief was the principal deputy to the chief of the General Staff, and all the other branch chiefs deferred to him.[72] Each of the other branches performed a set of associated functions that in some way supported the army's ability to carry out operations:

The Third and Twelfth Branches (Foreign Armies West and East, respectively) prepared studies on the capabilities of other nations' military forces, whether allied or potential enemy. Before the war these branches worked primarily with information supplied from the Attaché Branch (unnumbered), which placed German officers as observers with other armies as well as monitoring the activities of foreign military attachés in Germany.

The Second Branch (Organization) created the plans for the establishment and organization of the peacetime and wartime armies. The Second Branch also worked out the yearly updates to the army's Mobilization Plan and developed the army's requirements for matériel, aside from munitions and fuel. The Sixth Branch (Quartermaster) planned for and supervised the delivery of those supplies to the units of the field army.

The Fourth and Eleventh Branches were both responsible for questions of training. The Fourth, or Troop Training, Branch handled all elements of training for enlisted personnel, including the use of training grounds, the organization of exercises, and the training of reserve units. The Eleventh Branch concentrated on officer training, including that of General Staff officers. It ran the War Academy, prepared the selection exam for General Staff candidates, and prepared the *Handbook for General Staff Duty in War.*

The Central Branch (unnumbered) became part of the General Staff in 1934; before then it had been the P4 Group in the Army Personnel Office. It handled the General Staff's administrative affairs, including the organization of the Army General Staff and the selection and assignment of General Staff officers. It also played an important part in the assignment of commanders, especially from division level upward.

The other branches of the General Staff had narrower technical duties. The Fifth Branch (Transport) planned for the use of railroads and inland waterways in mobilization and deployment, not just for the army, but for the entire Wehrmacht. The Eighth (Technical) Branch worked together with the Army Weapons Office on all questions of military technology, including developments in other countries. The Tenth Branch (Fortifications) supervised the design and construction of defensive systems. The Seventh Branch (Military Science) specialized in the evaluation of past operations, with the goal of developing lessons to improve combat performance. And the Ninth Branch, called the Army Survey and Military Geography Branch, provided the General Staff with all its maps and regional guides, as well as studies relevant to particular operational plans.

Coordinating the work of all these branches was no easy matter, and it became more difficult as the army and the staff expanded. To assist him in that task, General Beck reintroduced the old position of Oberquartiermeister, which had not existed in the Reichswehr because the staff had been so small. Appearances notwithstanding, that title had nothing to do with the quartermaster or supply service; it is best translated as "assistant chief of staff." The role of each Oberquartiermeister was to coordinate the activities of related branches within the General Staff under the direction of the chief, thus relieving him of some of his workload. These officers had no official decision authority, nor did they change the relationship of the branch chiefs to the chief of the General Staff. In practice, however, they could and did exercise a good deal of power within their particular functional areas. Beck created three such positions in 1935 and another in 1937; Halder added a fifth in 1938.[73]

With the addition of the last Oberquartiermeister to the General Staff, the high command assumed the basic form that the Germans would keep through their most successful campaigns. Although form does not dictate function, the structures themselves do reveal four important points about the high command.

The first is that, within the Army General Staff, there was clear organizational continuity that linked the structure of 1939 with a process of bureaucratic evolution. A staff officer of 1914 would have felt right at home in the staff of 1939. Most of the office functions had changed little or not at all in a quarter century, despite the changes in warfare and politics that had taken place in that time span. Second, the structural continuity within the General Staff reflected a similar lack of change in its intellectual foundations. The Germans were maintaining their emphasis on operations, as the primacy of the General Staff within the OKH and of the Operations Branch within the General Staff both demonstrate. Third, at a higher level the OKW did represent something new—but only in theory. The establishment of a centralized armed forces command, if it had had real power, would have brought an unprecedented level of coordination to the German military. The reality was, however, little more than a continuation of old patterns of rivalry among top-level command organizations. That was the point at which formal and informal structures parted company most significantly. The fourth and most obvious fact was that Hitler was in charge. His official position gave him the legal authority to issue orders, an authority fit into a military tradition that looked to the head of state as the leader of the army. That fact would remain a key to the high command's role in the coming war.

THE BALANCE OF POWER

For the first five years of Hitler's rule, the army's senior leaders could tell themselves that they were gaining everything they had wanted under Weimar. Hitler was leading Germany back to a position of power on the world stage. Rearmament was well under way, without any annoying interference from a representative government. The internal Communist threat no longer existed. Furthermore, the Führer had demonstrated his willingness to protect the army's position as the sole bearer of arms within the state. For that the generals had quite willingly sworn their absolute loyalty to the dictator and had even put up with his elimination of some of their number. Additionally, those of the generals who cared could still believe that Hitler would dare not challenge their position in the state or their control of their exclusive military realm. In the course of 1938, however, even those certainties slipped away. Having left the army in relative peace for five years, Hitler had finally subdued it entirely; the process of *Gleichschaltung* was complete.

The Blomberg-Fritsch affair and its aftermath were pivotal. Hitler had taken personal command of the Wehrmacht, set up a stronger centralized command agency under his direct control, and driven many of his most important and powerful opponents out of their positions or from the army entirely. As Wilhelm Deist points out, "The tensions between the party, its organizations, and the state on the one hand and the armed forces on the other were resolved by the complete subordination of the latter to the purposes and aims of the former."[74] Above all, the failure of the army's leaders to defend Fritsch against a blatant political conspiracy doomed them, even assuming that the army could still have acted against the state at that late point. Many of the Nazi leaders did in fact fear a coup d'état.[75] Hitler was more confident that he had the measure of the generals, and he was right. After his February 4 address to the Wehrmacht's leaders, Hitler supposedly remarked to some SA men that every general was either cowardly or stupid.[76] Many of the more junior officers interpreted the events differently, but in a way that was just as damaging: they imagined that their leaders' inaction amounted to approval.[77]

The affair was a serious blow to that small group that was trying to organize a coup against Hitler's regime, and the diplomatic victory at Munich reduced their prospects further still. The group had already been in a difficult position. By 1938 Hitler was immensely popular in Germany and in the army. Most senior officers admired him; the only exceptions were a minority of those with whom he came into close contact. Manstein's letter to Beck indicates just how much even General Staff officers were in awe of the Führer; they tended to think that any problem lay with his underlings, not with Hitler himself. Meanwhile, the junior officers had already absorbed a great deal of National Socialist propaganda; the steady stream of additional Nazi material that they received in the army, with the full cooperation of men like Blomberg and Brauchitsch, only increased their devotion.[78] To those men who hoped to use the army against the regime, all of this meant that their venture was extremely risky, if not impossible. Other doubts crowded in on the conspirators as well. They thought back to the abortive Kapp Putsch of 1920, when popular opposition had defeated an army coup and badly damaged the army's reputation; another failure like that could be fatal, both for the conspirators and for the army as an institution.[79] They also knew that they would break a centuries-long tradition of the General Staff and the Prussian officer corps by acting against the legitimate head of state.

The lack of significant resistance, overt or covert, left Hitler in almost complete control. He had long since taken strategy out of the army's hands, beginning as early as the reoccupation of the Rhineland in 1936. Since then he had never made a single strategic decision in consultation with the army's leaders. Instead, he simply informed them of his decisions. Then, with the preparations for the invasion of Czechoslovakia, he had demonstrated his willingness to interfere in operational planning as well. Brauchitsch, hesitant though he was to challenge the Führer in any case, could only obey or resign, and the latter course offered no hope of affecting Hitler's decisions. He could not go to the other service commanders for support, and the OKW certainly offered none. Only unified action by *all* the army's leaders offered any hope at all, and that unity was not to be had.

Seen in this light, the battle to unify the command system under army leadership appears almost ridiculous. What would an army-dominated high command have enabled its members to do that they could not find a way to do anyway? The army wanted to have a voice in policy and strategy, as well as complete control over operations, but Hitler was not going to allow any of that. In fact, the battles over authority had merely served to increase Hitler's power. Many observers, then and since, have ascribed to Hitler a "divide and conquer" management style, in which he would encourage conflict among his subordinates in order to increase his own power. They have pointed to the seemingly chaotic and competitive nature of the entire Reich government as a reflection of that philosophy. How much of that chaos was deliberate, and how much a result of Hitler's lack of interest in administration, remains open to question. In any case, one underlying point is certain: Hitler was jealous of his power. The organizational squabbles among his generals were irrelevant. He never intended to let the army build up a powerful command organization with which to diminish his control. Nor was he willing to let the OKW become the kind of Wehrmacht General Staff that Keitel and Jodl wanted. The organization that existed after February 1938 corresponded to Hitler's desires exactly.

Not only had Hitler created a structure that suited him, at least for the moment, but he had expanded his ability to influence the army through the personnel system. The postings of Bodewin Keitel to head the Army Personnel Office and of Rudolf Schmundt to head the General Staff's Central Branch were of critical importance. Bodewin Keitel was still officially subordinate to the commander in chief of the army, and so there was not as yet any fundamental change in personnel policies. The close cooperation that had existed between the General Staff and the Personnel Office was a thing of the past, however. Schmundt came directly under the OKW as the Wehrmacht adjutant to Hitler, so his direction of the Central Branch was even less subject to army control. Those two postings allowed Hitler, usually with close cooperation from Brauchitsch, to rid the officer corps of generals who were openly critical of the regime. From now on, the only officers to receive promotions would be either loyal to the Führer or obedient, apolitical technocrats.[80]

Thus 1938 was the year in which Hitler solidified his control of the German army. He knew that there were still elements within it that opposed him, but he also knew that he did not have to fear them too much. He could now concentrate on the war that he knew was coming, that he wanted, that he saw as the key to deciding the fate of Germany. The fact that his generals considered the armed forces unready for war disturbed him not at all. He was a gambler, a talented amateur in the military field, with a growing sense that he could out-general his generals. Now he was ready and able to put his new military instrument to the test. His success would depend in part on the effectiveness of the command system and his role within it.

Hitler defined that role in large part according to one of his fundamental principles: the *Führerprinzip,* or leader principle, according to which authority is centralized and strictly hierarchical. That is, the commander makes the decisions, and his subordinates carry them out exactly and without argument. That tenet flew in the face of the "principle of joint responsibility" that had played such an important role within the General Staff since the middle of the nineteenth century, and also of the long-standing practice of assigning *Vollmacht* to a subordinate officer, even one who was not a commander. The interplay of conflicting principles was complex. The traditional command style remained in use within the army's lower levels, while Hitler insisted upon the absolute nature of his own authority right from the start. The two systems clashed somewhere in the middle, and the point of contact worked its way downward through the chain of command as the war went on.

The principle of joint responsibility was actually in a weakened state before the war started. The *Handbook for General Staff Duty in War* of August 1939 stated, "The commander bears the responsibility for the act. The General Staff Officer is an adviser and helper, the conscientious executor of the decisions and orders of his commander."[81] Halder, who completed the first draft of the new handbook in November 1938, removed the staff officer's right to record his opposition to a commander's decision. Halder insisted later that he made this change on his own initiative.[82] The reality was more complicated. The principle had first come into existence as a way to exercise control over commanders who did not have any particular skill or training in warfare, as was true of many royal appointees in the nineteenth and early twentieth centuries. After the First World War this ceased to be an issue, since all officers shared roughly the same educational background and standards of professionalism, and so the principle began to fade from use almost immediately. All Halder really did was to put the stamp of approval on a trend that already existed.[83]

This is not to say that the General Staff had capitulated to the *Führerprinzip,* or that Halder "sold out" to Hitler, as some later claimed. True, the right to record objections in writing or to appeal a decision up the staff chain had disappeared from the General Staff manual. However, in a real sense the staff officer's responsibility and authority had not diminished. As Christian Hartmann points out in his biography of Halder, the General Staff remained a powerful, cohesive, and influential elite within the army.[84] Unit war diaries show a regular give-and-take among General Staff officers at various levels, and staff members sometimes worked behind the scenes to alleviate problems between commanders. Thus the changes in the *Handbook for General Staff Duty in War* were a routine, almost cosmetic reaction to changing circumstances. Since the principal commanders and staff officers nearly all hailed from the General Staff, few of them saw any problem with the changes. They also believed they had sidestepped the conflict with the *Führerprinzip,* although on that issue they were in for a disappointment.

For the moment, at any rate, the command relationships appeared to have stabilized. At the most senior level a set of procedures had evolved that would carry Germany through the opening campaigns of the war. This is a rough outline of how the system worked: first Hitler would issue broad instructions personally to one or more of the service commanders. Sometimes he would have the OKW—in effect the National Defense Branch—prepare a background study first, but often not. The services' headquarters staffs would create draft operational plans based on Hitler's instructions, which the service commanders would then present to the Führer personally. Hitler would make his decisions based on the services' plans and any information prepared for him by the OKW. Then the National Defense Branch would prepare and issue a written directive, incorporating the services' plans in some detail. With this directive, the services' staffs would then prepare their own operations orders, while maintaining close contact to ensure that those orders did not conflict with one another. When the orders were complete, the service commanders would submit them to Hitler for final approval, at which point the Führer would resolve any differences that remained.[85]

Two aspects of this process deserve emphasis. First, the OKW did not have any command authority of its own; all it did was issue directives in Hitler's name, just as the Army General Staff issued orders on the authority—im Auftrag—of the commander in chief.[86] Second, the inclusion of operational details in Hitler's directives was not at this time the result of the OKW's staff work or Hitler's meddling. This is not to say that Hitler did not meddle. The briefings he received were quite detailed, and he sometimes—as in the planning for Case Green—altered the plans significantly. But the details themselves were the outcome of staff work performed by the services, primarily the General Staff. There was no way that the National Defense Branch, with twenty-some officers, could produce the detailed plans that the General Staff could with eighty-five officers and numerous officer assistants (still a remarkably small total, considering the workload). Those details were a part of the OKW's directives simply so that the services could coordinate their planning more easily.[87] In all the operations planned or carried out up to the start of the war, the General Staff remained dominant. Hitler's role in the direction of the armed forces was still limited; he did not yet have the full confidence in his own military abilities that he would have later.

The extent to which Hitler interfered in strategic and operational planning remains one of the most important issues connected with the command system. Although he had served with distinction as an enlisted man in the First World War, that experience had done nothing to prepare him for the highest echelon of command. Nor did his personality suit him for that role. In his work habits he was often impulsive, at other times dilatory, but he nearly always clung stubbornly to a decision once he made it. If presented with information that conflicted with his preconceptions, he usually rejected it out of hand. He had a remarkable memory, but he concentrated too much on minutiae at the expense of broad issues. At best he was a talented amateur, but one with absolute power. Again, however, one must be careful not to exaggerate Hitler's influence within the command system, especially before the war began. For all his power, he could not make the command function by himself. He was dependent upon the expertise of the officers under him in the planning and management of warfare.

Thus Hitler, his principal commanders, and their staffs all made up a complex organism; all the parts had to work together to achieve their common goals. That organism's development up to 1939 had been a process combining chaos and design, cooperation and conflict. A multitude of outside forces had acted upon that process. The result was not exactly what anyone would have predicted in 1919 or 1933 or even at the end of 1937. Now, however, the Germans were stuck with it, at least for the time being. War was coming, and so the senior officers set aside their debate over the command structure—or at least the debate became secondary to other issues. The tensions and conflicts of the 1930s did not go away; they would shape German actions throughout the Second World War, and with them the nature of the war itself.

4

The Onset of War and the Initial Victories, March 1939 to June 1940

By the beginning of 1939, Hitler had decided on a path to his long-term policy goal, the acquisition of Lebensraum in the east. He knew he would have to deal with Britain and France, and in order to do that he would have to secure his rear. By that spring, most of the states on Germany's eastern frontier posed no threat: Lithuania was too small, Hungary was subservient, and Czechoslovakia no longer existed. Only Poland represented a problem. Hitler had been pressuring that country for some time to join the German sphere, to no avail. When the Poles rejected a German ultimatum on March 21, 1939, Hitler decided that they should be his first target; then he could deal with the west.[1] The war that followed less than six months later would mark the end of the high command's peacetime development. Now it had to prove itself—and at first it appeared to perform brilliantly. Poland would fall, followed by Norway, Denmark, the Netherlands, Luxembourg, Belgium, and France, all within the first ten months of the war. The series of victories was astounding, hardly less for the victors than for the vanquished. Behind the triumphs, however, serious weaknesses were already appearing.

On March 25, 1939, Hitler instructed Brauchitsch to begin working out the plans for an invasion of Poland.[2] To his erstwhile strategic planning headquarters, the Führer said nothing; the OKW only received word of Hitler's intentions several days after he told Brauchitsch.[3] At Keitel's instruction, the Command Staff revised the "Directive for the Unified Preparation of the Wehrmacht for War 1939/40," in order to back up Hitler's order. The OKW issued the document on April 3, after Hitler approved it.[4] An annex to the plan covered the invasion of Poland, code-named *Case White,* and it was quite broad. It detailed the political circumstances under which the attack might take place, and it promised that the western powers would stay out of the fight. In operational terms, beyond stipulating that the Wehrmacht was to aim for the destruction of the Polish armed forces through a surprise attack, it said little.[5] For the most part Hitler was willing to let the services do the detailed planning. As he had with *Case Green,* however, the Führer insisted on a strict review process; the April 3 directive stipulated that the services submit their plans to the OKW for inclusion in a master timetable, which Hitler would approve. All preparations were to be complete by September 1.[6]

Halder began planning the invasion with something approaching glee. Many German officers considered Poland an eternal enemy; Halder commented that with the end of the artificial friendliness between the two states "a stone has fallen from our hearts." Intervention by the west or even the USSR was a minor concern if the Wehrmacht could defeat Poland in two or three weeks, as he confidently predicted it would.[7] In the course of the next two months, the army drew up its plans. Hitler hardly figured in this process, although the army did keep him informed. On April 26 or 27 Brauchitsch took the army's draft to the Führer, who approved it without making any important changes.[8] On May 1 the invasion force's two army group headquarters staffs received their missions; they submitted their plans on May 20 and 27, respectively. In the meantime, Halder had worked out many of the details of the invasion by making it the focus of the General Staff's annual staff ride, which took place from May 2 to May 11. The OKH released its final version of the plan on June 15. It reflected the fact that the army's primary concern was to finish Poland off as quickly as possible so that it could transfer units to the west. Despite Hitler's assurances that the western powers would stay out of the fight, the OKH was taking no chances.[9] The OKW, meanwhile, served as little more than a central registry. It gathered the services' plans and reissued them as directives, but it offered no guidance. Halder made sure his staff kept the OKW informed, but when any problem arose, the army did not hesitate to bypass the OKW and deal directly with the Führer. Virtually the only task that the OKW performed was the creation of a list of deadlines for the plan, and even this was based upon input from the services.[10]

Preparations went forward over the course of the summer on several levels. A series of camouflaged movements and maneuvers served to bring units to the eastern frontier as the date for the attack—originally set for August 26—approached. Hitler also kept up a propaganda campaign with which he hoped to inflame the German people while delaying his enemies' preparations. In addition, after intense negotiations he succeeded in obtaining a nonaggression pact with the Soviet Union, accompanied by a secret clause under which the two states would partition Poland. He was sure that this diplomatic coup, which he announced on August 23, would deter the western powers from intervening in the campaign; thus he was profoundly shocked when Britain signed a treaty of alliance with Poland on August 25. That treaty, along with Mussolini's reluctance to join in the fray, prompted Hitler to call his forces back literally in the last hours, but he soon regained his nerve and rescheduled the attack for September 1.[11]

While these last-minute maneuvers took place, the OKH had been implementing its mobilization plan, which had been a focus of attention for years. The chief of the General Staff and his senior assistants met regularly throughout the prewar period to discuss mobilization measures, including the shape that the OKH would take when Germany went to war.[12] Within the army's mobilization plan, Special Enclosure 3 dealt with the wartime headquarters organization; the General Staff's Second (Organization) Branch was responsible for producing it. The Second Branch presented drafts to the other branches and to any other agencies concerned, after which it incorporated their comments into the final plan. This process took place annually in peacetime.[13]

A mobilization plan for the headquarters was necessary because, despite the many structural changes that the OKH had undergone between 1933 and 1939, it was still not suited for running a war. Some of its elements dealt with activities—such as military history or personnel administration—that were not the concern of an operational headquarters. In addition, there were more levels of responsibility than the Germans considered desirable; they favored small, streamlined organizations that could react quickly to any changes in the military situation. Special Enclosure 3 took these considerations into account. With mobilization, some duty positions fell out, others took on different responsibilities, and still others came into being.[14]

The most significant change in the OKH was its division into two parts. Upon mobilization, Brauchitsch, Halder, and most of the General Staff moved to a headquarters complex at Zossen, outside Berlin, where the staff operated under Halder's direct supervision; this was the so-called Headquarters, OKH. All the other offices of the Army High Command stayed in Berlin under Major General Friedrich Fromm, whose post, chief of army equipment and commander of the Replacement Army, came into being as soon as the mobilization plan went into effect. In his supervisory role, Fromm had wide-ranging responsibilities: he oversaw the entire army administrative apparatus, including elements that handled personnel replacement (except for officers); financial and material resource planning; and equipment development, production, and distribution. He also controlled all the army's assets inside Germany that were not under the direct command of the operational headquarters.[15]

From Zossen, the General Staff assumed responsibility for the direction of the Field Army, as well as for supply, intelligence evaluation and dissemination, and other functions related to combat operations. In order to carry out these functions more efficiently, the staff went through its own organizational changes. The first series of these concerned the assistant chiefs of staff. The assistant chief of staff for intelligence (OQu IV), Brigadier General Kurt von Tippelskirch, retained his old duties, but he was virtually the only one to do so.

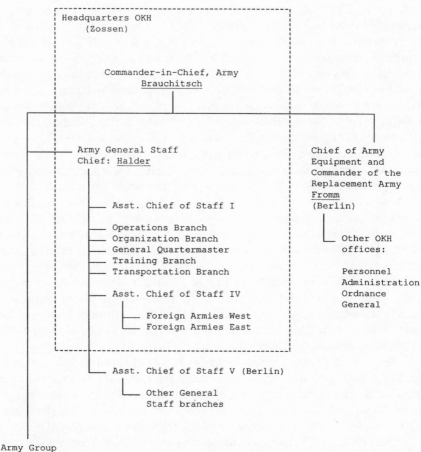

Figure 3. The German Army High Command (OKH) upon mobilization, September 1, 1939.

The positions of the assistant chiefs of staff for training and organization (OQu's II and III) were eliminated, and the branches they had supervised now came under Halder's direct control. The assistant chief of staff for military science (OQu V), General Waldemar Erfurth, stayed in the rear headquarters, where he supervised the activities of those General Staff elements whose responsibilities made them superfluous to an operational headquarters.[16]

The assistant chief of staff for operations (OQu I), Major General Carl-Heinrich von Stülpnagel, took on a special role with mobilization. He gave up any responsibility for specific branches; instead, he became Halder's roving deputy, providing assistance with whatever projects the chief deemed important. In

Friedrich Fromm. (Courtesy Bundesarchiv, photo no. 69/168/7)

that capacity he brought together the expertise he needed from throughout the staff, and he also worked with subordinate headquarters as well as other agencies in the OKH, the Wehrmacht, and even the Reich administration. The chief might put him to work to ensure that tactical lessons became part of training doctrine, to designate units for planned operations, or to visit the front as his representative. Many of these missions called for special skill and tact on Stülpnagel's part, since he often had to deal with people much senior to him in rank.[17]

On the branch level, the staff dissolved the Technical, Fortifications, and Officer Training Branches upon mobilization and gave their responsibilities to other elements. Meanwhile, the branch chiefs also reorganized their branches' internal structures to handle their new duties. The Operations Branch remained the focal point within the General Staff, and its structure was fairly typical. With Stülpnagel working on special projects, responsibility for purely operational matters now devolved upon the chief of operations, Colonel Hans von Greiffenberg. He no longer reported to Stülpnagel but reported directly to Halder, although he still had to keep the OQu I informed and act in accordance with his instructions.[18] The chief of Group I (known as the Ia), Lieutenant Colonel Adolf Heusinger, was Greiffenberg's deputy. The group's three subsections—each with its own geographic area of responsibility—collected reports, collated and analyzed the information in them, drafted plans and orders, and prepared studies. Groups II and III, meanwhile, supported the work of Group I by coordinating with other agencies, collecting additional information, and preparing maps, among other things. In addition, liaison officers from the navy, the Luftwaffe, and the chief of transportation formed a section inside the Operations Branch to facilitate any planning that involved their particular specialties.[19]

While the OKH was thus preparing for its role in the campaign, the OKW was making its own hasty arrangements prior to taking the field. In the Second World War's other combatant nations, the heads of state and their top command agencies remained in their respective capital cities, at least as long as they could. Not so Hitler; he was determined to lead from the front. His motives remain obscure, but the decision may have had to do with his view of himself as a frontline commander *("Feldherr")* and "first soldier of the German Reich"; he may also have seen the propaganda value of such a move.[20] Whatever his reasons, he boarded his special train, *Amerika,* on September 3 and headed east.[21]

Hitler's decision to direct the war from a headquarters train severely limited the capabilities of his command apparatus. For unknown reasons, the Führer had resisted every prewar plan for a field headquarters. No one had had the opportunity to lay out an organizational or technical framework for the OKW's activities in wartime, so after hostilities began there was no proven mechanism for doing the work and making the decisions that the situation demanded.[22] Moreover, there was a straightforward problem of manning: the Führer's train was too small to accommodate any but the most skeletal of staffs. With Hitler went Generals Keitel, Jodl, and Schmundt, and the three service adjutants; liaison officers from the SS, air force, and navy; Martin Bormann (head of the Party Chancellery and Hitler's private secretary); Press Chief Otto Dietrich; a representative from the Foreign Office; Hitler's two doctors; and a small number of orderlies and clerks. Jodl could bring only two officer assistants; the bulk of the National Defense Branch had to stay in Berlin.[23]

Fortunately for his staff, Hitler's role in the Polish campaign served to mitigate the impact of the headquarters' small size. The Führer spent most of his time either on excursions to the front or in handling diplomatic matters with the British, French, and Russians.[24] The offensive was over so quickly that he had little opportunity to involve himself in operational decisions. He did reserve all decisions for himself that he regarded as strategic, such as those concerning the naval war against Britain or the aerial bombardment of Warsaw. But although he stayed in close touch with Brauchitsch and kept himself informed of events, he rarely intervened in the battle, and so his tiny military staff was able to keep up.[25] Jodl now began to emerge as Hitler's primary military adviser, as Keitel distanced himself from operational matters and concentrated on administration, and soon a set of ad hoc working methods began to emerge.[26] Jodl conversed daily with Colonel Walter Warlimont, chief of the National Defense Branch, in order to transmit Hitler's instructions and plans. Warlimont and his staff met every morning so that the section leaders could report on the information they had received from the services. Then Warlimont would brief them on the Führer's intentions. Few orders needed to be written, so the officers of the branch busied themselves by maintaining contact with the service headquarters. The situation did not call for detailed planning or extensive coordination.[27]

From the OKH's standpoint, the relative inactivity at the OKW was entirely appropriate. As a strategic planning organ, the OKW should not have had much to say about the conduct of the campaign. Halder had warned Keitel and Jodl not to stick their noses into operations, and with Brauchitsch acting as direct liaison with the Führer, the OKH was free to get on with its job. Halder was able to report later that there was no friction between the OKW and the OKH during the opening phases of the offensive.[28] Likewise, an examination of the campaign reveals that the OKH maintained an appropriate command relationship with its subordinate army groups. Its proper role was to direct operations on all fronts, so it left the details of the Polish campaign to the army groups' headquarters for the most part, while it maintained a broad view. Halder's diary reveals that he kept close tabs on the situation in Poland, but that he and his staff also monitored military and diplomatic developments in the west.[29] They kept track of the situation down to division level but did not intervene unnecessarily in the spheres of their subordinate commands. The

OKH's orders remained general; they dealt with the disposition of the army groups and the direction of broad offensive thrusts.

The German plan for the Polish campaign called for an advance in depth, to dislocate Poland's defenses and surround and destroy its forces before they could withdraw. The Poles, for patriotic, geographic, and economic reasons, felt compelled to defend every acre of Polish territory; their dispositions ultimately made the Wehrmacht's task easier.[30] In fact, the offensive went even more smoothly than the Germans expected. Not until September 9 did they have to adapt their original concept to the developing situation.[31] This is not to say that they had no concerns. The declarations of war by Britain and France on September 3, though not entirely unexpected, were still a blow. Germany had fewer than half as many divisions as France on the western front. The German defenses were stronger than in 1938, but if the French attacked, they could certainly threaten the Germans' long-range plans. Allied miscalculation gave their enemies the breather they needed.[32] That said, however, the Germans' conduct of the campaign in the east was highly effective.

Two sets of events illustrate the command methods that the OKH employed. The first occurred after the 3d and 4th Armies met in the corridor between Pomerania and East Prussia on September 3. At this point General Fedor von Bock, commander of Army Group North, wanted to transfer the bulk of his 4th Army to the east for a wide drive around Warsaw. He argued that this move would prevent the Poles from retreating and regrouping in that area. The OKH refused; it wanted to keep forces in Poland as far west as possible, in case the British and French attacked.[33] This decision shows that the system was functioning properly: the OKH considered the views of a subordinate commander but kept the broader situation in mind and acted within its proper sphere of authority.

The other set of events took place on September 10–17. At this point the Germans were closing in on Warsaw: the 3d Army (part of Army Group North) from the north and the 8th Army (part of Army Group South) from the southwest.[34] The Poles' Poznan Army was attempting to retreat to the east toward Warsaw from the area between the Vistula and Bzura Rivers. On September 10 it launched an attack that threatened the left flank and rear of 8th Army. The OKH did not interfere; it left the decisions, quite properly, to the 8th Army and Army Group South commanders. However, the situation soon demanded that the OKH act. Parts of two army groups moved in to fight the encircled Poznan Army and converge on Warsaw. If no one coordinated their actions, the effectiveness of their attacks might suffer, or their forces might even fire on one another inadvertently. Accordingly, the OKH established a new boundary between the army groups and gave control of the attack against the Poznan Army to the 8th Army, in the process transferring command of some units from the 3d Army to the 8th.[35] Again the command system had functioned as it should: the OKH rapidly made a sound decision, thus allowing the army groups to perform their missions with maximum efficiency.

The only serious command problem of the Polish campaign developed on September 17, when the Soviets invaded from the east, in accordance with the Nonaggression Pact's secret clause. The timing of their advance came as a surprise to everyone. Hitler had been trying to persuade the Soviets to come in early, in hopes that such a move would further hamper intervention by France and Britain and might even lead them to declare war against the USSR. Josef Stalin saw through that maneuver, however, and chose his own moment to move. For the German military, the surprise was even more complete, since Hitler had not informed them of the secret military agreement with the Soviets at all. Furthermore, in the initial days after the Soviet advance began, there was some confusion over the demarcation line that would separate the two sides. Some German units were in combat with the Poles over one hundred miles beyond the line that the two sides eventually agreed upon. The OKH had to react quickly to avoid clashes between the two armies, and in any case German soldiers had already lost their lives to take ground that the army now had to give up.[36] For example, the Soviets declared themselves the liberators of the city of Lemberg, which German troops had taken. In his diary, Halder called this "a day of shame for the German political leadership!"[37]

Naturally, the army's leaders were incensed that Hitler had not informed them of a political decision of such importance. The affair must have confirmed their worst fears about their place in the command hierarchy. As Brauchitsch had already told Halder on September 10, "The separation of policy (OKW) from the army's leadership (OKH) has proven itself to be very disadvantageous. OKH must know the political line as exactly as possible, with its potential variations. Otherwise regular, planned action within our own sphere of responsibility is impossible. The leadership of the army cannot be torn away from policy; otherwise the army will lose its confidence."[38] In general, he was correct; an army that does not know the government's intentions stands to waste effort or—as in this case—suffer unnecessary losses.

The exact nature of Brauchitsch's argument deserves emphasis. He was not saying that the army should *influence* policy; that possibility had long since disappeared, and if the senior generals cared much about that, they hid their resentment well. Also, at the time when Brauchitsch made his remark to Halder, there *were* no discernible problems with the way Hitler was directing the war. Even after the Soviets intervened, moreover, the Germans had relatively little to gripe about; Hitler's political and strategic judgments appeared to have worked out well so far. What concerned Brauchitsch was not so much the army's purely instrumental position in the political and strategic spheres but the fact that it continued to lose ground in the battle for control of operations. Hitler's failure to keep the army informed boded ill for the future because it implied a lack of concern for the generals' operational priorities.

The issue came to a head within a week of the Soviet incursion: even while the last operations were going on in Poland, the Führer was beginning to express an interest in an offensive in the west.[39] On September 25 Halder heard the first hints; then, on September 27, Hitler told his three commanders in chief, without first consulting them, that time was on the side of the Allies, and that therefore Germany must strike just as soon as forces could be ready, in any case before winter.[40] On October 10 he repeated his arguments in another conference and released his Directive No. 6 for the Conduct of the War, together with a longer written explanation for his subordinates.[41] The directive specified that the attack would cross Luxembourg, Belgium, and Holland and that it must come as early and be as strong as possible. Its goal would be to strike at the most powerful part of the French and their allies' armies, and simultaneously to take as much territory as possible in the Low Countries and northern France for use in air and sea operations against England and as a buffer against Allied air attacks on the Ruhr, Germany's largest industrial area. Other than that, the directive offered no operational guidance for the army, but, as in the past, Hitler demanded that he be kept informed.

The Führer had seemingly good reasons for his decision to press the attack as soon as possible. The British blockade was hurting Germany's economy, not enough to interfere with current operations, but enough to hamper long-range plans. The Germans needed the resources of western Europe if they wanted to carry on the war.[42] Nevertheless, most senior army officers were aghast that Hitler would order an offensive so soon. Halder had been planning for a period of defensive warfare. Stülpnagel, his assistant chief of staff for operations, had just written a study stating that an attack in the west would be impossible before 1942.[43] The army needed time to rest, retrain, and make up its losses after the Polish campaign. And although many of the OKH's planners recognized the weaknesses in the French army, no one expected to defeat France as quickly as Poland; many expected a stalemate in the style of the First World War. Halder and Brauchitsch agreed that the attack methods used in Poland offered no recipe for the west; they would be no use against a well-knit army.[44] Halder and Brauchitsch argued against the idea in a meeting with Hitler on October 7, but they failed to convince him. Brauchitsch—at the urging of his army group commanders—tried once more on November 5, but all he received for his trouble was an enraged rebuff.[45] In the end, only the weather kept the Führer from launching the offensive until the following spring.

In the meantime, Hitler gave the army's leaders unmistakable signs that his leadership style was becoming more intrusive rather than less. His remarks in the October 10 conference were typical. He not only explained his version of the strategic situation ad nauseam but also expounded upon a range of other subjects, from the direction of offensive thrusts and the danger of sending armored units into cities to the tactical details of special operations and the need to conserve ammunition.[46] Hitler's directives and orders began to go into similar detail—and there were more of them, since Hitler was beginning to suspect that he could no longer trust the OKH to carry out the verbal instructions he had been giving to Brauchitsch.[47]

Hitler would play a key role in formulating the plan of operations for *Case Yellow* (the code name for the invasion of France), which was the subject of heated debates almost from the time that the Führer issued the first order. The original plan called for a straightforward advance into the Low Countries, in line with the goals that Directive No. 6 identified, but no one was happy with that concept. Impetus for the most radical changes to the plan came from two directions: on the one hand, from Hitler, and, on the other, from the commander of Army Group A, General Gerd von Rundstedt, and his chief of staff, Manstein. Coincidentally, both sides came up with the same embryonic idea: Why not shift the main point of attack farther south, break through, turn north, and strike at the enemy's rear?[48] Halder and Brauchitsch resisted the idea for a number of reasons, but gradually they came to see merit in it. By early January the General Staff had gone so far as to rewrite the plan so that they could shift the weight of the attack toward the Ardennes if such an action seemed worthwhile. Then, on January 10, 1940, an unauthorized courier flight got lost and landed in Belgium, and important parts of the plan fell into Allied hands; that event put still more pressure on the army to change the concept of operations. Halder, who by this time believed in the plan, presented a new order on February 24, which would be the basis for the phenomenal German success in May. Some credit, however, must go to the Führer: he began to see the possibilities before the General Staff did.[49] Here Hitler demonstrated that curious genius that marked his performance in the early years of the war: that of the inspired amateur.

While preparations were moving forward for *Case Yellow,* developments to the north had drawn Hitler's attention in that direction. At the end of November 1939, the Soviets attacked Finland, and the Führer became concerned that, perhaps as part of a move against the USSR, Britain might occupy Norway, thus threatening Germany's supply of Swedish iron ore. Admiral Raeder pointed out the threat to Hitler and also noted that submarine bases along the Norwegian coast would be extremely useful.[50] So, on December 12, Hitler ordered Jodl to prepare a study on the possibility of occupying Norway before the British could get there.[51] On January 24, 1940, the OKW set up a so-called Special Staff North to continue the study. Then, on February 21, at Jodl's suggestion, Hitler appointed General Nikolaus von Falkenhorst to command the operation, now code-named *Weserübung (Weser Exercise).* Falkenhorst brought a corps-level staff with him, into which he incorporated the OKW's working group.[52] Hitler's directive for the operation, which the OKW issued on March 1, stipulated that the forces for *Weser Exercise* would come under a "special command" and would not be available for other theaters.[53]

With the assignment of *Weser Exercise* to the OKW, the evolution of the command system had taken a significant new direction. For the first time, Hitler had given the OKW responsibility for operational planning, a responsibility that, until then, had been the General Staff's alone. Hitler justified this measure in several ways at the time. He claimed that *Weser Exercise* was too large an operation for the OKH to direct, since it would require the close cooperation of all three armed services. He also said that the OKW was better suited to coordinate the operation with the Foreign Ministry. Finally, he stated that the OKH needed to concentrate on the upcoming invasion of France.[54] The extent to which Hitler took these reasons seriously is unclear. He may have had no clear reason in mind. In any case, his rationale was weak on several counts, and this new wrinkle in the command system would highlight some old problems as well as creating new ones.

There was, first of all, the problem of the OKW's authority. Granted, it had a legitimate role as a coordinating agency for joint operations and as a liaison with other governmental agencies. At no time, however, had the OKW's intended mission included operational planning. The Luftwaffe and the navy had no intention of turning over that power to the OKW, and Göring and Raeder had the political clout to keep the OKW out of their spheres.[55] The army had no such influential figure, and so the OKW was able to take over a General Staff function. This fact introduced the possibility that the OKW-OKH rivalry could take on a whole new aspect, as the two became parallel operational headquarters. For the time being that problem would retreat into the background, only to reappear later. Another set of problems existed within the OKW itself. Contrary to Hitler's claim, it could not relieve the OKH of much work by taking over *Weser Exercise,* because the OKW was simply not equipped to be an operational headquarters, even with the addition of Falkenhorst's staff. Falkenhorst was able to create a maneuver plan in short order, but there was no way the OKW could oversee all the associated functions such as logistics and intelligence; it had to call upon the OKH for help. The General Staff's Supply, Transportation, and Foreign Armies West Branches had to formulate large parts of the plan, and their efficiency suffered from having two sets of superiors simultaneously.[56]

The army's leadership noted these new command arrangements with chagrin. Halder only found out about Falkenhorst's appointment indirectly, when the OKW bypassed the normal army channels and started assigning units to the operation.[57] Halder concluded—correctly—that Hitler and the OKW were usurping the OKH's proper role. He wrote in his diary, "Not a single word has passed between the Führer and ObdH (Oberbefehlshaber des Heeres—Brauchitsch) on this matter; this must be put on record for the history of the war."[58] There was, in any case, little more he could do. Brauchitsch was the person who, by virtue of his position, should have objected to the command arrangements, but there is no evidence that he did. Perhaps he recognized the futility of further argument, given his track record with the Führer.

At any rate, the operation went ahead: Germany invaded Denmark and Norway on April 9, 1940. Hitler supervised the operation closely from Berlin, and he displayed a startling lack of nerve.[59] As the battle developed, he became increasingly agitated over events and began issuing detailed and often contradictory orders. The worst example occurred on April 18 when, in a fit of nervousness over the situation at Narvik, in northern Norway, the Führer had Keitel draft an order for the force there to withdraw into neutral Sweden and allow itself to be interned. Only prompt action by a relatively junior officer salvaged the situation. Lieutenant Colonel Bernhard von Lossberg, chief of the Army Operations Group in the National Defense Branch, was filling in as branch chief for Warlimont, who was ill. When he received Hitler's order, he went immediately to the Reich Chancellery and confronted Keitel and Jodl about it. He insisted that he would not send the order, and that it reflected the same kind of crisis of nerves that had lost the Battle of the Marne in the First World War.

Keitel left the room immediately, without saying a word; doubtless he found the scene too uncomfortable. Jodl heard Lossberg out—they were good friends—but explained that he could not countermand the Führer's personal order. Finally Jodl agreed to let Lossberg delay the order, and the latter used the time to arrange with Brauchitsch for a congratulatory telegram to go out to the commander in Narvik. Jodl was thus able to go to Hitler the next day and explain that they could not very well order the withdrawal of a unit that the army commander in chief had just congratulated![60] In the end the force in Narvik held. Hitler's panic attack sent ripples of anxiety through the high command, however. Brauchitsch asked Lossberg how they were going to manage in the coming offensive in the west if the Führer was already losing his nerve in front of Narvik; it was a question for which Lossberg had no good answer.[61]

While *Weser Exercise* ran its course, the high command was putting the final touches on the preparations for *Case Yellow,* some of which concerned the organization of the command itself. The General Staff implemented a routine process by which it could adapt its structure to the new military situation. The changes in the Operations Branch were typical. A particular part of the branch—Group IVb—was responsible for the branch's internal organization. As the planning for *Case Yellow* got under way, this group began designing a structure to match the operation's order of battle. On April 6, 1940, the group published its new organizational plan, which would become effective the following day. Three groups in the Operations Branch—I, IIa, and IIb—would oversee the three army groups on the western front: they would collect and process reports, keep the branch chief and his assistant (Greiffenberg and Heusinger) informed, and draft orders. Group I also handled questions regarding the occupied territory in the east. Group III took care of liaison with other parts of OKH and with OKW, oversaw the army's reserves, and maintained the situation map. Group IV handled administrative matters.[62] Its other elements having reorganized themselves along similar lines, the Headquarters OKH moved to a location in western Germany, shortly before the offensive opened.

At the uppermost level of the high command, the changes did not have the routine nature of those within the OKH, since the OKW was still struggling to find the right structure. Jodl had not been satisfied with the ad hoc organization of September 1939, but his concern was probably greater than the Führer's; according to Warlimont, Hitler was perfectly happy with the command arrangements during the Polish campaign and was, in any case, not familiar with the needs of a modern headquarters.[63] However, he approved Jodl's request for an enlarged staff that would be part of a Führer Headquarters near the western front. His only stipulation was that the staff remain small enough to pack up and move on short notice.[64]

When Hitler moved to his headquarters outside Münstereifel, about fifty miles southwest of Bonn, on the night of May 9–10, 1940, a so-called Field Echelon of the National Defense Branch (Feldstaffel der Abteilung Landesverteidigung) went with him. This part of Jodl's Armed Forces Command Office (Wehrmachtführungsamt, previously the Amtsgruppe Führungsstab) was responsible for all military questions, for writing up all of Hitler's directives, and for keeping Keitel informed of military developments, among other things.[65] The Field Echelon consisted of three operations groups, one each for the army, navy, and air force, plus a political liaison group, a communications section, an administrative section, the keeper of the war diary, and several liaison officers. All told, with a small reinforcement to help with its expanded duties, the Field Echelon numbered approximately twenty-five officers and thirty to forty other ranks. One or two officers from each group stayed in Berlin, along with the groups that handled organizational questions and special projects. With this reorganization the military command apparatus in the OKW had achieved its final form; there would be no significant changes in structure for the rest of the war, and only minor increases in strength.[66]

During the campaign in France, Hitler spent more of his time dealing with strictly military issues than he had the previous September, and a work routine evolved in his headquarters that would remain relatively constant for much of the rest of the war. The schedule revolved around his daily briefings, which took place in the early afternoon and again at around midnight. By this time Jodl had come into his own as the Führer's military adviser. Hitler gave him the right of immediate access, something that few people had; in effect, Jodl became Keitel's equal rather than his subordinate.[67] He briefed Hitler personally on military developments during this first part of the war. If Brauchitsch or Halder was present, he would brief Hitler on the army's situation, but the two senior army leaders were not frequent visitors to the Führer Headquarters; Halder's diary shows that one or both of them met with Hitler only thirteen times during the French campaign.[68] Jodl's influence with Hitler grew accordingly; he did not in fact believe that army representatives needed to be present for the briefings, and before long he had arranged for the army liaison officers to be excluded as well. Jodl rarely even allowed his subordinate, Warlimont, to attend.[69]

Jodl is a difficult man to assess. He was extremely competent in a narrow technical sense, and very ambitious. He challenged Hitler's decisions on several occasions but was far more likely to acquiesce. His diary entries reveal that he was in awe of the Führer, whom he thought to be a political and military genius. He also shared his brother officers' limited view of strategy as well as their sense of duty. In his understanding of command relationships, however, he was much more a proponent of the *Führerprinzip* than a believer in the General Staff tradition. Lossberg wrote that Jodl "was taciturn by nature and did not hold with long discussions. He seldom accepted anyone else's advice. He would give his staff under Warlimont clearly defined jobs; even Warlimont was in his eyes merely a subordinate who had no authority to act on his own, as officers of a high-level staff would normally expect."[70]

According to Warlimont, Jodl often used the National Defense Branch merely as an organ to prepare orders, rather than expecting independent thought or advice. He often felt justified in bypassing the branch entirely; he would coordinate with the service commanders and draft orders himself, based on Hitler's wishes. Moreover, as part of Hitler's inner circle, Jodl often remained at a physical distance from his staff. Thus the staff became at times little more than a secretariat or records office, and Warlimont would hear secondhand of developments of which his superior should have informed him.[71]

Jodl briefed Hitler using situation reports that the National Defense Branch's operations groups prepared each morning and evening. The groups derived their summaries—which together often ran to thirty pages—from reports they received from the respective services. Once they had evaluated and summarized that material, they would brief Warlimont, who, in turn, would brief Jodl. The subject matter included the previous day's military events, foreign affairs, and economics. The process, which began at around 6:00 A.M. with the arrival of the first status reports, took the entire morning. Special supplements and updated situation maps accompanied the basic reports, which usually also included information on order of battle and unit strengths, equipment status, or any special projects in which the Führer had expressed an interest. Everything had to be meticulously accurate, because Hitler had an amazing memory for technical details and would become greatly annoyed at any discrepancies.[72]

In the course of a briefing, Hitler would often have some question for which he required an immediate answer. Jodl or one of his assistants would

Alfred Jodl. (Courtesy Bundesarchiv, photo no. 71/33/1)

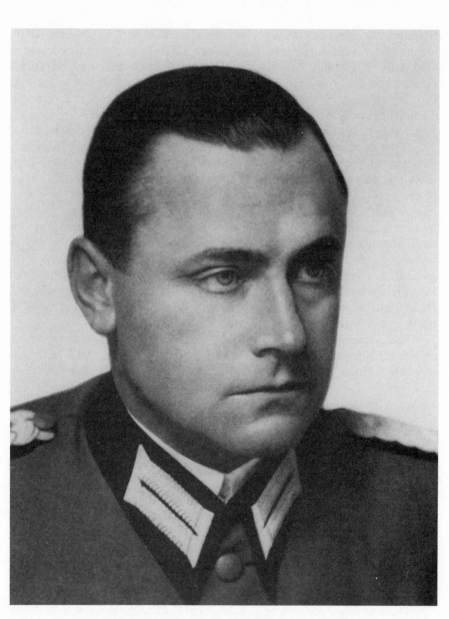

Walter Warlimont. (Courtesy Bundesarchiv, photo no. 87/104/27)

telephone the appropriate agency or headquarters and, if possible, get the information while the briefing was still in session. This was a source of considerable extra effort for the National Defense Branch and whatever other headquarters were involved; all other work had to stop while they handled the Führer's request, no matter how trivial. Such tasks were especially onerous during the midnight briefing; the staff knew that at 6:00 the following morning they would have to be back on duty again to start evaluating the new reports.[73]

Hitler often made decisions on the spot, either during his briefings or in separate meetings on special military problems. He would express these decisions through verbal orders that, during this early phase of the war, were often vague. Different listeners interpreted them in different ways—and usually to their own advantage. Moreover, Hitler did not always care to whom he directed his orders. Rather than work with the person or agency that normally handled a specific function, the Führer would simply give a task to whomever was handy. The results were often chaotic, as individuals and organizations, sometimes with competing interests, attempted to sort out what Hitler really wanted.[74] The only mitigating circumstance at this stage was that Hitler's intrusions into the military sphere were still not as common or as serious as they would become.

The problems with the command's working methods certainly did not escape the notice of those further down. The fact that the OKW was little more than Hitler's speaking tube, rather than any sort of Wehrmacht General Staff, was obvious. Hitler would not allow Keitel or Jodl to exercise any authority independently, as Brauchitsch allowed Halder to do. The directives issuing from the OKW were indeed more detailed and intrusive than before, but that reality was the result of two sets of inputs: Hitler's decisions and staff work done by the services, especially the Army General Staff.[75] At one point Halder wrote, "At any rate one can reckon on the fact that in thirty-six or forty-eight hours we will receive the ideas we briefed today as a higher directive."[76] Naturally this practice bred resentment; Halder had already expressed his disgust at orders for which the OKH had done the work, but which gave the outside world the impression that OKW was responsible.[77] The problems in the high command were certainly not limited to the realm of working methods, however. Hitler was determined to play an active role in the French campaign, and his idiosyncratic command style began to have serious consequences.

The attack in the west began on May 10, 1940, with thrusts into Holland, Belgium, and Luxembourg. Halder was looking forward to a great victory. On the train trip west to his headquarters he had stated that "this war is as necessary as the one of 1866, and at its end will stand the United States of Europe."[78] Within a week of the campaign's start, however, his supreme commander began to show signs of strain, just as he had a month earlier. Hitler had been one of the main proponents of a bold armored thrust, but now he became nervous about the possibility of failure. Any setback, he knew, would give the Allies not just a military but also a political boost of great value.[79] On May 17 Halder wrote: "A really unpleasant day. The Führer is terribly nervous. He is frightened by his own success, does not want to risk anything, and therefore would rather stop us. His pretext: concern for the left flank! The conversations that Keitel carried out with the army groups at his behest, as well as his own visit to Army Group A, have only created uncertainties and doubt."[80] And again the next day: "The Führer has an incomprehensible fear about the south flank. He rages and shouts that we are on the way to ruining the entire campaign and exposing ourselves to the danger of a defeat. . . . That is the subject of a most highly unpleasant clash in the Führer Headquarters between the Führer on the one hand and the OB [Brauchitsch] and me on the other."[81] Contrary to the picture that often emerges in the German generals' postwar accounts, however, Hitler was not alone in his fears.[82] As Hans Umbreit points out, a debate quickly emerged between the "progressives," mostly at the OKH Headquarters, who wanted to push on, and the "old school" commanders such as Rundstedt, for whom the headlong rush was proving too stressful.[83]

These tensions provided the basis, on May 24, for the first of the Germans' major operational setbacks, the halt before Dunkirk that has been the subject of so much debate. The German postwar accounts are nearly unanimous in blaming Hitler for the debacle, but the reality of the situation was more complex. Hitler did give the halt order on the twenty-fourth, but he was, in part, reacting to Rundstedt's pessimism. The armored units had suffered severely from enemy action and the long advance, and some of Rundstedt's subordinates were pushing for a rest; the commanders in Army Group A were apparently willing to leave the reduction of the Allied pocket to Army Group B. Göring had also boasted to Hitler that the Luftwaffe could finish off the Allies, and there is some thought that Hitler wanted to take some glory away from the army. Brauchitsch and Halder protested the halt strongly, and on May 25 Hitler gave Rundstedt the choice of whether or not to resume the advance, but Rundstedt held back for another day. By then the British had formed a more solid defensive line from which they held off the Germans while the bulk of their army escaped by sea.[84] Halder's diary reveals that both he and Brauchitsch were fuming at the delay and its results, but there was nothing they could do.[85]

The Germans' unease over the "miracle of Dunkirk" was limited, however; the rapidity of their victory over France served as sufficient consolation. By May 25 Halder and his staff were already deciding how to regroup for the second phase of the Battle of France. The necessary realignments began even before Dunkirk fell, and despite some disagreements with Hitler over the plan, the attack opened on June 5.[86] In less than three weeks the campaign was over. For the Germans the victory seemed almost magical. The goal that had eluded them for over four years in the Great War had fallen in their laps in less than seven weeks. Hitler had special cause to celebrate; for him, this was *his* victory. He forgot his nervousness, his mistakes, and his lack of command experience. He became convinced that his military talents were as great as those of his commanders, and his distrust of the General Staff grew apace with his faith in his own abilities. From this point forward, his willingness to listen to his best military minds would only diminish.

The German victories in 1939 and 1940 had deep roots. The Germans had developed tactical, operational, and command doctrines that were clearly superior to those of their enemies. Solid campaign plans, their enemies' mistakes, and the required amount of luck added to their advantages. But even as the Wehrmacht rolled on in triumph, stress fractures were appearing in the high command. Leaving aside questions of strategy (with which the next chapter will deal), it had performed reasonably well in the Polish campaign; each element worked efficiently within its sphere. From that moment of greatest promise, however, the command system began to degenerate along familiar lines. Friction between the OKW and the services and between Hitler and his generals increased. The OKW could do nothing to improve its position vis-à-vis the Luftwaffe or the navy, but the army was more vulnerable because it did not have Hitler's trust. With the assignment of *Weser Exercise* to the OKW, that rivalry took on new significance. Meanwhile, the army's leaders were determined to maintain their operational independence in the face of Hitler's growing confidence. They apparently believed that they could continue to avoid, ignore, or twist his orders to get what they wanted. That approach had its limits, however, which the Führer was already finding. These trends would become more serious as the war began to turn against the Germans. Thus was the pattern established: the worse the military situation, the less the high command was able to cope with it.

5
New Directions, New Problems:
June 1940 to June 1941

The year after their spectacular defeat of France was a momentous one for Germany's military leaders. Their initial position seemed enviable: they were in possession of the best army in the world; their remaining enemy was licking its wounds, apparently impotent; the resources of France awaited their exploitation; and the Soviet Union, the only power that might threaten them, was going to great lengths to stay on good terms. All that remained was to bring the war to a successful conclusion—and there lay the rub. For all their apparent advantages, the Germans still had far to go. In the course of the next year, Hitler and his advisers would struggle to find a way out of the strategic impasse in which they found themselves. In that year the Führer, whom his propaganda instrument now styled "the greatest commander of all time," would make some of his last great strategic decisions.[1] And in the meantime, the organization and functioning of the high command would continue to deteriorate in subtle but significant ways.

RESOLVING THE STRATEGIC DILEMMA

Following the signing of the peace treaty at Compiègne on June 22, 1940, Hitler took time off to tour Paris and the battlefields of his youth in the company of his closest associates. He wanted to savor his victory, and he could see no reason not to. After all, Great Britain was no longer a threat; like nearly everyone else in Germany, Hitler expected that the British would see the hopelessness of their situation and sue for peace.[2] When they did not do so immediately, Jodl prepared a memorandum that began from the premise that victory was just a matter of time; to achieve it, Germany had two options. The first was direct action against the British homeland, to be carried out by air and naval attacks on the Royal Air Force, manufacturing centers, supplies, and shipping, plus terror attacks on population centers (which Jodl justified as "retribution"). As a last resort, and only after the other attacks had weakened England fatally, the Wehrmacht could invade and occupy the island; preparations should begin immediately, in case the operation did indeed prove necessary. As an alternative to these direct attacks (or an expansion of them; the memo is not clear on this point), Germany could also strike at Britain's empire, with the help of whatever other nations might be drawn into an alliance for that purpose. Jodl suggested Italy, Spain, Russia, and Japan as likely candidates and wrote that attacks on the Suez Canal and Gibraltar would be the most effective opening moves.[3]

Hitler faced a difficult set of decisions. Like Jodl, he pinned his hopes on a political solution that would follow a collapse of British will. In the absence of such a collapse, none of the courses of action in Jodl's memo offered a quick military solution, his confidence notwithstanding, and there is every indication that Hitler knew this. Historians have produced thousands of pages of analysis over the last five decades—and thrown not a few barbs at one another—in an effort to understand how Hitler and his military leaders coped with this strategic dilemma.[4] The historical accounts have attempted to impose order upon a decision-making process that led the Germans from victory in France in June 1940 to the invasion of the Soviet Union a year later, but the picture they have created is, especially for the general reader, extremely confusing. Paradoxically, this is appropriate, because confusion dominated the high command during this period. Granted, the principal actors masked it well, even from themselves—this was a case of unconscious incompetence rather than true folly—but the fact remains that the German leadership did not know how to bring the war to a successful conclusion.

Hitler had neither the background nor the temperament for strategic decision making. He did have long-range goals that were never far from his thoughts: the destruction of the Jewish-Bolshevik state to the east and the simultaneous conquest of Lebensraum for Germany. In deciding on the means to those ends, however, he was an opportunist, and now he was out of clear opportunities. He was aware that he could not leave the British alone forever, but he could not see a way to defeat them. His military advisers, although their training was better than the Führer's in some respects, were equally out of their depth. Together they and their leader cast about for operational solutions to strategic problems, in the German tradition. In the face of a range of possibilities, Hitler chose at first not to choose; instead he tried to pursue several courses, in the vague hope that one of them would yield the desired result.

The Führer eliminated some options immediately. The Wehrmacht did not have the forces available to bring about a decision through bombing and blockade alone, and unrestricted submarine warfare threatened to bring the United States into the war, as had happened in 1917. Hitler also vetoed the idea of "terror bombing" for the moment; he did not want to alienate the British public, since he hoped that they would pressure their government into a compromise peace.[5] A political solution with Great Britain—albeit a temporary one—remained his foremost wish. Such a solution not only would save him time and effort but also would avoid the risk that the British Empire would collapse, to the net benefit of Japan, America, and others, rather than Germany.[6] He tried to offer the British an agreement whereby he would leave their empire undisturbed if they let him have the Continent, but in so doing he simply demonstrated his lack of understanding of British interests and commitment.[7]

An invasion seemed to offer the best hope for a rapid decision, but here too there were serious obstacles. The British army was a shambles in June 1940, but the Royal Air Force (RAF) and the Royal Navy remained formidable adversaries. The RAF had denied the Germans control of the air over Dunkirk and would doubtless put up an even stiffer fight over its own territory. Without air superiority, the Germans had little hope of defeating the Royal Navy, and so the chances of landing and sustaining an invasion force would be small indeed. Nevertheless, Hitler decided to prepare for this option. On July 2 he told his commanders that if they could create the correct conditions —chief among them being air superiority—then an invasion could go forward.[8] Two weeks later, after the army, through Jodl, had provided more specific planning guidance, Hitler expanded upon his original order in Directive No. 16, "Regarding the Preparations for a Landing Operation Against England."[9] In this directive the Führer ordered that the Wehrmacht prepare to land on a broad stretch of the English coast. Preparations were to be complete by mid-August at the latest. The operation, code-named *Seelöwe (Sea Lion)*, would take place if England, "despite its militarily hopeless situation," continued to be obstinate. Hitler would exercise overall command, with each of the service commanders in chief directing his arm; detailed instructions on each service's tasks followed.

Some doubt remains as to how serious he was. The risk of failure was great, as he well knew, and a failure would have serious strategic consequences. Moreover, as Hitler had indicated to Halder and Brauchitsch, even success carried risk; the collapse of the British Empire would not necessarily be to Germany's advantage. Perhaps for these reasons, attacks on the "periphery," as Jodl had termed them, also attracted the Führer's interest, even as the services were beginning to prepare an invasion. Hitler brought up the concept in nearly every major meeting that month: with his military advisers, naturally, but also with other officers and officials, as well as Italian diplomats; this was no passing interest.[10] He considered the idea of a continental bloc that would present a united front against Britain from the North Cape to Morocco. On July 21 he even indicated that he might try to bring the Soviet Union into an alliance.[11] His most immediate focus, however, was the prospect of acting with Spain to take Gibraltar.[12] The navy suggested this plan on July 5, independently of Jodl's initiative. Soon the OKW and the Abwehr (the German intelligence service) had both sent reconnaissance teams to Spain, while Hitler sent a personal representative to broach the idea to Spanish dictator Francisco Franco.

While plans for attacks on Britain and its imperial position moved forward, Hitler began to consider yet another possibility. As early as June 23 he said to Brauchitsch that, if Britain were to stay in the war—an event he considered highly unlikely at that point—it would do so in the hopes that the United States and the Soviet Union would eventually lend it their support.[13] As was the case with the peripheral strategy, Hitler's interest was clear from the frequency with which he brought up the subject. He did so again with Italian ambassador Dino Alfieri on July 1, once more with Halder and Brauchitsch on July 13, and yet again with Raeder and Brauchitsch on July 21. In that last meeting, he asked the army officers to begin considering a solution to "the Russian problem," if possible in the coming autumn. Brauchitsch was actually able at that point to brief Hitler on plans that the OKH already had in the works.[14]

All the various threads came together in the midday briefing on July 31, when Hitler met with, among others, Keitel, Jodl, Brauchitsch, Raeder, and Halder. The meeting opened with a discussion of *Sea Lion;* Raeder believed that the operation was still feasible, but he did not think it could be ready before September 15. Hitler approved the postponement and added that if the Luftwaffe had not achieved air superiority by that date, he would put off the invasion until the following May. He also said that he wanted to bring Spain into the war in order to take Gibraltar, and he reacted favorably to the army's suggestion that it send two Panzer divisions to support the Italians in North Africa. Then he launched into a monologue on the general strategic situation. He repeated his view that Britain was depending on help from Russia and America. Take Russia out of the picture, he said, and America would fall out too, because the removal of Russia would allow Japan the freedom to expand in east Asia. Then Germany would be the master in Europe and the Balkans. His decision: Russia must be eliminated, but in spring 1941 rather than autumn 1940, so that the conquest could be completed in one campaign. The goals of the operation, he said, would be "the destruction of Russia's vitality" and the acquisition of the Baltic States, the Ukraine, and White Russia.[15]

In the course of the next five months, Hitler would attempt to follow each of these strategic avenues, with mixed success. *Sea Lion* proved a chimera. The operation had always depended upon the Luftwaffe's ability to take control of the skies over southern Britain, and by the middle of September it had clearly failed. Hitler had the services continue their preparations, mostly as a way to put psychological pressure on the British. For their own information, he told his commanders on September 17 that the decision to invade was postponed "for the time being," and on October 12 he put off the invasion definitely until the following spring.[16] After that point there is little indication that the planners took the prospect seriously.

The peripheral strategy hung on a bit longer, with support from the navy, the OKW, and the Foreign Ministry. The navy, especially, had always had some doubts about *Sea Lion,* and in September Raeder began to push the Mediterranean option more strongly in his briefings with Hitler.[17] The plan for the conquest of Gibraltar (code-named *Felix*) went forward in anticipation of an agreement with Franco. The Spanish dictator had been willing to join the war back in June and remained enthusiastic right up into September, but in the end he could not get the concessions he wanted from the Germans. When Hitler met with him on October 23 in order to enlist his participation in *Felix,* Franco refused to commit himself.[18] Hitler did not want to give up on the idea completely, and planning continued, if only at a reduced level. In spring 1941 Hitler even added a further contingency plan—*Isabella*—for an incursion into Spain and Portugal to help repel a British landing. In the end, nothing came of any of these plans.

As an adjunct or alternative to the peripheral strategy, the idea of a "continental bloc" also remained under consideration for several weeks in late summer and early autumn.[19] Foreign Minister Joachim von Ribbentrop was the principal exponent of this approach, by which Germany would lead a coalition consisting of Vichy France, Italy, Spain, Japan, and the Soviet Union against Great Britain. The concept never really gained much strength, however. Spain proved too cautious and too greedy, and Vichy France was no more cooperative. Moreover, given Hitler's long-term ambition to destroy the Soviet Union and seize much of its land for Germany, an alliance with that country can never have been more than a temporary solution in his mind. By mid-November, in any case, strains in German-Soviet relations convinced the Führer to turn away from the "continental bloc" option.

Collaboration between Germany and Italy in the Mediterranean and North Africa would have been an important part of any peripheral strategy, but it remained problematic. Following the July 31 meeting, the OKW told the army to examine the technical issues involved in sending a force to Libya. Jodl believed that the time was ripe for Germany and Italy to work together to defeat Britain. The Germans offered their support to Mussolini at the beginning of September, but the Duce believed his forces could take Egypt on their own, and he refused.[20] Before long, however, Italian reverses would lead to a change in their leader's attitude. In North Africa, an Italian offensive toward Suez stalled; the British counteroffensive, which started on December 9, 1940, pushed the Italians halfway back across Libya in a matter of weeks.[21] At the same time, the Italians were fighting in Albania, from which they had launched an attack into Greece on October 28 and back into which the Greeks had soon pushed them.[22] As a result of these debacles, the Germans sent armored and air units to North Africa in January 1941 (Operation *Sonnenblume [Sunflower]*), drew up plans to send another force to Albania *(Alpenveilchen [Cyclamen]),* and began planning an invasion of Greece *(Marita)* for the spring.[23]

The German entry into the Mediterranean theater did not, however, represent a commitment on Hitler's part to an indirect strategy against Britain, although the navy would continue to promote that idea.[24] By the time the preparations began for the operations in the Balkans and North Africa, the Führer had his eye fixed firmly on the east. It is impossible, as Hans Umbreit and Andreas Hillgruber have pointed out, to say exactly when Hitler's decision to attack the Soviet Union became unalterable.[25] There is no doubt that the idea of a confrontation with Bolshevism was central to Hitler's thinking even before the war began, and his "decision" of July 31, 1940, certainly sounded final.[26] On the other hand, Hitler apparently did give the "continental bloc" idea serious consideration, and even as late as December 5, when Brauchitsch and Halder briefed Hitler on their plans for the invasion of the USSR, the Führer's comments led his advisers to wonder if he had really committed himself to it.[27] Their doubts were probably misdirected. By midautumn, Hitler had painted himself into a strategic corner. *Sea Lion* was dead in the water. The peripheral strategy remained just that; it could not provide the quick decision the Führer wanted. What remained was a blow at the USSR, which Hitler found attractive for political, ideological, economic, and strategic reasons.[28]

EMERGING PROBLEMS IN THE COMMAND SYSTEM

The strategic indecision that marked the latter half of 1940 thus came to an end, if more by default than by direction. Hitler had considered a number of options, major and minor, and had finally settled on the course toward which he had been inclined all along. In this strategic decision-making process his military advisers had exercised little influence upon their Führer. They presented him with options, some of which they had worked out in advance of his wishes, but he was the driving force. That fact created a problem for the planning organs of the high command: because Hitler was confused, neither he nor the topmost figures in the OKW could provide clear strategic direction. Halder's diary is full of references to this problem. On November 24, 1940, for example, he complains:

> Again there is too little liaison between OKW and us regarding the Balkan question. The matter seems to be developing further, and in fact with thought to a possible attack on our part against Turkey. Naturally that creates an entirely different picture than heretofore. We must be clear with ourselves about the fact that the possibilities regarding Russia will fade if we commit ourselves against Turkey. In our last discussion the Führer said to me: "We can only move against the Straits when Russia is

beaten." This thought forces the statement: we must avoid war with Turkey as long as Russia is not beaten. In our considerations our first assumption has been that our policy is to avoid conflict with Turkey by every means possible. If this conception has given way to another . . . then one has to shelve the Russian goal![29]

On the very next day, Halder's complaints continue: "On the whole this day highlights the wealth of unnecessary work which is expected of the General Staff because of a lack of clear leadership on the part of OKW."[30] Here Halder brought out an important point: Hitler's strategic indecision was a disadvantage not just because of any lost opportunities it represented but because of the extra work it created for the people under him. Moreover, this problem did not disappear when Hitler finally decided to attack in the east. In the year following the fall of France, the planners in the high command had to devote their energies to *Sea Lion, Sunflower, Cyclamen, Marita, Felix, Isabella,* the invasion of the Soviet Union, a possible invasion of Switzerland, operations against the Canary Islands and the Azores, the last-minute conquests of Yugoslavia and Crete, plans to occupy the rest of France, and military missions to Romania and Iraq, among other things. The workload that this collection of projects entailed was enormous.

Serious though this overload doubtless was, it represented only one aspect, and not the most important one, of the evolving problem with the high command. The period between June 1940 and June 1941 was one in which some important structural weaknesses also emerged. The relatively clear chain of command that existed in the Polish and French campaigns began to break down, and the process by which this breakdown occurred was itself not orderly or consistent from case to case. Each operation developed its own unique set of command arrangements that reflected interservice rivalry as well as Hitler's wishes.

In the planning for *Sea Lion,* for example, the army and the navy soon locked horns. The quick victory over France had caught everyone flat-footed; with the exception of some theoretical work by the navy, no one gave much thought to an invasion of Britain until operations in France were nearly complete. When the army and navy finally began detailed planning, their concepts for the operation proved incompatible.[31] *Sea Lion* entailed special difficulties, similar to those the services encountered in *Weser Exercise* but on a much larger scale. Neither service had much experience with amphibious warfare, and each had its own requirements. As had been the case with past plans, the directive for the operation (No. 16) was primarily the army's work. (On July 19, 1940, Halder wrote, "'Directive No. 16' has come in. For the most part it puts into the form of an order all that I briefed at the Berghof on July 13. . . . A whole lot of documents are required. From this body of thought, new directives will grow.")[32] Knowing the resistance that even the weakened British forces could mount, the army wanted a landing on a broad front. In late July the navy came to the conclusion that such an operation was beyond its abilities; it had neither the transport necessary to get the proposed force across the Channel nor the naval assets needed to protect it. Too many ships had gone down during *Weser Exercise* and subsequent operations.[33]

The difference of opinion became apparent in late July and early August 1940.[34] In the July 31 meeting that Hitler had with Keitel, Jodl, Raeder, Brauchitsch, and Halder, they discussed the plans for the invasion in some detail. Raeder argued, among other points, that the invasion should take place on a narrower front than that which the army proposed. Neither Hitler nor Brauchitsch offered any comment, and Raeder went away convinced that his argument had won the day. No sooner was he out the door, however, than Brauchitsch expressed grave doubts about the navy's plan. He persuaded Hitler to stick to the army's concept, at least for the time being, and Hitler sent out an order to that effect the next day. In the meantime, though, the Seekriegsleitung (the equivalent of the General Staff in the OKM) had been working out the concept as Raeder understood it.[35] The result was widespread confusion, and the OKW had to help sort things out. A series of meetings with the army and navy followed; the debates continued for nearly another two weeks. Meanwhile, the Luftwaffe complained that the dispute was interfering with *their* plans: they suggested that the OKW supervise the planning process more closely! The OKW really had no such power, however. It could encourage the parties to come to an agreement, but it could not issue orders. The final power of decision lay with Hitler. He finally settled the matter personally—in favor of the navy—on August 27.

This was exactly the kind of situation for which the OKW supposedly existed: someone needed to reconcile the services' conflicting concepts and coordinate their planning efforts. The OKW even had a precedent, albeit an imperfect one, in the planning structure for *Weser Exercise*. However, that structure had been Hitler's brainchild, and he opted not to set up another like it. Without his authority to back them up, the officers in the OKW again found that their role vis-à-vis the services was limited to informal coordination. Halder wrote, "We have the peculiar sight, that . . . OKW, which really has a joint operation to direct for once, is playing dead."[36] The remark was perhaps not quite fair. The OKW did try to smooth out the differences between the services, after all. Still, Halder had a point. Had the command system functioned properly, an operational issue such as the breadth of an invasion front would never have needed to reach Hitler's ears.

The problems with *Sea Lion* would arguably have given the Germans good reason to centralize and rationalize their command system, but in fact they moved in the opposite direction. By the middle of 1941, the OKW, rather than remaining a strategic planning organ, had begun to take on direct responsibility for more theaters itself, leaving the OKH eventually to control only a narrow operational zone in the east. The process began with the OKW's direction of *Weser Exercise;* Norway and Denmark remained under the control of the OKW thereafter. The trend would develop only slowly from that point—so slowly, in fact, that no one took any great note of it until much later in the war.[37]

Developments in the occupied west—France, Belgium, and Holland—demonstrate how gradually this split in the command system could emerge. The OKH had appointed a military commander in each of those countries shortly after they surrendered. In October 1940 the OKH also created the post of Oberbefehlshaber West (commander in chief west).[38] By early 1941, however, the OKW was already issuing operational instructions for the area. On February 2 it sent out a basic order concerning the defense of the coast from English attack in the case of major combat operations in the east.[39] Similar orders followed, until the OKW became the de facto operational headquarters for the west. No one issued a formal order transferring authority, and the OKH maintained a significant level of involvement to the end of 1941 and beyond.[40]

In other cases the change in responsibilities was more straightforward. Finland became an "OKW theater" in March 1941. The OKW, without consulting with the OKH, ordered a division from Norway into Finland for the upcoming invasion of the Soviet Union. Brauchitsch, who was piqued at this intrusion into the OKH's sphere of authority and still angry over the creation of the original OKW theater in Norway, insisted that the OKW take over responsibility for Finland altogether.[41] This display of petulance speaks ill of Brauchitsch, as Warlimont points out; for no good reason he abandoned a theater that would be important during *Barbarossa* (the code name for the upcoming invasion).

Command in the Balkans also went to the OKW, this time on Hitler's initiative. The process was more gradual than in the case of Finland but more straightforward than in the west. It began with the planning for Operation *Marita*, the invasion of Greece. In Directive No. 20, which the OKW issued on December 13, 1940, Hitler stipulated that "the especially great political effect of the military preparations on the Balkans demands the exact direction of all the relevant measures of the service commands." He went on to reserve for himself the right to approve all discussions with the Romanians, Bulgarians, or Italians, and he demanded reports from all the service commanders regarding their intentions.[42] Then, on March 27, 1941, shortly before the invasion of Greece was to take place, the government of Yugoslavia, which had just aligned itself with Germany, fell to an anti-Nazi coup. Hitler immediately ordered his forces to conquer Yugoslavia along with Greece.[43] In Directive No. 26, "Collaboration with the Allies in the Balkans," the Führer strengthened the guidelines he had provided for *Marita*. "I reserve for myself," Hitler announced in the directive, dated April 3, "the unified direction of this campaign, inasmuch as it concerns setting the operational goals for the Italian and Romanian forces." He justified this measure by stating that it was necessary to protect the sensibilities of the allied leaders. He would, he continued, personally send the army's and Luftwaffe's support requirements to the appropriate heads of state; meanwhile, the OKW would coordinate certain aspects of the allies' combined offensive.[44]

The OKW's role in the Balkans still did not entail operational control—the OKH ran *Marita* and *Unternehmen 25* (*Operation 25,* the Yugoslav campaign) with little interference from Hitler or the OKW—but Hitler stepped in again to adjust the command arrangements almost as soon as the campaign ended. On June 9, 1941, he issued Directive No. 31, by which he appointed Field Marshal Wilhelm List armed forces commander (*Wehrmachtbefehls-haber*) southeast. The order directed List to report directly to the Führer through the OKW.[45]

As an adjunct to *Marita,* the Germans also captured the island of Crete in May. The chain of command for that operation, code-named *Merkur (Mercury),* was unique. The operation would start with an airborne assault, but it would also involve forces from the army and navy. As with *Weser Exercise* and *Sea Lion,* this operation called for coordination by the OKW. Because the airborne and air-landing divisions belonged to the Luftwaffe, however, and because that service was eager to erase the embarrassment of its failure in the Battle of Britain, Hitler gave control of the operation to the OKL.[46] The result, due in part to the OKL's inexperience with land and naval warfare, was a Pyrrhic victory; Crete fell to the German assault, but the losses to the airborne forces were so high that Hitler refused to use them again until the war was nearly over.[47] As far as the postcampaign command arrangements were concerned, Hitler saw the island as an essential element in the air offensive in the eastern Mediterranean, so he left it under a Luftwaffe commander, who in turn was subordinate to List. This arrangement was problematic. According to Directive No. 31, List's command included all the forces within the theater, but in reality he—like other theater commanders—would have trouble exercising any authority over headquarters belonging to rival services.

One other major operation took place that winter and spring of 1941: Operation *Sunflower,* the German deployment to North Africa. The command situation there rapidly became the most complicated of all. Officially, the Italians controlled the theater. The directives on which the Germans based their intervention, issued in January and February, placed their forces under the control of the local Italian commander. The plans called for the OKW to coordinate with the Italians and oversee the use of German troops. The OKH had other ideas. It would provide the units and the commander, and it specified that while the Italians would exercise "tactical" command, German forces in Libya would otherwise remain under Brauchitsch's control.[48]

German leadership in the theater did nothing to simplify matters. The Afrika Korps—its later designation—deployed under the command of Major General Erwin Rommel, a talented tactical leader but also an acerbic and independent officer with a large reserve of faith in his own abilities. Rommel lionized Hitler and knew he had the Führer's support. He also knew that his force was going to North Africa to prevent an Italian collapse. Under the circumstances, the extent to which he would cooperate with the Italians—or with anyone else, for that matter—was open to question. The OKH, which had appointed Rommel, tried to keep a tight rein on him. Rommel was not popular with the senior army leadership. He was not a General Staff officer (he would become the only German field marshal in the Second World War who was not). His superiors also noted his popularity with Hitler and his willingness to use that popularity to avoid their instructions. Brauchitsch and Halder briefed him personally before he left for North Africa, but apparently that measure did not have the desired effect.[49] Rommel proved to be difficult for the OKH to control; at one point Halder even sent his assistant chief of staff for operations, Major General Friedrich Paulus, to Africa to "head off this soldier gone stark mad."[50]

The army was not alone in trying to direct Rommel's actions. Hitler and the OKW also issued orders for the Afrika Korps on a regular basis, either to Rommel directly or through the liaison officer with the Italian high command, Brigadier General Enno von Rintelen. These orders often contradicted not only the OKH's instructions but also those of Rommel's erstwhile superiors, the Italians, with whom Rintelen was hard put to maintain cordial relations at times. Thus, although Hitler never issued an order taking control of the forces in North Africa away from the OKH, which maintained a role in the theater, and although the Italians retained nominal authority, the OKW played an increasingly important role in directing the operations there.[51] Rommel put the confusion to good use, sometimes ignoring orders with which he disagreed, or appealing to whatever headquarters he believed would support him. His operational successes and his firm rapport with Hitler strengthened his bid for independence from the Italians and the OKH.[52] This multipolar struggle for command authority—among Rommel, the Italian Comando Supremo, the OKW, and the OKH—continued well into 1942.

One other command arrangement deserves attention, this one relating to *Barbarossa,* the preparations for which were well under way by late winter 1941. On March 13 Hitler issued—through the OKW—a set of "guidelines" on "special areas" to be defined during the campaign. In short, these guidelines restricted the OKH's responsibility in Russia to a narrow operational zone behind the front lines. Within that zone, the Reichsführer SS—Heinrich Himmler—would carry out "special tasks" on Hitler's authority, tasks that "arise from the struggle of two opposing political systems." Any occupied territory behind that zone would fall under the administration of Reich commissars, who would also receive their instructions from the Führer.[53] Hitler's rationale is clear: he meant to implement his racial and ideological policies in the east. The army leaders put up no resistance to the order, since it gave them the opportunity to cooperate fully while avoiding an open connection with the "special tasks" that the Führer had in mind.[54]

One remarkable point about the gradual shift in command responsibilities is that, at this stage, no one seemed to care or even to notice. Many officers criticized these developments later on, but at the time they apparently said nothing. The OKW and OKH records contain no comments at all on the command changes; nor does Halder's journal. Given the chagrin that the chief of the General Staff felt at the creation of the OKW theater in Norway, one would expect him to react strongly to these additional changes, had he thought them of any consequence. The vague and apparently temporary nature of the new command relationships may explain the lack of concern on everyone's part. The army still had an intact chain of command in the occupied west as well as strong links with the other theaters. With *Barbarossa* gearing up, perhaps the OKH saw some logic in letting the OKW handle the "quiet" areas. After all, nearly everyone thought the campaign in the east would end quickly, after which the OKH expected to pick up the reins in the west again for the final confrontation with Great Britain. Warlimont later stated that the OKW theaters were considered "exceptions to the rule" until 1942.[55] In fact this is a case in which hindsight can lead to false conclusions; at this early stage of the war, the problems engendered by the split in the command system were more potential than real.

With that said, however, the creation of the OKW theaters did have some immediate and detrimental effects. One was to further add to the high command's workload problem. The OKW soon found itself with a vastly expanded set of responsibilities. It had to brief Hitler on operations in all the theaters, prepare strategic directives, exercise operational command in its own theaters, coordinate military plans with allies and satellite nations, and handle whatever special projects—such as coast defense, long-range weapons, and guerrilla warfare, to name a few—in which Hitler took even a passing interest.[56] Furthermore, the new command arrangements created the same difficulties as those for *Weser Exercise* had, but on a larger scale. The OKW still did not have the manpower to handle its expanded duties; several branches of the General Staff and parts of other offices in the OKH had to support the OKW on a permanent basis. Their workload was that much greater and more difficult to organize because they had to respond to requirements from more than one set of superiors.

All these problems existed in the context of continuing organizational rivalry and personal antipathy between the OKH and the OKW. Unfortunately, there is not much specific information on the work flow and relationships between the two, but there is ample evidence of tension. "The relationship

OKW-OKH was miserable," wrote Lossberg after the war.[57] Johann Adolf Graf von Kielmansegg, who served in the General Staff's Operations Branch, related that when the officers in the OKH would see an officer on his way to report for duty at the OKW, they would ask one another, "How long will it be before he catches the OKW bacillus?"[58] References to meetings between Halder and Jodl, whose positions were roughly equivalent within the increasingly odd command structure, are conspicuously absent from both men's diaries. Jodl usually dealt with Halder's subordinates, the assistant chief of staff for operations or the chief of the Operations Branch, while Keitel was usually the one to speak with Halder; the two OKW staff officers probably felt more sure of themselves when they arranged their discussions that way.[59] At the lower levels the interactions may have been more professional, but interpersonal problems at the top were surely difficult to overcome.

Under the circumstances, disagreements and delays were bound to occur. The specifics are elusive, but some problems did make their way into the records. On March 1, 1941, for example, Halder drafted a memo to Keitel, in which he complained that the OKW was withdrawing trucks for Africa that the army needed for *Barbarossa.*[60] Then, at the end of April, another argument broke out between OKH and OKW over transport; the OKW wanted to move a division to Greece to take part in *Merkur,* but the move would have made a transport unit unavailable for operations in Russia. Representatives of the army, Luftwaffe, navy, and the Armed Forces Transport Office had to meet with Warlimont to work out the problem.[61] These disputes were minor, but they did interfere with the planning process, and they foreshadowed the more serious problems that the split in the command system would create later.

The rivalry between the OKH and the OKW also continued to manifest itself in bouts of organizational one-upmanship. Jodl still wanted to carve out an independent sphere of authority for the OKW, and Halder still considered the OKW to be a rubber-stamp agency. The evolution of the OKW theaters may have been one result of Jodl's ambition; one of the characteristics that General Staff officers all seem to have had in common, after all, was the desire to exercise operational control of forces in the field. Bureaucratic expansion was another means toward the same end. As one General Staff officer put it, "The military office that does not want to expand itself has not yet been invented."[62] Hitler's insistence on a small staff limited the OKW's ambitions in this direction, but one change did take place. On August 8, 1940, the keeper of the Armed Forces Command Office's war diary made this brief notation: "From today on, the Armed Forces Command Office is called the *Armed Forces Command Staff* (Wehrmachtführungsstab, or WFSt)."[63] The origin of the change goes back to July 19, when Hitler brought together many of his senior generals to reward them for their performance in the French campaign. In a conversation with Keitel before the ceremony, the Führer came up with the new designation.[64] On one level the decision seems almost meaningless: nothing changed aside from the title. The staff's mission, structure, and working methods all remained the same. On the other hand, the new title had important implications. In the German bureaucratic scheme of things, a "staff" is higher than an "office," so the name change carried a certain amount of prestige. Now the OKW's principal planning organ had the same designation as the one in the OKH. Christian Hartmann, in his biography of Halder, does not exaggerate when he characterizes the change as official confirmation that the Armed Forces Command Staff, not the Army General Staff, was Hitler's personal military planning organ.[65]

CONTINUING OPERATIONAL EFFECTIVENESS: YUGOSLAVIA

Amid all this talk of conflict and bureaucratic pettiness, however, one must bear in mind that the high command was still an efficient instrument at this stage of the war. One need only look at the Yugoslav campaign to see how smoothly the system could function. The coup against the Yugoslav government took place on March 27. By 1:00 that afternoon Jodl was already informing his staff by telephone that Hitler had decided to invade. With that done, he, Keitel, Brauchitsch, and Halder met with the Führer to hammer out a plan. Halder had already worked out some initial thoughts on his way from Zossen, based on studies that he had initiated earlier.[66] By 2:30 they were finished, and Jodl closeted himself with Lossberg and his counterpart from the Luftwaffe Operations Group to draft Directive No. 25. Hitler signed the directive that evening, and soon it was on its way to the services. Meanwhile, Halder had returned to Zossen to discuss the plan with the Operations Branch.[67]

Friedrich Paulus. (Courtesy Bundesarchiv, photo no. 226-P-25-9044)

On the following day, at 12:30, Halder took Paulus and Heusinger to meet with Hitler and go over the army's concept for the operation.[68] The Führer talked about several possible courses of action but apparently made no major changes to the plan. On March 29 the OKH issued the order for the invasion to its subordinate headquarters, while logistical preparations went forward; Halder discussed the operation twice that day with the army's chief supply officer, the general quartermaster, Lieutenant General Eduard Wagner. He also had to deal with Field Marshal List, then commander of 12th Army, which would execute the attack; List disagreed with part of Halder's plan. Halder spoke with Brauchitsch about the problem at 9:00 that evening and again at 8:30 the next morning, then with Hitler that afternoon; Hitler decided in Halder's favor, as the latter could not resist noting in his diary.[69]

In the meantime, efforts had been under way to define the roles of Germany's local allies in the operation. Talks went on at several levels about and with Bulgaria, Hungary, and Romania in the week following the coup. The Armed Forces Command Staff wrote up the results in Directive No. 26, which Hitler signed on April 3. This explained the various states' political goals and, in general terms, the military operations they would undertake in support of those goals. From there it set out the command arrangements by which the Wehrmacht could coordinate its operations with those of Germany's allies.[70]

On April 6 the attack on Yugoslavia went forward, along with the invasion of Greece. This was a mere ten days after the coup in Belgrade and eight days after OKH issued its first order. Within days the Yugoslav army had collapsed; unconditional surrender followed on April 17. Doubtless the earlier German preparations, as Martin van Creveld points out, helped their effort enormously.[71] All the same, one cannot fail to recognize the efficiency of a system that could put together an operation in such a short period, especially when, at the same time, the command was preparing for the invasion of the Soviet Union, keeping track of operations in North Africa and the Mediterranean, and organizing the defense of the occupied west, among other things.

Certainly the Germans themselves were well aware of their military prowess. They had defeated the Poles, Norwegians, Dutch, Belgians, Greeks, Yugoslavs, even the French and, on some fronts, the British. They believed they had no peers in the world, at least on land. In some respects that belief was true, but it was also dangerous. They had succeeded in bringing their strengths to bear against their enemies' weaknesses at the tactical and operational levels. Now, however, they had reached a point at which good tactics and a clever scheme of maneuver would no longer suffice. Their strategy had been weak from the start, and now their overweening pride would begin to compound the weaknesses in their operational concepts as well. If they had not yet begun to lose, they were at least about to stop winning.

6

Military Intelligence and the Plan of Attack in the East

In the last half of 1940 the Germans began their preparations for Operation *Barbarossa,* through which Hitler meant to achieve his long-held dream: to eliminate the Jewish-Bolshevik threat and give Germany the Lebensraum it needed to sustain itself. He also believed that the fall of the USSR would destroy Great Britain's hopes for a continental ally, and that was the goal upon which his military advisers concentrated. Inasmuch as they possessed any strategic vision at all, they believed that the strike against the USSR would be a way of obtaining the freedom and the resources they would need to fight the British Empire and perhaps the United States. That strategy might have worked, at least in the short term, but it contained a fatal flaw, in that it depended on a quick victory over the Soviets. Thus the failure of that strategy arose not so much from a lack of strategic vision, for which Hitler was exclusively responsible, but from inadequacies in narrower military calculations. This was the realm that the General Staff considered its special purview, and it had a point, in that its ability to plan and execute a maneuver plan was unequaled at this stage of the war. The problem was not with the scheme of maneuver, however, but with the less glamorous but no less important elements of the planning process: intelligence, logistics, and personnel management.

Germany stood little chance of winning the war once it committed itself to *Barbarossa.* If that fact was perhaps not apparent in the first half of 1941, then it certainly is in hindsight. Because the campaign determined Germany's fate to such a large extent, and because the root of the failure lay in the General Staff's inability to match the Wehrmacht's capabilities to those of its enemies, *Barbarossa* provides a particularly powerful case study in the high command's handling of the support functions. This chapter will therefore examine the military intelligence system and its role in the planning for *Barbarossa;* the next chapter will cover logistics and personnel, as well as the outcome of the invasion itself. These topics will introduce a new level of complexity into an already complicated story. Nevertheless, this investigation is essential to a complete understanding of the high command.[1]

OPERATIONAL PLANNING IN THE GLOW OF OPTIMISM

In their postwar accounts, the surviving German generals claimed that they opposed Hitler's decision to attack the USSR. The experience of the First World War, they said, had shown them the folly of opening a two-front conflict. Halder criticized Hitler in the harshest terms after the war for underestimating Russian strength and said that protests regarding the "complete inadequacy" of the information on the Soviet Union went unanswered.[2] Heusinger also said that the General Staff viewed the decision with extreme alarm.[3] Heinz Guderian wrote that he found the decision incredible, since Hitler himself had railed against the stupidity of the men who committed Germany to a two-front war in 1914.[4]

Given the catastrophe that grew out of the invasion, such claims are hardly surprising. Like so much of the information that senior veterans of the Wehrmacht provided, however, these protestations are a mix of truth, half-truth, and outright deception. It is true that many officers had misgivings about the coming campaign. In a meeting on July 30, 1940, the evening before Hitler made his intentions clear, Halder and Brauchitsch concluded that "one would be better off maintaining friendship with Russia."[5] Russian ambitions in the Dardanelles and the Persian Gulf posed no threat, they believed, and continued good relations with the Soviet Union would allow Germany to pursue victory against the British in the Mediterranean. Heusinger echoed this sentiment; moreover, in his view and that of most other staff officers, an attack on Russia would not make England surrender. The officer corps was also painfully aware of the fate that had met the French in 1812; a book by a French officer who had accompanied Napoleon into Russia was very well known at the time and gave some officers pause.[6] Apparently Keitel even tried to talk Hitler out of the idea, first verbally and then in a handwritten memo.[7] Jodl apparently shared his superior's doubts, though more quietly. Even as late as January 1941, Halder and Brauchitsch still could not see the sense in the operation; they did not believe that it was a valid way to strike at Britain.[8]

Thus the generals' postwar accounts gave an accurate impression of their strategic misgivings—misgivings that, in the end, proved prescient. However, the generals were less than honest when they claimed to have opposed *Barbarossa* on operational grounds. Most of Hitler's advisers agreed with his assessment that "a campaign against Russia would be a sand-table exercise in comparison [with the western campaign]."[9] Almost to a man, the senior German officers believed not only that a showdown with Bolshevism was necessary and inevitable but also that Germany could defeat Russia easily. On July 3—well before Hitler had announced his intentions formally—Halder ordered Greiffenberg to begin long-range planning for the operation; the primary consideration, he said, is "how a military strike against Russia is to be conducted in order to wring recognition of Germany's dominant role in Europe from them."[10] As Ernst Klink points out, there is no sign in Halder's diary of the shock he later said he experienced when he heard of Hitler's decision.[11] Guderian, even while claiming that he opposed the operation, admitted that both his own staff and the OKH found his objections surprising; he saw nothing but optimism in the army's senior ranks.[12]

The planning went forward smoothly in the last half of 1940 in this optimistic, almost lighthearted, atmosphere.[13] On July 4 Halder told Lieutenant General Georg von Küchler and the latter's chief of staff, Brigadier General Erich Marcks, to work out a plan of operations. (Küchler was the commander of the 18th Army, which was then stationed in East Prussia and Poland to cover Germany's eastern flank.) Marcks completed the plan and submitted it on July 9. This first version was defensive in nature; it envisioned an initial Russian attack followed by a German counteroffensive. That changed after Brauchitsch met with Hitler on July 21 and learned that the Führer wanted to solve the "Russian problem" that autumn. Over the next few days Halder and the principal staff sections created the basis for a new plan and then called Marcks back in to refine it. Marcks presented his "Operational Draft East" at the end of the first week of August. In it he calculated that the army might need as little as eight weeks of combat operations, perhaps as many as eleven, to take Leningrad, Moscow, and Kharkov, after which he expected no further organized Soviet resistance. To those figures the Germans added a three-week pause to rest and refit after the initial advance. The total would mean that a campaign begun on June 22 would be over by the end of September at the latest. Paulus worked with Marcks's concept after he became the assistant chief of staff for operations on September 3; he briefed Halder on the plan on October 29 and tested it further in a series of war games at the beginning of December. The end result went straight into the briefing that Halder gave to Hitler on December 5.

While the General Staff was working on its plan, Colonel Lossberg in the Armed Forces Command Staff was creating one of his own. He began the process in late June or early July 1940 by considering some of the operational factors involved. Then, on July 29, Jodl informed the principal members of the Command Staff that Hitler was determined to rid the world of the threat of Bolshevism "once and for all" by a surprise attack in May 1941.[14] Hitler's remarks on July 31 added further impetus to the planning process. The immediate result was an OKW order of August 7 entitled "Aufbau Ost" ("Buildup East") that called for infrastructural improvements in East Prussia and occupied Poland so that those areas could serve as a staging zone for the invasion force. Jodl also ordered an operational study, which Lossberg completed on September 15. There were some differences between the Lossberg and Marcks plans, but they shared the assumption that the Wehrmacht would have to destroy the Russian forces as far west as possible, so that they could not withdraw into the interior and prolong the campaign.[15] At no point in the planning process did Lossberg reveal any doubts about the feasibility of that goal; like Marcks, he assumed that the Russians possessed neither the operational skill to conduct a fighting withdrawal nor the reserves they would need to halt the invasion in the interior of the country.

Such confidence begs the question: Upon what did Marcks and Lossberg base their plans? These were not stupid men, and they had years of experience behind them. They believed that they had examined all the possibilities and that their conclusions were valid. The answer lies in two overlapping factors: the information that was available and the planners' interpretation of that information. In order to understand their decisions, therefore, one has to understand the mechanism by which the Germans gathered intelligence and, even more important, the planners' attitudes and beliefs toward military intelligence and toward their enemy.

THE INTELLIGENCE STRUCTURE

The OKW controlled several military intelligence-gathering and assessment organizations. First and foremost among these was the Amt Ausland/Abwehr or Office of Foreign- and Counterintelligence, under Admiral Wilhelm Canaris.[16] This office was responsible for, among other things, gathering information on foreign political and military affairs and disseminating it to the armed forces and various government agencies. It fed information directly to the intelligence officers in the Field Army, and it also maintained a liaison group, Gruppe A, in the OKH, attached to the staff of the assistant chief of staff for intelligence (Oberquartiermeister IV) in the General Staff.

Canaris's office comprised four main branches, only two of which are relevant to this study: the Foreign Branch (Abteilung Ausland) and the Counterintelligence Branch I (Abteilung Abwehr I). The first of these handled questions pertaining to the foreign policies and military affairs of other states. It collected information from a variety of sources, including the Foreign Office, military reports, and foreign press reports, and it kept Keitel, Canaris, the Armed Forces Command Staff, and the armed services informed of its findings. The official role of the Counterintelligence Branch I actually had nothing to do with counterintelligence; it was to generate secret intelligence for the army, the navy, and the Luftwaffe. In other words, it ran agents. It also worked in collaboration with the Secret State Police (Geheime Staatspolizei, or GeStaPo), the Foreign Office, and the other parts of the Office of

Foreign- and Counterintelligence to register and record all intelligence information of interest to the military.[17]

The organizational schemes within the Office of Foreign- and Counterintelligence followed both functional and geographic lines; the first set of subdivisions was functional.[18] In the Foreign Branch, for example, the main intelligence groups covered the following functions:

Group I: Foreign and defense policy
Group II: Relations with foreign militaries, and general
Group III: Foreign militaries; central reports collection for the OKW
Group V: Foreign press

Within the groups, the organization might be functional again, as in Group V, which contained departments *(Referate)* that evaluated foreign press reports and created summaries from them; collaborated with the reference archive; and translated documents from eastern languages. Group I's organization, on the other hand, was primarily geographic: its departments handled, respectively, general political questions, the British Empire, southern and southeastern Europe, eastern and northern Europe, western Europe (other than Britain), and America.[19]

Outside of the Office of Foreign- and Counterintelligence, the OKW also maintained a Cipher Group (Gruppe Chiffrierstelle OKW) in its Armed Forces Communications Branch (Abteilung Wehrmacht-Nachrichtenverbindungen) that intercepted and decoded both military and diplomatic traffic and passed on anything of interest to the services. Finally, the OKW's Defense Economy Branch (Wehrwirtschaftliche Abteilung) provided information on enemy production capabilities.[20]

Of course, in addition to using the OKW's assets, the army also gathered and evaluated information on its own, and not just within a narrow military realm. Up to mid-1941 the army's top leaders paid close attention to the broader context of the war. The reports that came in from the Office of Foreign- and Counterintelligence, either directly or through its liaison office in the General Staff, were one source of information, much of which came to Halder and Brauchitsch through Tippelskirch, the assistant chief of staff for intelligence.[21] In addition, Halder maintained outside contacts of his own. He met occasionally with Canaris personally, as well as with foreign representatives such as the Italian ambassador, Alfieri. He also stayed in frequent touch with representatives of the Foreign Office. Between the beginning of July and the end of October 1940, for instance, his diary shows no fewer than nine meetings with either Captain Hasso von Etzdorf, the Foreign Office's liaison officer with the OKH, or with State Secretary Ernst Freiherr von Weizsäcker.[22] (An interesting point in connection with many of these meetings, as well as with many of Halder's meetings with Brauchitsch, is that they focused on divining *German* intentions; this is another clear sign that the army's leaders had a hard time figuring out what Hitler had in mind.)[23]

Within the OKH, Tippelskirch supervised the army's intelligence assessment efforts.[24] He made sure that the intelligence branches performed all evaluations according to uniform standards and that their tasks did not overlap; in addition, he took care of any problems that fell outside the purview of any individual branch. He also summarized the branches' findings and disseminated them to all interested parties within the OKH, primarily to Brauchitsch, Halder, the assistant chief of staff for operations, and the Operations Branch chief, in the form of oral or written reports.[25] Tippelskirch was always present at Halder's briefings, and the two men also met separately once or twice a week.[26]

The General Staff's intelligence apparatus consisted primarily of two branches: Foreign Armies West and Foreign Armies East.[27] As the names imply, each of these organizations served as a central processing point for information on countries bordering Germany on one side or the other, although the division became less clear in the case of countries that lay farther afield. As of May 1, 1941, for example, Foreign Armies West covered, among other areas, the British Empire, including Iraq, India, and the British possessions in the Far East, as well as the United States and South America.[28] Foreign Armies East, meanwhile, was responsible not just for Eastern Europe, the Soviet Union, China, and Japan but also for some Scandinavian countries.[29] The need for a position such as Tippelskirch's becomes obvious in this context. Someone would later have to decide, for example, what branch would handle summaries of the conflict between the United States and Japan. For the most part there was some logic to the system, although Tippelskirch did assign some countries to one branch or the other simply to equalize the workload.[30]

The Foreign Armies branch chiefs divided their branches further into groups along geographic lines, but on the whole the groups, like the branches themselves, all performed the same functions and relied upon the same sources of information. In peacetime these sources included foreign official publications; military literature; press reports, radio, and movies; signals intercepts and radio direction finding; and information from military attachés and the OKW intelligence organs. In war some of those sources—such as the military attachés—would dry up, but others would become available: troop reconnaissance, prisoner-of-war interrogations, aerial reconnaissance, and captured documents. Twice every day the branch chiefs would summarize their findings in a report to Tippelskirch, who would then pass it along to Halder and Brauchitsch and up the chain to the OKW. The branches also produced enemy situation maps on a daily basis.[31] Finally, the two branch chiefs frequently met with Halder personally to brief him on some aspect of the intelligence picture.

The image that emerges to this point is that of an efficient hierarchy. Information flowed regularly up from the fighting units and reconnaissance assets in the army to the General Staff, where intelligence officers combined it with information that had come from the other services, especially the Luftwaffe, and from the intelligence organs of the OKW. The officers processed that information and disseminated it to everyone concerned, from corps headquarters to the army commander in chief and the OKW. Why, then, was there a problem with the Germans' intelligence assessments?

CULTURAL WEAKNESSES AND THE INTELLIGENCE INPUT TO *BARBAROSSA*

The problem with German intelligence was not really structural but attitudinal; it did not have so much to do with the quantity, or even the quality, of the information available, but with the ability of the high command to evaluate and use that information correctly. Actually, the flaw in the German intelligence system breaks down into two components. One of these was a subtle but pervasive bias against the intelligence function itself, a bias that intelligence officers themselves unconsciously shared to some extent. The other component was a tendency to accept convenient preconceptions in place of hard facts, especially when the analysis left the realm of operations and moved into political, economic, and social issues. Neither of these tendencies was unique to the Wehrmacht, but within that organization they took on particularly insidious and disruptive forms.

The bias against military intelligence was not usually evident in any open derogation of the function but instead manifested itself through more subtle mechanisms. Reinhard Gehlen, who took over Foreign Armies East in April 1942, later wrote, "Next to knowledge of comprehensive facts, the essence of the intelligence service lies in the ability to determine, predictively, the line that historical developments will take in the future."[32] That task never has been, and never will be, an exact science. Intelligence assessments are open to interpretation and debate, after all. Their power to convince is inherently weak. In the German army, moreover, intelligence efforts took place within a restrictive context, in which everything revolved around the operational concept or maneuver plan. In fact, the current wisdom held that operations officers could discern the enemy's intentions as well as intelligence specialists could. Such factors are not easy to isolate and examine. They are visible only, on the one hand, through the relevant regulations and personnel policies and, on the other, through an analysis of events (where the influence of the officers' preconceptions is also evident).

The bias against intelligence was visible, first of all, in the army's most basic regulation for officers: *Troop Command (Truppenführung)*. This manual was especially significant because it provided every German officer not just with specific tactical techniques but with the fundamental attitudes to carry with him throughout his career. *Troop Command* did not ignore intelligence; on the contrary, it emphasized the importance of that function to the decision-making process. At the same time it stipulated, quite properly, that uncertainty is the rule in combat and that the commander cannot wait for complete information before he makes a decision. It also enjoined the commander to consider the action that the enemy could take that would most seriously hinder the accomplishment of the mission. That is the decisive point, for by emphasizing the enemy's most *disruptive* act, the regulation removed the imperative to discern his most *likely* act. Thus it actually devalued the role of the intelligence officer, since the former task requires far less skill and subtlety than the latter.[33]

The *Handbook for General Staff Duty in War* addressed the intelligence function more directly than *Troop Command* did. The *Handbook* devoted more than two pages to the importance of intelligence and the role of the "Ic," as intelligence officers were called. However, it clearly identified the Ic as the assistant to the operations officer ("Ia") in the operations element, and it enjoined him to work closely with the Ia, not vice versa.[34] When the General Staff issued its first separate regulation governing the intelligence function—after a year and a half of war—it still made the Ic subordinate to the Ia and said, further, that "estimating the enemy picture is a matter for the commander in cooperation with the chief of staff or the Ia. The judgment of the enemy situation always proceeds from the command authorities, not from the Ic alone."[35] Thus there was no attempt to make the intelligence officer an equal of the operations officer, as the French and Americans did, at least nominally, by placing the two on the same level under a chief of staff.[36] If the structure in the OKH differed somewhat from that in a corps or army staff, the principle was the same. The intelligence officer remained first and foremost a supplier of information, not someone whose independent assessments carried special weight of their own. And since intelligence officers, especially the senior ones, had come up through the normal General Staff training program, with its emphasis on operations, they tended to share this fundamental attitude.

On the other hand, after the war some intelligence officers complained about the prevailing view of their role. From their standpoint, the bias against intelligence had some concrete effects. The officers held that the intelligence staffs in the OKH were too small, and the intelligence officers in the subordinate headquarters were too young, too inexperienced, and in some cases unqualified.[37] There is some merit to both of these complaints. There were, for example, only nineteen officers divided among the five groups in Foreign Armies West as of November 1, 1939, and only six of those were trained General Staff officers. No one would argue that nineteen is a generous complement with which to monitor military developments in Western Europe and the United States, especially with a major military campaign in the offing.[38] The problems with quality and experience among lower-level intelligence officers were equally serious. The position of Ic did not possess the prestige of the Ia. Officers generally wanted to move out of the Ic job as quickly as they could. Furthermore, as the war went on, the army filled the Ic positions more and more with reserve officers rather than General Staff officers. This move held the advantage that the reserve officers would probably stay in their positions longer, but these men were not as well trained as General Staff officers were. Their effectiveness also suffered from their status as reservists and their junior rank relative to the operations officers. Many General Staff officers looked down upon reservists, for one thing. For another, an intelligence officer had to be able to convince the commander and operations officer of the validity of his assessments. Even in the German army, in which rank differences carried less absolute weight than in other nations' forces, the intelligence officers were in a difficult position vis-à-vis their older, more experienced, and higher-ranking colleagues.[39]

This is the point at which to reemphasize, however, that the main problem associated with German intelligence was not that the operations officers ignored or belittled their compatriots in intelligence. The problem was that operations and intelligence officers on a staff formed a team of like-minded individuals; both parties shared the same attitudes and preconceptions, and so they often arrived at the same conclusions. The planning for Operation *Barbarossa,* which, as far as intelligence was concerned, centered on the trio of Halder, Tippelskirch (later Gerhard Matzky), and Colonel Eberhard Kinzel (chief of Foreign Armies East), illustrates how the flaws in the system worked out in practice. In this case the leading figures in the Army High Command, including the intelligence officers, when faced with a shortage of complete, accurate information on the Soviet Union, allowed their preconceptions to dominate the decision-making process. Here again, the point is not that they missed an opportunity to resist Hitler's strategic decision; Hitler never allowed them such an opportunity. The point is that, contrary to their later assertions, they supported that decision through their own assessments of the Russians' operational capabilities.

The Germans began with a long-standing image of Russia—the *"Russland-Bild,"* as Andreas Hillgruber terms it—and never really saw beyond it.[40] This image had two mutually contradictory faces. On the one hand, Russia appeared as a standing threat to the peoples of the west, a threat that the political philosophy of Bolshevism only intensified. Bolshevism, in addition to its inherent hostility to western political systems, had been a force behind the German collapse in 1918, and so the generals found it especially troubling.[41] On the other hand, the more dominant view was that Russia was a "colossus of clay": politically unstable, filled with discontented minorities, ineffectively ruled, and militarily weak. It would undoubtedly collapse at the first good blow.[42]

The Wehrmacht had little in the way of hard facts with which to check its assumptions. Soviet-German relations had become increasingly strained since the rise of the Nazi Party, and so many sources of information evaporated. The German military attaché in Moscow, Lieutenant General Ernst Köstring, complained to Halder that surveillance by the Soviet security forces made intelligence gathering nearly impossible.[43] The Abwehr had been trying for years—if somewhat halfheartedly—to insert agents into Russia, with no success. Foreign Armies East began looking seriously at Russia in autumn 1939, but it had few resources to bring to bear. The country was too vast for aerial reconnaissance to reveal much, although the Germans did make an effort, over Russian protests. Radio reconnaissance was the best source, but the effectiveness of Russian radio discipline and ciphers limited the usefulness of this approach.[44]

The paucity of intelligence sources left the Germans with little more than their general impressions. They observed Russian performance in Spain, Poland, and Finland carefully, and what they saw did not impress them. The operations revealed a number of serious problems in the Soviet army, and although the Germans also noted Russian efforts at remediation, they did not expect to see significant improvement for years.[45] Behind Russian ineffectiveness, they believed, lay the purges that Stalin had carried out in his officer corps in 1937 and 1938. John Erickson has estimated that between twenty and twenty-five thousand Soviet officers died, including most of the senior commanders.[46] Köstring estimated in September 1940 that the Soviets would need four more years to recover to the level of effectiveness they had held before the purges.[47] His deputy, Lieutenant Colonel Hans Krebs, later increased the estimate to twenty years.[48] In comparison with the French army, which the Germans had defeated with such apparent ease, the Soviets seemed an easy target.

Foreign Armies East was able to offer little of value on the strength and organization of Soviet forces. Halder first briefed Kinzel on plans for an attack in the east on July 22, 1940.[49] Four days later, Kinzel was back with his estimate of the enemy situation. Unfortunately, Halder did not record the details of Kinzel's briefing; he simply noted that it supported a plan to drive on Moscow and then attack into the Ukraine.[50] At any rate, the quality of Kinzel's briefing is open to question. Not only were sources lacking, but Kinzel himself had had no special intelligence training, did not speak Russian, and could boast of no special familiarity with that country. The fact that the Germans would entrust such a man with a task of such importance speaks volumes.[51]

When Marcks prepared the plan that he presented to Halder in early August 1940, he presumably used estimates from Foreign Armies East. He figured the Red Army's strength at 221 large units (infantry and cavalry divisions and mechanized brigades), of which 143 would be available in European Russia to resist an attack by 147 German divisions. Despite the relative parity of forces, Marcks was confident of the outcome. He not only forecast an operation that might be over in as little as eleven weeks but also openly regretted the fact that the Russians would not do Germany the favor of attacking first. In any case, he believed that, in contrast to 1812, the Russians would not be able to avoid a decision; the value of the industrial assets and resources in Great Russia and the western Ukraine would force them to defend those areas. Moscow was the key, he continued: take it, and the empire would fall apart.[52]

Foreign Armies East was more cautious in a report it submitted on October 17. The branch pointed out that the factors of time and space would be in the Russians' favor, and that the Red Army still possessed considerable defensive strength and therefore should be taken very seriously. The report went on to say, however, that the Soviets could not conduct a war of movement on a large scale.[53] In any case, there is no indication that this report had any particular effect on German operational planning, one way or the other.

The most wide-ranging assessment from Foreign Armies East appeared on January 15, 1941: "The Armed Forces of the Union of Soviet Socialist Republics, Status as of January 1, 1941."[54] The study estimated the peacetime strength of the Soviet army at about two million men; this figure would rise to four million—in two hundred rifle divisions plus other units—in wartime. The mechanized forces were the elite of the army, it continued, but Soviet tanks and armored vehicles either were obsolete or were modified versions of foreign models. Furthermore, although Foreign Armies East admitted that its sources of information were extremely limited, it nevertheless proceeded to draw broad conclusions about the Soviet order of battle, doctrine, capabilities, and intentions. It stated that the strengths of the Red Army lay in its size and the stoicism, endurance, and courage of its soldiers; these factors would make the Soviets particularly effective in the defense. Still, the Germans believed that the Soviets' weaknesses would more than cancel out their strengths. Russian training and doctrine were not up to German standards and would not allow the Red Army to carry out modern mobile operations. Moreover, Soviet officers were clumsy, unwilling to make decisions or accept responsibility, and too methodical, according to their German counterparts.

Foreign Armies East issued yet another assessment of the enemy situation on May 20, 1941.[55] By this time it had raised its estimate of Soviet strength in European Russia alone to 192 major units. The report disregarded the Soviet forces in the Far East, since the intelligence officers shared everyone else's assumption that the threat of an attack by Japan would not allow the Red Army to shift forces from that area. The May 20 assessment also repeated the claim that the Russians would be unable to withdraw to the interior of the country as had happened in 1812; thus, the Germans would be able to force a battle of annihilation close to the western frontier.

These assessments were flawed in several ways. First, they vastly underestimated the USSR's military potential, including the number of units available, the quantity and quality of equipment, and the skill and flexibility of the officer

Eberhard Kinzel. (Courtesy Bundesarchiv, photo no. 85/48/28)

corps. For instance, the army that Foreign Armies East estimated to contain 2,000,000 men at the beginning of January 1941 actually contained 4,205,000 already, and that figure would grow to 5,005,000 by June 22. The 10,000 tanks that the Germans expected would turn out to be 20,000 to 24,000 (against a German strength of 3,500), and they would include the T-34, which was better than anything the Wehrmacht possessed.[56] Also, the Germans undercounted the total number of Soviet units by a third, even while they *overestimated* the number in the western military districts by 30 to 50 percent.[57] Obviously, these miscalculations would act against the plan to defeat the USSR in one campaign. On top of these errors, the Germans badly miscalculated in the strategic realm by deciding that the Soviets would not move forces from the Far East. Finally, the Soviet Union would prove to be much more politically stable, economically robust, and psychologically strong than the Germans assumed.

Several authors have made the point that the Germans were not the only ones who underestimated the Russians. The British and American authorities also expected the Wehrmacht to roll over the Red Army. Their estimates of Russian resistance varied from as little as ten days to as much as three months—but no one expected the Soviets to win.[58] This only proves, however, that the Western powers experienced the same paucity of information and operated from many of the same assumptions. The key questions still remain: Should the Germans have come to some other conclusion? Given the information that was available to them—or *not* available, as the case may be—should the army's leaders have embarked upon the Russian campaign with such confidence?

In this context one should first note the information that German intelligence-gathering efforts missed, even though it was available. The existence of the Soviet T-34 tank, arguably the finest of the war, is the best-known example. These tanks caught the Germans completely by surprise, even though the Japanese had faced them at Khalkin-Gol in August 1939. That battle itself was also something from which the Germans could have learned, for it demonstrated that the Soviets were not so inept as most outside observers thought; the Soviet forces under General Georgi Zhukov showed that they were already learning the principles of mobile, combined-arms warfare. There is no indication that the Germans expressed any great interest in the battle, however.[59]

A more serious problem is discernible in the planners' reaction to intelligence that they had but that ran counter to their assumptions and plans. Such information definitely existed, almost from the moment the General Staff started planning the campaign. The first warning flag took the form of a document dated August 10, 1940, from the Military Geography Branch of the General Staff: "First Draft of a Military-Geographic Study on European Russia."[60] The study identified Leningrad, Moscow, and the Ukraine as the most valuable military targets. It also identified the Caucasus, with its oil, as a valuable goal but said that the area was far outside of Germany's reach. The study went on to say, however, that even if *all* these targets fell to the Wehrmacht, victory would not be certain. Asiatic Russia was no longer a wilderness; it contained forty million inhabitants, a good railroad network, agriculture, and a large percentage of the USSR's industry and raw materials. The study also pointed out that space and climate remained serious obstacles to any attack.

There is some indication that Marcks had access to an early version of the Military Geography Branch study. In any case, his plan loses its confident tone as it discusses the possibility that the Soviets might not surrender or collapse after the fall of Leningrad, Moscow, and Kharkov. If they held out, he stated, the army might have to pursue them to the Urals. Even then, with its most valuable European areas gone and without the ability to mount major combat operations, the Soviet Union could "maintain a state of hostilities for an indefinite period with support from Asia."[61] Thus, as Ernst Klink points out, Marcks "grasped the information in the Military Geography Branch's assessment, without deriving requirements for dealing with it."[62] As for Halder, he did not even address this aspect of Marcks's plan; he simply assumed that the destruction of the Soviet forces and the occupation of a certain amount of territory would end the war.

About four weeks after he submitted his first plan, Marcks went a step further. He gave Tippelskirch a broad strategic assessment that he had written on his own initiative. If Germany attacked Russia, it said, a coalition war would follow that the United States would eventually join. Germany would be cut off and vulnerable to an Anglo-American invasion combined with a Russian counteroffensive. Only if Germany could take over the prime industrial and agricultural areas of western Russia could it expect to survive against the "Red Coalition." The danger lay in the possibility that German forces would find themselves tied down short of their goals when winter arrived. Therefore, every effort had to be made to fight the decisive battles as far west as possible, so as to free the way for a rapid advance to the campaign's objectives.[63] Tippelskirch and Kinzel responded together to Marcks's concerns, but they did so superficially. They never actually addressed the prospect of a "Red Coalition." Both men believed that the Wehrmacht could fulfill Marcks's last requirement, thereby nullifying his earlier points. Tippelskirch did not even pass Marcks's memo on to Halder.[64] If he had, moreover, there is no indication that it would have changed Halder's plans.

One last example illustrates Halder's willingness to bend everything to his operational concept. Early in 1941 Hitler ordered a study on the Pripyat Marshes, an expanse of territory smack in the middle of the German advance that covers roughly twenty-eight thousand square miles and is impassable to vehicles. Foreign Armies East had a first draft ready on February 12, but apparently Halder found its conclusions unsettling; he did not want to give Hitler any excuse to meddle in his plans. Halder ordered a revision, which was ready on February 21. It toned down the dangers that the area might contain.

Hitler was not convinced; he told Halder on March 17 that entire enemy armies could move in the region.[65] Halder considered the Führer's concerns to be exaggerated, but Hitler was right. In more than three years of occupation, the Germans never managed to clear the Pripyat. Partisan forces operating from the area created serious problems for two German army groups. In the short term, though, Halder stuck to his original plan.

Clearly the upper echelons of the German military were not interested in information that did not match their plans and preconceptions. Michael Geyer's conclusion about Hitler can be broadened to include the senior military leaders: they did not gather information in order to make major decisions but only to plan the implementation of decisions they had already made.[66] For their part, the German intelligence services did well at evaluating doctrine and tactics, the areas closest to their own General Staff training, but when faced with an army whose doctrine was unfamiliar—such as the Soviets'—they relied upon old biases. Some of the lower-level planners, especially in the army groups' headquarters, foresaw problems with *Barbarossa,* as did the few true Russian experts such as Köstring, but their objections rarely reached the upper echelons, and, when they did, they received little attention. Thus the system accepted those "facts" that backed up its assumptions and rejected everything else. The leaders' confidence was ill considered, given the inadequate intelligence information they had at their disposal. The German army was about to march willingly into the largest battle in history without anything more than the flimsiest information regarding its enemy.

7

Logistics, Personnel, and *Barbarossa*

Solid information about the USSR and its armed forces was not the only thing that the Germans lacked when they invaded in June 1941. Men, munitions, fuel, equipment, and transport were all in short supply, especially considering the scope of the task. *Barbarossa* would fail in large part because the Germans simply did not have the resources to defeat the Soviets in one campaign. The postwar accounts placed the responsibility for this state of affairs squarely at Hitler's feet. Manstein, for example, said of the Führer that "he had a certain vision for operational possibilities, but he lacked an understanding of the prerequisites for the execution of an operational idea. He did not understand the relation of an operational goal to its time and force requirements, never mind the logistical needs."[1] Manstein had a point, but as was so often the case, he and the other generals went too far when they implied that their own expertise so far outstripped Hitler's. The planners were fully aware of the army's weaknesses, but they went ahead anyway, with complete confidence in victory. Both the weaknesses and the confidence reflected serious problems within the logistics and personnel administration systems.

LOGISTICS

Logistical planning was primarily an army affair; the OKW played only a limited role. Within the National Defense Branch there was a Quartermaster Group (Quartiermeister-Gruppe) that Jodl and Keitel had set up in November 1940 to supervise quartermaster activities throughout the Wehrmacht, under the leadership of Colonel Werner von Tippelskirch.[2] The pending deployment of German troops to Libya had made such an arrangement necessary. Rather than set up a separate staff, Jodl had Group IV in the National

Defense Branch restructured to handle the task; in any case, it depended heavily upon support from the service commands. The representatives of the various OKW offices that dealt with logistics, plus representatives of the armed services, also formed an Armed Forces Quartermaster Staff (Wehrmacht-Quartiermeister-Stab), but this met only occasionally to iron out particular problems.[3]

Within the army, both major divisions of the OKH—the General Staff and the elements under the "chief of army equipment and commander of the Replacement Army," General Friedrich Fromm—played important roles. In broad terms, the former set the requirements and the latter filled them.[4] More specifically, four agencies were involved: the General Army Office under the Replacement Army commander and, in the General Staff, the Transport and Organization Branches and the General Quartermaster. Here is how the process worked, in greatly simplified form: the chief of the General Staff discussed the current military situation and any upcoming operations with the chief of the Organization Branch, Lieutenant General Walter Buhle, and the general quartermaster, Lieutenant General Eduard Wagner, on an ongoing basis.[5] Both men or their representatives attended Halder's morning briefing.[6] Each of their branches then used Halder's guidance to work out the army's material requirements, that is, for transport, equipment, arms, food, fuel, fodder, and munitions. The Organization Branch planned for the formation and equipment of new units, while the General Quartermaster handled replacement equipment as well as supplies for units-in-being.[7] Both staff sections coordinated with the General Army Office to obtain the required items. In the case of the Organization Branch, the assistant chief of staff for operations often helped with that coordination.[8]

Once the General Army Office made the materials available, the next step was to get them to the proper location. The first stage in this process was the responsibility of the Transport Branch, whose chief, Brigadier General Rudolf Gercke, was simultaneously chief of Armed Forces Transport (Wehrmachttransportchef). He controlled all shipment by rail and inland waterway, in accordance with directions he received from the OKW. Regardless of any task that the OKW might give him, however, he was officially subordinate to Halder, so army requirements did receive some priority.[9] Once beyond the railhead, the supplies were Wagner's responsibility; he controlled all motor transport in the so-called zone of communications behind the lines. Like Gercke, he also wore two hats, since he was responsible for supplying army units in the OKW theaters and for providing certain classes of supplies to any units of the Luftwaffe, navy, SS, or attached organizations within any theater of operations.[10]

Wagner's organization deserves a closer look, since it "owned" the supplies as well as transporting them forward to the troops, and especially since it played the primary role in logistics planning. Its mission, as defined in 1935,

Walter Buhle. (Courtesy Bundesarchiv, photo no. 78/127/21)

Rudolf Gercke. (Courtesy National Archives, photo no. 242-GAP-101-G-5)

Eduard Wagner. (Courtesy Bundesarchiv, photo no. 81/41/16A)

was to "supply the army with everything that is necessary for its striking power" and "free it from everything that could detract from its capabilities."[11] To that end Wagner (whose nickname within his domain was "Nero") controlled the largest organization within the General Staff.[12] Under the Chief's Group (Chefgruppe), which included Wagner and his personal staff and which handled plans and personnel matters for the entire organization, there were two branches and five independent groups. The most important of these elements from the supply perspective were the Army Supply Branch (Abteilung Heeresversorgung) and the Army Supply Distribution Group (Gruppe Heeresnachschubführer); the other elements dealt with the administration of occupied territories and other, less critical responsibilities.[13] The Army Supply Branch did the actual logistics planning: how many tons of what supplies were needed where, and so on. It contained five groups, organized functionally; Group 3, for example, was in charge of munitions, vehicles, fuel, weapons, and equipment, while the so-called Technical Group handled engineering equipment, road construction, supply routes, and construction materials and equipment. The Army Supply Distribution Group oversaw the so-called *Grosstransportraum,* the transport regiments and battalions that bridged the gap between the railheads and the troop units.[14]

Two major sets of problems existed within this system. The first was structural: the lines of responsibility and authority were sometimes unclear or illogical. The most troublesome problem of this sort was that the individual services retained far too much independence; in fact, they even increased it as time went on. The navy, Luftwaffe, and SS set up their own supply organizations over time, even though the General Quartermaster was responsible for getting them their essential supplies. The resulting redundancy was a waste of matériel and manpower, and it also overburdened the transport system. In the area of transport itself, the services submitted their own requests for rail and inland shipping space separately, without any background materials. Thus the chief of Armed Forces Transport did not have the opportunity to prioritize requests properly. The services also built up and guarded their own transport assets. The General Quartermaster had no control of Luftwaffe or navy trucks, and the transport chief had none over aircraft or oceangoing ships.[15] Thus interservice rivalry and the relative powerlessness of the OKW again made themselves felt.

At this point in the war, however, the structural problems with the supply and transportation systems had still not become a great hindrance. As with military intelligence, the far more serious problem was attitudinal. All planning revolved around the maneuver concept; the operations officers would set that up first and then call in the logisticians. "According to our opinion," Halder told an interviewer after the war, "the material has to serve the spiritual. Accordingly, our quartermaster service may never hamper the operational concept."[16] That approach found perhaps its most blatant practical expression in a briefing that Colonel Kurt Zeitzler gave to a group of division supply officers before the French campaign. If ever there was an operation that depended upon logistics, he said, this was it. Then he simply demanded that all the divisions get over the Meuse; how the officers managed it was their business![17] The hierarchy within German staffs mirrored the dominant attitude: supply officers, like their counterparts in intelligence, were junior in rank and position to the operations officers. Their job was to support the operation however they could. Even the military's vocabulary gave away its assumptions. The term *Logistik* did not come into general use until after 1945; before that time, everything in that sphere came under the rubrics *Nachschub* or *Versorgung,* both meaning "supply," a much narrower term.

The Germans' approach worked well enough in France, but Russia would be another matter entirely. The logistical task there was enormous. In the briefing that Wagner gave to Halder on November 12, 1940, he spoke of a force of two million men, with three hundred thousand horses and five hundred thousand vehicles (including over two thousand different types).[18] That force would aim for objectives that were between six and nine hundred miles away. But because the railroad gauge was different in Russia than in Western Europe, there would be no way to bring supply trains forward initially. Special railroad units would follow behind the advancing armies to reset the rails to the German gauge and repair damage, but until they could catch up, the combat units would have to depend upon the *Grosstransportraum* and their own carrying capacity for their supplies. Moreover, the roads in Russia were few and poor; the planners figured on a maximum of two arteries for each army group.[19] (The standard up until then was one supply route per *corps;* there are at least four corps in an army group, but most army groups in Russia would contain more.) Those arteries would grow to hundreds of kilometers in length if the armies advanced at the planned rate, but the armies could not pace their advance to let the supply services keep up, or the Soviets would escape into the interior, thus invalidating the whole concept of the operation. The fast armored divisions would soon outpace the mass of the infantry, which in turn would clog the roads that the armored divisions' supply columns needed. And to top off all the other problems, some matériel was in critically short supply. Rubber tires and fuel were the most worrisome items; the latter might run short as early as July, according to some estimates.[20]

No one can claim that the Germans lacked creativity and diligence in their approach to these problems. Wagner set up supply headquarters that would be under his orders but would operate with the army groups for maximum efficiency. Each of these headquarters would control a "supply district" with a number of depots. Wagner also scraped together every truck he could find in Germany and the occupied territories to add to the *Grosstransportraum;* this allowed for the army's conservative minimum of twenty thousand tons of trucking capacity behind each army group. To deal with the different march rates of the infantry and armored divisions, Wagner decided to try to make the latter independent of any supply base for the initial thrust. To that end he directed them to carry extra fuel that they would dump behind their advance but in front of the infantry divisions, so that it would be accessible to the *panzers'* own truck columns. The plan also called upon the armies to live off the land to the fullest extent possible, and to that end each army group set up special centers to process captured supplies and transport of every description.[21]

The planners knew that these measures would not be enough to support an uninterrupted drive to Moscow and beyond. Paulus held a war game in early December 1940 to check out the plan of campaign that he had created, based on Marcks's study. The results dictated a three-week pause after the initial thrust, to allow the army to rebuild the railroad lines, replenish the combat units' stocks of supplies, and repair vehicles and equipment; the pause would take place roughly three-quarters of the way to Leningrad in the north, at Smolensk in the center, and at Kiev in the south. After the pause, Army Group Center would drive on for Moscow, even if that meant stopping the groups on the flanks for the last stages of the attack.[22]

At no time did Paulus, Halder, Wagner, or any of the other planners give any indication that they thought the Soviet Union might simply be too big a target, that Germany did not have the supplies or transportation assets to carry out the campaign as they envisioned it. In fact, the more the Germans found out about the difficulties of the campaign, the less time they estimated they would need to complete it. What at first guess had seemed to require five months—this at Hitler's July 31, 1940, briefing—Marcks predicted would take as little as eight weeks, plus replenishment time. By early December the planners believed they could do it in eight or ten weeks *including* a replenishment phase. And by April 1941 Brauchitsch was speaking of a tough battle at the frontiers that would last "up to four weeks," after which resistance would be negligible.[23] The army's leaders' attitude toward logistics was merging with their faith in a quick Russian collapse. Only with difficulty can one escape the conclusion that they were engaged in a gigantic effort at self-delusion.

PERSONNEL ADMINISTRATION

The Germans' illusions applied not just to logistics but also to manpower. One of the points that strikes the layman about Germany's position in the Second World War derives from simple arithmetic. How could a nation the size of Germany take on the British Empire, the Soviet Union, and the United States and hope to win, even with help from Italy, Japan, and several smaller allies? Of course the outcome of a war does not depend on population figures alone, but there is still an important point here. In his more reasonable moments even Hitler admitted that Germany would lose a long war against a large hostile coalition. When he and his generals forced just such a coalition to form, they did so in the expectation that they could win before their enemies could bring all their assets to bear. In terms of personnel, two interrelated issues bore on that expectation. The first was a straightforward shortage of manpower and especially of officers. The second was an emerging change in policy, as Hitler and the Nazi Party tightened their control over the army.

Halder and Brauchitsch both paid close attention to the personnel situation. Halder's diary shows regular meetings with Organization Branch Chief Buhle and Lieutenant General Bodewin Keitel, chief of the Army Personnel Office. Likewise, Brauchitsch worked through Keitel, who was officially his subordinate, on matters concerning the officer corps.[24] Appearances notwithstanding, however, Halder and Brauchitsch found their influence shrinking. On September 11, 1939, Hitler had taken control of postings to division command and above, and to corresponding positions in the high commands of the services. He also monitored every promotion to lieutenant general and above.[25] And Halder's diary reveals that the Führer was taking an ever more active role in the details of personnel policy. On October 19, 1940, for example, Bodewin Keitel delivered some pointed comments from Hitler on "frocking," on the establishment of so-called supernumerary officers, and on the awarding of decorations.[26]

One might expect to find the OKW behind such interference, but at this point in the war the initiative lay predominantly with Hitler himself, not with any bureaucratic agency. Personnel matters within the OKW were the responsibility of the Armed Forces Central Branch (Wehrmacht Zentral-Abteilung), which was directly subordinate to Wilhelm Keitel. This branch handled, in addition to issues concerning personnel in the OKW, questions that were general enough to cover all three services or that required Hitler's decision. Probably its most important function was to rule on the standards according to which the services selected, evaluated, decorated, promoted, posted, and dismissed their officers, again inasmuch as these standards applied to the Wehrmacht as a whole.[27] However, the Armed Forces Central Branch did not play a significant role in army personnel decisions at this early date. Hitler's personal influence was much more important.

In a 1990 study, Jürgen Förster pointed out the method to Hitler's meddling and the ways in which the Führer's philosophy on personnel matters differed from that of the army's elite.[28] The old Reichsheer of the interwar years was an organization in which an exclusive leadership group—the General Staff—dominated. They chose their personnel as much for specific views and attitudes as for ability; hence the Reichsheer never became an institution that represented all of Weimar society. Instead, it stood as "the modern model of the standing army from the age of Absolutism."[29] That was the model with which the army's senior leaders were most familiar, but it was not the model Hitler wanted. Although he had defended the army from Röhm's ambitions, his long-term goals were little different. For Hitler, the Wehrmacht, the state, and society were all to adopt the same organizing principles: race, personality, and competition. He wanted the army to be a people's army. To that end he demanded, among other things, that promotion into the officer ranks rest on performance alone, with no prerequisites. In war, that meant that a candidate's combat record would be most important. This idea went against more than a century of emerging professionalism in the army, and it reversed the standard that Seeckt had used in building the Reichswehr officer corps, but in April 1937 Blomberg accepted it as a guide for the Wehrmacht. Although full implementation within the army would not follow for several years, the trend was clear. Hitler was going to emphasize character over intellect, thus replacing the army's traditional elitism with Nazi egalitarianism.

Hitler's notion of "character" was in some ways similar to the army's, but it also contained—naturally enough—a strong National Socialist emphasis. One of the key attributes that Hitler demanded was personal loyalty; he wanted obedient servants within the context of the *Führerprinzip,* not independent thinkers. He got that loyalty, first and foremost, through his control of senior officer selection, promotion, and postings. The rewards for good behavior were obvious, as when, on July 19, 1940, Hitler promoted no fewer than twelve full generals to the rank of field marshal. On top of such rewards, moreover, Hitler also introduced systematic bribery that July, using money from a Chancellery discretionary fund. Army and Luftwaffe officers with the rank of full general or field marshal, as well as naval officers of equivalent rank, began receiving secret monthly tax-exempt payments that more than doubled their salaries. Hitler also made monetary gifts to various generals on special occasions, gifts that sometimes amounted to hundreds of thousands of reichsmarks at a time. The message to the officers who received these payments was crystal clear: raise a fuss over any Nazi policies, such as the elimination of Polish Jews and intelligentsia that was already taking place, and the money would disappear.[30] Of course, occasions on which this bribery altered a particular decision are impossible to pin down, and senior officers would still oppose Hitler from time to time, but their postwar attempts to hide the payments give some indication of the money's effect.

In contrast to the bribes, Hitler's broader personnel policies aroused some opposition at the time, partly because they threatened many officers' prospects for promotion. Resistance from the General Staff was especially strong, and it led to compromises and delays in the new policies' implementation. The policies affected staff officers severely because they often stayed in their positions for long periods and thus did not have the opportunity to distinguish themselves in the front line. That fact was, in turn, a reflection of a more immediate and serious problem. General Staff officers had to stay in staffs instead of taking commands because there were not enough of them to allow for the traditional duty rotation.

Halder controlled personnel policies for the General Staff personally, and so he was at the center of this issue. According to his duty instructions, the chief of the General Staff was

the superior to all General Staff officers and officers who have been attached to the General Staff for training; in this capacity he acts in the interest of the General Staff Corps. He bears the responsibility for the training of these officers. In collaboration with the chief of the Army Personnel Office he makes suggestions to the commander in chief of the army regarding the employment of the General Staff officers and of the officers attached to the General Staff for training. He can give his opinion on the assessments of these officers.[31]

Halder took this set of responsibilities very seriously. His diary shows that he met frequently with Colonel Gustav Heistermann von Ziehlberg, who was chief of the General Staff's Central Branch and thus responsible for the staff's affairs, including the selection and assignment of staff officers.

The army's expansion between 1933 and 1939 had already put a significant strain on the General Staff; the demands of war only made the situation worse. The Germans started the war with 415 fully qualified General Staff officers, plus 93 officers assigned for training and 303 with the War Academy, for a total of 811. When the war broke out, the academy closed so that the officers there could fill slots in active units. Even so, there was a shortfall of thirty-three General Staff officers; the army filled the empty slots with regular officers or with reactivated First World War General Staff veterans.[32]

As the war went on, the problem intensified, despite the best efforts of Halder and the Central Branch. With the War Academy closed, there was no source of additional General Staff officers. Obviously, that situation had to change, but there was no easy solution. Training a General Staff officer to the old standards took more time than the army had. Finally, in early January 1940, the General Staff began running shortened training courses, but the first course yielded only 44 officers. When the army began the buildup for *Barbarossa,* the need for General Staff officers went up again, to 1,209 by February 15, 1941. The staff tried to meet this demand by expanding its training classes, reactivating more veterans (by raising the age limit), and creating expanded training programs for officers at the unit level. In the end, though, still more staff slots had to be filled by regular and reserve officers who had received no special staff training. Intelligence slots (Ic) were the first to be filled this way; most Ic officers at the division level were reservists by mid-January 1941. Ziehlberg reported at that point that the division supply officers (Ib) would be next.[33]

In the face of such shortages, the General Staff was hard put to maintain its training standards, but it did try to hold on to certain core principles. Officers whom their units nominated for General Staff duty had first to serve at the front for at least six months; only proven combat officers could go further in the program. Six months of on-the-job training with a division-, corps-, or army-level staff would follow, thus allowing a reduction in the period of formal training to six months. Once the formal training was over, the officers often went through a series of assignments to further test and develop their skills. A new General Staff officer usually received a posting as a Ib with a division staff first, so that he could prove his ability to handle supply matters. Then, if possible, he received a Ia (Operations) slot. Based, then, on his performance and wishes, the Central Branch would decide if he would continue his service in operations, supply, intelligence, or one of the specialty areas such as organization, training, or transport. If he had shown himself to be particularly adept at operations, the Central Branch would observe him carefully and move him into operational positions in army or army group headquarters or within the OKH itself.[34]

Two principles governed the whole training process: the need to place assistants of high personal worth and extensive military knowledge with commanders, and the need to guarantee unity of thought in the staff corps. One key part of the first task was to ensure that the commander's personality and that of his chief of staff meshed. Strong-willed commanders needed quiet, thoughtful, but strong personalities to advise them; commanders who tended to hesitate needed daring, direct chiefs. The Central Branch usually did not consult with a commander regarding the choice of a chief. If frictions did develop between the two, the Central Branch would replace the chief, but this hardly ever happened, especially in the first years of the war.[35]

Halder worked to maintain unity of thought within the General Staff by reviewing all fundamental writings and orders personally, as well as by overseeing the training program. One of his constant concerns was to see that the staff put its wartime experience to good use, and to that end he promoted a constant exchange of ideas between the OKH and the subordinate commands, right down to the lowest levels. And in further pursuit of that goal, he insisted that all General Staff officers report to him personally if they came near the OKH while in transit to or from their assignments. After the war Halder wrote that, since command responsibility lay solely with the commander, these measures could only ensure unity in the advice their staff officers provided. He maintained, however, that such advice was enough to ensure unity of leadership within the army.[36]

Halder's point is debatable; especially in the later stages of the war, some officers would place their own interests above those of the General Staff. Moreover, unity of thought can be a questionable goal. Within certain narrow bounds the General Staff's unity served it well, as in tactics, operational maneuver, organization, and staff procedures. However, it also locked some attitudes in place—toward intelligence, logistics, and strategy, for example— that were definitely disadvantageous. The General Staff was not a place for radical thinkers. To be fair, most military organizations (and many civilian ones) share that attribute; the balance between creativity and organizational unity—both important goals—is difficult to find and maintain.

The General Staff's elitism and intellectual consistency were all the easier to maintain because of the Germans' conviction that staffs should remain small. The example of Foreign Armies West in autumn 1939 is worth reviewing here: nineteen officers to monitor Western Europe and the United States, with a major ground offensive set to begin in the near future. The Operations Branch was no better off. Its organizational chart of June 1, 1941, shows only thirty-one officers and officials, ten of them General Staff officers. Moreover, of that number, only eleven officers handled the entire eastern front plus Denmark, Norway, Sweden, Finland, Poland, Czechoslovakia, Romania, and Hungary.[37] The shortage of General Staff officers might appear as a plausible explanation for this phenomenon, but on the contrary, this was a matter of principle, even if it was never written down. The Germans believed that smaller staffs were more efficient; that they cut down on paperwork, briefings, and unnecessary detail work; and that they allowed for the clarity that comes from personal interaction. The emphasis on smallness also mirrored the Germans' belief in the qualitative superiority of their work; they did not need large staffs such as the Allies had, they reasoned, because their officers were better.[38] As is true of the bribes that senior officers accepted, any attempt to identify this policy's broader effects would rest on pure conjecture. Certainly the size of their staffs did not prevent the Germans from conquering most of Europe—but neither did it allow them to keep what they conquered. Most significantly, the problems that did result tended especially to exacerbate failings in the other support functions. The operations sections functioned well with small staffs, but logistics and intelligence elements did not; nor did personnel management agencies.

In the case of personnel management, as with logistics, the system functioned through the interplay of several different staff elements: the Army Personnel Office, which was directly subordinate to the commander in chief of the army, the General Staff's Organization and Central Branches, and the General Army Office under the Replacement Army Commander. The Central Branch took care of General Staff officers, as noted earlier. The Army Personnel Office worked on all other officer personnel matters, such as education, evaluations, promotions, assignments, discipline, honors, and awards. It also determined officer requirements and supervised the officer replacement system, in cooperation with the Organization Branch and the General Army Office. The Organization Branch worked out the personnel requirements—officer and enlisted—for all new units, according to guidance provided by the chief of the General Staff. In addition, it allocated enlisted replacements to the units of the Field Army, in collaboration with the General Army Office. That last organization had a broad role. First, it regulated the distribution of replacement personnel to all the services, under the direction of the OKW. Then within the army's sphere, it sent recruits to training units and worked with the Organization Branch to regulate the allocation of trained men, both to fill new units and to replace combat losses in established ones.[39]

In the planning and preparations for *Barbarossa,* the Germans ran into problems in the personnel arena that were just as serious as those connected with intelligence and logistics. In general terms (and this was something that applied on the logistical side as well), one of the army's greatest sources of difficulty was the fact that it had to alter its structure radically in the months leading up to the invasion of Russia. On May 28, 1940, in expectation of imminent victory in France, Hitler had told Brauchitsch that he wanted to reduce the army to a peacetime level, and he ordered that thirty-five divisions disband. In mid-July he lowered the figure to seventeen and sent the men from the others on leave. Then the decision to attack the USSR turned the whole idea on its head; now the army had to grow from 120 to 180 divisions (later 207, including 19 instead of 9 armored divisions).[40] Manning, training, and equipping the extra units was no simple matter, especially with the preparations for the invasion of England under way simultaneously. The enlargement was complete by the time *Barbarossa* began, but the army was definitely not, in qualitative terms, what it had been in May 1940.

The army's overall personnel situation on the eve of *Barbarossa* was not encouraging. Fromm reported to Halder on May 20, 1941, that there were 385,000 soldiers available in the Replacement Army, plus 90,000 in the field replacement battalions. His office predicted 275,000 casualties in the border battles, then 200,000 more in September. Thus the army could run out of trained replacements in October, he continued, unless the OKH called up the next year group of recruits early. He saw no need to do that, however; the risk that the army could find itself in the middle of a campaign with no pool of trained manpower "could be borne." If Halder had any problem with that statement, he did not record it.[41] He apparently assumed that the campaign would be over before the supply of troops ran out.

As Ernst Klink has noted, the problems in manning and equipping the army turned the leaders' assumption of a short campaign into an obligation. The Germans simply could not afford to allow serious reverses that would lead to a winter campaign; they made no preparations for such an eventuality before June 22, 1941, when the attack began.[42] One can only add that, given the gaps in German intelligence regarding their opponent, the leaders' confidence becomes difficult to comprehend. The fact that the General Staff could generate such an exercise in wishful thinking is a damning indictment of their professional standards. Their actions did not even agree with the principles by which they had been trained: "In war the situations are of unlimited variety. They change often and suddenly, and they can only seldom be seen clearly in advance. Unknown quantities are often of decisive influence. The independent will of the enemy encounters your own will. Friction and error are everyday phenomena."[43] Naturally, the army's senior officers would have disputed the accusation. The actual course of Operation *Barbarossa*, however, substantiates it. That operation has been the subject of careful and detailed treatments in the literature of the Second World War, especially from the operational side.[44] There is certainly neither space nor need to review the campaign in detail here, but two themes do require attention: the respective roles of Hitler, Brauchitsch, and Halder in directing operations—centering on the conflict that developed between the Führer and the army on that subject—and the results of German miscalculations regarding their and their enemy's capabilities.

BARBAROSSA

The conflict between Hitler and his senior army advisers over the campaign's goals had been building since December 1940. Halder believed that Moscow had to be the primary target. Not only was it the seat of the Soviet government, a major industrial center, and a transportation hub, and thus a valuable objective in its own right, but Halder believed that the Soviets would commit the largest and best portion of their remaining forces to defend it, thus ensuring the Red Army's complete destruction. Hitler had other ideas. He believed that the economic targets in the Ukraine and the Soviet forces in the Baltic region were equally important. That difference of opinion would be the centerpiece of the conflict to come, and it would illustrate the workings of the two men's relationship.

Hitler put the primacy of Moscow into question as early as December 5, after Halder briefed him on the army's plan, but the two men left the issue unsettled at that point. On December 18 Hitler signed Directive No. 21, "*Fall Barbarossa*," which defined the goals of the operation as follows: the destruction of the Russian armed forces as far to the west as possible, in order to prevent their retreat into the vast interior; then an advance to a line that would prevent Russian air attacks from reaching the Reich; and finally an advance to a line stretching from Archangel to the Volga River, from which the Luftwaffe could dominate the last Soviet industrial areas beyond the Ural Mountains. The directive went on to place the main thrust *(Schwerpunkt)* of the offensive north of the Pripyat Marshes. Further, it stated that the southern army group in that thrust, that is, Army Group Center, which would advance toward Moscow, must be prepared to swing north and assist the attack into the Baltic region before taking the Soviet capital.[45]

Halder's reaction shows that he had adopted a new approach in dealing with his Führer. He knew better than to argue, at least at this early stage; such efforts got precisely nowhere. Instead, he worked patiently to create an operational plan that matched his own concept. Where his plan differed from Hitler's, he simply ignored the differences and carried on as if he and Hitler were in full agreement. He even had Lossberg insert a sentence into Directive No. 21, at the start of the section that discussed the army's operations, which said, "In approval of the intentions briefed to me [Hitler]"— even though that was hardly the case! The army's deployment and attack orders, which came out at the end of January 1941, differed significantly from Hitler's intentions, but Halder glossed over this fact in his briefings. Apparently, he expected that his concept would win out, once the campaign got under way.[46]

The confrontation over the invasion's operational goals did not come up in the first weeks of *Barbarossa;* the stunning initial successes were the focus of everyone's attention. By July 10, only three weeks after the attack began, German forces were nearly halfway to Moscow and Leningrad and had almost reached Kiev. Hundreds of thousands of Soviet prisoners were in German hands, along with vast stocks of matériel. On July 4 Hitler declared, "Practically speaking, he—the Russian—has already lost the war." He gloated over the fact (as he understood it) that the Wehrmacht had already destroyed the Russian armor and air forces: "The Russians cannot replace them." With his prompting, Jodl and Brauchitsch started to work out the form the army would take after the conclusion of the campaign.[47] Halder shared in this confident mood. On July 3 he wrote:

> On the whole one can indeed now say that the mission to destroy the mass of the Russian army forward of the Dvina and the Dnepr [Rivers] is fulfilled. . . . Thus it is not too much to say when I maintain that the campaign against Russia was won within fourteen days. Naturally it is not over yet. We will yet be occupied for weeks with the expanse of the territory and with stubborn resistance, conducted with all means. . . . Once we have crossed the Dvina and the Dnepr, [the campaign] will have less to do with the destruction of enemy forces than with [the task of] taking away the enemy's industrial cities and thus hindering him from forming a new army from the output of his industry and his inexhaustible reserves of manpower.[48]

On the same day Paulus sent a memorandum to the branches in the General Staff, laying the groundwork for the operations to follow *Barbarossa.*[49] On July 23 Halder predicted that in another month the army would be in Leningrad and Moscow, at the beginning of October on the Volga River, and one month after that in Baku and Batum in the Caucasus oil region.[50] The collapse that so many authorities had predicted seemed to be taking place.

In reality, Halder's boast was an indication that he did not understand either the enemy's strength or his own logistical situation. His belief that Soviet forces were nearly exhausted is perhaps understandable; he was still working with the woefully inadequate estimates that Foreign Armies East had produced before the campaign. His belief that his armies could advance hundreds of miles more in a little more than three months is harder to fathom. The armies were already howling about supply shortages. Abwehr maps had proved totally inadequate; they showed dirt tracks as main roads.[51] Bad roads and enemy action had reduced the strength of the *Grosstransportraum* by 25 to 30 percent in less than a month. Railroad conversion crews were not keeping up. Captured food supplies and transport never reached expected quantities, and Russian gasoline and coal proved useless due to its poor quality. Aerial resupply to some forward units had become necessary to make up critical shortages of fuel and ammunition.[52] By mid-July the German thrusts had stalled almost exactly where the precampaign planning had forecast, but their preparations for the next phase progressed much more slowly than expected. In that light alone, Halder's goals fell in the realm of sheer fantasy.

The first cracks in the high command's confident facade began to appear before long. On August 6 Warlimont produced a "Brief Strategic Overview on the Continuation of the War After the Campaign in the East." In it he said that the German military leadership must reckon with the fact that the Wehrmacht would not reach its operational goals—a line from the Caucasus oil region to the Volga and on to Archangel and Murmansk—in 1941, and so an open front would remain in existence.[53] On August 11, moreover, Halder confided to his journal:

> Regarding the general situation, it stands out more and more clearly that we underestimated the colossus Russia, which prepared itself consciously for the war with the complete unscrupulousness that is typical of totalitarian states[!]. This statement refers just as much to organizational as to economic strengths, to traffic management, above all to pure military efficiency. At the start of the war we reckoned with 200 enemy divisions. Now we already count 360. These divisions are not armed and equipped in our sense, and tactically they are inadequately led in many ways. But they are there. And when a dozen of them are destroyed, then the Russians put a new dozen in their place.[54]

Hitler's behavior was another source of concern for the chief of the General Staff. The Führer insisted on playing the role of field commander. The OKW War Diary shows that the Armed Forces Command Staff was tracking the situation in the east in great detail and that both Jodl and Schmundt were offering suggestions to Hitler about the conduct of the operations there.[55] Hitler issued directives to the army group commanders and sometimes visited their headquarters. He also used Keitel as a go-between. On July 25, for example, the chief of the OKW met with Field Marshal Fedor von Bock, the commander of Army Group Center, to pass on the Führer's message that large, operational encirclements would not work in Russia; the army needed to stick to smaller, tactical encirclements.[56]

Halder's reaction was, once again, to resist passively to the fullest extent possible. As early as June 25 he wrote, "In the evening an order arrives from the Führer about the conduct of operations by Army Groups Center and South, in which the worry is expressed that we are operating in too much depth. The old song! Nothing in our conduct will be changed that way."[57] Then, on June 29, he commented on the need to take bridgeheads over the Dniepr to open the way to Smolensk and Moscow, and added: "One hopes that the middle levels of command will do the right thing by themselves without express orders, which we may not issue because of the Führer's instructions to [Brauchitsch]."[58] And again on July 3 he wrote:

> We hear the usual noises from the Führer headquarters again, via ObdH and the Operations Branch. It is in a great state again, because the Führer is fearful that the eastward-moving wedge of Army Group South is threatened by flank attacks from north and south. Naturally this concern is not unjustified, tactically speaking. But that is why the army and corp commanders are there. The man in the top position [Hitler] does not understand the trust that we have in our organs of command, which is one of the strongest sides of our leadership, because he is not conscious of the strength of our leadership corps' common training and education.[59]

Apparently, the irony of his position did not occur to Halder. He wrote of trust, while at the same time he and Brauchitsch were counting on their subordinates to disobey orders that they themselves were unwilling to support but unable to resist. What is more, Halder would prove later that he was just as willing as Hitler to disregard the opinions of those under him.

Brauchitsch was the point man in the campaign of dissemblance that the OKH carried out against the Führer. He divorced himself from the nitty-gritty of operations to a large extent and instead served as a buffer between Hitler and Halder while the latter ran the campaign.[60] Before long, however, Hitler interceded in the direction of the campaign in a way that Brauchitsch could not deflect and Halder could not ignore. Beginning with Directive No. 33 ("Continuation of the War in the East") of July 19, he issued orders that redirected forces from Army Group Center to the north and south, essentially halting the drive on Moscow.[61] For the next month various army generals, including Brauchitsch, Halder, Bock, and Lieutenant General Heinz Guderian, the noted expert on armored warfare, attempted to change Hitler's mind, but he remained adamant. Even Jodl tried, using studies that the Armed Forces Command Staff prepared, but he had no luck either.[62] On August 25 the Germans launched a great battle of envelopment in the Ukraine that netted a reported total of 665,000 Soviet prisoners as well as depriving the Soviets of one of their most productive regions. The main cost for the Germans was to delay the resumption of the attack on Moscow until October 2, and within three weeks after that date the autumn *rasputitsa* began, that period when rain makes movement on the unpaved Russian roads nearly impossible.[63] The German drive, its supply columns stuck in the mud, had to halt and wait for the ground to freeze. Wagner wrote to his wife on October 20, "It can't be kept a secret any longer: we are hung up in muck, in the purest sense."[64]

Up until that point, the atmosphere in the OKH had remained overwhelmingly positive. Before the October offensive began, the Germans were convinced that the remaining Russian divisions could only be "scrap and refilled skeletal units."[65] As late as October 5 Wagner still believed that

the last great collapse stands immediately before us. . . . Operational goals are being set that earlier would have made our hair stand on end. Eastward of Moscow! Then I estimate that the war will be mostly over, and perhaps there really will be a collapse of the [Soviet] system. . . . I am constantly astounded at the Führer's military judgment. He intervenes in the course of operations, one could say decisively, and up until now he has always acted correctly. The great success in the south is his solution.[66]

There was certainly no talk of halting the offensive. In fact, plans were still under consideration for an attack through the Caucasus, starting in November, that could reach the passes from Iran into Iraq late in 1942, thus threatening the British position in the Middle East.[67] Not until October 24 would Paulus announce to the assembled General Staff branch representatives that the attack would have to wait until the following spring.[68] On the same day Wagner wrote to his wife, "In my opinion it is not possible to come to the end [of this war] this year; it will still last a while. The how? is still unsolved . . . [the fact] that this war would still be long and hard was already clear at the end of last year."[69]

Paulus's announcement and Wagner's letter are indications that the halt engendered by the *rasputitsa* was forcing the Germans to take a long look at their prospects for the first time since the campaign began. On November 7 Hitler finally admitted to Brauchitsch that Germany could no longer hope to reach the farthest objectives, such as Murmansk, the Volga River, and the Caucasus oil fields, in 1941.[70] On the same day, Halder informed the army group and army chiefs of staff that he was planning a conference in the town of Orsha in about a week's time to discuss the situation. In the supporting paperwork, Halder included a map with two boundaries drawn on it, to mark the "farthest" and the "minimum" advance for which the army should strive. The minimum boundary started from a point well east of Leningrad and ran southward, 160 miles east of Moscow, to Rostov on the Don River. The farthest boundary extended another 75 to 90 miles east in the northern and central sections of the country, to cut off Murmansk and take the Vologda and Gorki industrial areas, and moved the southern sector 30 miles farther east to Stalingrad and over

200 miles southeast to the Maikop oil fields. Halder admitted, however, that the war would continue into 1942. Even he had to recognize at last that the dream of destroying the Soviet Union in one campaign had disappeared.[71]

The conference at Orsha took place on November 13. In that meeting, and again in another with his assistant chiefs of staff on November 23, Halder stated that he and Hitler were both inclined toward a strategy that, rather than simply conserving strength, would aim for the maximum possible gain with what was available. "It is possible," he said,

> that the war is shifting from the level of military success to the level of moral and economic endurance, without changing the military's mission, that is, to use all available means to damage the enemy as severely as possible. . . . The military power of Russia is no longer a danger for the reconstruction of Europe. . . . The enemy . . . is not yet destroyed. We will not achieve his full destruction *in this year,* despite the efforts of our troops, which cannot be recognized enough. What with the endlessness of the territory and its inexhaustible supply of manpower, we definitely cannot reach 100% of that goal. Naturally we knew that from the start.[72]

At Orsha he argued initially that the army would have to take some risks so that it could reach the farthest boundary if possible, or at least the minimum boundary. Under pressure from the assembled staff officers, he ended the day by admitting that such far-flung goals were not realistic. He still, however, expected that all three army groups would push on until mid-December, and that Army Group Center's forces would take Moscow, even if they did not get too far beyond it. He expected six weeks of cold but dry weather, from mid-November until the end of December, in which to carry out the operations. (To be more exact regarding Moscow, the plan was not to take the city but to surround it, starve its citizens to death, and flatten it. Hitler ordered on October 12 that Army Group Center not accept the city's surrender even if offered.)[73]

Halder's—and Hitler's—determination to continue with the attack shows yet again the inadequacy of the intelligence they were receiving, plus an astounding willingness to gamble with limited resources. Foreign Armies East estimated in mid-November that the Russians possessed 200 major units but added that those units' combat effectiveness was under 50 percent because more than half of their officers and men were untrained. Actually the Soviets had 373 major units, and some of the ones in the west were of high quality because the Soviets had—contrary to German predictions—begun transferring units from the Far East.[74] On the German side, according to Halder's diary, personnel losses by November 10 amounted to 22,432 officers and 663,676 enlisted men killed, wounded, and missing.[75] The Organization Branch rated the 136 German divisions as having the fighting strength of only 83.[76] The transport system was still in crisis; the frost had set in around November 7 in Army Group Center, thus freezing the mud and making the roads passable again, but the damage the cold caused to vehicles and locomotives canceled out the improvement in road conditions.[77] Bringing up supplies for continued offensive operations would mean that winter clothing and equipment would have to remain in depots far in the rear.[78] However, when Colonel Otto Eckstein, then chief supply officer for Army Group Center, pointed out the precariousness of the situation to Halder at Orsha, the latter clapped him on the back and replied, "You are certainly right to be anxious, based on your calculations; but we don't want to hold Bock up, if he thinks he can do the thing; indeed it takes a little luck, too, to conduct a war."[79]

The Germans launched their attacks around the flanks of Moscow on November 15 and 16. At first they made decent progress, but by the end of the month they had run out of steam. On November 27 Wagner told Halder that the German army was "at the end of our personnel and material strength."[80] Bock reported to Brauchitsch shortly thereafter that the expected Russian collapse was a myth, that he could not encircle Moscow, and that the time had come to decide what to do next. He stayed on the attack for the next few days, because he believed that was better than losing the initiative. But on the morning of December 4, with the temperature below zero degrees Fahrenheit, the Soviets launched a massive counteroffensive. Surprise was total; neither Bock's staff nor Foreign Armies East had thought that the Russians possessed the forces to mount such an attack. By December 6 the Germans were struggling, not to advance, but to hold on to what they had.[81]

While the Germans were still reeling from the initial shock of the Soviet attack, new information reached them that would prompt Hitler to make his last great strategic decision. On December 7 Halder made one brief notation in his diary: "Japan opens hostilities against America."[82] On December 11 Hitler declared war on the United States. Historians have wondered at Hitler's hubris ever since, but in truth, as Gerhard Weinberg has pointed out, Hitler had believed for years that he would have to fight the United States eventually. His determination to do so had even helped to shape his policy decisions and plans after the fall of France.[83] Hitler knew that his navy was too weak to take on the Americans directly—but with Japan on his side he would have an ally with a powerful fleet. Thus Germany's declaration of war represents neither a change in German policy nor a great risk from the point of view of the Wehrmacht's leaders. As subscribers to the "stab in the back" myth, most of them did not believe that the United States had contributed much to Germany's defeat in the First World War, and so they easily dismissed the threat that America now posed. Raeder was positively eager for the fight, while the army and the Luftwaffe paid hardly any attention at all. Halder, who still occasionally noted international events in his journal, had nothing to say on the subject of the German declaration. Whether because he was too wrapped up in the crisis in the east, or because he had completely given up on strategic thinking, he failed to comment on the event that all but sealed Germany's fate.[84]

Granted, Halder did have a lot on his mind. The crisis on the ground was something new for the Wehrmacht, and it produced a crisis in the high command, centering on Brauchitsch. His position had become more and more difficult over the course of the campaign. The Führer was above him, insisting that he knew how to run a campaign better than anyone else. As Hitler said at the end of October, "I am the field commander against my will; I only concern myself at all with military things because at the moment there is no one who could do it better."[85] Any reverse, any perceived failure or hesitation, was enough to bring Hitler's wrath down upon his army commander in chief, who meanwhile also had to face Halder and his other subordinates. Brauchitsch frequently agreed with their assessments and intentions, but he was powerless to affect Hitler's opinions, and few below him were slow to notice that fact. On July 31 Halder wrote, "The OKH's implementation orders for the Führer's last 'directive' [for the diversion of forces from Army Group Center] go out. The commander in chief is unfortunately unable to arrange to place even a hint of his own will in this order. It is dictated out of the concern that it suggest no contradiction of those above."[86] The strain told on him more and more as the campaign went on. On November 10 Halder recorded that Brauchitsch had suffered a severe heart attack the night before, but the commander in chief continued to work even from his hospital bed, and in less than three weeks he was back on duty. As the crisis on the eastern front developed, the pressure on Brauchitsch intensified. Halder noted his dilemma on December 7: "The commander in chief is hardly even a messenger boy anymore. The Führer goes over his head to the army group commanders."[87] In the meantime, rumors of Brauchitsch's powerlessness were spreading in the headquarters.[88] On December 15 Halder reported that Brauchitsch was "very depressed and sees no way to save the army from its difficult situation."[89] His heart ailment continued to trouble him, and his nerves were fraying. On December 19 Hitler relieved him at his own request. "I'm going home," Brauchitsch told Keitel after meeting with the Führer; "he has relieved me; I can't do any more."[90]

In contrast to the situation of February 1938, when Blomberg had suggested that Hitler take over as war minister, this time Hitler needed no urging; he immediately took command himself. The Führer saw the chance to blame the emerging debacle in the east on Brauchitsch and the OKH (and on the three army group commanders and other senior officers he would relieve during this period), while he could appear as the savior of the situation.[91] The army's reaction is illuminating. In retrospect many officers would see this latest coup as the final death knell for the army's independence, but at the time no one expressed any such misgivings. On the contrary, this appeared to be the perfect solution to the army's problems.[92] Even Halder did his best to accommodate himself to the new situation, in the hope that he could work with

Hitler more successfully than Brauchitsch had.[93] And, in truth, there was some cause for the army's initial burst of enthusiasm. With Hitler in command, for example, the civilian railroad authorities within the Reich suddenly became more responsive to the army's needs.

The wider ramifications were more negative. For one thing, Hitler now occupied too many positions. He was simultaneously head of state, commander in chief of the Wehrmacht, and commander in chief of the army, and in that last role he was taking an active part in directing operations. The Führer could not hope to juggle all those responsibilities successfully, even if he delegated away nearly all of his authority—and delegation was not one of his strong points. By attempting to keep so much control, Hitler was in fact forfeiting much of it. While he was busying himself with the details of operations, investigating the designs of new weapons, and otherwise concentrating on minutiae, vast portions of the governmental and military bureaucracies were becoming essentially autonomous. Normal bureaucratic ambition plus Nazi unscrupulousness led to competition rather than coordination. Only common practices, assumptions, and goals kept the disparate parts of the system functioning.

Below Hitler's level, the high command structure became less rational with this latest change. For the OKW, Hitler's assumption of army command brought with it more work and less organizational clarity. Hitler identified more with the role as army commander than with that of commander in chief of the Wehrmacht, while at the same time he focused his attention almost entirely on the east. For those reasons he tended more and more to see the OKW—specifically the Armed Forces Command Staff—as another operational command element, on a par with the Army General Staff. That latter organization, meanwhile, became even less the strategic command organ that Beck had envisioned. Instead Hitler, to whom it was now directly subordinate, restricted it more and more to the eastern front.[94] This moment in the war would in fact have been a good one in which to reunify the command structure, but instead Hitler was heading in the opposite direction.

The administrative changes that went with this new command setup only muddied the waters further, and in the end the army found itself losing more power vis-à-vis the OKW and the Nazi Party. Inasmuch as the army had been a unified institution, separate from the OKW, it had possessed some limited ability to resist inroads into its authority. Now that changed. Hitler had no intention of overseeing all the administrative matters with which Brauchitsch had occupied himself, so all the associated agencies that had been subordinate to the commander in chief of the army, such as the Replacement Army commander, the Army Personnel Office, and the Army Ordnance Office, went to Keitel to administer.[95] Not only did Keitel have trouble handling the new responsibilities on top of his old ones, but the organizations in question were now open to increased influence from Hitler's immediate circle and other Party functionaries.[96] Their chiefs also got to see less of their nominal commander in chief than they had under Brauchitsch.[97] Moreover, the changes produced additional tension between Keitel and Halder, as the latter attempted to defend his influence with Hitler and within the army.[98]

The new command arrangements also affected the army itself. The direct effect upon operations was minimal, since Halder still ran the General Staff, but the indirect impact and the potential for future harm were significant. The General Staff had been "first among equals" within the OKH; now its influence was considerably less. It no longer had the same prominent voice in policy decisions governing issues such as replacements, organization, and weapons procurement. In effect, the OKH had ceased to exist as a unified organization.[99] A seed had been planted that would bear bitter fruit in the last years of the war.

Again, however, little or none of this was apparent in December 1941. At that point most Germans were far too concerned about the current situation in the east to pay much attention to such matters anyway. The reversal of their fortunes made a huge impression on many officers. At the beginning of August 1941, for example, Ulrich de Maizière, then a thirty-year-old supply officer with the 18th Infantry Division (Motorized) in Army Group Center, had written to his mother, "By the beginning of September the Russian army will be destroyed." On October 10 he wrote, "The campaign is not yet over." On December 12: "Because of the war against America I figure on a significant extension. There will be no peace within the next three years, in my opinion."[100] De Maizière's remarks highlight the range of emotions that the Germans experienced between June and December 1941. In June they had gambled on a quick victory, although in truth many of them believed that there was no gamble involved; this looked like a sure thing. The victories of July and August seemed to confirm their faith. Over the course of the next three months, they kept the Russians on the ropes, but by early December even the most confident of them knew they could not achieve a knockout blow. Then the Russians struck back, and many Germans asked themselves, often for the first time, what they had gotten into.

Debate rages to this day over the conduct of *Barbarossa*. The significance of the battle of Moscow and of Hitler's earlier decision to divert forces away from Army Group Center have received most of the attention. Some historians maintain that Germany had only to take the Soviet capital to knock Russia out of the war, and many of them blame Hitler for fatally weakening the central thrust just when victory appeared certain.[101] Certainly, the army's leading generals felt the same way: at the time they argued against the diversion, and after the war they continued to maintain that Hitler made a fatal blunder that summer. There are several reasons that their argument is not convincing, but the most important is that the Soviets were showing no sign of the political collapse upon which the Germans were depending. If anything, reports of German barbarity in occupied Russia were strengthening resistance. The Soviet administrative apparatus behind the front was functioning, contrary to German expectations, and the Russians still had significant industrial assets beyond the Urals (as the Germans knew before they attacked).[102] On the eve of the last German offensive against Moscow in November, the Soviets were already preparing a further line of defense far to the east.[103] Desperate though this measure was, it indicates that they were not ready to give up. The Germans were by then at the end of their resources (as they had known they would be); in fact, any additional gains in the east would have only put them in a worse position. The Wehrmacht had depended upon operational success to overcome a strategic risk. Now the Germans' miscalculations had caught up with them. With the failure of *Barbarossa* and the entry of the United States into the war, only a miracle could stave off defeat.

Unsurprisingly, this fact was not apparent to many at the time. To the Allies, victory seemed anything but a foregone conclusion. Certainly the Germans, though discouraged, did not consider themselves beaten. They ruled most of Europe, and their enemies appeared weakened or distant. More than three years of even bloodier fighting yet remained.

8

The System at Work: A Week in the Life of the High Command

In military histories the "great man" approach is difficult to avoid. After all, military commands are relatively strict hierarchies; the commander does indeed determine, as much as any one person can, where his force goes and what it does. In reality, though, the commander cannot do his job alone. He has to have information before making a decision, and the complexity of modern warfare is such that all but the most junior officers rely on others to tell them what is going on. Then, once he makes a decision, a senior commander relies upon a whole succession of intervening authorities to process it into ever-more-specific orders before it becomes reality. Thus a military organization, as much as it might appear to be the creature of one person's will, is really a complex system in which the separate parts have to function properly if the whole is to do the commander's bidding.

The case of the Wehrmacht in the Second World War is certainly no exception. In describing the war, one can present a picture that makes Hitler seem almost the sole decision maker. (Indeed, many surviving German generals tried to do exactly that.) Not only is that picture incomplete, however, but even the addition of figures such as Keitel, Jodl, Brauchitsch, and Halder does not take us far from the image of individual minds controlling vast, faceless forces. This chapter will attempt to escape that image, to connect the organizational descriptions and narrative that have dominated this book so far and glimpse the system as it functioned in detail. The glimpse will be imperfect; that is unavoidable. For one thing, the records do not exist that would enable anyone to piece together the activities of every person in every staff during every moment. For another, such a description, even if the sources existed, would be impossible to comprehend completely. Even a fully trained staff officer, with years of experience, needed months to become proficient at a new job on the General Staff, and that proficiency did not give him anything like a view of the whole. Nonetheless, an opportunity exists to enter the world of the high command and gain some understanding of its workings.

To that end, this chapter will focus upon a one-week period, from December 15 to December 21, 1941. This was a time of crisis, when the Wehrmacht was suffering its first great setbacks on the eastern front and the pressure of the situation at the front was making itself felt throughout the command system. Hitler and his advisers struggled to keep ahead of developments, make the decisions that would avert catastrophe, and maintain some broader view of events. Under them, a host of people struggled just as hard within their own narrower realms to keep up with their leaders' demands. They had little time for broad thinking, but the stress of the situation filtered through to them anyway. And if their circumstances represented something new for them, that would not be the case for long. Crisis was going to become a familiar state of affairs within the high command.

THE BACKGROUND

By December 5, 1941, the Germans held a front that stretched from west of Rostov on the Black Sea north past Moscow to Leningrad, for a total of something like 1,250 miles—roughly the straight-line distance from Boston to Miami. That first week of December saw them reach the farthest limits of their advance for the year. Army Group South had already been kicked out of Rostov on November 28, prompting Hitler to relieve its commander, Rundstedt. At Moscow the Soviets launched counterattacks on December 5 and 6 to stop the German offensive against the capital.[1] The initial attacks did just that; the Germans made minor withdrawals ahead of the Soviet counteroffensive, which itself was slow to develop. At the same time Army Group North, under Field Marshal Wilhelm Ritter von Leeb, had to fall back a short distance under strong Soviet pressure. On December 8 Hitler and Brauchitsch issued separate orders for the entire eastern army to go over to the defensive.[2] Hitler's order specified that there were to be no withdrawals except to prepared positions, but in several places the Soviets were denying his troops that luxury. By December 15 the Russians had eliminated German salients north and south of Moscow and were preparing to open fresh thrusts there and in the north of the country. The Germans had already lost large numbers of men and masses of equipment to enemy action and the bitter cold, and their confidence had taken a severe blow. The supply situation was critical, and there were no reserves. The army seemed to be near the breaking point. Halder described the situation as "the worst crisis in the two world wars."[3]

Of course, Russia was not the only place where the Germans had forces; they occupied territory from Norway to central France and were still engaged against the British in Libya (where a major German withdrawal was under way). Nowhere was the situation nearly so serious as in the east, though, and nowhere else were the stakes so high.

Monday, December 15, 1941

Well before first light on this Monday morning, in the headquarters compound of the OKH, "Mauerwald," messages began coming into the Operations Branch of the Army General Staff. The branch had reorganized itself before *Barbarossa* began. Under the branch chief (Brigadier General Heusinger) and his assistant (the so-called Ia, Lieutenant Colonel Helmuth von Grolman), there were now three groups. Group I, the "Eastern Group" under Major Gehlen, comprised three subgroups (IN, IM, and IS), each of which oversaw the operations of an army group.[4] Now, by phone and Teletype, the army groups were sending in their morning reports. The reports were short; they dealt solely with events that had occurred since midnight. The officers in the subgroups used that information to update the more comprehensive reports that had come in several hours earlier, reports that contained, among other things, information on the friendly and enemy situations, intentions, losses, troop strengths, supplies, and weather. In each of the Operations Branch subgroups the same officer handled the reports every day, to ensure consistency and rapidity in their transcription. When the reports came in by phone, the officers worked with preprinted forms that matched the reports' format.[5]

With the new information in hand, the subgroup leaders (Majors Detlev von Rumohr for Army Group North, Heinz Brandt for Center, and Alfred Phillippi for South) entered Heusinger's office one at a time and briefed him on the situation, using updated 1:300,000-scale maps to do so. Heusinger also had a 1:1,000,000-scale map that showed the entire eastern front, and his deputy, Grolman, had an overview of the enemy situation that Foreign Armies East had prepared. In this way Heusinger became thoroughly familiar with events in the smallest possible amount of time. By 9:30 the entire process, from first reports to Heusinger's briefing, was complete.

At that point Heusinger joined a small group for the morning General Staff briefing. Halder was there, of course, as were his assistant chiefs of staff for operations and intelligence, Paulus and Matzky, along with Kinzel (Foreign Armies East), Gercke (Transportation), Buhle (Organization), and Colonel Alfred Baentsch from the General Quartermaster's office (Wagner usually did not attend personally). Heusinger led off the briefing with a summary of the friendly situation as it had developed during the night; Kinzel followed with his estimate of the enemy's status. The other branch chiefs added their input in turn. As the briefing went on, Halder added his own thoughts, posed questions, and assigned new tasks. In this way, all the principals in the

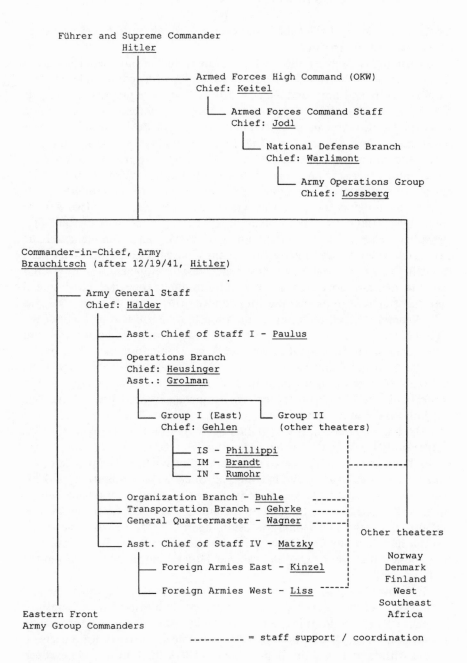

Figure 4. Key operational command elements and personnel in the German high command, December 1941.

General Staff learned what the situation was and what tasks they and their colleagues had to carry out.[6]

Normally Halder and the principal branch chiefs would next have given Brauchitsch an abbreviated briefing, at which the army commander in chief would have issued any fundamental orders that were necessary.[7] On this day, however, Brauchitsch was not yet in the headquarters; he was en route from the front, where he had been consulting with Bock and his subordinates, Field Marshal Hans von Kluge (who commanded 4th Army) and Guderian (commanding 2d Panzer Army).[8] Therefore, the group split up, each to accomplish his separate tasks. For all of them, this meant a further succession of conferences, telephone conversations, reports, and orders.

Halder's activities were fairly typical. Between noon and 1:00 P.M. he spoke by telephone with each of the three army group chiefs of staff: first Brigadier General Hans von Greiffenberg (Center), then Major General Kurt Brennecke (North), and finally Lieutenant General Georg von Sodenstern (South). In each case Halder went over the latest developments on the ground and the measures that the army group should take. After the last call Heusinger arrived to discuss the situation at Army Group Center. Then, at 1:20, Fromm stopped by to report on a meeting he had had with Hitler the night before and to discuss two special programs—code-named *Walküre* and *Rheingold*—with which the Replacement Army would form more units in the homeland. At 1:30 Gercke came in to brief Halder on some problems with the railroads; Göring was being difficult, and the next day he and Gercke would confer with the Führer on the matter. Brauchitsch arrived as Gercke was finishing, and Halder updated him on the day's events.[9]

The biggest concerns for both men were the situations at Army Groups Center and North. In the former case, Bock wanted to take the entire army group back sixty to ninety miles to a new defensive line. The problem was that no defenses existed on that line, as Bock himself admitted, and his troops would have to leave large quantities of heavy equipment behind them. Hitler had rejected the idea on December 14 for exactly those reasons, but apparently there was some confusion regarding that decision. Heusinger told both Halder and Greiffenberg on the afternoon of the fifteenth that he had spoken with Jodl, who had relayed Hitler's permission for a limited withdrawal.[10]

In Army Group North's area, Leeb wanted to pull back and set up a line behind the Volkhov River. He communicated that wish to the Operations Branch at 10:15 that morning, but all the senior officers were in their briefing at that point. At 4:45 P.M. Brennecke called Heusinger to ask for a decision on the withdrawal as soon as possible, and less than an hour later Leeb spoke directly with Hitler, who was in Berlin. The Führer was convinced that the proposed withdrawal would allow the Russians to raise the siege of Leningrad, but he seemed hesitant to contradict Leeb and left the issue unresolved. Keitel made a follow-up phone call at 7:00 P.M. in which he told Leeb that Hitler still could not make up his mind. He had asked if the army group could not mount a counterattack, Keitel continued; Leeb said that was impossible. Keitel then asked that Leeb meet with the Führer the next day to discuss the matter. An hour later Jodl read Brennecke a paragraph from an order that the OKW was releasing that night, to the effect that Hitler would make a decision on the retreat the next day when he met with Leeb; until then the army group could pull its armored units behind the Volkov, but nothing else.[11]

Actually the point was all but moot by then. The Army Group North war diary indicates that Leeb had decided during the morning to make the withdrawal; his personal calendar notes and Halder's summary of the evening situation report both show that the army group headquarters gave the order that day.[12] At this point in the war some field commanders were still willing to circumvent Hitler's wishes, and sometimes they got away with it.

Back in the OKH Headquarters, the day continued more or less as it had begun, with each person going about his assigned tasks. In the afternoon Halder met briefly with the chief of the Central Branch, Ziehlberg, to go over matters pertaining to the General Staff. At 6:00 P.M. he met with Brauchitsch for an hour and a half to discuss the situation at the front. This was the occasion on which the commander in chief struck his chief of staff as being "very depressed" and seeing "no way out"; Halder had no idea that Brauchitsch had requested relief over a week before.[13] Then, at about 10:00 P.M., Halder got together with Heusinger and Paulus to go over the army groups' interim reports and issue a few final orders.[14]

By the time Halder finished up his meeting, Hitler and his advisers were on the train from Berlin, where the Führer had declared war on the United States on December 11, to the field headquarters just east of Rastenburg, in East Prussia. Jodl took the opportunity to sit down for a talk with his old friend Bernhard von Lossberg, head of the Army Operations Group in the National Defense Branch. Lossberg was very critical of Hitler's handling of the war. He believed that the Führer's unwillingness to allow any withdrawal on the eastern front was a mistake. He called for the erection of a massive "east wall" along a defensible line in the rear, to which the armies could retreat in need. And he said that the strategic direction of the war should be given over to an "outstanding soldier," to whom Hitler would have to listen; Lossberg suggested Manstein for the post. Jodl was noncommittal. He could see that an orderly withdrawal in the east would have advantages, he said, but he tended to agree with Hitler's view that the dangers outweighed them. Moreover, while Jodl agreed that some leading general needed to take over command, and that Manstein was probably the best candidate, he maintained that Hitler would never approve such a change. There the two men left the matter and said good night.[15]

Tuesday, December 16, 1941

Early in the morning of December 16, Hitler's special train pulled through Rastenburg and into the little station of Görlitz, which was now a part of the Führer's headquarters, code-named "Wolfsschanze" (loosely translated as "Wolf's Lair"). The Germans had built this compound during the planning for *Barbarossa*. Except for several weeks spent at another compound in the Ukraine in 1942 and 1943, "Wolfsschanze" would be Hitler's headquarters from June 1941 to November 1944. It existed in an area of woods and "breezeless, fetid swampland" measuring roughly 1.5 by 2 kilometers and surrounded by minefields and thick belts of barbed wire.[16] More barbed wire separated the interior of the compound into three inner security zones, or *Sperrkreise*. Sperrkreis I contained a large aboveground bunker where Hitler lived and worked, as well as a bunker for Keitel and a brick-and-concrete house for Jodl. Colonel Schmundt, Major Engel, Commander Karl-Jesko von Puttkamer, and Major Nicolaus von Below (Hitler's Wehrmacht, army, navy, and Luftwaffe adjutants, respectively) also lived within the compound, but aside from a few junior assistants, they were the only military personnel to do so. The rest of the Armed Forces Command Staff lived and worked nearly a kilometer away, in Sperrkreis II.

Both the location and the layout of Hitler's headquarters were problematic. To begin with, the government's offices and the military's administrative apparatus had to remain in Berlin, mostly for reasons of space; by retreating to a remote headquarters compound, Hitler cut himself and his staff off to a large degree from those critical organs. He was in fact the only head of state in the Second World War to isolate himself in such a way. Keitel complained about this state of affairs in his memoirs; because he could not be in Berlin, he wrote, he had to give the OKW's offices there a lot more independence than he otherwise would have.[17] Of course, the headquarters staff in East Prussia did take steps to stay in contact with the offices in Berlin. The "Wolfsschanze" had all the most modern communications gear. Daily flights carried couriers back and forth, and officials also traveled between the two nerve centers on a nightly train, accompanied by bags of correspondence. Moreover, the field echelon of the Armed Forces Command Staff included liaison officers from several other offices in the OKW.[18] These measures were at best only a partial solution, however.

Keitel's complaints notwithstanding, problems that arose because of the Führerhauptquartier's isolation are difficult to document. Sometimes there were delays in reaching and implementing decisions, because of the time needed to travel between the headquarters and Berlin. Doubtless many small errors occurred because the people involved did not have personal contact with one another on a regular basis; the Germans may have been especially prone to such problems, since they kept their staffs small and relied on personal coordination to such a large extent. Some other problems arose simply because the headquarters did not have support services available that would have been on hand in Berlin. The Armed Forces Command Staff, for example, had no map service or print shop available; its own draftsmen had to draw all its maps and charts by hand.[19]

The most important problem with Hitler's choice of headquarters, though, may well have had to do with the effect it had on the leaders' understanding of events. There is more than symbolic meaning in the picture of Hitler and his closest advisers sealed in their own little world, separated by barbed wire from events and people outside.[20] Jodl once described the atmosphere inside the Führer's compound as "a mixture of cloister and concentration camp."[21] Hitler's isolation allowed him to fully understand neither events at the front nor developments in the homeland. Moreover, Hitler, Keitel, and Jodl were cut off not only from the outside world but also from the Armed Forces Command Staff itself. Days would go by without any personal contact at all between Jodl and Warlimont, on or off the job.[22] Jodl's physical separation from his staff heightened his tendency toward aloofness, and gradually the Armed Forces Command Staff's advisory role disappeared. It became more and more an organ that served simply to put Hitler's and Jodl's wishes onto paper, or even just to register orders that Jodl drafted himself. The free flow of ideas and information that is the hallmark of good staff work did not exist within the OKW's headquarters compound.

The physical environment in the OKW compound was also a hindrance. The "Wolfsschanze" was hot and humid in the summer, cold and damp in the winter. Dampness was a special problem in the concrete bunkers where much of the work took place. The cramped rooms received little sunlight because of the thick pine forest and the bunkers' small windows. Additionally, the ventilation system set up a constant racket. For these reasons the staff officers much preferred to live and work in the compound's wooden barracks if they could.[23] Overall, this setting was not conducive to good work. If its effects were perhaps minor, they were nonetheless real.

At any rate, with Hitler's reentry into his "cloister" early that Tuesday morning, the work there could return to its normal flow. The first major event on the Führer's schedule was the meeting with Leeb, who flew in from Army Group North that morning. Leeb found the mood "gloomy"; Jodl compared the situation at the front to that of 1812. The meeting ended to Leeb's satisfaction, however: he was able to persuade Hitler to allow the army group's northern wing to withdraw—without mentioning, of course, that the pullback was already under way.[24] Hitler was not happy at having to make the decision, and with Brauchitsch listening on, he blamed Army Group North's predicament on the OKH. Then Leeb left and went on to "Mauerwald" to brief Halder, while Hitler turned to the situation at Army Group Center, where Russian pressure was intensifying. At some point in the morning he had the Armed Forces Command Staff begin drafting a Führer Order to the army and Luftwaffe general staffs, the Replacement Army commander, and the Wehrmacht transport chief. This order laid out the actions that each of the army groups was to take and identified reinforcements that would be sent to the front as soon as possible.[25]

At about the same time, Schmundt, who was then in the area of Army Group Center, responded to an urgent appeal from Guderian for a meeting. The two spoke for half an hour at the airfield at Orel, behind Guderian's sector. Guderian tried to convey to Schmundt how serious the situation had become, and he asked that Schmundt relay his impressions to the Führer.[26] Schmundt's activities in this instance illustrate the idiosyncratic way in which Hitler gained information about events at the front. The OKH often sent its officers forward to investigate the situation there; Brauchitsch's own trips serve as an obvious example, but many lower-ranking officers made such trips as well and then reported their findings back to their superiors. Hitler, however, rarely allowed officers from his military staff to leave the headquarters for any length of time, and Jodl, for reasons of his own, also frowned on such trips by his subordinates. Therefore, Jodl and the officers in the Armed Forces Command Staff almost never had an opportunity to find out firsthand what was going on in the combat zone. On the other hand, as the war went on Hitler *did* send officers to the front—or call commanders back to his headquarters—when he believed that their reports would support his views against those of the General Staff. To that end he tended to use men such as Schmundt or officers from the Luftwaffe or SS upon whom he could count to take a position hostile to that of the OKH.[27]

While Hitler was working on the crisis at Army Group Center from his end, Halder called Bock to give him the approximate text of an order that he said Hitler would be releasing later. According to Halder, the Third and Fourth Panzer Groups, which were trying to hold on a line northwest of Moscow, could fall back gradually if they had no other choice; the other armies would have to hold.[28] If Halder was talking about the order that the Armed Forces Command Staff was even then drafting, however, he cannot have known its contents. That order went out to the Operations Branch at some point during the evening. The subgroups then adapted it for each subordinate headquarters and sent it on; Army Group Center got its copy at 1:05 A.M. on December 17.[29] It called on the officers there to force their troops into "fanatical resistance . . . without consideration for enemies that have broken through to the flanks and rear."[30] Only through such resistance could the army win time to bring up reserves, it said.

At about 10:00 P.M. Schmundt called Greiffenberg and said that Hitler had "turned off" Brauchitsch during that day's discussion of the situation, and that he (Schmundt) would be staying in close touch with the army group for the time being. As Bock saw his forces' position growing even more serious that night, he called Schmundt back. He wanted to know if Brauchitsch had relayed his report on the situation to Hitler; Schmundt said he had not. At that, Bock read the report to Schmundt over the phone; it said that Hitler had to decide whether or not to retreat, but it did not hold out much hope either way. Bock doubted if the army could retreat and still have enough strength to hold on a line farther back, since it would have to leave so much equipment behind. Schmundt then said that Hitler did not believe he could sacrifice everything because of a couple of breakthroughs; he had taken everything into his own hands, Schmundt continued, and was doing all he could to get more men to the front. He then added, "It is extremely regrettable that . . . the Führer has not been properly briefed about the seriousness of the situation"! Then Bock pointed out, as he had to Halder at noon, that he had absolutely no reserves left. He closed by saying that his health was hanging "by a silken thread" and that, if the Führer believed that a fresh mind was needed there, he should not hesitate out of consideration for him (Bock). Schmundt said that he understood and would pass Bock's report on to Hitler. This exchange certainly places Hitler in a better light than many later accounts do. Bock obviously had no solutions to offer; he appears to have been trying to find someone to take responsibility for the untenable position in which he had helped to place his army group.[31]

Obviously the army's senior leadership was losing power as the crisis deepened. Hitler was dealing with army group and even army commanders, both directly and through OKW staff officers. He had shut Brauchitsch out of the decision-making process altogether, and he was now working, if not at odds with Halder, then at least parallel to him. Senior people in both the OKW and the army were beginning to comment that this state of affairs could not go on much longer.

Wednesday, December 17, 1941

The passing of Tuesday to Wednesday went almost unnoticed in the high command, as most such transitions usually did. It was a chronological formality, after all. On the basis of sleep periods, Tuesday was not yet over. Shortly before midnight, Brauchitsch, Halder, and Heusinger had reported in at Sperrkreis I in the "Wolfsschanze," and the guards had passed them through to Hitler's briefing room. Normally Hitler's midnight briefing was a smaller affair than the one that took place at midday; Jodl usually handled the briefing itself alone.[32] In this crisis, however, Hitler had ordered the army officers to attend.

Halder recorded the main points of the meeting in his diary. For the most part they agreed with the order that the OKW had just issued. There is to be no talk of retreat, Hitler said. The enemy has broken through in only a few places. Talk of building positions in the rear is fantasy. The only thing wrong with the front is that the enemy has more men. He is much worse than we are in all other respects. New Luftwaffe units would deploy to support the battle. New divisions are on the way. The number of trains is limited, so infantry replacements with light weapons and antitank guns must have first priority; everything else can wait.[33]

A series of follow-up calls with Army Group Center followed the briefing proper. First Hitler called Bock at about half past midnight. He had, he said, just heard Bock's report from Schmundt. He went on to explain his reasons for demanding that the troops hold: if they retreated, in a few days they would find themselves in the same predicament, but without any heavy weapons or artillery. There is no choice but to hold, he said. Bock replied that he had already issued such an order, but that the situation was so tense that the army group's front might be torn wide open at any moment. Hitler said that he himself would have to accept responsibility for that. With that the conversation ended, but both Hitler and Keitel would speak with Bock again before the night was out.[34]

With the briefing over, Brauchitsch, Halder, and Heusinger boarded the trolley that ran between "Wolfsschanze" and "Mauerwald" for the trip back to their compound. Like the OKW headquarters, the OKH's was subdivided. All the men in the General Staff had their offices and living quarters in that part of the field headquarters code-named "Fritz," except for the offices of the General Quartermaster, which occupied the other half of "Mauerwald," code-named "Quelle" ("Source").[35] The entire complex was enormous; Ferdinand Prinz von der Leyen, then a captain in the Army Supply Distribution Group, wrote later that one could easily get lost within the compound, especially at night, and that after four years of service there he still did not know where some staff elements' offices were.[36]

Halder did not record the time at which he and his assistants left "Wolfsschanze," but if one assumes that they left after Hitler's first phone call to Bock, they could not have started back on the trolley to "Mauerwald" until nearly 2:00 A.M. The distance to the OKH compound was about ten miles, so they probably arrived there before 2:30. That would have put them in their quarters and asleep—assuming that they did not take time for any last-minute work, as frequently happened—by 3:00 or so. This was not unusual for the senior army leaders or the men in the key staff sections. Halder's adjutant, Captain Conrad Kühlein, wrote of him, "He was a tireless worker who put his health at stake, in that he was active until the early hours of the morning for months at a time. I repeatedly saw him leave his desk at 7:00 in the morning when I arrived in the barracks for the early situation briefing. Then at 9:00 he would reappear for duty."[37] More typically, Halder arrived for work at about 8:00 A.M., worked until well past midnight, and then read for some time before retiring.[38] In this sense he tried to personify Moltke the Elder's dictum "Genius is diligence," and he expected no less from those who worked under him. There were no "shifts" in the German headquarters as there were in American staffs; everyone was on duty twenty-four hours, at least in theory.[39]

Naturally, the staff officers did not spend every waking hour in work, and there were some limited opportunities to put the stress of their roles aside, however briefly. In a period of crisis such as the one that this chapter describes, those opportunities were virtually nonexistent, but sometimes in less stressful periods the officers could take time for a walk or a ride, or to participate in sports. The choice of activity was the individual's; there were no mandatory activities such as physical training. On occasion the officers also received leave, although, with the staffs already so small, their superiors could not spare them often or for long. To some extent the amount of free time depended on the staff section in which one worked. Some staff elements worked on longer-range projects that events at the front did not drive; their personnel worked more regular hours.[40]

The social environment in the high command was both important and complicated. Friendships and animosities, mutual support and petty jealousies all played roles in the work as well as in the officers' social activities. At times service loyalties came into play, at other times tension between reserve and General Staff officers did so, but mostly the individuals' personalities and ambitions were the key elements. The situation inside the "Wolfsschanze" was the most complex. For one thing, many of the people in the area were engaged in their own private power struggles, and that fact carried over into the social realm. For example, one Foreign Office official who held SS rank canceled an invitation he had extended to Warlimont, with whom Himmler had apparently forbidden all SS personnel to socialize because of his "anti-SS attitude."[41] Then there was the special challenge of dealing with the Führer himself. At one point, for example, Schmundt decided that a staff officer from the Armed Forces Command Staff should join Hitler's dinner party each evening. At first the officers—especially the younger ones—were very keen on this idea. Later, however, Schmundt had to direct officers to go, since there were hardly any volunteers.[42] Hitler's table offered only vegetarian dishes, smoking was prohibited, the atmosphere could be icy if the news from the front was bad, and the Führer's hours-long after-dinner monologues were famous for their somnolent effect.[43]

The interpersonal relationships within the high command, as well as the length and stressfulness of the workday, are not factors that lend themselves to easy analysis. Lack of sleep and leisure time—both outgrowths of the small size of German staffs, but also common to armies everywhere—may have adversely affected German performance, but those effects are nearly impossible to isolate. Social relationships were important, as in nearly any organization. Officers learned quickly that official ranks carried only limited meaning within the command structure. Knowing the right people meant that an officer could accomplish much that the hierarchy made nearly impossible, or at least that he could accomplish the possible more quickly.[44] Again, however, specific examples that demonstrate the importance of such contacts in everyday staff work are difficult to find. They were certainly not the focus of any official record keeping, and the mentality of the General Staff emphasized process over personality. Especially in a crisis such as that which the Germans faced in December 1941, the men in the high command would have been focused on the tasks at hand.

On this Wednesday, those tasks were many and detailed. The leaders had made the major operational decisions that the situation demanded. What remained for the moment was to implement them. The main job was to get reinforcements—both complete units and infantry replacements—to the front. Actually this was not a new mission; the Germans had been struggling with it for weeks to some extent, and with increased urgency for the previous few days. Their efforts are worth noting in detail.

On December 15 the Armed Forces Command Staff had sent out an order to the Armed Forces commander southeast and the German generals in Rome and Agram, initiating steps to bring more Italian and Bulgarian forces into the Balkans, in order to release German forces there for service in Russia.[45] Also, Hitler's order of that night directed that several unspecified divisions be sent to the front and that the 7th Mountain Division be sent to Finland as soon as possible.[46] Word on the transfer of the 7th must have come down to the General Staff earlier, actually, because Paulus and Heusinger were already at work on it. Heusinger had checked with the Training Branch on that unit's status; its reply indicated that the 7th was not combat-ready.[47] Heusinger sent the document on to Paulus with a note saying that the 7th could not deploy yet, and he asked that Paulus reply as soon as possible, since the OKW was expecting a report. Paulus sent back word the same day. He wrote that he had spoken with Warlimont, who had said that Hitler wanted the northern theater reinforced right away. The 7th would have to go, but the report to the OKW should note that the division would need more training time in Finland, Paulus added.[48]

Work on the reinforcement issue continued on December 16. Operations Branch subgroup IIa, which was responsible for Army Group D (also the headquarters of commander in chief west), sent that headquarters a memorandum that provided the dates for five divisions' departures for the eastern front; it also asked for the army group's assessment of the effect these transfers would have on its mission.[49] Operations IIa also informed Army Group Center that one division's transfer would be delayed.[50] In both these cases information copies went to the Transport, Central, Organization, and Training Branches, Halder's adjutant, the General Quartermaster, the Army Personnel Office, and Operations Ia, I, and III. This was the standard pattern: the Operations subgroups coordinated the unit transfers between the giving and receiving headquarters, and information on every decision went to any other staff sections that needed it. To keep track of all the transfers, the subgroups in Operations maintained charts showing the units and their status.[51]

Hitler and the OKW took a direct role in the reinforcement situation again on December 16. First Hitler met with the Wehrmacht transport chief, Gercke, to relay his thoughts regarding the railroads' priorities. The front needs men, Hitler said; therefore, the railroads have to give priority to infantry replacements rather than formed units. Gercke passed this guidance on to Halder, who informed the other branch chiefs.[52] Additionally, that day's Armed Forces Command Staff order to the army groups, while it further emphasized the immediate need for riflemen, identified five infantry divisions that would arrive at Army Group Center between January 1 and February 1, 1942. The OKW did not pick these units out of a clear blue sky, of course; two of them had been included in the previous day's memo from Operations IIa, regarding Army Group D's readiness. Obviously the OKW and the OKH were working closely together on this matter.[53]

Now, on Wednesday, the General Staff went to work to implement the Command Staff's order. Immediately after the morning briefing, Halder met with Paulus, Heusinger, Baentsch, Buhle, and Kinzel to go over the order and the guidance that Hitler had issued in the briefing the night before. Their primary mission was to organize transport to get infantry forward as quickly as possible.[54] When that meeting had broken up and the various staff officers were embarking on their tasks, Halder spoke briefly with Brauchitsch on several issues, including the transfer of an additional one thousand trucks to Army Group Center.[55] Later he met with Brauchitsch again, this time together with Fromm; once again, replacements and reinforcements were a focus of the discussion.[56]

While Halder had his meetings with Brauchitsch and Fromm, his people got to work. Heusinger drafted a plan to transport replacements to the front, according to which infantry would be separated from their parent divisions and sent forward first. In addition, *Walküre* personnel, that is, men gleaned from the Replacement Army, would go into the divisions on the front rather than forming new divisions themselves. In the meantime, Gercke met with Hitler and State Secretary Kleinmann, the Reich traffic minister. The three of them had agreed on a plan to increase the number of trains to the east from the current 122 per day to 140 by January 1 and to 180 by March 1, 1942.[57] And Gehlen, head of the "Eastern Group" in the Operations Branch, got on the phone with the Operations Officer for Army Group Center, Lieutenant Colonel Henning von Tresckow, at 11:15 that morning to discuss the transport chief's plan to replace several supply trains with troop transports. Surprisingly, Tresckow rejected the idea; he said that the difficult supply situation would not permit such a measure.[58] Reinforcing the front would not be a simple matter, apparently.

Thursday, December 18, 1941

The daily and morning reports for this day revealed no great change in the Germans' situation. In Army Group South the attack on the Black Sea port of Sevastopol, which had opened the day before, was making progress against heavy resistance; the army group's other fronts remained quiet. The Russians were making local attacks against Army Group North, which was nevertheless completing its withdrawal without great difficulty. Army Group Center remained the danger point. Twelve new Russian divisions had appeared. Northwest of Moscow, 4th Army had fallen back and had hopes of holding in its new positions; on its left, however, the Russians seemed to be preparing an attack against 9th Army that would bypass the 4th. South of Moscow, gaps existed that the Germans could not close, and 4th Army had just barely repelled attacks on its front in that sector. The Germans were outnumbered everywhere, and their supply services remained on the brink of collapse. Only a fraction of the needed matériel was getting through. Fuel, food, and ammunition were all in short supply, and winter clothing had reached only one-third of the troops because more important supplies had to have priority.[59]

Naturally, events at the front, especially at Army Group Center, remained the focal point for everyone on this day. Halder spoke several times with Greiffenberg and once with Brennecke. In that last case, he warned the Army Group North chief of staff that the situation on the northern flank of Army Group Center could soon spill over, and he asked what additional resources Brennecke's army group might need.[60] He also spoke twice with Bock, whom Hitler had decided to replace with Kluge; Brauchitsch passed that message along to Bock in the evening.[61] However, Halder also took time to step out of the trees and look at the forest. He heard from Matzky and Etzdorf about international affairs, including the conflict in the Pacific, possible cooperation with Japan, and the mood in Turkey. He met with General Harald Oehquist, the Finnish liaison to the OKH, on a variety of issues relevant to that officer's homeland. Lieutenant General Erich von Gündell, the OKH Headquarters commandant, saw Halder briefly about a Christmas celebration on December 24. And Ziehlberg met with him about General Staff matters, including the release of all General Staff officers from duty as corps intelligence officers, in order to use them for other purposes.[62]

Within the Operations Branch the staff officers were dealing with matters that were more mundane but no less important. At 9:45 that morning Captain Thilo, who worked under Phillippi in the Operations Branch subgroup IS, called the Army Group South headquarters to tell them that they had to give up the Generalkommando LI (a corps headquarters) and its associated corps troops to Army Group North as soon as possible.[63] This "order" touched off an interesting exchange that bore more hallmarks of a negotiation than one might expect. At 10:20 the army group operations officer, Colonel August

Winter, spoke with the Operations Branch Ia, Grolman, about the order. Winter said that the army group could not possibly provide the corps headquarters in question, but Grolman persisted, and Winter finally said he would try. At 5:30 P.M. the two men spoke again, but Winter had no solution as yet. Not until nearly 10:00 P.M. did the army group send a Teletype message to the Operations Branch with word that it would send Generalkommando LV in place of Generalkommando LI.[64] This series of communications shows how coordination should and often did work: the higher headquarters was flexible in its request, while the lower level provided a solution that achieved the basic goal. Also, junior staff officers carried out all of the work, thus leaving their superiors free to deal with larger issues.

For the captains and majors in the Operations Branch, and also for Heusinger and Halder, all this careful work would have been impossible without information. Information is the currency of staff work. Some of it can be transmitted by word of mouth in the course of normal coordination when the subject is discrete enough, as in the case just cited. Modern warfare is too complex to depend upon such means, however; it generates far more information than people can keep in their heads. Therefore, the Germans created a carefully organized reporting system. For *Barbarossa,* the OKH defined the necessary reports in an order of June 6, 1941.[65] The first type of report that it required was the normal situation report, which the Operations Branch subgroups received from the army group operations sections. The army groups had to submit three of these every day: the Morning Report (due by 8:00 A.M.), the Interim Report (7:00 P.M.), and the Daily Report (2:00 A.M.). These reports concentrated on operational information, such as significant events, current friendly positions, and intentions for the immediate future. The OKH defined the scope and format of these reports very exactly.

The OKH also required other, more narrowly focused reports. Enemy Situation Reports (also called Ic-Reports) came in to the Foreign Armies East Branch direct from army and panzer group headquarters, together with whatever elaboration the army group headquarters deemed necessary. Reports and questions from the supply services came in to the general quartermaster, and every day the army groups were to report to the OKH's chief of communications on various matters related to his sphere. The order of June 6, which Halder signed personally, emphasized that punctuality was essential if the OKH was to keep the Führer and the commander in chief of the army up to date on events and requirements. It went on to stipulate the exact time frames during which the reports had to arrive, so that report traffic would not overburden the communications nets. The subordinate headquarters were to use Teletype whenever possible and otherwise to keep telephone conversations and radio reports as brief as possible. (The staffs at every level tried to get the information up the chain as quickly as possible, so that the senior commanders could make their decisions in a timely manner, but even so the lag time from the front line to the OKH was usually five to seven hours when the front was unstable.)[66]

The OKH also received reports from other theaters, although often not in the quantity that the eastern armies and army groups had to submit them. Army Group D/commander in chief west, commander in chief Balkans, and the Afrika Korps were responsible for the same reports as the eastern forces. The Armed Forces commander Norway was not under the OKH, but the OKH still requested that it submit the operational daily and interim situation reports. Likewise, Liaison Staff North (on the Finnish front) was to report both to Foreign Armies East and to the Operations Branch. In addition to those reports, the OKH also received periodic input from the navy and Luftwaffe. The latter had several daily reports to submit, since its operations were tied so closely to those of the army. The former sent two daily situation reports each to the OKH and the OKW.[67]

Once the OKH had the reports in hand from all its subordinate headquarters and other sources, it could get to work producing its own reports and other documents. The Operations Branch kept a war diary, which covered the events of the day down to corps and sometimes division level and served as the basis for other reports.[68] Operations subgroup IIIb prepared a daily summary of events on the eastern front for liaison staffs in Finland, Italy, and Hungary. The summary was brief, only a sentence or two on each army group, but it was not so brief as the OKH's input to the daily Armed Forces Report, which the OKW published for public consumption. The army's part of that report covered the eastern front and North Africa in a couple of sentences.[69] Operations IIb also produced a daily report, for distribution within the OKH, on events in Africa and the Mediterranean, drawn from reports it received from the German staffs in Africa and Rome.[70] This was one of several such situation reports that circulated within the command system; obviously not every staff element wanted or needed every report from every individual headquarters, but every staff wanted to be kept informed on the overall situation.[71]

The intelligence organs within the OKH produced their own reports as well. Foreign Armies West produced a daily situation report that covered British and French forces at home and overseas. These were detailed reports. British operations in North Africa received daily attention, while other areas came up less frequently, as the situation required.[72] Foreign Armies East produced a variety of reports on the Soviets. These included a daily report entitled "Important Features of the Enemy Situation (Eastern Front)" that went to most of the staff sections in the OKH as well as to the subordinate commands.[73] In addition, the branch produced a daily report on the strength and disposition of Soviet forces. This consisted of a series of charts showing raw numbers of Soviet units (corps headquarters; infantry, cavalry, and armored divisions; and armored brigades), in front of each army group and in total.

They also showed units discovered up to a certain date, units no longer to be found, and units in other theaters of the USSR. Accompanying documents showed newly discovered units and units that had reappeared.[74] One point of interest about these reports is that Foreign Armies East usually did not try to forecast enemy intentions; instead, it provided raw information on enemy movements, reinforcements, and the like. Sometimes it cited reports of prisoner interrogations that indicated upcoming attacks, but in general its reports did not look beyond the immediate future. The Foreign Armies branches also created more general reports on a weekly, monthly, or as-needed basis. Foreign Armies West published a monthly guide to the British army's combat-capable units, for example.[75] Another report, this a onetime affair, went from Foreign Armies East to the Army Weapons Office on December 15; it dealt with Japanese weapons.[76]

Within the OKW the system worked in much the same way. The Armed Forces Command Staff received reports of various kinds from the services, such as the ones mentioned earlier. It also received separate reports from some of the theater commands, reports that were often quite broad. The December 16 report from the Armed Forces commander in the Netherlands, for example, reported on air activity (the number of overflights, bombing attacks, damage, and casualties), ground and sea activity, special incidents, and the political situation (attacks on German soldiers and administrative personnel, the capture of Jews, and the mood of the Dutch people, which the report described as "depressed and hostile").[77] The OKW used such information to keep its war diary up to date and as a basis for its own reports.

Along with all the various reports that circulated within the high command, one other kind of internal document deserves special mention: the *Vortragsnotiz,* or "briefing paper." This kind of document was common throughout the command system; it was an all-purpose memorandum, used to present information to a commander or senior staff in order to elicit or support a decision. It could be broad or narrow in scope and contain anything from details on one particular situation to a broad strategic analysis. Sometimes it would serve as the basis for generating orders; at other times it would guide their implementation. One such document, for example, went from the Training Branch to Heusinger on December 17, with information on the training status of the 7th Mountain Division (see earlier discussion). The Operations Branch III sent another such to Halder, Paulus, and the Operations subgroup IN on December 22. This one contained two points. First, it noted that the OKW wanted to know which so-called army troops (that is, special supporting units that the OKH controlled directly) would be available for use with the 7th Mountain Division. Second, because of changes in the situation in Finland, the branch suggested that a reorganization of the command system there might be a good idea, and it offered suggestions on the form the new system should take.[78]

This overview of the internal reporting system suggests just how much work the few people in the staffs had to do. Merely tracking the paperwork on one particular action was complicated, and the role of the OKH's staff elements required them to look after dozens, if not hundreds, of such actions at a time. Even with typists to produce the documents themselves, there was an enormous volume of creative and editorial work of the most detailed kind. Any given decision might require input from half a dozen different staff elements, each of them requiring the most accurate information possible. And behind it all lay an awareness that the stakes were high: any confusion at the top would grow exponentially as the orders went on down the chain of command, and confusion led to delays, mistakes, and needless casualties.

Friday, December 19, 1941

On Thursday the Soviets opened the second phase of their counteroffensive against Army Group Center with attacks against the central portion of the front. When Halder got to the army group in his first diary entry for Friday, he simply wrote: "Attacks everywhere."[79] The Germans counted four more new Russian divisions and two more armored brigades in the sector that day. By evening Halder knew of Soviet breakthroughs in three places. "Situation very tense," he wrote.[80] He spoke with Greiffenberg, Kluge (who was now commanding the army group), and Lieutenant General Günther Blumentritt (chief of staff at 4th Army, which was bearing the brunt of the attack) to gain their appreciation of events. Blumentritt was especially discouraged. He reported that the troops were becoming apathetic, that the Russians attacked by night and were behind the forward positions by daybreak. There was little of consequence that Halder could do from East Prussia, however, except lend encouragement. He did brief Hitler on the army group's predicament in the early afternoon, but the Führer had no practical solution at hand either. The OKH was already working as hard as it could to get reinforcements and replacements to the front. Realistically, all that Army Group Center could do was try to hang on.

As tense as the circumstances were, another event on this day all but overshadowed them, at least for a small group of officers in the high command. This was the day on which the Führer accepted Brauchitsch's resignation. At 1:00 that afternoon Hitler summoned Halder to his headquarters and gave him the news, saying, "Anyone can handle the little task of directing operations. The task of the commander in chief of the army is to train the army in a National Socialist sense. I do not know a general in the army who can fulfill this task as I wish. Therefore I have decided to take over command of the army myself."[81] Hitler informed Halder that he would keep him on to oversee operations as chief of the General Staff, but that Keitel would take over all the administrative duties that Brauchitsch had fulfilled. Hitler also said that he expected Halder to brief him daily.[82] Then, having delivered the big news, the Führer proceeded to lecture Halder in typical style. Two mistakes had been made up to that point, he said. The first was that the phrase "rearward position" had been allowed to take hold among the troops. Such positions were not available and could not be created. The second mistake was that not enough preparations were made for the winter. The army works too schematically, he added as an aside; as a contrast, Hitler pointed to the Luftwaffe, which he said Göring had trained much differently. As far as the front was concerned, the thing to do was to hold, without fear of threats on the flanks.[83]

That evening Hitler released an Order of the Day, announcing his decision to take over command of the army:

> Soldiers of the army and the Waffen-SS!
> Our people's fight for freedom is approaching its climax.
> Decisions of worldwide importance are imminent.
> The army is the foremost bearer of the struggle.
> As of today I have therefore taken over command of the army myself.
> As a soldier in many World War battles I am united with you in the will to victory.[84]

Brauchitsch also released an Order of the Day of his own, in which he said how proud he was of the soldiers who had fought under him and how glad he was to see the Führer taking command.[85] Halder spoke with Brauchitsch that afternoon but did not record the contents of that conversation; "No significantly new viewpoint" was his single cryptic remark.[86] That evening the chief of the General Staff called his officers together and informed them of the change in command and the new work routine that the change engendered, but again there is no record of his exact remarks. The mood of the moment, however, seemed to be that Brauchitsch had reached the end of his endurance, and that the army would benefit by having Hitler at the helm.[87]

Saturday, December 20, 1941

If Halder had any illusions about the nature of his relationship with Hitler—and there is every indication that he did—this day should have at least cast doubt upon them. Likewise, Halder would receive a strong indication of the impact that relationship would have on his work. Up until this point he had only occasionally taken part in the Führer's briefings; now they would become a regular part of his life. The briefings themselves not only used up an inordinate amount of time but also disrupted Halder's (and his staff's) entire morning schedule, since he required detailed notes from which to make his presentation. Moreover, while he had sometimes taken issue with Hitler's decisions in the past, there was usually a buffer, in the person of Brauchitsch, to shield him from the full force of the Führer's megalomania and stubbornness. Now he was on his own.

The form of Hitler's midday briefing changed when he took over as commander in chief of the army. Before this point Jodl had briefed the situation on all fronts by himself, except on those infrequent occasions (once or twice weekly) when Brauchitsch or Halder had been present. Now the OKH submitted its situation reports to the Armed Forces Command Staff as before, and the staff worked them into Jodl's notes, but only in a general form. In the briefing Jodl would cover the overall situation, including the western and southern theaters in detail and an overview of the east, for which last task he used a 1:1,000,000 map. Then Halder would brief the eastern front in detail, using 1:300,000 maps and extensive notes that covered the situation down to army and sometimes corps or even division level.[88] Heusinger and one or two other General Staff officers would be present to provide any additional detail that Hitler required.

From this description the briefings might appear to have been orderly affairs, but in truth they were not. Disruptions often came from Hitler's so-called inner circle. This group consisted of those members of the OKW, the armed forces, and the Party who were regularly in the Führer's company at the briefings. On the OKW side, Keitel, Schmundt, the service adjutants (Engel, Puttkamer, and Below), and an SS representative were usually present. Sometimes Göring or his personal representative, Lieutenant General Karl Bodenschatz, would also attend, and there were frequently one or more senior Party officials there as well. Keitel, living up to his nickname, usually restricted his remarks to the occasional *"Jawohl, mein Führer!"* or some similarly subservient sentiment, unless Hitler asked him a direct question. Jodl remained quiet for the most part during Halder's portion of the briefing, except to throw in an occasional remark in support of something Hitler said. The others felt free to interject remarks or questions at any point, and Hitler often took their comments more seriously than Halder's. Army group or theater commanders also called regularly during the briefings, in hopes of getting a favorable decision from the Führer on some matter. And Hitler himself often called some headquarters at the front, especially when he wanted to contest some fact that Halder had presented.[89]

As Warlimont pointed out, Hitler's personal style was probably the factor that wore on Halder the most during their daily interactions. Not only was the Führer endlessly caught up in details, but at any point he might launch off into a monologue on any subject old or new, important or not, constantly repeating himself, sweeping away concrete questions and suggestions with an unrestrained, rushing stream of talk.[90] This side of Hitler's personality shows up in the extensive notes that Halder took during the briefing on December 20, although on this occasion the Führer did restrict himself for the most part to comments about the eastern front. He gave instructions for the defense of particular points and directed the actions of certain armies and corps. He demanded that the army construct heated strongpoints between villages, and that the Luftwaffe destroy enemy-held towns. He directed that the OKH issue orders to counteract the psychological impact of the enemy's offensive. The phrase "Russian winter" should be stricken from everyone's vocabulary, the Führer insisted. Going on, he designated reinforcements for particular sectors and addressed problems with the railroads and the organization of the supply services. He gave tactical guidance on antitank warfare and the construction of positions. He even pointed out the need to supply the troops with stoves. Finally, he directed that the army send tanks and antitank weapons to Africa. Altogether Halder's abbreviated record of Hitler's remarks for this one meeting runs to over three pages in printed form.[91] No great amount of imagination is needed to guess how Halder and the other General Staff officers felt about this use of their time.

The orders that came out of Hitler's briefings could take a number of forms.[92] The broadest were his "directives" (Weisungen). These gave strategic and—increasingly—operational guidance to the services, and their intended time span extended as far as possible into the future. In theory they left the implementation to the services, although in practice Hitler interfered in that with growing frequency. Often an individual directive showed the influence of one service or another, especially in the details, which the services had to provide in any case. At other times Hitler plainly went against the armed forces' wishes, as in the orders of July and August 1941 that redirected the focus of the eastern campaign away from Moscow. In addition to the Weisungen there were several other written forms of order. They are often difficult to differentiate in terms of content, but they did tend to stay within certain bounds most of the time. The "special directives" (Sonderweisungen) usually went to Armed Forces commanders in separate theaters and dealt with special tasks. "Battle instructions" (Kampfanweisungen) provided operational and tactical guidance, especially for the war in the east. "Duty instructions" (Dienstanweisungen) defined the positions of senior officers (this was a common form of order throughout the command system). "Guidelines" (Richtlinien) most often covered economic, administrative, or supply matters. Normal orders (Anordnungen or Befehle) were the most common type; of these, the Führerbefehle carried the most weight and urgency. Grundsätzliche Befehle ("fundamental" or "basic orders") were also very broad and powerful.

One important point about these written orders is that Hitler still issued them through the OKW to the General Staff, although as commander in chief of the army he had the right to issue orders directly to the army group commanders (and in fact did so on occasion, telephonically).[93] Thus at this stage of the war the OKW remained closely involved in the operations on the eastern front, just as the General Staff continued to monitor events in the other theaters.

Following the briefing on December 20, Hitler took the opportunity to back up his instructions to Halder with a written document. He had Jodl's staff draw up a draft memorandum that same day; the approved copy went out on December 21, addressed to the Operations Branch of the General Staff. The memo did not carry one of the normal order designations; instead, its first line identified it simply as a "compilation of the army's tasks for the coming period, as explained by the Führer to the chief of the General Staff of the Army on Dec. 20." It covered nearly all the points that Hitler had made in the briefing, albeit in a more logical order, plus some additional information. Among other things, it defined some particular units to be sent to Army Groups North and South, with all remaining reinforcements to go to Army Group Center. (The memo also called on the army to strip all local inhabitants and prisoners of war of their winter clothing "ruthlessly.")[94] Apparently Hitler did not trust Halder to remember everything he had said—or perhaps to implement everything he remembered.

While the staff at the OKW was busy drafting that memorandum, Halder, Heusinger, and the others returned to "Mauerwald" to resume their work. Army Group Center was still the crisis point; the situation was "still very tense," as Halder described it.[95] The Russians were mounting strong local attacks along the whole army group front, and although the Germans managed to fend off many of these, others broke through, and there was no hope of closing the large gaps that the Red Army had already made in the lines. Halder had already spoken with Kluge once, at 11:00 that morning. At 3:45 in the afternoon they consulted again, and Halder passed on the news that Hitler had forbidden any withdrawal whatsoever; the Führer would not give Kluge the freedom of action that he sought. Kluge emphasized that his forces were weak and he had no reserves; the Führer must be clear on the consequences, he said. At 6:00 that evening the two men talked again, but Halder could only echo Hitler's objections to any pullback. The two also discussed Guderian, who was just arriving at the "Wolfsschanze," having gone over Kluge's head to appeal directly to Hitler for permission to withdraw. Kluge told Halder that Guderian was not following orders, that he had "lost his nerve" and was preparing to retreat.

Guderian met with the Führer for nearly five hours that evening, with only a couple of interruptions. Keitel, Schmundt, and several other officers from the OKW were there. No one from the OKH was in attendance, although Halder had briefed Hitler on the situation at Army Group Center and on Guderian's intentions just before the latter went in. Guderian told Hitler what was happening at his command and then began to describe the pullback he had planned. Hitler immediately forbade any such pullback. Guderian duly reported that the move was already under way (he maintained in his memoirs that Brauchitsch had approved the retreat six days earlier, and that he was shocked to discover that Hitler did not know that). The two men argued back and forth—Halder later described their discussion as "dramatic"—but the Führer would not budge.[96] In the meantime, Schmundt called Kluge to reinforce the message that his armies must not pull back. Keitel called Halder at 8:00 P.M. with the same message: Guderian's retreat had to be stopped. Halder, in turn, called Greiffenberg and let him know. Later Jodl called Halder to pass the order along yet again. At 9:30 Halder spoke with Kluge once more, and the latter reported that he had countermanded Guderian's order.

The situation that evening, as Halder recorded it, was "in general unchanged"—but that did not mean it was good.[97] Heusinger spoke with Greiffenberg at 11:10 and learned that the Soviets were continuing to advance on the left flank of 4th Army, northwest of Moscow.[98] Farther south, new Russian forces appeared to be approaching 2d and 2d Panzer Armies and gathering in the gaps they had made earlier. Soviet cavalry was massing more than thirty miles behind the front line of December 16, and things looked black.

Sunday, December 21, 1941

The morning did not bring better news. Soviet attacks against Army Group Center continued to gain ground. Overnight the Soviets had forced their way into a major supply center for 4th Army. South of there, a fifty-mile-wide gap was developing across the boundary of 2d and 2d Panzer Armies. Pressure against the southern portion of the 2d Army front had made some local withdrawals necessary. The same was true along the 4th Army front. "The commanding generals report," wrote Halder, "that their troops are exhausted and not up to further attacks. The order to hold is given."[99] Attacks against 9th Army had less success, but there, too, the troops were reaching the end of their strength. Army Group North faced strong attacks as well, although it was able to defend against them successfully.

As part of the effort to shore up the front, Halder took a new step. He sent five senior officers from the OKH to headquarters on the front and in the rear areas to raise the commands' self-confidence and restore order.[100] (Hitler had suggested something like this measure in the briefing the day before, but that suggestion may or may not have been the origin of the men's mission.) None of the men Halder chose had any special qualifications—their current positions had nothing to do with operations or logistics—but Halder must have counted on their common General Staff training and experience to allow them to spot problems and take corrective action. "Wem Gott ein Amt gibt, dem gibt er auch den Verstand," as the saying went in the staff circles: "To whom God gives an office he gives also the necessary understanding."[101]

One wonders if Halder thought of that saying as he contemplated an order that appeared on this day, actually a supplement to the one by which Hitler took command of the army on December 19. The heading was "Oberkommando des Heeres," but the signature on it was Keitel's. The order said that the Führer had decided to issue orders directly to the Replacement Army commander and to the chief of the Army Personnel Office on all fundamental matters. Further, it said that for special tasks Hitler also would use his Wehrmacht adjutant, Colonel Schmundt (or, in his place, Major Engel), who would maintain a close link to a new staff, the Staff OKH. The Staff OKH, the order continued, would be formed from the former office of the army commander in chief's adjutant, in order to help with the army-related tasks that Keitel now had to carry out; to that end it would be a liaison element with the Army General Staff. Lieutenant Colonel Heinz von Gyldenfeldt, Brauchitsch's former adjutant, would be in charge of the Staff OKH.

This liaison arrangement on the administrative level was certainly a prudent measure, since Keitel was overburdened already and Hitler was not interested in most administrative matters. In general, any measure that increased cooperation between the OKW and the OKH was a good thing, because that cooperation was lacking at times.[102] At some levels the two staffs collaborated closely. The OKW was becoming increasingly dependent upon the OKH for many supporting staff functions, especially those having to do with intelligence and logistics; in these areas the two headquarters worked well together at this stage of the war. Some officers, of course, such as the chief of transportation, occupied positions in both realms. Their work went smoothly so long as both sets of superiors agreed. And even within the operational elements—the Operations Branch and the National Defense Branch—the relationship was still strong at the lower levels. There was as yet still no great split between the two headquarters, as would develop later. However, at the very top of each organization there was a definite lack of mutual effort. At that level the clash of personalities was too great, especially between Halder and Heusinger on the one hand and Keitel, Jodl, and Warlimont on the other. These men saw each other frequently, they heard each other's briefings, they were fully informed on each other's spheres—but there was no bond, no true exchange of ideas and intentions. As yet this fact was more a nuisance than anything else, since there was not yet any great point of contention between the two sides, but that would change before long.

EPILOGUE

Midnight on Sunday arrived without any sign that the crisis on the eastern front would end anytime soon, despite Halder's confident assertion to Greiffenberg that if everyone could just hold for another fourteen days the whole thing would be over, that the enemy could not possibly keep up his frontal attacks much longer.[103] For purely practical reasons, however, the examination of the command system's day-to-day functioning has to stop here, artificial though the quitting point is. Now is the moment to step back and see what broader conclusions stand out.

To begin at the top: Hitler's style of command, and especially the so-called *Führerprinzip,* or leader principle, was beginning to have insidious effects on the command system. According to the *Führerprinzip,* every commander held sole responsibility for decisions within his command, and he was also duty-bound to obey every order he received from his superior commander. The Führer himself stood, of course, at the top of the hierarchy; his will was quite literally law.[104] Every senior commander (and more junior commanders, too, as the war went on) knew that Hitler had the power to issue or change any order. More and more often they began to appeal to him directly, as Guderian did on December 20, and his personal style was such that he allowed such behavior, even though it clearly violated the chain of command.

That aspect of Hitler's role corresponded perversely with the principles and practices of the General Staff. On the one hand, Halder himself had promoted the idea that "the commander alone bears the responsibility for his sphere of command."[105] He wanted to return the General Staff officer to the proper role, as he saw it, of adviser. On the other hand, many other senior officers—and one must remember that General Staff officers dominated the senior ranks—clung to the idea that they should be able to appeal an order that they did not believe made sense. Properly seen, their actions were a perversion of the original practice, which was meant to circumvent the decisions of unqualified commanders. With the standardization of professional education for officers, the need for such action had disappeared; that, in any case, had been Halder's rationale when he rewrote the *Handbook for General Staff Duty in War* in 1939. However, the urge to appeal a decision obviously still existed. By encouraging it, Hitler undermined both his own *Führerprinzip* and the authority of his immediate subordinates. His army group commanders, in turn, reacted by turning on *their* subordinates, as Kluge would turn on Guderian a few days hence. This was the natural outgrowth of a system that allowed anyone to go straight to the top with their complaints.[106]

That problem in the chain of command intersected with another issue that, if it does not exactly jump out of this look at one week's activities, certainly forms a strong undercurrent. All of the officers in the high command seem to have shared an illusion of control, the idea that, with the communications means at their disposal, they could orchestrate developments on the ground hundreds of miles away. This is a difficult attitude to document. Wagner, the general quartermaster, was the only officer who actually left a record that expressed it. On September 29, 1941, he wrote to his wife, "Without a doubt *I will bring* Army Group South to the Don [River], [and Army Group] Center to Moscow."[107] And on October 10: "I sit far from the shooting but I notice that my arm is long enough to keep all the people moving at top gear, even the chiefs of an army group and two armies!"[108] Otherwise the attitude showed up only in subtle ways. Probably its clearest indirect expression was the stubbornness with which the senior military leaders refused to recognize the seriousness of the situation at the front, but even that tendency is difficult to gauge. It came out through references to subordinate commanders "losing their nerve" and to the need to reinstill "order" and "confidence." Mostly, however, it took the form of an underlying frustration with a dichotomy, the dichotomy between supposedly perfect knowledge and great operational skill, on the one hand, and inadequate results, on the other. That frustration, in turn, led to ever-greater efforts to direct the battle from the top.

The illusion of control was definitely not a new phenomenon in 1941; Geoffrey Parker has demonstrated, for example, that Philip II of Spain operated under it in the sixteenth century.[109] It was in fact a danger that some of Germany's military leaders seemed to recognize. Surely they should have. Carl von Clausewitz, the nineteenth-century military philosopher whose work *On War* the staff officers pretended to know, warned of the "fog of war" and a force he called "friction" that could make the best plan go awry. No less a figure than Moltke the Elder had also written of the danger of interfering needlessly in subordinates' decisions. Despite all the warnings, however, Germany's leaders, and especially Hitler, tended to intervene more and more frequently as the war went on.

The seeming efficiency of the Germans' staffs, and the modernity of the communications technology that supported them, were two factors that helped to support the illusion of control. Staff organization and procedures were two of the Germans' greatest strengths, if one ignores the problems at the top between the OKW and the OKH. Information flowed up the chain regularly, smoothly, and in great quantity. At each stage the recipients recorded it, processed it, and made sure it got to the people who had to make the decisions. Once the decisions were made, the system then allowed for their rapid and thorough dissemination and implementation.

The smallness of German staffs came into play here. The people who manned the command system were remarkably junior in most cases. Hitler's role aside, only the most fundamental questions reached the top levels of the army hierarchy at this stage of the war; the lower-level staff members took care of all the routine work and let their superiors get on with the more important tasks. Just as the Germans themselves maintained, in a small staff a subordinate can more easily go to his superior with a question or problem if necessary, and the superior can more easily stay informed of what is going on throughout the hierarchy. Thus both parties can be comfortable with a system in which relatively junior officers handle much of the work. The fewer the levels in the hierarchy, the faster and more reliable the information flow. Thus the parts of the system could function with an apparent smoothness that lulled the Germans into overconfidence.

The problems that staff size created are difficult to identify from a day-by-day account such as this. Perhaps the most obvious hazard was that everyone had to work long hours, and the resulting fatigue could lead to errors. Unfortunately, even the most detailed of the existing records are not detailed enough to show such a problem, and the few personal accounts by staff officers do not address the issue either. The Germans might also have suffered from the lack of certain specialist officers such as meteorologists, but again the documentation is lacking.[110] The most serious problems arose in connection with longer-range planning, and so they do not show up in an examination of one week's activities.

In general one can say that, at this point in the war at least, the German staffs kept up well with the daily demands of operations. The organizational and procedural expertise that the Germans had built up over the preceding century were serving them well, if only in terms of the staff elements' internal mechanisms. The potentially fatal problems existed in the higher realms. Deep flaws were emerging in the larger high command organization, flaws that the personal leadership styles of Hitler and many senior commanders exacerbated. When one adds strategic incompetence and weaknesses in personnel administration, intelligence, and logistics to the mix, one can see why the course of the war was turning against the Third Reich. From the end of 1941 forward, these problems would only get worse, until they overwhelmed the efficiency of the staff system completely.

9

The Last Grasp, 1942

By the end of 1941 the war had changed dramatically for Germany. The effort to defeat the Soviet Union in one campaign had failed, and German forces there seemed on the brink of collapse. The initial efforts to eject the British from their position in the Mediterranean had likewise faltered. Not only did Britain, backed up by its empire, still sit unconquered in the Germans' rear, but the United States had now entered the war, bringing with it a potential more vast than even its own citizens could appreciate at first. Yet despite these facts, the mood in the upper echelons of the high command was one of cautious optimism. Germany's leaders knew that the war was far from over and that the events of the coming year would be decisive. With one more campaign, they believed, Germany could still place itself in a position to win the war eventually. By the end of 1942 that vision would lie in ruins. Its failure and the further degeneration of the German command system would go hand in hand.

PLANS FOR THE YEAR TAKE SHAPE

The Germans' initial optimism grew from a study that the Armed Forces Command Staff released on December 14, 1941: "Overview of the Significance of the Entry of the U.S.A. and Japan into the War."[1] Despite some errors, the document's appraisal of the enemy situation was remarkably accurate. It stated that Japan's entry and its initial successes had thrown the western Allies' strategic plans out the window, and that the Allies could not regain any kind of strategic initiative until autumn 1942 at the earliest. Beyond that point they would have three options: to concentrate on Europe and the Atlantic, to concentrate against Japan, or to hold and stabilize on all

170

fronts until they had built up their strength. Each option presented the Germans with advantages and risks; for planning purposes, the assessment assumed that the Allies would choose the first (and, for Germany, worst) course. Decisive operations under that option would not be possible in 1942, since the United States would not yet have mobilized fully. The most serious threats would be against northwest Africa or Norway, where Allied successes could further restrict the German strategic sphere and offer the Allies a variety of additional possibilities.

The study went on to draw conclusions for the coming year's operations, and here the staff proved less astute. While the western Allies were still impotent, they said, Germany could bring its operations in the east to a close and build its strength for a long defensive phase. Specifically, the staff suggested that operations in the Soviet Union aim first to cut off the ports of Murmansk and Archangel and second to take the oil region in the Caucasus. With the Soviets thus unable to receive significant amounts of supplies from the west, and with Germany's supply of petroleum secure, Germany could hold off its enemies for the foreseeable future. The Caucasus would also make an excellent jumping-off point for a drive into the Allied position in the Near East. With that in mind, and in consideration of the general need to defend the periphery of Germany's strategic position, the paper also recommended that Germany and Italy act to stabilize the situation in the Mediterranean, in part by bringing Spain and France into closer cooperation. The staff knew that Germany's forces were insufficient to provide a continuous line of defense over this entire sphere, but they counted on the formation of mobile reserves and improvements in internal communications to make up the difference. Exactly how France and Spain could be persuaded to cooperate, or how all this would lead to victory, the study did not explain.[2]

Hitler's analysis was similar in many respects.[3] The Führer was determined to continue the campaign in the east, and he had long known that the Caucasus oil fields were essential to the German war effort. Up until late in 1941 he had wanted to press forward again on the whole front, but he realized by December at the latest that Germany no longer had the capacity to carry out such an ambitious offensive. Both manpower and equipment were lacking, the latter especially since Hitler had shifted production priority to the Luftwaffe and navy in July 1941 in anticipation of a quick victory; he would shift that priority back to the army in January 1942, but months would pass before the effects would become apparent. Therefore, Hitler decided to make the main thrust in the south, with perhaps a subsidiary attack against Leningrad. He still expected that Britain might give up if its position became hopeless; a German victory in Russia, combined with Japanese advances in the Far East, ought to bring the British around. As far as the United States was concerned, Hitler had no idea how to defeat it, but he covered his uncertainty with bluff and bluster. Beneath it all, he had come to recognize that the war was going to last for years and, without expressing it clearly, he had decided on a continental, defensive strategy.

In the OKH, all this strategic thinking was far from people's minds. The Soviet offensive that opened around Moscow on December 18 broadened in the new year to include points along the entire line, although the crisis in the center remained the most serious. Hitler at first continued to insist that every unit hold where it stood, regardless of the circumstances. Even Halder had begun to argue with the Führer on that point, but to no avail. Hitler responded with harsh accusations against the OKH for, among other things, having "parliamentarized" the army and for not leading it strictly.[4] He also relieved two army commanders—Guderian on December 25 and Hoepner on January 8—for having the temerity to order withdrawals without authorization. Leeb asked on January 15 to be either relieved or given freedom of action; Hitler chose the former. Halder, his arguments with the Führer notwithstanding, told Brennecke, Leeb's chief of staff, to "extirpate this mania for operating. The army group has a clear order to hold and the highest command will assume all the risk."[5] A day later he exhorted the General Staff officers on the eastern front not to give in to a "numbers psychosis": "I ask that in the preparation of the enemy situation reports, the one-sided overestimation of the numbers of enemy units be resisted, and that a critical evaluation of the circumstances that determine the actual enemy fighting strength be set in its place and made the basis of command decisions."[6] Hitler eventually gave in and allowed Army Group Center to make a limited withdrawal in the fourth week of January, but the Soviets soon advanced beyond the proposed stop line, and the situation remained in a desperate state of flux for weeks. The Germans managed to hang on, but only barely, aided as much by Soviet incompetence and difficulties as by their own efforts. Finally, the spring *rasputitsa,* the mud season that arrived with the snowmelt, put an end to operations.

ORGANIZATIONAL CHANGES AND TENSIONS

While the winter campaign on the eastern front was at its height, a minor but illuminating change took place in the organization of the high command. On January 1, 1942, in accordance with an order that Keitel had issued two weeks before, the designation "National Defense Branch" disappeared.[7] Major General Warlimont, who had headed the branch, became the deputy chief of the Armed Forces Command Staff, under Jodl. The Defense Branch's operations groups became branches in their own right. Now their chiefs were directly subordinate to Jodl and received new designations. Instead of being the Army Operations group leader, for example, Colonel Freiherr Treusch von Buttlar-Brandenfels was the "first general staff officer (army) in the Armed Forces Command Staff."[8]

This change in organization is illuminating because of its limited nature. It did not represent a real change in the manning or missions of the Command Staff. Keitel's order stipulated that there would be no change in working methods, and the staff did not increase in size right away, although it would do so later. A comparison of the duty instructions of 1939 and 1942 reveals no significant differences. Warlimont admitted that he himself prompted the change purely to give the colonels under him titles commensurate with their ranks. He also claimed that Jodl favored the new organization, since it placed the branch chiefs directly under him, and he saw that structure as more appropriate to a higher-level command staff.[9] In fact the change was completely cosmetic; it fed some bureaucratic ambitions and nothing else.[10]

Perhaps the reorganization of the Command Staff satisfied the officers' need for status, but they can hardly have claimed that it helped them overcome the challenges they faced. Their responsibilities were still increasing, while the size and authority of the staff remained the same. Fortunately, the level of activity in the OKW theaters of war had not yet picked up, but the OKW was still struggling to define its place in the command system. On December 8, 1941, for example, Keitel had to send a memorandum out to his subordinate offices and to the services, stating that "the growing inclination of the armed forces offices subordinate to OKW to turn to the Armed Forces Command Staff in connection with every question that concerns them is leading to an overburdening of the staff with matters that do not belong within its sphere. The result is the growth of correspondence in which the WFSt can only play the role of a go-between."[11] Keitel went on to say that the Command Staff regulated only those questions that dealt with deployment, command, or quartermaster issues. In all other cases, the staff was to be called upon only if the matter could not be settled among the services or other agencies involved; when questions of deployment, command, or supply were significant; or when specially ordered. Three weeks later, in a seemingly contradictory move, Keitel sent out another memo, this one saying that the Führer's assumption of command over the army had not changed the basic relationship of the OKH to the OKW and to the other services. All questions from the OKH that related to the other services or to the Wehrmacht as a whole still had to go through the OKW.[12]

These memorandums are evidence of rather minor problems, but in the early spring of 1942 there were indications that the rivalry between the OKW and the services was heating up. In April the Armed Forces Command Staff produced a memorandum that defined Keitel's authority over units and staffs under the OKW's control. Specifically, Keitel reserved for himself the right to issue orders dealing with organization, training, equipment, employment, discipline, and several other matters. At the same time, he held the services responsible for administration, personnel, replacements, and resupply.[13] Even in those realms, moreover, the OKW tried to stake a claim. In May the General Staff's

Organization Branch noted a clear tendency on the part of the OKW to set up administrative structures in parallel to existing army staffs. The OKH could see no reasons for these efforts; they seemed only to "serve the expansionist needs of a specialist branch in a higher authority," and the OKH was determined to resist them.[14] That resistance may well have prompted Keitel to send this notice to the three service headquarters on May 14: "The Führer has ordered: 'All supporting materials that are necessary for the direction of the armed forces and that are requested for this purpose are to be provided to the OKW, as my military working staff, on demand and without reservation. The decision on the form of submission lies, in cases where there is any doubt, with the offices of the OKW.'"[15] Such was the nature of the continuing rivalry. As yet, however, there was still nothing of any great significance over which the command elements needed to argue, since the OKW theaters were mostly quiet. More than anything else, these squabbles simply reflected normal bureaucratic empire building, albeit in an atmosphere of deep distrust.

OPERATION *BLAU*

As the winter battles slid to a halt in the mud of the *rasputitsa,* the high command put the finishing touches on its plans for the summer offensives. Before it could move forward, though, the Wehrmacht had to make up the losses it had already suffered. Between June 22, 1941, and the end of March 1942, the Germans lost over 1.1 million men killed, wounded, or missing. Since the beginning of November alone, the Germans lost roughly 900,000 men, including those who fell out due to illness, and gained only about 450,000 back, even with the most strenuous efforts. Alone in the eastern army, the OKH calculated that it lacked no fewer than 625,000 men as of May 1, 1942, most of them in combat units.[16] The material situation was no better. As of March 20, 1942, the army had suffered *net* losses of over 115,000 transport vehicles, 3,100 armored vehicles, and 10,400 artillery pieces in the east. In addition, in the winter months the army lost over 180,000 horses killed, wounded, or sick and could bring in only 20,000 replacements. In that period it also expended nearly 572,000 tons of munitions and over 176 million gallons of fuel.[17] The Luftwaffe was in a similar state; despite a clear qualitative superiority in the first nine months of the Russian campaign, in March 1942 it had nearly six hundred fewer aircraft than in June 1941 and—amazingly—forty fewer than it had possessed in September 1939.[18] The Germans would funnel enormous quantities of men and matériel into the east in May and June, but there was no hope that the German economy could make up what the Wehrmacht had lost or support the same rate of consumption in the coming summer. Any German effort in 1942 would have to be on a much smaller scale than in the year before.

After the war Halder and his associates would maintain that he opposed the renewal of offensive operations in the east in 1942. A postwar footnote to his diary entry of February 15, 1942, for example, states that Halder wanted Germany to stay on the strategic defensive in 1942, in the belief that the army needed lots of time to recover from the losses it had sustained.[19] If Halder really believed that, however, there is no record that he said so at the time. In contrast, many other officers believed that an attack was foolish. These included Rundstedt and Leeb, who both suggested a withdrawal, perhaps as far back as the Polish border. Fromm, Wagner, and Thomas (head of the OKW's Military Economics and Armaments Office) all opposed an offensive as well, as did many in the General Staff's Operations Branch; they all believed that Germany did not possess the forces to achieve Hitler's goals. Some, such as Canaris, were even suggesting—quietly—that the war was already lost.[20]

Such a sudden outburst of realism might logically have come from improved performance on the part of the German intelligence network, but that was not the case. Nor was Halder's continued optimism based on hard information, although he did create some changes in the army's intelligence system. By the spring of 1942 he had become dissatisfied with the information he was receiving from Foreign Armies East. On March 31 he spoke with Ziehlberg about a replacement for Kinzel, "who does not meet my requirements."[21] On the next day Halder took Lieutenant Colonel Reinhard Gehlen from the Eastern Group in the Operations Branch and put him in charge of Foreign Armies East. The choice is illuminating. The two men knew each other and worked well together, but Gehlen had no special qualifications for his new position.[22] Halder told Gehlen that he expected not just a thorough analysis of the daily situation but also long-range assessments of enemy capabilities and intentions.[23] Soon Gehlen had embarked on a reorganization and reorientation of the branch. Under the new system, Group I handled the daily assessments; it contained one subgroup for each army group on the front, and the officers in those subgroups worked in close cooperation with their counterparts in the Operations Branch. Group II handled the long-range projects concerning the Soviet Union.[24]

The conduct of combat operations against the USSR had opened up new sources of information, and the day-to-day picture of Soviet units on the front lines had improved considerably from that which existed before the start of *Barbarossa*. However, there were still gaps in German knowledge, and those gaps became wider as the intelligence organs attempted to divine long-term Soviet capabilities and intentions. That effort did not even begin until near the end of the winter battles, since the intelligence officers had at first shared the belief that the campaign would be over in one season. In late March 1942, though, even before Gehlen took over at Foreign Armies East, the first comprehensive estimates of Soviet personnel and material resources became available.[25]

Those estimates and their impact demonstrate two points. First, they show that the task of estimating the resources of a nation such as the Soviet Union in wartime was well-nigh impossible. Both sets of estimates were inaccurate. The one on industrial potential, especially, encouraged the Germans to believe that they could render the Russians all but powerless with one more successful campaign. The study on personnel, on the other hand, even as it underestimated Soviet potential, should have created some doubts, for it clearly showed that the USSR was nowhere near the end of its strength. Beyond the question of accuracy, moreover, the timing of the studies' appearance highlights the persistence of the high command's fundamental attitudes, both toward the Soviet Union and toward the intelligence function. The Germans had already decided to launch another offensive before the new studies came out, and there is no indication that they reexamined their assumptions afterward. Hitler had made his attitude toward intelligence clear when, on March 17, he issued an order to the OKH, saying that all comprehensive evaluations of enemy plans and capabilities had to agree with his opinion before they went to subordinate commands.[26] He was convinced that the Soviet Union had nearly exhausted its military capabilities. On April 2 he stated baldly that he believed, based on the Russians' industrial capacity, that they probably could not form any substantial new armies—and that was *before* he saw the OKW study.[27] Likewise, if his diary is any indication, Halder did not think the studies worthy of note.[28] Planning for the operation went forward without a pause.

The General Staff, under Hitler's close supervision, had begun hammering out the concept for the summer's operations at the end of 1941.[29] However, the prolonged crisis during that winter made more concrete planning seem irrelevant. Bock, now commander of Army Group South, prepared a "theoretical study into the operational possibilities" at Halder's suggestion and submitted it to Hitler on February 20, but the Führer took no immediate notice of it.[30] On March 28, 1942, Halder briefed Hitler on the army's deployment plan. The Führer approved it and went on to give Halder his goals for the offensive, beginning with the usual broad strategic appraisal. The overall situation, he believed, was significantly less tense. The greatest dangers could come in the form of landings in Norway or France; Allied operations against Spain, Portugal, or northwest Africa were less likely. The situation in Africa remained unclear; logistical problems were still a key factor. In any case, the war would be decided in the east. The goal there would be to take the Caucasus and hold through the next winter along the Don River. In reaching those goals, he continued, the army must be careful to avoid deep penetrations and instead concentrate on smaller tactical encirclements.[31]

On April 5 Hitler signed the directive for the drive in the south, which he code-named *Blau (Blue)*. In the preamble, which certainly reflected Hitler's own thoughts, he defined the campaign's objectives more broadly than he had in the briefing with Halder on March 28. The goal of the operation, he stated, would be to "destroy the Soviets' remaining fighting strength and take away his most important sources of militarily significant economic power."[32] The operational details in the directive were in part reflections of the army's work, primarily Bock's study. However, Hitler's growing confidence in himself as an operational commander shows up in the fact that he worked through the directive personally and made several significant changes and additions.[33]

The directive called, first, for a series of preliminary operations designed to stabilize the front and release forces for the main attack; these included operations to clear the Crimea. When the preliminaries were complete, the main attack would go forward, but in a series of phases, since the Wehrmacht did not have the resources to execute an offensive on this scale all at once.[34] The first phase would take the Germans east from Kursk in a pincer movement to the city of Voronezh, three hundred miles north of Rostov. Once Voronezh fell, part of the forces there would head southeast along the Don and meet with another thrust that would start southeast of Kharkov. A third phase would take those combined forces east to the area of Stalingrad, where they would unite with those of yet another spearhead that would break through the Soviet lines northwest of Rostov. Only then, in a fourth phase for which Hitler gave no details, would the Wehrmacht head south to take the Caucasian oil fields. The directive did not specify a date by which the offensive was to begin, but it did direct the army to continue the operation into its final phase without delay, so that the onset of winter would not prevent the Wehrmacht from reaching its final goals.[35]

The operation to clear the Crimea got under way on May 8. In the east it went well, but the siege of Sevastopol dragged on longer then the Germans had expected, bringing the total length of this preliminary phase to six weeks and the Wehrmacht's losses to one hundred thousand. In the meantime, the Soviets had launched an ill-conceived offensive of their own against Kharkov, not knowing that the Germans were concentrating in that sector. The strength of the Soviet blow caught the Germans off guard, but they soon recovered and turned the tables. In the end the Red Army gained no territory, lost one hundred thousand dead and two hundred thousand prisoners, and were weak when the German campaign opened.

Operation *Blue* began on June 28, and the Wehrmacht gained ground rapidly.[36] The first phase was complete by July 6 and the second by July 15, with the Germans suffering only light casualties. The Soviets performed better than they had before, however, while the Germans displayed unusual operational ineptitude. Each of these phases ended with a very small bag of Soviet prisoners and with the German forces poorly positioned for the next stage. The Soviets had changed their operational practices; they no longer stood in place and let the Germans surround them but instead retreated out of harm's way. The plan for *Blue* had called for small tactical envelopments, per Hitler's directive, but such maneuvers closed mostly upon thin air. Nevertheless, Hitler believed that the Wehrmacht was winning a great victory.[37] He decided to change the concept of the operation entirely; instead of sending all his forces to Stalingrad in Phase III, he would split them. In his Directive No. 45 of July 23, he ordered that Army Group A turn south into the Caucasus right away while only Army Group B continued on to the east.[38]

Hitler's involvement in the operation indicates another small but noticeable step forward in his willingness to exert personal control. He not only insisted on detailed briefings—which, after all, had been the norm for some time—but also issued orders with growing frequency and in increasing detail. This was not a role for which Hitler was suited. His occasional bursts of inspiration during the first two years of the war were no replacement for real operational expertise, and as flawed as the General Staff's performance sometimes was, Hitler's was even worse. The effect on operations was serious, as were the tensions the new situation created within the command, especially between Hitler and Halder. The latter's hopes for a constructive working relationship must have been wearing thin by this point. Halder wanted to be *the* operational mind for the army, but Hitler insisted on the superiority of his own ideas. Moreover, when those ideas failed, he was always ready to cast the blame onto others. On July 23 Halder wrote:

> After he himself ordered the concentration of mobile forces around Rostov on July 17 and the transfer of the 24th Panzer Division to Sixth Army on July 21, both against my will, it is obvious even to the layman's [Hitler's] eye that there is now a senseless jumble of mobile forces around Rostov while the important outward wing at Tsimlyanskiy starves for them. I warned insistently against both. Now that the result is as plain as the nose on his face, [he exhibits] fits of rage with the gravest accusations against the leaders.
>
> The chronic underestimation of the enemy's capabilities is gradually taking on grotesque forms and is growing dangerous. It is becoming less and less bearable. One cannot speak of serious work any more. This so-called "leadership" is characterized by pathological reaction to the impressions of the moment and a complete lack of judgment in assessing the command apparatus and its capabilities.[39]

Halder fought not only with Hitler but also with Keitel and Jodl, who seldom did more than parrot the Führer's opinions. Halder's lack of respect for the officers in Hitler's entourage shows up more frequently and with striking clarity in his diary entries for that summer. The one for July 6, for example, includes this comment: "In the course of the day, phone conversations with [various people, including Hitler and Keitel], always about the same questions. This telephoning back and forth about matters that should be thought out quietly and then incorporated in clear orders is agonizing. The least bearable is Keitel's senseless chattering."[40] And likewise on July 30:

> At the Führer's briefing Jodl is allowed to speak and pronounces grandiosely that the fate of the Caucasus will be decided at Stalingrad. Therefore a transfer of forces from Army Group A to B is necessary, and that as far south of the Don as possible. With that a thought that I briefed to the Führer six days ago, when the 4th Panzer Army was crossing the Don, is served up in a new turnout; when I gave it, though, no one in the illuminated society of the OKW grasped the idea.[41]

Clearly the chief of the General Staff was becoming fed up with the way Hitler and the OKW were running the operation, but, just as clearly, he was completely powerless to do anything about it. One should not take his objections at face value, however. There is little evidence that Halder would have been able to win the campaign he had planned and supported since the previous winter.

As the summer waned, the Germans' situation began to worsen, and not just in Russia. There they continued to make good progress until late August—fuel shortages slowed them more than enemy action—but by the end of the month Soviet resistance had stiffened in the Caucasus Mountains and on the outskirts of Stalingrad; the advance was slowing to a crawl. The Germans' spearheads were widely separated from one another and from their bases of supply, and those in the Caucasus were still well short of their goals, the oil fields at Grozny and Baku. On top of that, Russian attacks against Army Groups North and Center had nipped German offensives there in the bud. In North Africa, Rommel tried to break through the British position at El Alamein at the end of August, without success. At home in Germany, the British air campaign was becoming increasingly effective. In late May a thousand-plane raid by the British devastated Cologne, and by August the Germans already had 38 percent of their fighters deployed in the west. Finally, Hitler was becoming increasingly worried about the possibility of an Allied invasion of the Continent, to the point that he began to withhold powerful divisions from the east.

THE COMMAND DEGENERATES FURTHER

The growing tension soon led to another crisis in the high command. Hitler tried to push his eastern armies forward through force of will, and he took out his frustrations on any perceived source of resistance. His distrust of the army in general continued to grow and even affected the officers in his inner circle. On September 7 a break came over developments on Army Group A's front. Hitler had been pressing the army group commander, List, to push a spearhead through one particularly mountainous area, and List was resisting the idea because his forces would be too vulnerable and difficult to supply. Jodl finally flew out at List's request, reviewed the situation, and returned to report that he agreed with List completely. Hitler was infuriated. The exact nature of his complaint against Jodl is still somewhat in doubt; he may have believed that Jodl was blaming him for the campaign's weaknesses.[42] In any case, his reaction was immediate, broad, and petty. He considered relieving not only Jodl but Keitel and Warlimont as well.[43] For months afterward he refused to shake Jodl's or Keitel's hand or have the two of them at his dinner table. He also insisted that two stenographers be present at every meeting and briefing from now on, so that his officers could not twist his words against him.[44] On September 9, moreover, he had Keitel contact Halder to say that List ought to resign his post.[45] List did so the next day. The Führer did not replace him, however; instead, he took over command of the army group himself, and kept that position until November 22. Now he occupied four levels in the hierarchy at the same time: head of state, commander in chief of the Armed Forces, commander in chief of the army, and commander of an army group that was operating roughly eight hundred miles from his headquarters.[46]

Keitel, Jodl, and List were not the only targets of Hitler's ire. His relationship with Halder had become impossible, and some members of the "inner circle," especially Göring and Himmler, were urging him to dump his General Staff chief. Hitler frequently made jokes about Halder behind his back and ridiculed his recommendations to his face. Halder did his best to hide his frustration and contempt, but his bearing irritated Hitler unceasingly.[47] He could see the campaign approaching a bad end, but he had become little more than a mouthpiece in Hitler's eyes.[48] He tried to alert the Führer to the growing danger of the German position; the front was now roughly twenty-five hundred miles long, and the Soviets' operational reserves had still not put in an appearance. Foreign Armies East was beginning to provide more accurate—and sobering—assessments. Hitler would hear none of it, and the more Halder pressed his case, the harsher Hitler's outbursts became.

The tension finally boiled over on August 24. Halder had been trying to make the point that a Soviet offensive then striking Army Group North presented a real danger; he wanted to allow the headquarters there to pull back and thus release reserves by shortening the front. Hitler responded, "You always come to me with the same suggestion to withdraw, Halder. . . . We must remain firm in the best interests of the troops. I demand the same firmness from the leadership as I do from the front." Halder lost his temper and said, "I have that, my Führer. But out there brave riflemen and lieutenants are falling in the thousands as senseless victims, simply because their leaders may not execute the only possible decision and their hands are tied!" Hitler stared at Halder for a moment and then screamed, "What do you want, Herr Halder, you who only, and in the First World War too, sat on the same revolving stool, telling me about the troops, you, who have never once worn the black wound badge?!"[49]

After that episode, everyone in Halder's circle believed that he would have to resign; Heusinger actually advised him to do so.[50] In fact, although Halder recognized the hopelessness of his position, the final break did not come until a month later. Keitel dropped hints when he spoke to Halder about List on September 9, to the effect that Hitler was considering several personnel changes in the high command and that Halder might be one of those who would lose his position.[51] By September 17 Halder already knew that he would be going in less than a week.[52] Finally, on September 24, at the end of the normal midday briefing, Hitler and Halder parted company. The Führer said that Halder's nerves were used up and also that his own nerves had suffered from their confrontations. Halder listened silently, then got up and left, saying only that he would announce his departure.[53] An emotional scene followed at "Mauerwald" late that afternoon. The officers of the General Staff gathered under a tree outside the Operations Branch. Halder came over to the group, slowly, looking gray. He did not say much; he was nearly overcome by his feelings. After his short speech, in which he presumably expressed his gratitude and pride to the assembled officers, he left the headquarters.[54]

Ironically, in dismissing Halder, Hitler got rid of one of his most fundamentally optimistic military leaders. Even at this late date, Halder was unable to grasp the seriousness of Germany's position. In a letter of September 21 to the commander of Army Group North, Field Marshal Georg von Küchler, Halder wrote, "The numerical superiority of the Russians is a fact that we will continue to face, despite the lack of personnel on his side that is gradually becoming discernible. It will be balanced out through the high value of the German soldier."[55] He expressed similar sentiments to Weizsäcker a week after his dismissal, although he also admitted that the threat from the west concerned him.[56] Most incredibly, he maintained an unrealistic view even after Germany went down in defeat. Perhaps the most damning indictment comes from a letter he wrote six years after the war ended: "The question [put by an American historian], of when the last war had to be seen as lost, makes no sense. A war is a political act and can be militarily hopeless for the longest time while it still offers political chances. Such chances can even come up unexpectedly, as the Seven Years' War [1756–63] proved. So the correct answer remains: a war is only lost when one gives up."[57] Here Halder applied eighteenth-century strategic principles to a modern mass war in exactly the way that Hitler himself did. Thus, despite his differences with Halder, the Führer could hardly have asked for a more like-minded chief of staff. Had the two men been able to work together, there can be little doubt that Halder would have carried on in his post to the bitter end.[58]

Halder's successor, Kurt Zeitzler, was already on the scene when Halder left. His selection illustrates Hitler's desire for someone who would be

Kurt Zeitzler. (Courtesy Bundesarchiv, photo no. 185/118/14.)

Halder's antithesis. Before coming to the OKH, Zeitzler was chief of staff to the commander in chief west, Field Marshal Rundstedt. He was eleven years younger than Halder and relatively junior in rank, having become a brigadier general only that April. However, he was known personally to Hitler, in part for his role in defeating the Dieppe raid in August 1942; he was also a former subordinate of Jodl's and a close friend of Schmundt's.[59] According to Keitel, Schmundt was the one who suggested Zeitzler as Halder's replacement, although Göring may have done so as well.[60] In any case, Hitler sent Schmundt and Blumentritt to Paris on September 17 to bring Zeitzler to the Führer's headquarters in the Ukraine.[61] When Zeitzler arrived in the early morning hours of September 22, Hitler met with him immediately. At that point Zeitzler heard for the first time that Hitler was promoting him two grades and making him chief of the General Staff.[62]

Zeitzler was indeed a different sort of man from Halder. Whereas Halder was professorial and pessimistic, at least in Hitler's eyes, Zeitzler was confident and energetic to the point of impulsiveness. His nickname—"Kugelblitz," or "ball lightning"—says much for his leadership style.[63] When he first met with the officers of the General Staff, immediately after Halder's farewell address, he opened the meeting with a loud "Heil Hitler!" and went on from there to demand a new atmosphere in the headquarters. Organization, improvisation, and faith in the Führer would be the keys to victory, he said. He backed up that verbal message with a notice to all General Staff officers; it is worth quoting in detail:

> I demand that the General Staff officer radiate faith. Faith in our Führer, faith in our victory, faith in our work. He must radiate this faith to his colleagues, to his subordinates, to the troops with whom he comes in contact and to the troop commanders who seek him out. . . .
>
> I demand that the General Staff officer be hard. Hard on himself, hard on his colleagues, and hard—where it is necessary—on the troops. . . .
>
> I demand that the General Staff officer use every means at his disposal that will lead to victory. He must outgrow the traditional means and constantly devise and discover new ones. He must be a master and artist at improvisation. . . .
>
> I demand that the General Staff officer display an absolute and fanatical love of the truth in his reports and in the compilation of his General Staff materials. . . . Some people seek, through false representations, to force the command to make a decision that they want but which is wrong for the command as a whole. I will take action against such calculated reports on the part of General Staff officers with the strongest means possible. . . .
>
> I demand that the General Staff officer be the truest and most reliable

assistant—I emphasize the word "assistant"—to his Führer, chief of the General Staff, branch chief, or commander.[64]

From this statement the reasons for Zeitzler's rise become obvious. His emphasis on the importance of will as well as his overt allegiance to Hitler made him the Führer's favorite, at least for a while.

Zeitzler's elevation had a noticeable effect on the atmosphere in the General Staff. His enjoinder to the staff corps was not just a collection of empty words, meant to impress the Führer. Zeitzler had the reputation of being a "Nazi general" even before he arrived at "Mauerwald," and he did everything to strengthen that reputation once he got there.[65] He used the greeting "Heil Hitler!" at every opportunity and had a sign mounted in the Operations Branch that declared, "The German General Staff officer greets with 'Heil Hitler!'" Perhaps more important, his impulsiveness and passion for speed and brevity sometimes encouraged inexact and incomplete work. Moreover, Zeitzler brought with him a tendency to focus only upon his own narrow sphere; thus he would now fight to gain priority for the eastern front above all else.[66]

Zeitzler began his time in office with a series of changes to the General Staff's organization. He eliminated the offices of the assistant chiefs of staff for operations, intelligence, and military science within the first few weeks after he took up his post.[67] The reasons behind these changes remain unclear. Walter Görlitz wrote that Zeitzler merely wanted to simplify the General Staff's organization.[68] Erfurth contends that Zeitzler eliminated these positions because of the shortage of more senior General Staff officers, and that was in fact the reason that Zeitzler himself gave later on. Zeitzler added that he could spare these officers because the creation of the OKW theaters had lessened the workload for the General Staff.[69] Erfurth points out, however, that sixteen or seventeen separate branch chiefs now reported to the chief of the General Staff directly, and that such a workload was too much for any one man to handle.[70] In addition, on the intelligence side the new organization meant that the high command's view of the war became more splintered, since Foreign Armies West worked primarily with the Armed Forces Command Staff and there was no longer anyone in the General Staff to provide the chief with a unified assessment of Allied capabilities and intentions.[71]

In addition to cutting specific positions from the General Staff, Zeitzler also slashed staff strengths across the board. On October 1, 1942, he issued Fundamental Order No. 1, which called upon every staff section in the OKH and in every major command to reduce its strength by 10 percent and to justify every remaining position.[72] The rationale for this order was that too many officers were occupying staff positions while the front starved for leaders. The officers whom the staffs released were to take up positions as troop commanders. Six days later, Zeitzler issued a supplementary order that, among other things, exempted the Operations Branch and Foreign Armies East from the reductions.[73] Unfortunately, there is no record of the reactions that the or-der elicited within the General Staff. Without a doubt, however, Fundamen-tal Order No. 1 did two things: it increased the pressure on the already small staff sections, and it increased the command system's inherent structural bias against the support functions, since operations officers would certainly have been the last to go.

As radical as these orders might seem, they were of minor importance compared with the structural changes that Hitler made in the high command at the same time that he put Zeitzler into office. In a supplement to the order by which he took over command of the army the previous December, the Führer now assumed direct authority over the chief of the Army Personnel Office.[74] At the same time he replaced Bodewin Keitel in that position with Schmundt, whom he also kept on as his Wehrmacht adjutant.[75] Finally, he at-tempted to give Schmundt control over General Staff officer affairs. Zeitzler apparently tried to oppose this last measure, but in the end he was only able to negotiate for a say in those officers' postings.[76] On November 15, 1942, Zeitzler transferred the corresponding sections of the General Staff's Central Branch over to the P3 Branch of the Army Personnel Office.[77]

These organizational changes coincided with a fundamental shift in the personnel policies within the army, especially those concerning officer recruit-ing and promotion. In part this shift had to come about, simply because the old system could not function under the strain to which the war exposed it. The army had entered the war with approximately 89,000 officers; by October 1, 1942, that number had risen to well over 180,000, and in the meantime thou-sands of officers had become casualties. One result was, naturally enough, ac-celerated promotion: time-in-grade as a captain decreased 40 percent between September 1939 and April 1942, while the total time required to reach the rank of major dropped 61 percent.[78] In addition, the army had to bring in thousands of new officers. In both promotions and recruiting, the huge demand forced the army to be less choosy than it had been in the past.

That fact dovetailed exactly with Hitler's—and Schmundt's—wish to force a change in the nature of the officer corps. Under their direction, the se-niority principle fell more and more into the background as a criterion for pro-motion; performance in a duty position, and especially at the front, became the most important consideration. The change was gradual. New personnel regu-lations had come into force in February and June 1942, but they had little ef-fect until Führer Orders of October 4 and November 4 strengthened them. From then on, officers who performed well in combat would receive promo-tions more quickly, while those who occupied positions away from the front would be promoted according to the old system of time-in-grade and seniority. The new system allowed men such as Erwin Rommel, Friedrich Paulus, and Walter Model to receive army commands in their early fifties, while most officers of that station were fifty-five or older.[79] Likewise, at Schmundt's

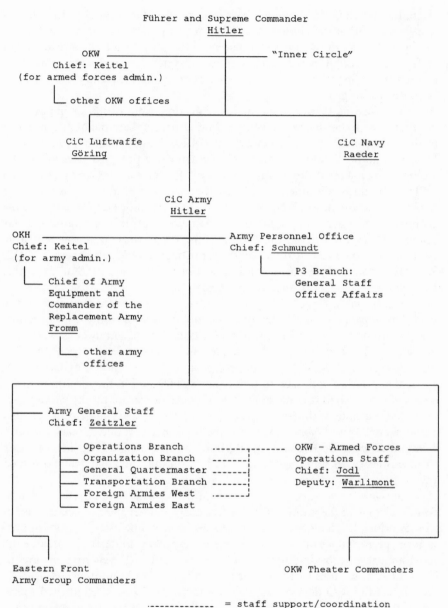

Figure 5. The German high command, December 1942, showing the effective split between the OKH and the OKW; a simplified diagram.

suggestion Hitler agreed to drop the long-standing requirement that officer candidates possess a secondary education, since it did not agree with the National Socialist emphasis on equality and achievement (the *Leistungsprinzip,* or "achievement principle"). From this point forward, any senior German enlisted man who could demonstrate character and effectiveness in front of the enemy would have the right to become an officer.[80]

Not all of Hitler's and Schmundt's ideas produced immediate results. Hitler emphasized that "there is only one officer corps."[81] That meant, for example, that he wanted to eliminate the distinctions that set the General Staff apart from the rest of the officers, including the carmine stripe that ran down the pants leg of the General Staff uniform. Military institutions are conservative by nature, however, and the German officer corps was no exception. Hitler knew, first, that the General Staff would oppose such measures and, second, that he could afford to let their status symbols remain in place for the moment, so he decided to bide his time. He and Schmundt also had to compromise on the promotion issue, however strict their regulations might seem. Since General Staff officers did not command troops, they stood to suffer under the new system, and there were never enough of them to allow for frequent rotation between line and staff positions. The Personnel Office therefore put measures into place to ensure that members of the General Staff would receive promotions on a more rapid basis than other noncombat officers.[82]

All the same, the changes that took place that autumn were real and significant, especially because of their connections to ideology. Schmundt was an excellent assistant to Hitler in this sphere because he shared the Führer's attitudes and gave substance to his often rather vague ideas.[83] Keitel, too, took many steps on his own in Hitler's interest. National Socialist principles were key elements in these men's program, above and beyond any emphasis on equality and performance at the front. Keitel had already released a decree on March 2, 1942, stating that the war effort required much closer cooperation and collaboration between the Wehrmacht and the Party; full trust and an exchange of ideas were necessary, he wrote.[84] On October 10 the Personnel Office issued an order declaring that an officer's views toward Jewry were a "decisive part of the officer's National Socialist attitude."[85] Hitler also insisted that adherence to Nazi ideals would be a prerequisite for posting into a troop command, which was in turn, of course, necessary to achieve rapid promotion.[86] Furthermore, since nominations from the front were to steer personnel policy to such an extent, Schmundt established the position of senior adjutant in each headquarters from division level up. These men would handle personnel matters, and National Socialist beliefs played a central role in their selection.[87]

The true extent of Nazism's penetration into the General Staff at this point is difficult to gauge. The postwar memoirs are full of anecdotes, humorous and otherwise, that illustrate the distance that supposedly separated many General Staff officers from the Nazi Party. Leyen wrote that many officers summed up their attitude toward politics with the statement "Thank God we have nothing to do with that business."[88] He also credited André François-Poncet, the prewar French ambassador to Germany, with saying that there were three characteristics common to the Germans: honesty, intelligence, and National Socialist convictions. No German possessed all three, the saying continued: he who was honest and intelligent was no National Socialist, he who was honest and a National Socialist was not intelligent, and he who was intelligent and a National Socialist was not honest. But, Leyen points out, this view was overly simplistic. His own superior in the Personnel Office combined all three characteristics. When Leyen asked him, after the war, how he could have done so, he responded that he simply could not believe that Germany's leaders would lie so incessantly.[89] That answer might not be a perfect or all-inclusive one, but it certainly indicates the dilemma that so many Germans in and out of the military faced. They wanted to believe in National Socialism, they shared many of its values and goals, and they were not prepared to question those elements of the Nazis' program with which they disagreed.

In any case, one thing is sure: National Socialism was gaining ground in the officer corps as a whole and gradually tearing away at the traditional position of the General Staff. Any officer who wanted to get ahead had to demonstrate, on paper at least, that he was a good National Socialist. If there were still ways around that, and if the officers' personnel records are not a perfect indication of their underlying beliefs, as Leyen maintains, the point remains that National Socialist principles were becoming the dominant force in the officers' careers.[90] If we cannot say exactly what percentage of officers remained resistant to those principles, we can say that it was small and that its influence was shrinking steadily.

Zeitzler helped the advance of National Socialism considerably. He was especially interested in the emphasis on frontline duty, since that principle matched his own dynamism. In addition, of course, he was a fervent supporter of Hitler. For these reasons and because of his enthusiastic service under Jodl earlier on, Keitel and Jodl both hoped for close collaboration with the new chief of the General Staff.[91] Hitler also believed he was getting an officer who would prove more cooperative than Halder had been. For all of his faith in the Führer, however, Zeitzler was not simply a yes-man, and his narrow focus ensured that he would fight anyone who tried to pull resources away from "his" front or intrude upon "his" sphere. According to Zeitzler, he had to fight off several attempts by the OKW to reorganize the General Staff, as when, for example, the OKW tried to take the Foreign Armies branches away and put them under the Foreign- and Counterintelligence Office.[92] In general one must treat Zeitzler's statements—all of which date from after the war—skeptically. His accounts are full of courageous confrontations with Hitler, the OKW, and others in the Nazi regime. He conveniently forgot to mention such things as his pro-Nazi memo-randum to the General Staff. One cannot take others' criticisms of him at face value; he was not a popular man. But his loyalties were clear.

When he accepted his office, Zeitzler knew that influence with Hitler would be the key to success. He also knew that the Führer believed in him, and, like Halder before him, he thought that he could make Hitler see reason. He was highly distrustful of Keitel, Jodl, and the others in Hitler's circle; he con-sidered them to be sycophants who would isolate him if he did not follow their lead.[93] He was also aware, however, that Keitel and Jodl were personae non gratae with their leader at the moment. Thus Zeitzler had a window of oppor-tunity in which to gain some independence. He arranged to precede Jodl in the midday briefing, and he began to appear regularly at the evening briefings as well.[94] He even tried, with some success, to brief Hitler alone in the evenings on events on the eastern front, so that the members of the "inner circle" would not be able to exercise any influence.[95] From the standpoint of the men in the OKW, Zeitzler had shut them out of any role in the east whatsoever.[96]

Although the new chief of the General Staff might well have viewed his rivals' exclusion as a victory—and with some justification—his actions did not bode well for the unity of the high command. In fact, the final split be-tween the OKW and the OKH dates from the autumn of 1942. Up until this point, both staffs had kept themselves informed of broad developments in the war. A section of the General Staff's Operations Branch had devoted itself solely to monitoring events in the OKW theaters, and Halder had also re-ceived reports personally from officers whose duties gave them insights into those areas.[97] In addition, Hitler had been issuing his operational orders for the east through the Armed Forces Command Staff to the Army General Staff, which then modified them and sent them on to the army groups.[98] After Zeitzler took over, however, Hitler only used the Command Staff to issue or-ders that applied to the OKW theaters or—in increasingly rare cases—to the war as a whole, while he sent his orders for the east directly to the army group headquarters, using the General Staff as the issuing agency.[99] From this point forward, no single organization could pretend to control the army on all fronts. The divide in the high command was complete, and just when the need for unity was becoming greatest.

DEFEAT AND REACTION

The last quarter of 1942 would see the failure of Hitler's "strategy" for the year. In addition, it would mark the end of the time in which Germany could concentrate on one land front to the near exclusion of all others. On October 23 the British under Field Marshal Montgomery attacked at El Alamein, and within twelve days the remnants of the German Panzerarmee Afrika were streaming to the west, despite Hitler's attempts to make Rommel hold. On November 8 the British and Americans landed troops in northwest Africa and began to advance eastward to trap the Germans between themselves and Montgomery's force. Less than two weeks later, on November 19, the Soviets launched their own offensive north and south of Stalingrad. They broke through the weak Romanian forces on the flanks, and within four days they had surrounded parts of two armies plus support troops.

Even before this string of calamities began, the high command had been casting about for ways to deal with the worsening situation. On October 14 Hitler issued Operations Order No. 1, in which he stated that the campaign had been concluded except for some operations still under way—meaning those in the Caucasus and Stalingrad. He called on the rest of the eastern army to prepare winter positions, which he described in excruciating detail, and he informed them that he would not allow any retreats or evasive maneuvers. Every commander, he continued, would be personally responsible to him for the "unconditional execution" of those orders. Hitler was convinced that the halt orders of the previous winter, which he had issued under desperate circumstances, were now the correct operational doctrine for all defensive situations.[100] Zeitzler backed up that order with a supplement on October 23. He repeated Hitler's call for resistance to the last man and the last bullet, but he reassured the army that "the Russian is at this time hardly in a position to begin a large offensive with long-range goals."[101] Obviously, the German intelligence apparatus was not working well.[102]

One of the Germans' highest priorities was to get more men to the front, and here they hit upon a disastrous solution. A study by the Organization Branch and the General Army Office showed that the army had reached its peak strength and from this point forward would not be able to make up its losses. When Zeitzler briefed Hitler on the study, the latter rejected it and offered Zeitzler two hundred thousand troops out of the Luftwaffe. Göring intervened, however; he said he did not want his National Socialist youths going to the reactionary army. He instead offered to form ten so-called Luftwaffe Field Divisions. The army would have to equip these divisions, but the Luftwaffe would provide all the personnel, including officers. This measure not only came at the cost of the army, which needed both the manpower and the equipment, but also spelled certain doom for the inexperienced Luftwaffe personnel who would now have to fight as infantry, without proper training or leadership. Lieutenant Colonel Burkhart Müller-Hillebrand, then chief of the Organization Branch, thought this idea so outrageous that he protested strenuously, in writing and verbally, until Zeitzler finally sacked him at the end of October.[103] Enemy pressure and the shortage of resources were beginning to take their toll even within the General Staff itself.

Now the split between the OKW and the OKH began to create real problems in the direction of the war. In mid-October Zeitzler asked for the first time that Hitler transfer additional units from west to east; Engel relates that he and Schmundt had to laugh, because when Zeitzler had been chief of staff to the commander in chief west he had always presented exactly the opposite request.[104] Developments in Africa as well as Hitler's concerns about the west made such transfers increasingly unlikely, in any case. After the Allies landed in Algeria and Morocco, Hitler ordered the occupation of the remainder of France and then decided to reinforce his army in Africa; by the end of the year he would send fifty thousand German and eighteen thousand Italian troops there, with significant amounts of equipment and air support. Jodl, meanwhile, finding himself excluded from decisions concerning the eastern front, began to lobby exclusively for the other theaters.

From this point forward two factors would dominate the Germans' war effort: an inexorable strategic squeeze as their enemies gained strength, and conflict within their own command apparatus. The relative importance of these two factors to the overall situation is something that must remain in the foreground. Barring some absolute miracle, the Germans could no longer win the war. From that standpoint, then, the command apparatus was completely irrelevant. No matter how well or poorly organized it was, it could not change the situation in any fundamental sense. Its organizational evolution and performance during the remainder of the war remain of interest, however, for two reasons. First, they provide a window into the National Socialist state; an examination of the high command will reveal the growing power of the Nazi Party. And second, the performance of the high command, although it could not affect the basic outcome of the war, is an essential element in explaining the war's nature and length after 1942.

10

A Command Divided Against Itself, January 1943 to July 1944

In his Order of the Day for January 1, 1943, Hitler reassured his troops: "The year 1943 will perhaps be difficult," he wrote, "but surely no more difficult than those past."[1] He promised them better equipment and more munitions, and he asked them to have faith in final victory. Many soldiers still believed him, but their faith was misplaced. In 1943 the Allies would begin to bring their full strength to bear against the Axis. As the disparity in the two sides' capabilities became more and more apparent, the Germans would begin a desperate scramble to come up with the forces they needed to win or—more realistically—to keep from losing. That effort suffered, however, from the organizational weaknesses in the high command, as well as from a simple lack of means. The Germans had missed the chance to unify their command system, and now the divisions within it became a serious obstacle to sound staff work, thus making a bad situation even worse.

LEAD-UP TO KURSK: THE BLIND LEADING THE HOBBLED

Hitler's confident words notwithstanding, New Year's 1943 can have brought little cheer to the members of the German high command. On the ground, they still controlled nearly as much territory as they had a year before, but their prospects were far worse. The second campaign in the east, upon which they had placed so much hope, had failed. The Soviets were on the offensive again, and if the German troops were better prepared for winter combat, their opponents were stronger, better equipped, and more capable than they had been a year before. In Africa the Wehrmacht had beaten the British and Americans to Tunisia, but the situation there did not look hopeful; supplying that force and Rommel's army in Libya was already proving difficult in the face of Allied aerial and naval interdiction.[2] The Germans faced a two-front war in the coming year, and although they controlled far greater resources than they had in the First World War, those resources still could not match those of their enemies.

In one respect the situation in January 1943 was much the same as in January 1942: the leading members of the high command still viewed their position unrealistically. Hitler's New Year's Order of the Day is one clue to their thinking. Another is the study by Warlimont and his staff that Jodl presented on December 12, 1942: "Overview of the Strategic Situation."[3] This study offered a mostly realistic, accurate assessment of the Allies' situation, but with an evaluation of Germany's prospects that bordered on the fantastic. Even though the German 1942 offensive in the east had failed badly—by the time the study appeared, the Soviets had already encircled Stalingrad—Jodl and Warlimont called for the Wehrmacht to renew its offensive in the east at the earliest possible moment, with the same goals as in the previous summer![4] The economic resources of the Caucasus, they said, would be the key to victory, along with the U-boat campaign. The study stipulated that Germany must hold North Africa as a glacis for Europe. If the Allies took it, they would next attack in the Balkans, so the defenses there would have to be brought up to strength immediately, just in case. All in all, the document, which met with Hitler's approval, displayed an attitude that would dominate the high command's military planning for the remainder of the war: great emphasis on "must" without much explanation of "how."[5]

Indeed, the "how" was becoming an increasingly difficult question. The Soviet offensives had all but eliminated the armies of Germany's allies, which had numbered half a million. Total German losses—killed, maimed, missing, and sick—for 1942 totaled over 1.9 million men.[6] Tens of thousands more would join the lists in the first two months of 1943. In the east, the Soviet winter offensive that began on December 16, 1942, forced the Germans to abort a relief operation aimed at the Stalingrad pocket. On February 2 the last resistance there ceased, and over 200,000 men vanished from the German rolls. In the meantime, the Wehrmacht had had to give up nearly all its gains in the Caucasus, and additional Soviet thrusts farther north had taken large areas west of the Donetz River. In Tunisia an attempt to break through the Allied lines in mid-February failed. Warlimont had visited the theater the week before and described the German position there as "a house of cards," mostly because of the shortage of forces and supplies.[7] From this point on, the situation there and in Libya, where the Germans were trying to slow Montgomery's advance, would deteriorate steadily.

By late winter 1943 Hitler had had to abandon any thought of resuming the offensive in the Caucasus that summer, partly because the Wehrmacht simply did not have the resources to carry it out and partly because of the threat of an Allied invasion of western or southern Europe. Instead, he opted for a more limited mission. Manstein was in the process of stopping the Soviet winter offensive with a series of counterstrokes; that impressed Hitler. At the same time, a planned shortening of a portion of Army Group Center's line promised to free up some units. Instead of forming a central reserve to counter any Soviet offensive, which was Zeitzler's suggestion, Hitler decided upon a spoiling attack, à la Manstein, right at the end of the spring *rasputitsa.* He would direct Army Groups Center and South to pinch off a large salient west of the city of Kursk; the attack would be code-named *Zitadelle (Citadel).*[8] If it succeeded, the army could form a more defensible front and weaken the Soviets, thus opening up an opportunity to pull some mobile units out of the line and send them west to repel any invasion.[9]

On March 13 Hitler released Operations Order No. 5, in which he stated his intentions. He wanted to seize the initiative as soon as the ground dried, before the Soviets could launch their own offensive.[10] However, the operation ran into a series of snags. Because of the weather and various other considerations, the earliest possible attack date fell in late April. As that date approached, the generals involved began to bicker. General Walter Model, commander of Army Group Center's thrust, wanted to wait until June, when new tanks would be available. Manstein, commander of the southern thrust, warned that the delay would benefit the Soviets more than the Wehrmacht, and Zeitzler agreed. Guderian tried to talk Hitler into canceling the operation entirely. Hitler decided not to decide, although in practical terms that meant a postponement. For weeks the debate continued while the Führer waffled. On June 18 the Armed Forces Command Staff recommended abandoning the operation and using the forces thus freed to form two strong central reserves.[11] Hitler rejected the idea and finally set July 5 as the start date for the operation. By that time, though, the situation had changed dramatically. Not only had the Soviets had time to prepare for the German attack, but events had been moving forward on other fronts as well.

In North Africa the German efforts were faltering, both because of Allied action and also from disputes with their erstwhile allies and within their own hierarchy. The command system in the theater had been a mess at the start, and it had not improved with age. In late January 1943, for example, the Comando Supremo, which still held nominal authority in the theater, sent Rommel an order from Mussolini, in which the Duce ordered that the current withdrawal in Libya be carried out as slowly as possible, in order to win time in which to build up more forces. The Italian headquarters also sent a copy to the OKW via the German liaison officer, Rintelen, with the request that the OKW send an identical order to Rommel as well; the Italians knew how uncooperative he could be. The OKW responded, through the commander in chief south (Field Marshal Albert Kesselring), with its own ideas on how to fight the battle, and it also said that it did not feel it should be sending orders direct to Rommel but only recommendations through the Comando Supremo.[12] Three weeks later a dispute arose between the Italians and Kesselring; the former wanted to reduce the size of Kesselring's liaison staff with their headquarters, but Kesselring wanted to make sure that his hosts could not send out a single order pertaining to North Africa without his agreement.[13] The two parties finally settled that issue themselves, but in the meantime tensions had erupted again between the Italians and Rommel. In late February the Comando Supremo asked the OKW to find employment elsewhere for the Desert Fox, and Hitler decided to go along with their request, both for political reasons and because Rommel's assessments of the situation in Tunisia were growing too pessimistic.[14]

With or without Rommel, the Germans' days in North Africa were numbered. The Axis simply could not get the required quantities of supplies across the Mediterranean. By May 13 the fighting in Tunisia was over, and more than 275,000 Axis prisoners fell into Allied hands. Hitler was shocked; he had apparently never accepted the possibility of defeat in the theater. Even before Tunisia fell, however, the question arose: Where would the Allies strike next? The most likely targets seemed to be Sicily, Sardinia, and Corsica in the western Mediterranean and the Peloponnesus and Dodecanese in the east. On May 12 the Armed Forces Command Staff sent out an order to all the relevant commands to strengthen the defenses in those areas, with priority going to Sardinia and the Peloponnesus.[15] Between then and early July, not much changed in the German plans, although the OKW did begin to see Sicily and Sardinia as the most likely initial targets, with a landing in Greece to follow. A landing on the Italian mainland struck them as unlikely, since Italy would be much easier for the Axis to reinforce.[16]

Whatever the western Allies' plans, the Germans faced a problem: there were not enough resources to go around. The high command embarked upon a series of partial, stopgap solutions, a kind of management-by-crisis system in which the operational hot spot of the moment received priority while the other theaters went short. At the beginning of February the General Staff's Organization Branch presented its plan for meeting the army's personnel and material requirements up until the coming autumn. The plan called for the reestablishment of the 6th Army, which had disappeared at Stalingrad, with fourteen 3,000-man "battle groups" as well as six full divisions (most of them in the west at that point) by April 1. Along with the formation or rebuilding of other divisions in the west, the plan also called for units to be formed in, or sent to, Russia, North Africa, the Balkans, and Norway. The strain on the command was evident, however; the plan made frequent use of phrases such as "as soon as possible," "as the situation allows," and "within the limits of the possible."[17]

With the resource situation worsening, the long-standing rivalry between the General Staff and the OKW took on new meaning and form, as the two staffs tried to balance requirements in the east with those in the OKW theaters, especially Africa and the Mediterranean. There were frequent disputes over force allocations or supply shipments, and in many cases Hitler had to adjudicate. In late February, for instance, the commander in chief west, Rundstedt, complained to the OKW that the General Staff had ordered a division to move out for the east on April 3; he said that the unit was not yet ready for combat in Russia. The Armed Forces Command Staff then reminded the General Staff that, in accordance with the Führer's policy, only the Command Staff could determine departure dates for units in the OKW theaters. Finally the problem went to Hitler, after which the OKW notified the General Staff that the division would be available on April 4—one day later than the General Staff's original target date.[18] Such were the quarrels that were taking up an increasing amount of the staffs' time.

Hitler could have simplified the structure and so avoided these disputes to a large extent, but instead he added a new wrinkle. He wanted to bring his beloved and invaluable armored forces back up to strength. Not only were they numerically weak from the battles of the past two years, but their opponents' equipment, especially on the Soviet side, now outclassed them. To deal with those problems he appointed Lieutenant General Guderian to a new position as "inspector general of armored troops" on February 28, 1943. Guderian had been in Hitler's eye for years; he was one of Germany's foremost experts in armored warfare. Schmundt also reminded the Führer that Guderian, whom Hitler had relieved over a year before, was "one of his [Hitler's] truest followers among the generals."[19] (Even Goebbels, who did not generally hold army officers in high esteem, liked Guderian, whom he believed was "certainly an ardent and unquestioning disciple of the Führer.")[20] According to his new duty instructions, Guderian would be directly subordinate to Hitler, not to Keitel, Fromm, or Zeitzler, although he would have to "coordinate" with the chief of the General Staff. The Führer gave Guderian full authority to direct vehicle design, procurement, and allocation, as well as doctrine and training for all armored and motorized units, according to Hitler's instructions.[21]

Later assessments of Guderian's role vary. On the one hand, Guderian himself claimed that he did a sterling job, and he criticized other military figures for failing to cooperate with him, but his opinion is open to question.[22] In the opposing camp, a number of officers criticized him for *his* lack of cooperation. Moreover, they held that the creation of yet another entirely independent command element under Hitler contributed to a progressive disorganization of the command system.[23] The truth is that nearly everyone had a hand in creating friction and strife. Guderian locked horns with Fromm, Zeitzler, Jodl, and anyone else whose sphere appeared to overlap with his.[24] At one point later in 1943, for example, the Organization Branch had to ask Guderian to stop sending suggestions direct to units but to work through the branch.[25] The effect of such disputes is difficult to pin down, but one thing is certain: there was now one more officer who had direct access to Hitler, an officer who would not hesitate to offer advice on any subject,

Heinz Guderian. (Courtesy National Archives, photo no. 242-GAP-101-G-2)

including the conduct of operations, and who also added his voice to the debates over resource allocation.

Those debates took on new urgency because of the delays in the start of Operation *Citadel*. By late spring, German intelligence was reporting indications that the Allies would move soon against Europe's southern flank; Hitler's plan to win a quick victory in the east and then move units to parry the Allied attack looked increasingly risky. The OKW prepared plans—code-named *Alarich* and *Konstantin*, respectively—to occupy Italy and the Balkans if the Italian government and army collapsed, as Hitler strongly suspected they would. In May and June the Germans began moving divisions into Italy, ostensibly to help defend it, but if necessary to take it over. However, the Führer had no intention of pulling forces out of the east for that purpose; the divisions that went to Italy came primarily from the west, which was alarmingly understrength already. Only after the completion of *Citadel* or in a dire emergency would Hitler transfer units from the east to one of the OKW theaters, even though there are indications that the OKW was planning on several eastern divisions to form its reserve.[26]

Citadel went forward on July 5, 1943. It ran into strong Soviet opposition immediately; the Red Army had been preparing for weeks. Progress was slow for the first few days, then virtually nonexistent. On July 12 the Soviets launched their own counteroffensive on the flank of the Germans' northern pincer, and the next day Hitler announced that he had decided to cancel *Citadel* entirely. The decision came too late to be of much immediate help to the west, however: the British and Americans had invaded Sicily on July 10.

One setback followed another for the rest of the year. By mid-August the western Allies had taken Sicily, and while the battle there was under way, King Victor Emmanuel III removed Mussolini from power and had him arrested. Italy signed an armistice on September 3, and the Allies invaded the mainland the same day. The Germans promptly occupied the country, freed Mussolini, and allowed him to set up a Fascist regime in the north. Their only consolation lay in the fact that the Allies were unable to advance far through the easily defensible terrain.[27] Meanwhile, the British and Americans also stepped up their air campaign over the Reich; they devastated several cities, including Hamburg, where an estimated forty thousand people died in a series of raids at the end of July. And Admiral Karl Dönitz had to call off the U-boat campaign in the central Atlantic, which had looked so promising earlier in the year, after losses became prohibitive.[28] The effort to strangle Britain and prevent American forces from reaching Europe was at an end, at least for the moment.

In the east, the Germans proved unable to either predict or halt the Red Army's thrusts. On July 25 Gehlen confidently forecast that the Soviets would be satisfied with the local gains they were making in the counterstroke to *Citadel* and that they would rest up between September and November.[29] Two weeks later the Red Army attacked Army Groups Center and South; the expected mud season did not appear that year, and the Soviets continued their advance right through the autumn. By the time they stopped in December, they had pushed Army Group Center back to the Pripyat Marshes, breached the Dniepr River line, and cut off the Crimea. In places they had advanced over two hundred miles, and when the offensive was over, Germany had lost some of the most economically valuable areas of the Soviet Union. The unexpected success of the Soviet offensive threw Gehlen into a fit of pessimism in which he predicted that the entire eastern front could collapse.[30]

THE BATTLE FOR RESOURCES

Given the situation on the ground, the fact that the high command sank into a nearly constant state of crisis in the latter half of 1943 is hardly surprising. Conflicts over units, supplies, replacements, and equipment came to dominate the command's work as never before. Naturally the Germans continued to issue operational instructions, but these are hardly worth scrutinizing, since in this period they were mostly reactive and reflected a decision-making process in which Hitler was beginning to be almost the sole voice. The organizational issues show up more clearly in the succession of discussions, memorandums, reports, and orders having to do with force distribution and manpower procurement. Those pieces of evidence also point to an atmosphere of unreality and desperation that was growing in direct proportion to the threat to the Reich. In fact, Hitler and his subordinates were caught between two stools: the east and Italy both needed more resources, but the other theaters could not give any up without becoming even more vulnerable themselves. In that summer and autumn of 1943, Hitler and his advisers sent out a series of directives and orders in an effort to scrape together all available forces and place them where they would do the most good. At times, to judge from the records, the leaders' wishes seem to have changed almost daily.

In July the dominant trend in the flow of units was toward Italy and the Balkans. The question was: Who was to give up what units to whom? No command wanted to suffer a net loss, or even to dispatch a unit before a replacement was on hand. The complexity of the resulting negotiations would be difficult to exaggerate, as a single entry from the OKW war diary illustrates. On July 8 the OKW stated that the threat of an invasion in "a mountainous area" (such as the Balkans) called for the release of two mountain divisions, the 3d and the 5th, from the east. The General Staff wanted the 65th and 113th Infantry Divisions from the west in exchange, but the OKW had already addressed that idea in a briefing paper on June 29. The paper said that when the OKH had given up the 100th Jäger Division to the southeastern theater, the OKW had sent the 328th and 355th Infantry Divisions from the west, for which that theater was also to have received the 5th Mountain Division in exchange. The loss of the 65th and 113th would weaken the coastal defenses too much, the paper continued, because their replacement units either were untrained or had been assigned to *Alarich*. Moreover, the 3d and 5th Divisions were currently so weak that they would hardly be a fair exchange for the 65th and 113th. The diary goes on to indicate that negotiations continued throughout the first week of July, with each side trying to gain an advantage. The OKW was prepared to give up the 113th for the 5th (which the General Staff would first have to bring up to strength), but it wanted to move the 3d Mountain Division to the southeastern theater without providing a replacement. Finally, the OKW issued an order on July 8—for which the staff must have obtained Hitler's backing—that represented a compromise between the two sides' positions. Like most compromises, it satisfied no one completely.[31] In any case, the burden that this dispute created for the staffs is clear—and this was only one of many such conflicts.

In Hitler's midday briefing on July 25, Jodl presented his staff's plan for the division of forces up until autumn.[32] Jodl believed at that point that the forces in France were adequate; presumably, he expected no attack in that theater in the near future, since the Allies were heavily engaged in Sicily. He planned to transfer several divisions to the Italian theater, including, from the eastern front, the II SS Armored Corps with two or three divisions. He also addressed the status of units that were in, or intended for, Army Group E (Armed Forces Command Southeast), as well as an army group that was forming around Rommel's headquarters for possible use in the Balkans. Hitler commented that Jodl's plan looked as though it would work, and Jodl agreed, provided that the army could stabilize the eastern front. That was the point of contention for Kluge, commander of Army Group Center, with whom Hitler met the next day. Kluge was not at all pleased to hear that he would soon lose some of his best units. He argued that he needed them to fend off the Soviet counteroffensive that was gaining ground in the Orel salient north of Kursk, but he could not change Hitler's mind. "Nothing else is left to us," said the Führer; "I can only do something down there [in Italy] with really first-class units that, above all, are also politically reliable, Fascist units."[33]

Hitler remained determined to withdraw units from the east, even after the Soviets launched their main summer offensive on August 3. As the Soviets advanced, however, he began to cast around for alternatives. So did Zeitzler and the men under him. Schmundt had already told Fromm that officers would have to be culled out of the OKW and OKH organizations for service at the front, and the General Staff had also issued a basic order that directed all commands to give up 4 percent of their supply troops to bolster their frontline strength.[34] Jodl and his staff, meanwhile, as well as the OKW theater commanders, opposed any reduction in their forces, especially after the Allies landed in Italy on September 3.

The relationship between Zeitzler and Jodl now reached a new low as they competed with one another and with others—including Guderian, Keitel, Himmler, Göring, Dönitz, Speer, and various Party officials—for every new asset that became available or any existing unit that one headquarters wanted from another. New units, replacements, tanks, ammunition, and fuel were the objects of heated disputes. A single trainload of supplies might spark an argument that would continue, off and on, for days. The subordinate staffs became involved as well, especially those such as the General Quartermaster, which had to try to meet the conflicting demands of two sets of superiors. In nearly every case Hitler finally had to make the decision, since he was the only one at the top of the command structure, the only one with authority over each of the competing agencies.[35] Since everyone recognized that fact, they came to him first when they could, and he tended to side with whomever had offered the latest proposal. The conflicts became so serious that, on September 11, he had to issue an order regulating his conferences with Jodl and Zeitzler. From then on, both men had to be present whenever one of them wanted to discuss any measure that would affect the other's strength.[36] On a more personal level, Schmundt offered to mediate between the two men, so acrimonious had their correspondence become, but Zeitzler rejected the idea.[37] The two were not completely selfish in their actions; Jodl, especially, recognized the seriousness of the situation in the east. Still, their rivalry was beginning to overshadow any hope of collaboration.

Not every detail of the resource debates made its way into the records, but evidence of the debates' nature and pervasiveness is easy to find. For instance, Jodl and his staff frequently prepared force distribution studies of one kind or another, sometimes at Hitler's instigation and sometimes in support of some point that Jodl or Warlimont wanted to make to the Führer or to others in the high command. One of these, dated September 14, went to Zeitzler and his counterparts at the navy and Luftwaffe high commands, among others. On the cover letter Jodl wrote that the study "should correct the false opinion that forces have been withheld from the hard-fighting eastern army without good reason. The Führer has approved this assessment of the situation."[38]

Jodl may have been overstating his case, for Hitler was determined to reinforce the army in Russia. On September 1 the Führer ordered large personnel transfers from the OKW theaters to the east. Warlimont pointed out the imminence of an Allied attack in the west and the lack of reserves with which to meet it, but to no avail. Hitler seemed to reverse himself on September 23; after Jodl briefed him on the balance of forces, he ordered the formation of five divisions under Army Group D (commander in chief west), as well as the creation of a central reserve in the west. But on October 2 Hitler ordered a further set of transfers from west to east, since the earlier reinforcement had not been enough; now the Armed Forces Command Staff had to rework its force calculations yet again. At this point even the OKW appears to have recognized the need to give priority to the east. On October 4 it recommended that the forces in Italy pull back to the Apennines in order to release some units, and on both October 5 and 18 it suggested other formations that the east could have.[39]

By the end of October, however, the pendulum seems to have swung suddenly back toward the west. The OKW now argued that its forces in the Mediterranean needed to be at full strength, contrary to what the General Staff maintained, since the enemy forces there were fresh, unlike those on the eastern front. Foreign Armies West, meanwhile, pointed out that the current strength of German forces in France and the Low Countries offered the Allies no reason not to attack; indeed, the British and Americans now appeared to be preparing to do just that. Hitler reacted by ordering the reinforcement of the Channel coast.[40] He followed that up with Directive No. 51 on November 3, which stated in part:

> The danger in the east remains, but a greater danger is emerging in the west: the Anglo-Saxon landing! . . . That is why I can no longer accept the responsibility for the fact that the west is being further weakened in favor of the other theaters of war. . . . None of the units and formations stationed in the west and in Denmark . . . may be withdrawn for other fronts without my authorization. . . . All responsible parties will watch that time and manpower are not wasted in questions of jurisdiction.[41]

Within days the General Staff's Organization Branch was taking steps to implement the order by sending reinforcements to Army Group D.[42] As for Hitler's enjoinder to his command not to waste time on "questions of jurisdiction," he was fooling himself if he thought it would make any difference.

Meanwhile, efforts continued to get more men to the front. In late November and early December, Hitler and Zeitzler sent out a number of *Führerbefehle* and *Grundlegende Befehle* (Führer and basic orders) to that end. The first of these, which the Armed Forces Command Staff issued on November 27, introduced measures to increase the fighting strength of the combat troops.[43] Specifically, it pointed out the imbalance—as Hitler saw it—between the number of troops at the front and the number in the rear areas.[44] It called for the armed services and the Waffen-SS to combine duty positions, comb through their support services, simplify the system by which they rated men's fitness for duty, dismantle unnecessary projects, reduce the recovery time for wounded and sick men, and limit paperwork, with the goal of finding an additional one million men for frontline duty. (The results would be disappointing. Even though the Germans formed special battalions that conducted surprise raids on their own rear services, the bag reached only four hundred thousand.)[45] Zeitzler reissued Hitler's order as Basic Order No. 22 on December 5.[46] On that same day he also released Basic Order No. 20, which set up so-called Special Staffs *(Sonderstäbe)* to work within the OKH and at the army group level to comb out excess personnel.[47]

TRUST AND INFORMATION

On December 7 Zeitzler issued Basic Order No. 23, in cooperation with Guderian; this one dealt not with personnel but with tank losses.[48] The order required that each division commander submit a report to Zeitzler, with a copy to Guderian, for every lost armored vehicle. The report was to include, among other things, detailed reasons for the loss of the vehicle, the name of the person who gave the order to abandon it, the condition of the vehicle when abandoned, and the present whereabouts of the radios and weapons. On its face, the order is astonishing. Zeitzler's and Guderian's expectation that a commander could retrieve such information in the chaos of combat indicates a serious divorce from reality.

In a wider sense, Basic Order No. 23 is significant because it points to the growing atmosphere of mistrust between the high command and the commanders at the front, especially in the matter of reports and their connection to battlefield performance. This was not a new phenomenon. Halder told his staff on December 25, 1941, for example, to emphasize to the army group and army headquarters the need for truthfulness in their reports.[49] Zeitzler brought up the problem in his first order to the General Staff, and on November 7, 1942, he issued a basic order on the subject to all commands. It began: "The Führer has noticed that, despite *constant* instructions, reports are still being purposely colored and are not fully honest and true, and that they are also being passed on as is without examination."[50] It then went on, predictably, to demand that such practices cease.

The issue of accuracy in the reporting system leads in two directions. The first is related to Hitler's suspicion, as Halder expressed in his notes, that commanders were falsifying reports in order to avoid his instructions. Efforts to circumvent the Führer's wishes were not uncommon; since at least 1940, various people, including Halder and Jodl, had withheld information from Hitler or interpreted his orders in such a way as to achieve a particular result.[51] Warlimont wrote that the Command Staff could sometimes change the form or content of an order so as to give the commander on the spot some leeway; subordinate commands referred to these as "rubber orders," and certainly the commands would have had to doctor any corresponding reports.[52] Such *"Führen unter den Hand"* (roughly: "underhanded leadership") became more difficult, however, as Hitler's orders went into more detail, thus leaving his commanders less and less freedom of decision.[53] Demands for more accurate and detailed reports were simply the complement to Hitler's command style. His desire to keep a tight rein on his subordinates might also explain his order of March 23, 1943, in which he stipulated that no higher command could be prevented from reporting directly to him as supreme commander. Such reports would also go to the sender's next higher headquarters, so that it could add to the report as it saw fit, but that headquarters could not block the report.[54]

The other facet of the reporting problem, one that did become more common as the war went on, had less to do with resistance to the Führer and more with self-interest and competition. As the military situation worsened and operational and tactical orders became less realistic, the pressure on commanders rose. They knew that their superiors would hold them responsible for every setback; Zeitzler's order on armored vehicle losses was typical in that sense. That pressure was one of the negative sides of the *Führerprinzip,* and it encouraged commanders to exaggerate both the enemy's strength and losses. At the same time, they also knew that they could benefit by overstating their own weakness, since by so doing they could make their units'—and their own—feats of arms more impressive while at the same time obtaining higher levels of reinforcement and resupply. Competition from the Waffen-SS and the Luftwaffe, which Hitler looked upon as his elites, heightened the temptation at the upper levels of the hierarchy. Thus reports from different agencies on the same subject could vary widely.[55] In any case, whatever the reasoning behind it, inaccurate reporting cost the command system time and reduced its ability to make sound decisions.

Naturally the availability of reliable information is a prerequisite—or at least an advantage—in any decision-making process. In the case of the German high command, postwar reports from its former members have emphasized not the flaws in the reporting system but the shackles that they said Hitler placed upon it. According to their accounts, the Führer had a mania for secrecy that interfered with their ability to manage the war. The problem first became serious in January 1940, they claimed, after an officer carrying part of the plan for the German offensive in the west crash-landed in Belgium, thus compromising the operation. Hitler reacted by issuing Basic Order No. 1, otherwise known as the Secrecy Order. It stated in part, "No one . . . may learn more about any secret matter than he absolutely must for official reasons."[56] This was a reasonable and necessary measure of the sort common to all armies, but it became a handy catchall excuse for some officers. They complained that the order prevented them from finding out what was going on in other theaters or even in neighboring sectors of their own front. Zeitzler, for example, wrote that he surely would have received reinforcements from Rundstedt if the latter had known what the situation in the east really was. Further, he maintained that he and his staff could not know what was happening in the OKW theaters.[57]

At their best these arguments are highly exaggerated. The records are full of instances in which information flowed freely between commands. The officers at the top—Jodl and Zeitzler, especially—attended Hitler's briefings, and thus had the opportunity to learn about the situation in each others' theaters in depth; Hitler's order of September 11 made their attendance mandatory. At all levels there was, moreover, a great deal of informal discussion among General Staff officers, who, after all, still formed a tightly knit group within the Wehrmacht. And last but not least, official reports—such as the one that Jodl released on September 14—gave detailed information on every unit to all the command elements.

This is not to say that misconceptions and suspicions did not exist. One of the reasons that Jodl prepared his studies on unit strengths and dispositions was to combat the belief, apparently widespread in the eastern army, that there were large numbers of units in the OKW theaters that were essentially on vacation. "Fifty-three percent of the army is fighting in the east for the existence of the German people," ran one chestnut. "Forty-seven percent is standing around doing nothing." Another such comment: "In 1918 we lost the war because of the 'navy in being'; we will lose the present one because of the 'army in being.'"[58] Such sentiments existed mostly at the lower levels, however. The people who were in positions to influence policy had access to plenty of information. Their mutual antipathy and shortsightedness were the greater problems.

STRUCTURE, STRATEGY, AND IDEOLOGY

The structure of the high command exacerbated the conflicts that existed within it. The effects of the split between the east and the OKW theaters, in addition to the existence of so many agencies operating in parallel under Hitler, were coming home to roost. The Führer continued to follow the course of operations in minute detail and to think that he could control everything from his headquarters.[59] His twice-daily briefings covered the gamut, from political, economic, and strategic developments and intentions to tactical guidance, weapons capabilities, and the status of individual units (sometimes down to battalion level!). Efforts to fix the system and persuade the Führer to take on a more sensible role failed utterly. Manstein suggested in February 1943 that Hitler appoint a new commander in chief of the army, or at least a commander for the eastern front. Failing that, he said that the Führer should end the split between the OKH and the OKW by combining the military staffs under one chief. Hitler put Manstein off on every point, saying he did not know a single general to whom he could entrust so much responsibility.[60] Keitel made similar proposals that spring and received the same response, and the same thing happened to Zeitzler.[61] In October 1943 the Organization Branch went so far as to prepare a study and briefing for Zeitzler on his position within the command system as it existed at that point, in which the branch suggested possible changes that would give Zeitzler more authority, but all the work came to nought.[62]

For the Armed Forces Command Staff the split in the high command meant a heavier workload, as combat operations or the potential for them spread into more of the OKW theaters. By the end of April, there were forty-four agencies and commands under the OKW, including the commanders in chief west, southeast, and south; the Armed Forces commanders in the Netherlands, Norway, and Denmark; the military commander for Belgium and North France; an army headquarters in Finland; and the German generals with the high commands of the Romanian, Italian, and Slovakian armed forces.[63] Further, the command relationships within the theaters were becoming more complex rather than less. A supplement to Directive No. 51, for example, highlights the problem in the west. In this order Hitler forbade any unit transfers out of Denmark or the area controlled by the commander in chief west. However, he excepted the reserve divisions under the control of the Replacement Army commander and training units under the services and the Waffen-SS, and he said he would make decisions on a case-by-case basis on the armored units controlled by the inspector general of armored troops, the assault gun units under the Replacement Army commander, and units of the navy and Luftwaffe.[64] The increasing scope and complexity of the structure under the OKW meant that the volume of reporting traffic and orders expanded steadily, and the latter, especially, required more detail work than had been the case earlier. The constantly changing plans to transfer units or form new ones, along with the associated negotiations with other agencies, added to the strain. And, as ever, there were the "jurisdictional questions" that the Führer had said he wanted his staff elements to avoid. On October 27, for instance, the OKW sent out a notice to a slew of other agencies, including the General Staff, the Replacement Army commander, the Army Personnel Office, and the SS, saying that the Command Staff must draft or approve any order that affected the strength of the OKW theaters.[65]

Until midsummer 1943, the Command Staff was still attempting to do all that work with the same number of officers as in 1940. On July 24 Jodl finally approved Warlimont's request to expand the Army Operations, Quartermaster, and Intelligence Branches. Even after the expansion was complete, however, the staff was not generously manned; it contained fifty-two officers and officials, including twelve each in the Army Operations and Quartermaster Branches and four in the Intelligence Branch.[66] The Command Staff remained dependent upon various branches of the Army General Staff for support in such areas as intelligence and transportation.

While the staff's operational responsibilities expanded, its original role as a source of strategic guidance was fading away. One cannot help noting, however, that this was no great loss to the German war effort. Toward the end of 1943, in one of its increasingly rare forays into the strategic realm, the staff proved that it did not grasp the seriousness of Germany's position. On November 7 Jodl delivered an address to the regional Party bosses, the Gauleiter, using notes that the Command Staff prepared for him.[67] He opened by saying that he believed, in consideration of Hitler's Secrecy Order, that the political leaders needed the most complete information available, since they needed to

fight the rumors and pessimism that were spreading in the homeland as a result of enemy propaganda. "All the cowards are seeking a way out," he said,
"or, as they name it, a political solution." But he added: "Capitulation is the
end of the nation, the end of Germany."[68]

Jodl went on to give a talk that encompassed three main points: the most
important developments to date; the situation at present in each of the theaters, including the east; and the basis for trust in final victory. His descriptions of prior developments and of the current situation were, on the whole,
sober and accurate. In the last section, however, Hitler's foremost military adviser refused to acknowledge the significance of the information he had just
imparted. Although he characterized the situation as serious and said that he
reckoned on further crises, he built his faith, he said, on a number of points.
"At the summit," Jodl proclaimed, "stands the ethical and moral basis of our
struggle, which leaves its mark on the entire attitude of the German people
and makes the armed forces an absolutely reliable instrument in the hands of
our leadership."[69] He went on to contrast that ideological foundation with the
moral, political, and military disunity of Germany's enemies. The most important source of his faith, however, was the man who stood at the top of
Germany's command structure, the man who would lead the German people
into a bright future. Jodl closed by saying that "we will win, because we must
win—because otherwise world history will have lost its meaning."[70] If there is
one single moment that best demonstrates the power of ideology within the
high command of the Third Reich, Jodl's speech is surely it.

Still, reality does have a way of interfering with the most firmly held ide-
ologies at times. In order to maintain their Weltanschauung, Jodl and Hitler
both knew that they would have to find a way to defeat the Allied invasion in
the west. "There is no doubt at all," the Führer told Jodl on December 20,
"that the attack in the west will come in the spring. . . . When they attack in
the west, then that attack will decide the war. . . . When that attack is beaten
off, the story is over. Then we can take forces away again without delay."[71]
This was Hitler's strategy for 1944, in a nutshell. First he would have the army
hold in the east until the Anglo-American invasion failed. That would set the
western Allies back for the foreseeable future; in the meantime, the Wehrmacht would turn on and destroy the Soviets.[72]

The quality of the Germans' strategic calculations had obviously not improved after four years of war. Moreover, the instrument that Jodl thought
so reliable was crumbling at its edges. Industrial production was actually increasing, so armaments were still available, if not in the quantities the army
needed. Manpower was a major problem, however; the officer corps, especially, had suffered serious losses. All told, the Field Army was lacking eleven
thousand officers by mid-October, and Schmundt reported that the distinction between the officer and noncommissioned officer corps was becoming
blurred because the latter was merely serving as a preliminary stage for filling

the great gaps in the former.[73] On top of that concrete problem, moreover, there were signs that the army's will was beginning to waver. Schmundt noted as early as the end of March 1943 that, since the fall of Stalingrad, officers in the homeland were not displaying the proper degree of support for the military and political leadership.[74] Six months later he recorded the fact that the Soviets had "turned" several high-ranking officers whom they had captured. Those officers were now beaming propaganda to the Reich as the "National Committee 'Free Germany.'"[75]

In part as a reaction to these developments, the Germans further strengthened the ties between the army and the Nazi Party. Hitler demanded that the Wehrmacht employ only those generals who radiated faith and demonstrated their approval of the National Socialist Weltanschauung. He also emphasized that every officer must be a political educator.[76] Schmundt backed up such efforts with the publication of a pamphlet entitled *"Wofür kämpfen Wir"* ("What We Are Fighting For"). But the most significant step was the creation of the National Socialist leadership officers, a cadre of men whose main task would be to indoctrinate soldiers in National Socialist ideals, much as the Red Army's political commissars inculcated their men with Communist philosophy. The idea was an extension of earlier efforts to bring political education into the Wehrmacht on a more consistent basis. Schmundt's idea to create a corps of senior adjutants had not been a success. Those officers tended to be General Staff rejects, and too many people were aware of that fact for the corps to have much credibility. High rates of loss and the stress of combat at the lower levels also tended to interfere with political education. Many commanders simply felt that there were more important things to do.[77] The Party was not slow to recognize the army's "failure" and take advantage of it.

The first step was to create a National Socialist Leadership Staff at the top, in the OKW, with direct access to Hitler. Martin Bormann, head of the Party Chancellery, led the drive, in the process outmaneuvering both Keitel and the Party's semiofficial ideologue, Alfred Rosenberg. By the end of 1943, Keitel had to accept the Party's full participation in the selection and training of the new officers; this was the first time that it was able to intervene directly in Wehrmacht affairs.[78] Lieutenant General Hermann Reinecke took over as the head of the National Socialist Leadership Staff in the OKW on January 1, 1944, and work began to build an organization that would extend down to battalion level. By the beginning of February the OKH also had a National Socialist Leadership Staff, and on March 15 Lieutenant General Ferdinand Schörner took over as its head; he, too, reported directly to Hitler.[79] Schörner was one of the most rabid Nazis in the entire officer corps; in his first decree he stated that "wars of this size are decided neither by numerical nor by material considerations" and that "the political education of fanatical National Socialist soldiers" would be his organization's task.[80]

Despite Schörner's enthusiasm, the new program met with some skepticism in the lower levels of the army. Many officers believed that political education offered an essential tool to counterbalance the Allies' superior strength, but they apparently objected to the imposition of such education from above. Some troops referred to the program as "the Führer's Salvation Army."[81] Whatever its effect at the lower levels, though, the program was a sign that National Socialism was becoming ever more important within the military command structure. Loyalty to National Socialism, and especially to the person of Adolf Hitler, would be the basis for future command decisions; professional military skills would be secondary in importance.

DEFEATS IN THE EAST AND WEST

As the Germans grasped at political straws, the military situation was becoming more desperate. The Soviets continued to advance in a series of offensives that began in January 1944 and lasted right through the spring *rasputitsa*.[82] At the end of March, Hitler gave command of Army Group North Ukraine to Model and that of Army Group South Ukraine to Schörner, but even the efforts of two such blindly obedient commanders could not stop the Soviets.[83] By the time their offensives ran out of steam in mid-April, they had nearly reached the Carpathian Mountains and Poland in the south and had pushed the Germans one hundred miles back away from Leningrad in the north. German units had to occupy Hungary to keep its government from pulling out of the war. The Wehrmacht was holding well against the British and Americans in Italy, but the pressure on the forces there was heavy, especially after the western Allies staged a new landing at Anzio on January 22. And the air war over the Reich was draining resources away from the front; most of the Luftwaffe was already defending Germany, and there would come a point in 1944 after which half of all German artillery would be "at home pointing skyward."[84]

The serious threats in the east and south—especially the former—played the devil with the strategy that Hitler had decided upon for 1944. He was determined not to give up any ground in the east, even as he spoke of giving priority to the west. Therefore, he refused to allow his commanders on the eastern front to engage in withdrawals that could have conserved their strength. Instead he began to designate cities in the Soviets' path to be "fortresses," each of which he ordered to hold to the last, the idea being that they would tie down additional Soviet forces.[85] In the meantime, he kept funneling units to the east that should have gone to the OKW. Jodl, Zeitzler, and Guderian—as well as their staffs—continued to clash.[86] Hitler decided again and again in favor of the east, and the strain of such decisions was beginning to show. At times he tried to avoid responsibility for them; he would put them off, or shift blame for them onto someone else. At one point Major General

Walter Buhle, who was "chief of the Army Staff with the chief, OKW," challenged Hitler's priorities. "But when we take everything from the west!" Buhle protested. "I have hardly put something together when it is gone again!" "To whom are you saying that?" Hitler retorted. "I will not allow you to accuse me of always taking units away. On that you must speak with Zeitzler."[87]

At first the east's reinforcements consisted of newly formed units from the Reich, but in March Hitler approved transfers out of commander in chief west's area, including several infantry divisions, an entire SS armored corps, and several assault gun battalions. In exchange he ordered that the General Staff bring some units in the west up to strength, but the Organization Branch argued that this was impossible because of equipment shortages.[88] Then, at the end of the month, Zeitzler ordered the Transport Branch to prepare to transfer the 1st Mountain Division to Hungary to guard the passes through the Carpathian Mountains—this despite the fact that the division was nominally under control of the OKW. Jodl went to Hitler yet again. He explained that the 1st Mountain Division was absolutely the last unit that the OKW had at its disposal; every other formation was tied to a particular theater or front command. He gave the Führer yet another overview of the balance of forces and reminded him of the units that the OKW theaters had already lost. The two men agreed on a compromise, but, more important, Hitler tasked Jodl to prepare the most comprehensive report yet on the distribution of forces in the OKW theaters, to include their capabilities, lengths of front held, and mobility and personnel status, down to battalion level.[89] The report prompted Hitler, at long last, to allow the OKW to form a central reserve of units under its own control.

Because of that last-minute decision (it came, after all, less than six weeks before the Allies landed in Normandy) the Germans were able to build up their forces in the west to some extent. In fact, despite the extensive Allied aerial interdiction campaign, the Wehrmacht forces in the west actually narrowed the gap between their own strength and that of the invasion force before D-Day. However, their intelligence services failed them, and their dispositions gave the initiative to the Allies, who managed to secure a beachhead. After that, Allied air superiority and German logistical problems made the outcome predictable, for all the hard fighting that took place in the next two months.[90] Moreover, on June 22 the Soviets opened their summer offensive. They had fooled German intelligence once again; Gehlen and his colleagues believed that the Soviets would strike at Army Group North Ukraine, but instead they launched a gigantic pincer attack against Army Group Center.[91] Within twelve days, twenty-five German divisions—at least three hundred thousand men—disappeared, and for the moment the Germans possessed nothing to throw in front of the advancing Red Army. The Soviets only stopped in mid-July to bring up supplies and repair the transport net before pushing on; they had already advanced more than two hundred miles.

This was the point at which, all hindsight aside, anyone with knowledge of the situation and a modicum of intelligence would have been able to see that Germany had lost the war. Many people did. Rommel, who at that point was a field marshal commanding an army group in Normandy, even tried to warn Hitler; in a Teletype of July 15 he tried to make the Führer understand that there was no possibility of victory in the west, that soldiers were dying needlessly by the thousands every day, and he asked him to "draw the conclusions from this situation without delay."[92] Six weeks later, Kluge, by then commander in chief west, made a similar appeal. Hitler commented that it was "childish and naive" to expect reasonable terms for a political settlement under the circumstances. "Such moments can [only] arise when one is successful."[93] And despite the mental gymnastics that such a point of view demanded, Hitler still believed that success was possible—not just the success needed to strike a bargain, but that needed to win the war. Hitler still believed that his destiny was to lead the German people to victory and mastery over the earth. In fact, by the time Kluge wrote his appeal, the Führer's confidence was stronger than ever, because of an event that had occurred in the meantime. On July 20, 1944, Providence had spared him, seemingly, from certain death, saving him to complete his task. At the same time, the events of that day doomed Rommel, Kluge, and many others, and sent the high command into its final chaotic decline.

11
Collapse, July 1944 to May 1945

The last stage in the high command's descent into oblivion began on July 20, 1944. On that day, Colonel Claus Schenk Graf von Stauffenberg planted a bomb a few feet away from Adolf Hitler as he took part in his midday briefing. The Führer escaped the explosion with only minor injuries, and within the next few hours he came to the conclusion that his survival was an omen. As he said to Mussolini that afternoon, "After my miraculous escape from death today I am more than ever convinced that it is my fate to bring our common enterprise to a successful conclusion."[1] He would hold on to that conviction almost to the end. After the war, Hitler's surviving subordinates criticized him in the harshest possible terms for insisting that the Wehrmacht fight on against all hope. In fact, those same men actively supported that fight and thus helped to bring another full measure of destruction and pain down upon the German people. Germany's military leaders were determined to demonstrate their loyalty to the Führer, even as he second-guessed their every move and encouraged the Nazi Party to make further inroads into their sphere. The result was chaos. Ever-changing command arrangements and continuing competition for resources all but paralyzed the high command. Only the military's blind dedication to a lost cause allowed the machine to function at all.

THE AFTERMATH OF THE COUP ATTEMPT

The attempt on Hitler's life had immediate and grave consequences for the command system. Most of the principal conspirators were members of the General Staff. Hitler now had added reason to strike out against the institution, starting with its chief. He and Zeitzler had argued two days before the assassination attempt; Zeitzler had offered his resignation and then, when Hitler refused it, had reported sick. The Führer's first reaction was to declare that, from now on, no officer would be allowed to give up his post voluntarily.[2] Heusinger stood in for Zeitzler, on the theory that he would be back before long, but after the bomb attack Hitler no longer trusted him, so he placed him in the inactive reserve and began looking for a successor.[3] His first choice was Buhle, but Buhle had been injured in the bomb blast. To fill in for him while he recovered, Hitler chose Guderian, who had been unstinting in his criticism of Zeitzler and whose actions on July 20 indicated that he was not part of the conspiracy.[4]

Guderian presented himself after the war as a military genius and a staunch opponent of Hitler; he was perhaps the most successful of the Wehrmacht's former leaders at creating an anti-Nazi image for himself. His memoirs (recent editions of which are readily available in German bookstores) and other postwar writings are full of righteous indignation at the role that Hitler and the OKW played in the last months of the war. He wrote that he accepted this latest assignment because "I was ordered to," and because he would have thought himself a coward if he had not tried to save all the innocent civilians and brave soldiers in eastern Germany from the Russians.[5] There is barely a hint in any of his writings that Guderian might ever have been attracted to Nazism, while he implies again and again that he could have saved Germany if only Hitler and the OKW had listened to him. In fact the new chief of the General Staff was one of the Führer's most ardent admirers, even if the two did not always agree on military matters. Furthermore, Guderian shared the same strategic myopia, the same callous determination to fight to the last, as the other members of the high command.[6]

He also shared a desire to deal quickly with the July 20 conspirators. On August 2 Hitler ordered the formation of a "court of honor" to review the case against each army suspect and, if the evidence so warranted, dismiss him from the service and hand him over to a so-called People's Court. Keitel, whom Hitler assigned to set up the panel, named Rundstedt to head it; Guderian and four other officers filled it out.[7] Guderian claimed in his memoir that he did not want to serve on the court and that he tried to save as many men as he could. But in practically the same passage he condemned those who had taken part, and he added:

Naturally the question will be brought up again and again: What would have happened if the assassination attempt had succeeded? No one can say. Only one thing is certain: at the time a very large part of the German population still believed in Adolf Hitler and was convinced that the would-be assassins would have eliminated the only man who would still perhaps have been in a position to bring the war to a mild end. This was the odium with which the officer corps, the generals, and the General

Staff above all would have been burdened, during the war but also afterward. The hatred and the contempt of the people would have turned itself against the soldiers who, in the middle of a life-or-death struggle, had broken their word of honor and made the threatened ship of state leaderless through the murder of the head of state.[8]

The implication is that Guderian did not share those feelings, that he no longer believed in Adolf Hitler or in Germany's final victory. Even in his postwar writings, however, there is evidence to the contrary, and his actions in 1944 cast him in a very different light indeed. Here, for example, are excerpts from the order that he released to all General Staff officers on August 24, which did not appear in his memoir:

> The 20th of July is the darkest day in the history of the German General Staff.
>
> Through the treason of several individual General Staff officers, the German army, the entire Wehrmacht, yes, the whole greater German Reich has been led to the edge of ruin. . . .
>
> Do not let anyone surpass you in your loyalty to the Führer.
>
> No one may believe more fanatically in victory or radiate that belief more than you. . . .
>
> Be an example to others in your unconditional obedience.
>
> There is no future for the Reich without National Socialism.[9]

In addition to releasing this order, Guderian appointed a "National Socialist leadership officer with the chief of the General Staff"; Guderian's order stated that this officer, one Colonel Langmann, was directly subordinate to Guderian and acted on his behalf.[10] These were certainly not the acts or statements of a devoted anti-Nazi, and they provide the context for Guderian's behavior as chief of the General Staff. They also reflected the attitudes of most senior German officers, very few of whom had shown any inclination to join in the coup, at least until it had won.

Within the OKH itself, the investigation of the July 20 coup attempt had a chilling effect. The number of arrests eventually ran into the hundreds—no one knows the exact number—and included the families of the conspirators. The Nazis tortured their prisoners, "tried" them in a People's Court (actually the authorities often determined the sentences beforehand), and executed many of them, often by slow hanging.[11] Some conspirators, such as the general quartermaster, Wagner, killed themselves rather than submit to such an ordeal and run the risk of incriminating others. For those General Staff officers who remained free, the tension in the workplace was palpable. Often an officer's arrest or suicide would only become known when someone tried to call him and learned that he could "no longer be reached."[12] Those who remained found that relationships had become strained. Men who thought they might be under suspicion often avoided contact with their friends who seemed to be in the clear, in order to avoid tainting them. At the same time, officers who had been friends of the accused found that many of their colleagues shunned them.[13] The Gestapo controlled the headquarters complex; every man had to show identification simply to go to his own duty station. Luftwaffe Lieutenant General Werner Kreipe, chief of the Luftwaffe General Staff as of August 1, reported that the mood in the Army General Staff was "very depressed. . . . An open word is only still possible among old friends."[14] While the consequences are impossible to document exactly, the absence of some key officers and the breakdown in communications among the others, along with the heightened stress level, must have interfered with the staffs' work.

More concrete problems also demanded solutions in the immediate aftermath of the attack. For one thing, Guderian needed to fill some serious gaps in his staff. Heusinger was among the injured (and would soon come under suspicion of having known about the plot). Many other officers, including the chief of the Organization Branch, the general quartermaster, and the chief of army communications, were under arrest; their positions could not remain empty for long.[15] In the case of Heusinger's position, a replacement came on board quickly: Major General Walter Wenck took over as chief of the Operations Branch at the same time that Guderian took up his post. Within six weeks he and Guderian instituted a reorganization of the General Staff. They formed a "Command Group" *(Führungsgruppe)* that included the Operations, Organization, Foreign Armies East, and Fortifications Branches, "in order to place the entire operational apparatus in one hand."[16] Wenck took over as its chief; his role resembled that of the old assistant chief of staff for operations. Colonel Bogislaw von Bonin took over as chief of operations at that point.

As the empty slots in the OKH began to fill up, one less tractable problem remained: too many of the key staff officers were new to their jobs. There was a shortage of institutional knowledge. Wenck was a staff officer, but he had never worked above the army group level. He and Guderian knew what they wanted, and they were familiar with staff procedures in a general sense, but neither knew the ins and outs of "Mauerwald." Guderian also had a long-standing bias against the General Staff, stemming from his stubborn and unfounded belief that the institution had opposed his attempts to introduce modern armored doctrine to the army back in the 1930s. The Operations Branch Ia, Colonel Johann Adolf Graf von Kielmansegg, was the most senior man with any experience in the OKH; he had been there since May 1942. Guderian and Wenck relied on him heavily, and he was able to temper Guderian's attitude toward the General Staff to some extent. But the Gestapo arrested Kielmansegg on August 8, and so his expertise disappeared as well.[17]

THE FINAL STUGGLE FOR THE REICH

The disruptions in the high command could not have come at a worse time. In France the western Allies had secured a beachhead in Normandy, and by the end of July they were poised to break out. The Soviets, meanwhile, were still advancing into the gap where Army Group Center had once stood. But as Hitler explained to Jodl, Warlimont, and several other advisers on July 31, he did not believe that Germany's situation was really that bad.[18] As usual Hitler rambled, and his line of thought is difficult to follow, but a few points do emerge. The Reich controlled enough territory to stay in the war, he said, and now it would not have to have such a huge organization in the rear. The first problem, he said, would be to stabilize the eastern front; he was confident the Wehrmacht could do that. The Wehrmacht would also have to hold in Italy and the Balkans. Italy was useful because it tied down Allied forces with a minimal investment of resources. The Balkans were very important for the raw materials they provided. Both theaters would have to give up forces, however, if a crisis developed in the west, since that theater was decisive. Hitler ordered the Wehrmacht to prepare a defensive line in eastern France and to turn every harbor into a "fortress," in order to deny its use to the Allies. He wanted to launch a counterstroke in the west, but he recognized that he lacked the air assets and mobile ground forces to do so in the short term, so he ordered the concentration of such forces against the day when the opportunity might present itself. Hitler stipulated—and here the effect of the bomb plot came to the fore again—that his staff was to reveal none of his long-term plans to the commander in chief west (Kluge, at the moment), lest the Allies get word of them. Instead, Hitler told Jodl to set up a special staff in the OKW to oversee the preparations. (Jodl avoided that task by appointing one man to the "staff"; he did not want to see any division of the Armed Forces Command Staff's authority.)[19] Kluge would receive orders to make certain units mobile by whatever means necessary, but he would not learn of their intended use.[20]

In neither the east nor the west did the battles of the next months develop as Hitler wished. The Soviets widened their initial drive with attacks against two other army groups, "North" and "North Ukraine," starting in mid-July. By the end of the first week of August, they had nearly cut off Army Group North from the rest of the front, and from there south had reached the border of East Prussia, the Vistula River below Warsaw, and the Hungarian border along the Carpathian Mountains. (Eventually the Germans had to accept the fact that they would not be returning to the Ukraine. In September they redesignated two of their army groups: "North Ukraine" became "South," and "South Ukraine" became "A.") Later in August the Soviets advanced into Romania. The Romanians opted not to fight, and the Germans lost over 380,000 men in about two weeks of fighting withdrawal. Over the course of the next three months, the Soviets occupied Bulgaria—which declared war on

Germany as soon as the Russians arrived—and advanced northwestward from Romania (now with Romanian help) across Transylvania into Hungary; by mid-December they were threatening Budapest. The Germans had to evacuate the southern Balkans in October because their position there was no longer tenable. In the meantime, the Red Army had also driven Army Group North out of most of the Baltic States and trapped the remainder on the Courland Peninsula.

In the west the British and Americans broke out from the western end of the Normandy beachhead, beginning on the very night when Hitler was explaining his intentions to his staff. Hitler ordered a counterattack that only succeeded in trapping much of the attacking force. All told, another 250,000 men disappeared from the German order of battle as a result of the invasion and the breakout, and now the Wehrmacht collapsed in the west. By the middle of September, the Allies had liberated nearly all of France and in places stood on the western border of Germany. Only supply shortages, which Hitler's order to hold the ports did much to engender, kept the Allies from advancing farther.

Throughout this series of defeats, Hitler clung to hope. As he stated on August 31, "We will continue this fight at all costs until, as Frederick the Great said, one of our accursed enemies becomes too tired to fight on, and until we achieve a peace that secures the life of the German nation for the next fifty or one hundred years and which above all does not disgrace the German honor a second time, the way it happened in 1918."[21] The Führer placed his faith in his secret rocket weapons and jet aircraft, in new U-boat models that the navy was trying to bring into service, and most of all in the counterstroke that he still planned to deliver in the west.[22] He hoped that, by delivering a severe blow to the Allies, he could break up their coalition. On August 19 he told Jodl to plan for an attack in November, when bad weather would neutralize Allied airpower. Within less than a month, he had chosen the Ardennes as the sector for the attack, into which he would throw some thirty new divisions. The offensive would hit the junction between the American and British armies and drive through to Antwerp, with the goal of forcing the British into a second Dunkirk. Guderian protested because of the crisis in the east—in his memoir he insisted that the Wehrmacht could still have stopped the Soviets if Hitler had listened—while Jodl objected because of Allied air superiority, but Hitler was adamant.[23] Again he stated that bad weather would nullify the Allies' advantage in the air. And he still insisted that Rundstedt, who would direct the attack, could not learn of it as yet.[24]

Hitler, Jodl, Keitel, and a select group of other officers spent the next three weeks working out the details of the plan. On September 25 Hitler explained his concept to Jodl and Keitel in more detail. He tasked the former to prepare an operational draft with exact force requirements, as well as special orders regarding deception and secrecy. He told Keitel to work out the fuel and munitions requirements.[25] The three men met again to discuss the operation on October 9. Jodl briefed the Führer on five possible operations, only one of which corresponded to Hitler's original concept. With the other four options Jodl was trying his best to set more realistic goals for the operation, although in doing so he eliminated even the scant hope of strategic benefit for which Hitler was striving. In the end Hitler combined his concept with one of Jodl's proposals, and Antwerp remained the objective.

Over the next two weeks Jodl worked out a detailed operations plan, while the OKW told Rundstedt to concentrate forces to meet an expected American attack and added that those forces would become part of the OKW reserve. Not until October 22 did Hitler inform Rundstedt's and Model's chiefs of staff of his plans—and only after they signed oaths to maintain the strictest secrecy.[26] On November 2 Jodl followed up on the briefing with highly detailed written orders. The subordinate headquarters had to prepare their own operations plans, but these were actually implementation orders, not true planning documents. Neither Rundstedt nor Model believed that Hitler's plan would work, but they could not depart from it, despite repeated requests. The contrast with the planning processes for the offensives of 1939 to 1941 was marked.

On December 12 Hitler addressed the division commanders who were to lead the Ardennes offensive, which would begin in four days. "Wars are finally decided through the recognition by one side or the other that the war as such cannot be won," he told them. "Therefore the most important task is to get this recognition across to the enemy."[27] When one is on the defensive, he continued, one has to hit back occasionally, so that the enemy will conclude that he can never force a capitulation. He referred—again—to the political events that saved Frederick the Great at the end of the Seven Years' War, and he pointed out that there had never before been an alliance so heterogeneous as the one now confronting Germany.

The Germans did achieve surprise, and the weather did indeed keep Allied airpower from intervening—at first. However, there was never any real hope that the Wehrmacht would reach Antwerp, just as there was never any sign that the Allied coalition would break up. The Allies did have their differences, to be sure, but their determination to defeat the Nazi regime was enough to forestall problems for the time being. By the end of the month, the Americans had contained the German offensive and were beginning to reduce the "bulge" for which they named the battle. A subsidiary German thrust in Alsace in January 1945 suffered a similar fate. (Ever efficient, the OKW sent out an order on December 24, 1944, noting that the General Staff's Organization Branch had forbidden further leaves to Lorraine.)[28]

In the opening weeks of 1945, the Allies continued to tighten the ring around the Third Reich. On December 31, 1944, Guderian had sent a telex to the Hungarian high command in which he maintained that the relief of

Budapest was the Germans' highest priority. He also insisted that the Russians could not gain any more territory in Hungary.[29] In January Hitler ordered an offensive to relieve Budapest, which the Russians had cut off in late December, but the attack failed. On January 12 the Soviets launched their own offensive farther north, and within a month they had closed to the Oder River, less than forty miles from Berlin. Between then and the middle of April, they went on to clear most of East Prussia, Pomerania, and parts of Silesia, and to advance through the rest of Hungary and on to Vienna. Meanwhile, the British and Americans had been making steady progress. After they reduced the "bulge" and another pocket near Colmar, they cleared most of the left bank of the Rhine by the end of the third week of March. Luck gave them a bridge at Remagen, south of Cologne, on March 7, and they added two more bridgeheads by the end of the month. By then they had captured nearly three hundred thousand German soldiers and killed or wounded sixty thousand more. By April 4 they had cut off Army Group B in the industrial region of the Ruhr; another three hundred thousand troops soon fell into Allied hands, and Model, their commander, shot himself. Farther south, the Americans fooled the Germans by heading southeast into Bavaria instead of east toward Berlin. On April 25 they met the Soviets at Torgau on the Elbe River; meanwhile, the Red Army was battering its way into the German capital. The noose had closed.

GÖTTERDÄMMERUNG

As the war closed in on the Reich from the summer of 1944 on, the atmosphere within the high command became increasingly unreal. Hitler set the tone. By this time he was a wreck physically and psychologically. He remained shut away in his headquarters bunkers, first in East Prussia and then deep under the Reich Chancellery in Berlin, with no breaks, no fresh air, no natural light. The weight of his responsibilities and the reality of his situation were grinding him down. He suffered from insomnia; he could manage three or four hours of sleep per night only with the aid of heavy doses of sedatives.[30] During his waking hours he relied upon equally heavy doses of stimulants that his doctors provided. One young officer described Hitler this way in February 1945: "His head was slightly wobbling. His left arm hung slackly, and his hand trembled a good deal. There was an indescribable flickering glow in the eyes, creating a fearsome and wholly unnatural effect. His face and the parts around his eyes gave the impression of total exhaustion. All his movements were those of a senile man."[31] Any bad news or argument could bring on fits of rage, some of which were so severe that he became nearly incoherent. But even if he was not in control of himself or of the military situation, the Führer did maintain his authority (one could say "spell") over his staff officers and subordinate commanders. Ulrich de Maizière, by then the "Ia" of the General Staff's Operations Branch, confirmed the impression of senility, but he added that, once a briefing began, the picture would change drastically. Hitler often seemed to come out of his daze; he listened attentively, added to the discussion, and posed amplifying questions.[32] His entourage seems to have grasped at these moments of lucidity like a drowning man at a life belt.

The extent to which Hitler truly maintained his belief in victory in this final phase of the war remains a mystery. Certainly, the objective circumstances could not support such a view, but Hitler apparently worked himself into a level of self-deception that bordered on the incredible. He clung to the hope that the Allies would collapse at the last moment. When Franklin Roosevelt died on April 12, 1945, the Führer was sure that the "Miracle of the House of Brandenburg" was about to repeat itself.[33] That hope, like so many others, proved illusory. More and more, Hitler sank into cynical depression. If Germany could not emerge victorious, he reasoned, then the nation should sink into oblivion with him. He had already demonstrated his ultimate contempt for the German people by ordering the destruction of everything that could be of value to the enemy—and which, coincidentally, might enable Germany to survive as a modern state after the war.[34] Now he prepared to direct the final battle for the Reich and, if need be, to take his own life rather than fall into enemy hands.

Throughout this period, Hitler became ever more hateful and distrustful, especially toward the army. The assassination attempt had provided fuel for his paranoia and an explanation for all the setbacks up to that point. On July 31, 1944, he said that it was a symptom of the "blood poisoning" that had taken hold in the command.[35] One can hardly expect the soldiers at the front to win the war, he continued, when the people in the highest positions are traitors. Certainly, the Russians could not have improved so much in so short a time; the traitors in Germany must have been helping them for years. The Führer cited letters he said he had received from the front, in which soldiers wrote that they could not understand what was happening, that treason was the only possible explanation for their defeats. "There must come an end. This won't do. We must knock off and drive out these vile creatures that dragged the soldier's uniform into this affair, this riffraff that emerged from times gone by."[36] With the traitors defeated, Hitler concluded, Germany's true moral and military superiority could once more come into play. Within his entourage, such rantings found a ready audience. The Führer's midday briefings were crowded with competing personalities, many of them from outside the military entirely.[37] Göring, Goebbels, Speer, Bormann, Himmler, Dönitz, and others all competed for his attention; they vied against one another and engaged in a constant campaign of rumor and slander against the army.

Even before the July 20 attack, the Nazi Party had been gaining ground in its struggle for more power within the military sphere. Himmler and the SS were the primary beneficiaries. Their most recent victory had occurred on July 15, when Hitler gave Himmler "all authority in questions of education, National Socialist leadership, disciplinary matters, and jurisdiction, as over the SS," for the fifteen so-called "Grenadier divisions" that were then forming.[38] On July 20, in the wake of the coup attempt, Hitler added to Himmler's power base by making him commander of the Replacement Army, which had been one of the conspirators' strongholds. The Reichsführer-SS, in turn, appointed a longtime crony of his, SS-Obergruppenführer and General of the SS Hans Jüttner, to run the Replacement Army in his name. Under their direction the Grenadier divisions became "People's Grenadier" (Volksgrenadier) divisions, and in October the Army Personnel Office set up a special branch, under SS control, to see to it that the officers in these units would display the proper National Socialist spirit.[39]

In October 1944 Hitler widened the Party's authority yet again by creating the Volkssturm, or Home Guard. His decree of October 20 enlisted every man between the ages of sixteen and sixty in the Volkssturm as a last-ditch measure to assist the Wehrmacht in those areas where the enemy had set foot on German soil. The Nazi Party raised and administered the units, under the direction of Martin Bormann and the Gauleiter, while Himmler and the SS controlled the new formations' military organization, training, and employment.[40] The Volkssturm never amounted to an effective fighting force—in fact, it achieved little except to bring an awful death to thousands of boys and old men. For Himmler, however, it was another military organization under his control, one that he could add to the Waffen-SS, which by the end of 1944 would reach a strength of 590,000 men, in twenty-four divisions plus special units, twelve corps headquarters, and an army headquarters.[41]

Nor was that the limit of Himmler's ambition—he also began holding operational commands in his own right. In an order of September 19, 1944, Hitler had made him responsible for defensive measures along sections of the North Sea and Baltic coasts; he worked through a new command, the Operations Staff North Coast (Führungsstab "Nordküste").[42] Then, at the end of November, Hitler named him commander in chief Upper Rhine, with authority over all units of the army, Waffen-SS, and Luftwaffe between Bienenwald and the Swiss border.[43] With his appointment, command effectiveness reached a new low. Himmler was a man of no military talent whatsoever; he could neither exercise command properly himself nor choose good commanders or staff officers to serve under him. He took after his Führer by meddling endlessly in the smallest details. At one point in late 1944, he went so far as to issue an order for the deployment of a single artillery piece![44] But although Himmler failed utterly in the west, Hitler later gave him command of the newly formed Army Group Vistula, which was responsible for the defense of the approaches to Berlin. His employment was proof, if such was needed, that Hitler valued loyalty over ability.

That being the case, the Führer should perhaps have looked more positively upon his subordinates in the army. Their reaction to the worsening crisis was, first of all, to back up Hitler's demands for absolute obedience and discipline. The *Führerprinzip* came into its own as Hitler's and the generals' orders became ever more detailed and strident. Guderian issued a directive to the commanders of "fortresses" in the east on November 23, 1944, in which he emphasized that "leaders of all grades are personally responsible for carrying out the orders that I issue in the Führer's name for fortresses on the eastern front, conscientiously, meticulously and without delay."[45] Two days later Hitler ordered that any commander who wished to surrender had to first offer his subordinate officers, noncommissioned officers, and finally his enlisted men the opportunity to fight on. If anyone accepted the offer, that person became the commander of the unit, no matter what his rank.[46] On December 5 he stated that, should any position fall because of negligence or a lack of vigor on the part of officers or troops, this would constitute "a crime of unpredictable consequences" for which he would hold every guilty party responsible. To that end he demanded that the commander in chief west report every bunker that fell, along with a count of missing soldiers who were or might have been deserters.[47] And on January 19, 1945, Hitler ordered that all commanders down to division level inform him of every planned significant movement or action in time for him to have a say in the decision. Furthermore, he again emphasized that every commander and staff officer was responsible for seeing that every report contained the unvarnished truth; in any case in which something was disguised or distorted, whether intentionally or not, the guilty parties could expect severe punishment. And finally, every commander was responsible to Hitler for seeing that the communications links to the higher headquarters continued to function—presumably so that commanders could not use communications problems as an excuse for failing to report.[48] The senior commanders passed these orders on assiduously and added their own strict disciplinary measures, usually centering on the frequent use of the death penalty.[49]

Other changes reinforced the Nazification of the army. In some cases the changes were largely symbolic, though significant nonetheless: on July 23, 1944, for example, the Nazi salute officially replaced the old-style military salute throughout the Wehrmacht, at Göring's suggestion.[50] Most new measures were more substantive, however. Goebbels created a special post office box at the end of July to which anyone, including soldiers, could write postage-free with denunciations or with complaints about lax execution of Nazi educational programs.[51] On September 24 Hitler approved a change to the basic Defense Law to allow members of the Wehrmacht to maintain their Party affiliation throughout their time in service. The new law called upon soldiers to work in the spirit of the National Socialist Weltanschauung and upon officers, noncommissioned officers, and officials to educate and lead their subordinates in a National Socialist sense.[52] The army's leaders matched the Party's measures with their own protestations of ideological enthusiasm. On November 6, 1944, Guderian told a Home Guard assembly that they would prove to the enemy that there were "85 million National Socialists who stand behind Adolf Hitler. We took our oath voluntarily, and after centuries they will speak of the invincibility of our generation, which protected justice against all enemies."[53] Guderian's approach was typical of the way in which the senior generals backed up discipline with ideology to bring out the last desperate resistance from their troops.

NEW LEVELS OF STRUCTURAL CHAOS

The developing military catastrophe engendered a spasm of organizational changes that only increased the complexity and exacerbated the competition within the command system. First of all, as the Soviets moved into southeastern Europe, the OKW's and the OKH's spheres began to collide. Five army groups faced the Soviets at the end of 1944. Army Group North was bottled up in the Courland Peninsula, while Center held East Prussia and northern Poland. Army Group A stood along the line from central Poland south to the Carpathians, South held Hungary, and Army Group F held parts of Yugoslavia. That last command was the army group headquarters for the commander in chief southeast, an OKW theater commander. Even though that command was now fighting the Red Army, the OKW was not willing to give it up to the General Staff, and so the completely arbitrary boundary between Army Groups South and F was also the boundary between the OKW and the OKH. Local commanders on that boundary had to work through the higher commands in order to get anything of importance done. For instance, when the commander in chief southeast learned in December 1944 that a Soviet drive on the General Staff's side of the boundary was vulnerable to a counterattack, the OKW had to *suggest* to the General Staff that Army Group South launch the thrust.[54]

The command organization in the southeast must have seemed simple, however, next to the structures that developed as the Allies entered the German homeland. The Gauleiter in each separate German state controlled such matters as resource mobilization and civilian evacuation, and each one guarded his authority jealously. The military could not simply ignore these men in the process of organizing their defenses. In addition, economic assets came under other civilian authorities, who also wanted a say in decisions that touched on their spheres. As early as July 1944, Keitel had stipulated that the Wehrmacht would have to restrict itself to purely military tasks in the homeland.[55] Hitler also issued orders regulating the command relationships in those areas of the Reich that would become war zones. Under those orders, the local military commander would share power with a Reichs defense commissar (for liaison with civilian economic authorities) and the local Gauleiter (for Party matters).[56]

Such arrangements looked clear enough on paper, but they were often a nightmare to implement. For example, an order from the General Staff of January 10, 1945, organized an "Operations Staff East Coast" (Führungsstab Ostküste) to take over responsibility for defense of the Baltic coast in Defense Region II, that is, from the western border of Mecklenburg to the eastern border of Pomerania and for a depth of twenty miles from the shore. An SS general would lead the staff, which would be subordinate to the OKW but would have to accept the General Staff's directives regarding certain defensive zones and fortresses.[57] The General Staff issued just such a directive on January 21; it dealt with the construction of positions to ward off the expected Soviet attack on Berlin. As such it did not concern the Operations Staff East Coast per se, but a copy went there nonetheless. Copies also went to the Armed Forces Command Staff in the OKW; the Luftwaffe General Staff; the Commander of the Replacement Army (Himmler) and his staff in charge of fortifications; Army Group Center; Army Group Vistula (Himmler again); the chief of the Reich Chancellery (Bormann); the leader of the Party Chancellery; the Reich interior minister; the Reich minister for armaments and war production; the headquarters of the Volkssturm; and the Gauleiter in Stettin and Berlin—and that list does not include the OKH's internal information copies![58] Obviously, such a command arrangement was susceptible to countless deadlocks and delays, as each agency pursued its own agenda.

And pursue them they did. Above all, in addition to the conflict between the military and civilian authorities, the OKW and the OKH were still fighting one another for resources. As Hitler gathered forces for the offensives in the Ardennes and Alsace, Guderian continued to plead for reinforcements for the east, where new Soviet attacks were in the offing. He made his case in face-to-face meetings with the Führer on December 24, again on New Year's Eve, and yet again on January 9; he also pleaded with Jodl for support.[59] Hitler rejected the arguments, with backing from Jodl, who, according to Guderian, believed that the Wehrmacht had taken the initiative away from the western Allies and needed to keep it.[60] The only exception, again according to Guderian, took place on December 31, after he had gone to Rundstedt and obtained his approval to remove four divisions from the west. That took the wind out of Jodl's sails and brought the Führer around as well, but even so, Hitler did not send the divisions where Guderian wanted them, but instead included them in the ill-fated attempt to relieve Budapest.[61]

The continuous strife among his staffs and senior generals became so bad that Hitler even complained of it to a group of more junior commanders:

There can hardly be a fourteen-day period of quiet or without a major battle on the eastern front, and already the commander of the army group in the west comes and declares: in the east there are still armored units available; why do we not get them? But there is hardly a bit of quiet in the west, but the same commander in the east would immediately say: in the west there is absolute quiet, we can certainly get at least four to six armored divisions in the east. I hardly have a division free anywhere, but there are already glances being cast at it from some other place.[62]

In fact—and especially in the case of the 1944 and 1945 offensives—the controversy over resource allocations has persisted to this day. After the war many former Wehrmacht officers, Guderian foremost among them, blamed Hitler for using up Germany's last reserves on such useless enterprises. Many otherwise astute historians have jumped on the bandwagon. All of them missed the point that even an extra twenty or thirty divisions were not going to change the outcome for Germany at that stage.

To add to the larger organizational problems within the high command, the General Staff continued to experience severe personnel problems, especially in the form of turnover. Guderian lost his position at the end of March 1945. He and Hitler had such a vehement argument on one occasion that they nearly came to blows; Göring finally had to lead Guderian from the room.[63] Guderian was becoming, according to Goebbels, "hysterical and fidgety."[64] Hitler relieved him on March 28 with the reason (which he often used) that the latter needed to recoup his health. He put Guderian on six weeks' leave. (At that point Hitler asked the general where he wanted to go. Keitel recommended Bad Liebenstein, saying, "It's very beautiful there." Guderian had to remind Keitel that the Americans had already occupied the area.)[65]

Guderian's successor was Lieutenant General Krebs, a man of "unquenchable optimism" and a "chameleonlike ability to adapt to the views of his superiors."[66] At the next level down, Wenck had lasted as chief of the Command Group until the middle of February, at which point he fell victim to an automobile accident. Krebs succeeded Wenck for a few weeks before moving up. Then Brigadier General Erich Dethleffsen held the job for a month. In the Operations Branch, meanwhile, Bonin was chief until January 18, when the Gestapo arrested him and his deputy, Colonel Wasmod von dem Knesebeck; Hitler ordered the arrest after learning from Guderian that the two men had approved the evacuation of Warsaw.[67] After Bonin, Brigadier General Kurt Brennecke was chief for a little more than a month, Brigadier General Ivo-Thilo von Trotha for less than two weeks, and after that, the position remained officially vacant.[68] The next place down in the hierarchy, that of "Ia" in the Operations Branch, saw even more turnover. The Gestapo arrested Kielmansegg in August 1944; then Bonin took over until he became chief of the branch on September 1. Knesebeck took over at that point. After his arrest, the post remained vacant for nearly a month.

The next Ia was Lieutenant Colonel Ulrich de Maizière, whose story

Hans Krebs. (Courtesy Bundesarchiv, photo no. 78/111/10A)

sums up the status of the General Staff in the last weeks of the war. He was not quite thirty-three years old when he took up his post, and yet for the last two weeks of his tenure (April 10–24, 1945), he was the de facto chief of the Operations Branch. In an interview in 1996 he emphasized that he would not have been qualified for that post as it had existed earlier; he was not experienced enough to plan major operations. However, by this point in the war there were no such operations to plan. De Maizière was extremely busy, but his role was almost clerical. The Operations Branch collated the situation reports and updated the maps as always. Hitler reviewed the reports in his briefings and made his decisions, which de Maizière would record and issue as orders. Beyond a very narrow technical realm, then, his qualifications, like those of the men above him, were largely irrelevant.[69]

Most officers in the General Staff were not blind to the irrelevance of their work, which derived both from Hitler's authority and character, on the one hand, and from the general military situation, on the other. Leyen wrote of the "as-if" work with which the staff busied itself in these final weeks: planning impossible movements of nonexistent troops into imaginary positions. Many people clung to the work, he noted, as the only way to avoid confronting the nearness of total collapse.[70] The workload was tremendous, and frequent air raids interrupted the routine. De Maizière wrote that he went through this period of his life in a mixture of alertness and trance. The staff was not getting enough sleep. Everyone was tired, tense, and irritable.[71] The officers' resentment even began to spill out onto the pages of the Operations Branch war diary. The diary shows the branch's recommendations and then Hitler's decisions; the two were almost always at odds, and the diary keeper was not shy in his criticisms of the latter.[72] De Maizière went so far as to hang a sign on the back of his office door that quoted a line from a movie, one that had provoked grim laughter from the staff officers who saw the film: "It is not my place to think about the senselessness of the tasks that are assigned to me."[73] Nazi ideology, meanwhile, was losing some of its appeal. On December 30, 1944, Guderian had to remind the officers in the OKH of the importance of National Socialist education; he stipulated that their attendance at weekly Nazi lectures was a duty, not an option.[74] Most officers recognized, though, that no amount of indoctrination was going to make a difference. Even Jodl recognized the hopelessness of the situation. At the end of March he confided to his diary, "When one no longer has any reserves, fighting to the last man makes no sense."[75]

One must note that, for all the dissatisfaction in the high command, there was no more talk of rebellion. No one resigned his post. No one—in the upper levels of the military, at any rate—tried to find a way to make peace. (This in contrast to some of Hitler's closest associates, such as Himmler, who tried to negotiate peace through Count Folke Bernadotte of Sweden.)[76] As the Allied armies swallowed up the Reich, the men leading the Nazi military machine continued to carry out their duties. The mix of motives at work in their minds is difficult to discern. A few may have remained blind to the approaching catastrophe. Some may have believed that Hitler had one last trick up his sleeve; others, perhaps, were psychologically unable to face reality. Fatalism certainly played a role in many cases, as did fear: these men knew that individual action would mean imprisonment, torture, and death, and in the end would do nothing to change Germany's fate. Discipline and loyalty were important factors as well; one did not run away from one's duty, pointless though it might be. And so the staff officers escaped into the details of their work; they avoided unpleasant strategic realities in much the same way they had since before the war began, if with more difficulty.

THE FINAL DISSOLUTION

In the last month of the war, the Germans again made adjustments to the high command's structure, in a last attempt to overcome the chaos of defeat. On April 11 Keitel redefined the command responsibilities for the commanders in chief southeast, southwest, west, and northwest, respectively, and for the General Staff, with several special stipulations. The commander of Defense Region III, for example, was to be directly subordinate to Hitler for the defense of the capital.[77] The Führer had decided to become his own fortress commander in Berlin. By the middle of the month, he recognized that the American and Soviet thrusts might cut him off from a portion of the Reich, and so he designated commanders to lead the final defense wherever he could not do so personally. If he were in the north, Field Marshal Kesselring would command in the south; if he were in the south, Dönitz would take over in the north.[78] Accordingly, on April 20, Hitler's birthday, the Armed Forces Command Staff split into two elements.[79] Command Staff North (A), under Jodl, moved first to Krampnitz and from there eventually to Mürwik, near Flensburg in Holstein. Command Staff South (B) moved to Berchtesgaden; this staff came under the direction of Jodl's deputy, Major General August Winter.[80] Four days later Hitler clarified his intentions: he would command the forces in the north himself, directly from his bunker in Berlin, while he worked through Command Staff B to control the forces in the south.[81] Thus the northern headquarters never really performed any command functions while Hitler was alive, and Kesselring still had to submit all fundamental orders to the OKW for approval. Also by the same order, after nearly seven years of peacetime and more than five of wartime development, Hitler finally unified the command: he gave overall control of operations to the OKW and placed the General Staff's Command Group officially under Jodl's control.[82] As Heusinger said later, in the last fourteen days of the war, the Germans had the perfect high command organization. (In fact, the OKW had never stopped pushing for this solution. As late as April 7, 1945, the Organization Branch of the Armed Forces Command Staff had presented a briefing paper on a possible new high command structure under the OKW.)[83]

Of course, all of this constituted exactly the kind of "as-if" work to which Leyen referred. The Soviets launched their attack on Berlin on April 16.[84] When Hitler issued that last order regarding the command structure, Russian artillery shells were already bursting in the Chancellery courtyard above his head. On the same day, Keitel, who had been shuttling back and forth between Berlin and Krampnitz, found himself cut off from the capital by enemy action, so he returned to Command Staff A's location and there led a briefing for the first time in the war. Dethleffsen briefed him on the eastern front, Jodl on the rest; then Jodl radioed Hitler and received his approval for the measures upon which Keitel had decided. Keitel spent the next few days trying to organize the relief of Berlin and getting caught up in the action. At one point he even stopped to organize the defense of a village![85] Hitler, meanwhile, remained in Berlin with Krebs, Burgdorf, Bormann, and various other luminaries, trying to direct the defense of the city, sending out radio messages to armies that no longer existed, and dictating his will and his political testament (in which he blamed the generals, among others, for his defeat). On April 29, with all hope of relief gone, he committed suicide.[86]

Admiral Dönitz now took over as Hitler's designated successor. The Führer might be dead, but the war was not yet over. The German leaders' primary goal at this point was to allow as many people to escape the Russians as possible. To that end Dönitz attempted to negotiate a separate peace with the western Allies, but, predictably, they turned him down.[87] Failing that, the Germans tried to delay the Soviet advance for as long as they could.[88] They even continued their reorganization of the command system in obedience to Hitler's last directive on the subject.[89] On May 8, however, the Wehrmacht's leaders had to accept their situation and sign a surrender with all the Allied powers.

Still, like an ant that has lost its head, the command took some time to die.[90] The Americans had overrun Command Staff B at Berchtesgaden and taken its members prisoner, but the Allies allowed Command Staff A to continue to function for a time, in order to assist with the execution of the surrender terms. Jodl wanted to reunite the southern and northern elements of the headquarters, but the Allies refused to allow him to do so. On May 10 and 13, Keitel sent out orders to reorganize the OKW in order to perform the tasks required by the capitulation agreement.[91] Finally, on May 23, the Allies took the members of Command Staff A into custody along with Dönitz and the Reich government.

The German high command had ceased to exist.

12

The German High Command: An Assessment

When then-Major Stauffenberg referred to the German high command structure as "idiotic" in December 1941, he could hardly have guessed how much worse it would become. Nor did he show that he understood the forces that had shaped the command up to that point. If we are to go beyond Stauffenberg's assessment—which, after all, is clever and entertaining but not particularly useful—we must review the development and functioning of the high command more systematically. The most constructive way to do so is to revisit the myth that grew up around the command during and after the war, and to use it as a central theme while we answer the questions with which this work opened. In that way we can draw out some of the broader lessons, identify the command's strengths and weaknesses, and come to some conclusions regarding the German officer corps' responsibility and the validity of the myth itself.

Adolf Hitler remains the story's central figure. According to those of his generals who survived the war, and to many of the historians who have written about that conflict, he bore almost complete responsibility for the disaster that befell the German state and military. Indeed, there are arguments in support of that view. One can safely say that no other individual had nearly so great an effect on the structure of the high command or on Germany's overall war effort. From the "great man" perspective, there simply was no figure to rival the Führer. That statement says as much for the flaws in the "great man" approach, however, as it does for Hitler's role. True, he dominated or eliminated every competing individual personality. Try though he might, though, he could not work without a command system, a collection of individuals bound together by common values, ideas, and practices. The system itself emphasized, through a culture that had evolved over centuries, the individual's subordination to the collective whole. In that sense it helped Hitler to maintain control, since the system did not produce individual rivals. But that whole also constituted an entity in and of itself, one that Hitler could neither discard nor completely dominate. He could not be the sole voice in the command system, much though he wanted to be. Despite his jealous dislike of much that defined it, the system's culture and ideas permeated every sphere they touched: political, strategic, operational, and organizational. That fact limited Hitler's power, but it also pulled the rug from under the generals' postwar apologia, because the evidence shows that most of the time the high command strove to work *with* the Führer, not against him. The command's values and ideas were not nearly so different from those of Hitler and the National Socialists as the myth would indicate. The dominant military culture was ripe for cooperation before the Nazis ever became a factor in German politics. For all the talk of conflict that arose after the war, the two sides both contributed to Germany's downfall.

The political sphere was the first in which the parties came into contact. To judge from the postwar memoir literature, the army's leaders found Hitler and his plans distasteful and dangerous from the start, and they kept their distance as best they could. In this version of history, Hitler pushed rearmament at a frantic pace, over his generals' objections. Eventually he dragged Germany into another world war, in spite of his officers' moral misgivings and against their expert advice. Later, as the war turned against the Third Reich, the generals resisted as best they could, but their sense of duty and their (regrettable but unbreakable) oath of loyalty, together with the forces of the totalitarian state arrayed against them, made resistance all but impossible.

On the whole this story seems entirely plausible, but it was one of the first to break down under scrutiny. In political terms the military's leaders demonstrated from the start that their goals and those of the Nazi Party coincided. Just as much as Hitler, they wanted to see Germany become powerful again, to see the terms of the Versailles treaty dismantled, and to retake the territories lost at the end of the Great War. Throughout the Weimar years they had maintained the fiction that the army was apolitical, but in that time they had deliberately undermined the constitution they had sworn an oath to uphold. They wanted an authoritarian government; they believed that only such a system could bring about the necessary militarization of Germany. When the Nazis appeared on the scene, the generals thought they had the perfect instrument. They believed Hitler could harness the power of German society and industry for them, without threatening their monopoly on armed force, and Hitler naturally encouraged that belief. He even sacrificed his old comrade Röhm to demonstrate his fidelity to the army, and in return the army swore personal loyalty to him.

That loyalty would prove remarkably strong, even after the army's leaders could see that their position in the state was not nearly so secure as they had thought. When the Nazis killed army officers in the course of the coup against the SA, the army accepted the loss with barely a murmur. The reaction was the same when Hitler and his cronies framed Fritsch and purged the officer corps in 1938. In fact, Hitler did more to distance himself from the army's senior generals than vice versa. With time came increasing hubris and distrust on the dictator's part, along with a corresponding disinclination to take the army's side in any dispute. Through it all, though, most army officers strove to demonstrate their loyalty, to prove themselves worthy of Hitler's respect and trust. The exceptions—those behind the July 20 coup attempt and other conspiracies—were notable as much for their small numbers as for their courage. Most of their comrades either opposed their efforts or stood by to await the outcome. The army did not lose the political battle so much as it failed to offer one.

The same was true of Germany's strategic efforts: the army handed over control of strategy to Hitler with remarkably little fuss. Granted, there was some resistance at first. The occupation of the Rhineland in 1936 took place over many generals' protests. Likewise, a few were nervous when Hitler ordered the army into Austria on such short notice in 1938. Then came Beck's vociferous but futile protestations over the plan to invade Czechoslovakia. In each case, however, most generals were finally unwilling to put their careers on the line to resist the Führer. Halder's acceptance of Beck's job sealed the bargain; never again would the generals challenge Hitler's strategic judgment in any serious way.

Two related factors contributed to their acquiescence. The first was the string of successes following one after another from 1936 right up through spring 1940. There seemed little cause to argue with the man who engineered the Rhineland reoccupation, the *Anschluss* with Austria, and the bloodless victory over Czechoslovakia—even less after the easy victories over Poland, Norway, Denmark, the Low Countries, and especially France. That is the reasoning that the postwar accounts offer, and there is some merit in it. Germany's success blinded its military leaders to some extent.

Hidden below that superficial argument, however, lies the Germans' fundamental inability to make sound strategic judgments. This was a problem with deep historical roots that, at the very least, stretched back to Schlieffen and the senior officers and officials of his era. With almost no exceptions, the Nazi-era military and government were devoid of people who could correctly balance means and ends in order to come up with a realistic strategic plan. They welcomed war with Poland, despite the certainty of conflict with Britain and France. Likewise, they believed that they could conquer the Soviet Union easily. Then, they not only failed to recognize that effort's collapse in front of Moscow but also simultaneously accepted a war with America without batting an eye. From there the strategic picture rapidly became hopeless, but the generals drove their troops to fight on. The myth of the high command focuses on

Hitler's lack of strategic acumen, but in this respect he was in good company. The generals' postwar protestations of innocence and their attempts to place sole responsibility on Hitler's shoulders now stand out as obvious falsehoods. At best, they deceived themselves. At worst, they cynically tried to deceive everyone else.

The situation in regard to operations was somewhat more complex. On the one hand, Hitler was definitely an amateur, and many of his forays into this realm were just as disastrous as his generals later claimed. On the other, Germany produced some of the greatest names in operational maneuver to come out of the war. Rommel, Guderian, Rundstedt, and Manstein remain some of that conflict's best-known commanders, and many other generals and lesser officers earned high praise for their mastery of the operational art. Their superiority won them relatively easy victories from 1939 to 1941. Eventually they faced enemies whose size or isolation robbed the Wehrmacht of operational opportunities, and later their enemies used their own doctrines against them. Even so, the Germans continued to demonstrate formidable operational abilities almost to the end of the war, and their reputation after war's end reached nearly legendary proportions.

The problem with the Germans' image—like their operations to begin with—is that it is one-dimensional. It emphasizes the positive aspects while glossing over the negative. As far as Hitler's performance is concerned, one must give him credit for his successes, which often occurred in the face of opposition from his subordinates: his support for the thrust through the Ardennes in 1940 and his "no retreat" order in the winter of 1941–42 come immediately to mind. Admittedly, the balance of inspired versus foolhardy decisions stands firmly against Hitler. But what of men who served under him, whose operational genius is still so often lauded to the heavens? Their record is much less positive than most people know. Operations consists of more than the ability to maneuver forces on the battlefield. To be effective operationally, an army must be able to figure out what its enemies are doing, disguise its own intentions, and keep its formations properly manned and supplied. In these respects the Germans proved themselves to be woefully inadequate. Their intelligence efforts were a cruel joke. They consistently misjudged their enemies' capabilities and intentions, especially on the eastern front. At the same time, the Allies were quite regularly able to discern German plans. In terms of logistics and manning, as was true of strategy, the Germans could not balance ends with means. The underlying fault was the officers' fixation on the maneuver plan and their unwillingness to integrate the support functions into the planning process.

The problems with politics, strategy, and operations had their counterpoints in the organizational realm. Political, strategic, and operational ideas and events helped to shape the structure. The structure, in turn, offered opportunities and imposed limitations on the command system, and so helped to define the political, strategic, and operational possibilities that were open to it. Small staffs, for example, were an outgrowth of an intellectual climate that emphasized maneuver above all else. Having developed in that climate, they proved excellent for the rapid decision making and coordination that mobile combat demands, but they also could not support extensive intelligence analysis or logistical planning. On a higher plane, the overall structure of the high command evolved through a process that involved far more political competition than reason. The result was a system in which the so-called armed forces high command was really a weak operational headquarters; the army high command lost organizational coherence as the war went on and controlled operations in only one theater; and the two other service headquarters and the SS went their own ways. Such a system would have been patently incapable of creating and executing a coherent strategic plan, even if the people within it had been able to imagine one. Instead, the structure encouraged the internecine strife that threatened to paralyze the command in the last years of the war.

Taken together, the high command's weaknesses, from the political to the organizational, represent one layer or aspect of the problem as a whole. Another consists of the ideas, the deeper background, that existed under the surface manifestations. Here, too, the disconnect with the myth stands out markedly. The flaws in this realm did not begin with the Nazis, by any stretch of the imagination; they had a long history. The Nazis added some ideological wrinkles, but even so, their contributions were not so very different from mainstream military thought, as it existed before they came to power. What the Nazis did, indeed, was to encourage and strengthen some of the worst cultural and intellectual trends within the military. Those trends encompass three sets of issues: character versus intellect; the *Führerprinzip* versus joint responsibility and "command by directive"; and the illusion of control.

The competition between character and intellect as guiding principles for officer education and training had been going on since the early nineteenth century. By the beginning of the twentieth, that competition had reached a point of relative stability in which both principles had a place. A rigorous program prepared officers for their duties in an intellectual sense even as it selected for those who had the requisite strength of personality to perform well under the strain of combat. Certainly this system had its advantages. No Allied commander in the Second World War would have downplayed the Germans' ability to pull together operations under the most difficult circumstances; that ability grew largely out of the skill of the staff officers at all levels of command. At the same time, however, the dual focus on intellect and character led in some dangerous directions, because the Germans perverted both of them to some extent. The General Staff's intellectual approach proved narrow and mechanistic, and it contributed to the problems—already noted—at the strategic and operational levels of war. Their emphasis on character, meanwhile, led them into hubris. Because of it they were ripe to buy into the Nazi credo that, with enough strength of will, no obstacle was insurmountable. Thus we have the picture of Halder, whose dedication to rational planning seemed total, pushing for further effort at Moscow and writing, twelve years later, that no war is lost until one gives up—and he is but one example that illustrates the atmosphere within the officer corps as a whole.

After 1945 the surviving generals made much of the conflict between Hitler's top-down command philosophy, the *Führerprinzip,* and the long-standing General Staff traditions of joint responsibility and "command by directive." There is no question that such a conflict existed. The history of the war is replete with examples in which Hitler refused to allow a subordinate commander any flexibility whatsoever in the execution of an order. Conversely, the Germans gained advantage throughout most of the war from the latitude that lower-level leaders habitually allowed their subordinate commanders and staff officers. Where top-down and bottom-up clashed, however, the former almost invariably won, and the point of conflict between those two approaches moved downward, gradually but inexorably, through the chain of command until a company could hardly move from one position to another without obtaining permission from the OKW or an army group headquarters. The key question is: Was this somehow Hitler's fault? In order to believe that, one has to accept that he forced his commanders to adopt his style of command against their will, but the evidence clearly contradicts that interpretation. The senior officer corps adopted the *Führerprinzip* with only occasional token resistance. For whatever combination of reasons—duty, fear, loyalty, and ambition among them—they proved only too willing to enforce absolute obedience on their subordinates, in many cases under threat of death.

The triumph of will over reason and of obedience over initiative went hand in hand with the illusion of control that came to permeate the high command. Obviously, in order to believe that moral strength can overcome any obstacle and that the superior officer's orders should always take precedence over those of his subordinates, one has to believe that the superior has a better understanding of the situation and can communicate his desires perfectly to the commanders under him. By the Second World War, modern technology seemed to offer realistic opportunities for just such a system to work. Detailed reports went from the lowest levels to the highest in a matter of hours; orders could travel even faster in the opposite direction. The idea of war as a chaotic phenomenon, subject to only very limited control, seemed to have faded from the Germans' consciousness. Here again, this was not only Hitler's problem. While the "great man" approach to history, as well as the postwar memoir literature, would emphasize the Führer's role, he operated at the top of an entire system that aided and abetted him in his style of command. That system, quite aside from its opinion of Hitler's decisions, clearly fell into the same trap that he did, in believing that it could command from hundreds miles behind the front.

The Second World War is now sixty years behind us. The ranks of those who remember it thin daily; few indeed survive who experienced it at the policy-making level. Already the literature is the only reliable guide to its history, and here the record is spotty. The myth persists of a supremely talented, if politically naive and ambitious, German officer corps being led unwillingly into war and defeat by a ruthless dictator, a megalomaniac with no understanding of the military art. Clearly that myth has little basis in fact. Germany's senior military leaders supported the rise of an authoritarian government whose policies they expected would lead to a war of aggression. Weaknesses in their professional culture and ideas contributed to serious flaws in their strategy and operations. They made strategic decisions, independently and in support of Hitler's, that started a war that Germany had little chance of winning, and they continued it long past the point when the futility of the effort should have been obvious. They willingly gave up their authority over all but the most mechanistic tasks. Their intelligence, personnel, and logistical systems were too weak to support their broader operational goals, which fact they never recognized. The strengths of their staff system and tactics, combined with a shared ideology and their enemies' greater initial weakness, were all that allowed them to get as far as they did. As those advantages weakened or disappeared, the Germans' advances turned inevitably into retreats. Thus, although Hitler does remain central to the story of the German high command, we can now place him in the proper context, at the center of a flawed system that supported him almost unconditionally.

Appendix: A Note on the Documents and Translations

The following guidance, along with the list of abbreviations at the beginning of the work, will assist the reader in deciphering the references to German documents.

The best approach is to work with examples. Here is one from chapter 2, note 79:

> Der Reichskriegsminister und Oberbefehlshaber der Wehrmacht. W.A. Nr.1571/ 35 geh. L I a, 24.8.1935, *Betr.:* Unterrichtung des W.A., *Bezug:* Nr. 90/34 g.K. W II b v. 31.1.34, Ziffer 3 und W.A. Nr.1399/34 g.K. L I a v.17.10.34, in BA-MA RH 2/134, 48.

The first part ("Der Reichskriegsminister und Oberbefehlshaber der Wehrmacht") is the title of the authority issuing the order, in this case the Reichs war minister and commander in chief of the Wehrmacht, Blomberg. Next comes the issuing office: "W.A.," or Wehrmachtamt, the Armed Forces Office. Next is the document number, with the last two digits of the year following the slash. Next is the security classification, in this case "geh." for *geheim,* "Secret." Following that is more specific information on the issuing office. In this case, "L I a" means Group Ia of *Abteilung* L, the National Defense Branch. The date follows; the German system puts the day before the month, so this document is dated August 24, 1935. Next comes the subject; *"Betr."* stands for *Betreff* and serves the same function as "Re:" in an English-language document. The memo then refers to two earlier documents (*"Bezug"* means "in reference to"). "BA-MA RH 2/134, 48" is the location information: Bundesarchiv-Militärarchiv (Freiburg), record group RH 2, volume 134, page 48.

Often the format of the headings differed in some small way from one document to another. Frequently, for example, the office designations appeared together, as in "Chef OKW/WFSt/Op(H)": Chief OKW/Armed Forces Command Staff/National Defense Branch/Operations Group (Army).

The translations in the work are mine, except as noted. For the sake of clarity, I have avoided the use of German terms in the text as much as possible, with the exception of some words such as "Wehrmacht," "Führer," and "Luftwaffe" that most readers will recognize. One further point about translations is particularly important. The Germans standardized the designations of their staff elements, but the English translations of those terms often vary from work to work. The result is that one author's "office" might be another's "department" and a third's "branch"; this is a problem of which any reader in the subject must be aware. As far as this study is concerned, the following translations will apply:

Leitung	directorate
Abteilung	branch
Stab	staff
Gruppe	group
Amt	office
Referat	department
Sektion	section

I have used the following rank equivalents throughout the study:

Generalfeldmarschall	Field marshal
Generaloberst	General
General (*der Infanterie*, etc.)	Lieutenant general
Generalleutnant	Major general
Generalmajor	Brigadier general
Oberst	Colonel
Oberstleutnant	Lieutenant colonel
Major	Major
Hauptmann or *Rittmeister*	Captain
Oberleutnant	First lieutenant
Leutnant	Second lieutenant

Notes

1. Ulrich de Maizière, *In der Pflicht. Lebensbericht eines deutschen Soldaten im 20. Jahrhundert* (Herford: E. S. Mittler & Sohn, 1989), 74.
2. For an overview of the historiography on the Wehrmacht as a whole, see Rolf-Dieter Müller, "Die Wehrmacht—Historische Last und Verantwortung. Die Historiographie im Spannungsfeld von Wissenschaft und Vergangenheitsbewältigung," in *Die Wehrmacht: Mythos und Realität,* ed. Rolf-Dieter Müller and Hans-Erich Volkmann (Munich: Oldenbourg, 1999).
3. Gerhard Weinberg, *A World at Arms: A Global History of World War II* (New York: Cambridge University Press, 1994); Militärgeschichtliches Forschungsamt, ed., *Das Deutsche Reich und der Zweite Weltkrieg* (Stuttgart: Deutsche Verlags-Anstalt, 1979–90), printed in English as *Germany and the Second World War* (New York: Oxford University Press, 1990–99). The MGFA series is not yet complete, unfortunately. The German edition (six volumes so far) covers the war up to the early part of 1943. Four volumes of the English translation are ready; they cover the war up through the campaign in Russia in 1941.
4. Christian Hartmann, *Halder: Generalstabschef Hitlers 1938–1942* (Paderborn: Schöningh, 1991).
5. One such work has a reputation as one of the standard sources for this topic: Walter Görlitz, *Der deutsche Generalstab. Geschichte und Gestalt 1657–1945* (Frankfurt am Main: Verlag der Frankfurter Hefte, 1950). An English edition is available as *History of the German General Staff, 1657–1945,* trans. Brian Battershaw (New York: Praeger, 1953). This work contains some valuable material, but the lack of citations reduces its value. The reader must exercise extreme caution when consulting it, especially in connection with the Nazi period. Two other works with similar problems are Trevor N. Dupuy, *A Genius for War: The German Army and General Staff, 1807–1945* (Englewood Cliffs, N.J.: Prentice-Hall, 1977); and Matthew Cooper, *The German Army, 1933–1945: Its Political and Military Failure* (Chelsea, Mich.: Scarborough House, 1990).

6. I am following the definitions of strategy and operations in Allan R. Millett, Williamson Murray, and Kenneth H. Watman, "The Effectiveness of Military Organizations," in *Military Effectiveness,* ed. Allan R. Millett and Williamson Murray (Boston: Unwin Hyman, 1989), vol. 1, *The First World War,* 1–30. See also Bradley J. Meyer, "Operational Art and the German Command System in World War I" (Ph.D. diss., Ohio State University, 1988), 2.

1. THE ROOTS OF THE GERMAN COMMAND SYSTEM

1. The reader should be aware from the start that the term "General Staff" can refer either to a central bureaucratic structure within the army command (as used here) or to an elite body of trained staff officers, many of whom served outside of the central command.

2. The best examination of the General Staff's first century is Arden Bucholz's *Moltke, Schlieffen and Prussian War Planning* (New York: Berg, 1991); Bucholz's work is especially valuable for its theoretical framework and for the wide range of sources it brings to the investigation. See also Gerhard Ritter, *The Sword and the Scepter: The Problem of Militarism in Germany,* vol. 1, *The Prussian Tradition, 1740–1890,* trans. Heinz Norden (Coral Gables, Fla.: University of Miami Press, 1969); Wiegand Schmidt-Richberg, *Die Generalstäbe in Deutschland 1871–1945: Aufgaben in der Armee und Stellung im Staate* (Stuttgart: Deutsche Verlags-Anstalt, 1962); Gordon Craig, *The Politics of the Prussian Army, 1640–1945* (New York: Oxford University Press, 1956); J. D. Hittle, *The Military Staff: Its History and Development* (Harrisburg, Pa.: Military Service Publishing, 1949); Herbert Rosinski, *The German Army* (New York: Praeger, 1966).

3. Field Marshal Helmuth von Moltke is known as "the Elder" to differentiate him from his nephew, who was chief of the General Staff from 1906 to 1914.

4. See Holger H. Herwig, "The Dynamics of Necessity: German Military Policy During the First World War," in *Military Effectiveness,* ed. Allan R. Millett and Williamson Murray, vol. 1, *The First World War* (Boston: Unwin Hyman, 1989), 81–82; also Herwig, "Strategic Uncertainties of a Nation-State: Prussia-Germany, 1871–1918," in *The Making of Strategy: Rulers, States and War,* ed. Williamson Murray, MacGregor Knox, and Alvin Bernstein (New York: Cambridge University Press, 1994), 243–45.

5. See Schmidt-Richberg, *Die Generalstäbe,* 49–52; Holger H. Herwig, *The First World War: Germany and Austria-Hungary, 1914–1918* (New York: Arnold, 1997), 259–66; and Herwig, "Strategic Uncertainties," 272; also Martin Kitchen, *The Silent Dictatorship: The Politics of the German High Command Under Hindenburg and Ludendorff, 1916–1918* (New York: Croom Helm, 1976).

6. On Groener, see Craig, *Politics,* 345–50; Johannes Hürter, *Wilhelm Groener: Reichswehrminister am Ende der Weimarer Republik (1928–1932)* (Munich: Oldenbourg, 1993); also Wilhelm Groener, *Lebenserinnerungen: Jugend-Generalstab-Weltkrieg* (Göttingen: Vandenhoeck & Ruprecht, 1957). On Seeckt, see Hans Meier-Welcker, *Seeckt* (Frankfurt am Main: Bernard & Graefe, 1967), 236–40; James S. Corum, *The Roots of Blitzkrieg: Hans von Seeckt and German Military Reform* (Lawrence: University Press of Kansas, 1992), 33–37; Waldemar Erfurth, *Die Ge-*

schichte des deutschen Generalstabes von 1918 bis 1945, 2d ed. (Göttingen: Muster-schmidt, 1960), 61–63. Technically, the army under the Weimar regime bore the name Reichsheer, but as was later the case with Wehrmacht, many people then and since have used the broader term Reichswehr.

7. Manfred Messerschmidt, "German Military Effectiveness Between 1919 and 1939," in *Military Effectiveness,* ed. Allan R. Millett and Williamson Murray, vol. 2, *The Interwar Period* (Boston: Unwin Hyman, 1990), 220–21.

8. Admittedly, cultural and intellectual elements overlap. For the purposes of this study, I have included the General Staff's fundamental beliefs about the nature of war, as well as other deep-rooted practices and attitudes, under "culture," and placed its debates over operational doctrine, strategy, and politics under "ideas."

9. For a concise overview of this conflict over values, see David Fraser, *Knight's Cross: A Life of Field Marshal Erwin Rommel* (New York: HarperCollins, 1993), 10–11. See also Bucholz, *Prussian War Planning,* 22–23; and Karl Demeter, *Das deutsche Offizierkorps in Gesellschaft und Staat, 1650–1945,* 2d ed. (Frankfurt am Main: Bernard & Graefe, 1962), 69–71.

10. There is still no wholly satisfactory examination of the early reforms, but the following sources are worth consulting: Craig, *Politics;* Demeter, *Das deutsche Offizierkorps;* Hittle, *Military Staff;* Rosinski, *German Army;* Gunther E. Rothen-berg, *The Art of Warfare in the Age of Napoleon* (Bloomington, Indiana: Indiana University Press, 1978); William O. Shanahan, *Prussian Military Reforms, 1786–1813* (New York: Columbia University Press, 1945); Charles Edward White, *The Enlightened Soldier: Scharnhorst and the Militärische Gesellschaft in Berlin, 1801–1805* (New York: Praeger, 1989).

11. See Demeter, *Deutsche Offizierkorps,* 27; for a broader survey of the relevant literature, see Bucholz, *Prussian War Planning,* 3.

12. See David N. Spires, *Image and Reality: The Making of the German Officer, 1921–1933* (Westport, Conn.: Greenwood Press, 1984), 5, 21, 28–29.

13. German officers used Clausewitz selectively, if at all. They wanted practical guidelines by which to conduct operations, not the contemplative theories that Clausewitz offered. Thus his influence was indirect. See Jehuda L. Wallach, "Misperceptions of Clausewitz' *On War* by the German Military," *Journal of Strategic Studies* 9 (1986): 214; and Williamson Murray, "Clausewitz: Some Thoughts on What the Germans Got Right," *Journal of Strategic Studies* 9 (1986): 269–70.

14. Alan Beyerchen, "Clausewitz, Nonlinearity, and the Unpredictability of War," *International Security* 17, no. 3 (1992–93): 70.

15. Carl von Clausewitz, *On War,* indexed edition, edited and translated by Michael Howard and Peter Paret (Princeton, N.J.: Princeton University Press, 1984), 108; emphasis in original.

16. The longer quote is from Heinz-Ludger Borgert, "Grundzüge der Landkrieg-führung von Schlieffen bis Guderian," in *Handbuch zur deutschen Militärgeschichte: 1648–1939,* ed. Militärgeschichtliches-Forschungsamt (Munich: Bernard & Graefe, 1979), 9:556. The edition of *Truppenführung* that Borgert cites appeared in 1933; that fact demonstrates the longevity of the command principles that emerged in the nineteenth century.

17. Germany, Heer, H.Dv.300/1, *Truppenführung* (Berlin: E. S. Mittler & Sohn, 1936), 3. Mittler was the official publishing house for the General Staff.

18. Germany, Heer, *Heeresdienstvorschrift* 92 (HDv 92), *Handbuch für den General-stabsdienst im Kriege, Teil I, II, abgeschlossen am 1.8.1939* (Berlin: der Reichsdruck-erei, 1939), 2-3.

19. Quoted in *Truppenführung,* 9.

20. Spires, *Image and Reality,* 36, 47.

21. Hansgeorg Model, *Der deutsche Generalstabsoffizier: Seine Auswahl und Ausbildung in Reichswehr, Wehrmacht und Bundeswehr* (Frankfurt am Main: Bernard & Graefe, 1968), 17; Bradley J. Meyer, "Operational Art and the German Command System in World War I" (Ph.D. diss., Ohio State University, 1988), 60.

22. See Spires, *Image and Reality,* esp. 2-6, 105.

23. Craig, *Politics,* 63; White, *Enlightened Soldier,* 168; Rolf Elble, *Führungsdenken, Stabsarbeit. Entwicklung und Ausblick—ein Versuch* (Darmstadt: Wehr und Wissen Verlagsgesellschaft, 1967), 57. The first official mention of command by directive, or *Führung durch Direktiven,* as Moltke called it, occurs in a regulation of 1806; see Martin Samuels, *Command or Control? Command, Training and Tactics in the British and German Armies, 1888-1918* (London: Frank Cass, 1995), 11.

24. Quoted in Walther Görlitz, *Der deutsche Generalstab: Geschichte und Gestalt, 1657-1945* (Frankfurt am Main: Verlag der Frankfurter Hefte, 1950), 100.

25. See Meyer, "Operational Art," chap. 5; also David T. Zabecki, *Steel Wind: Colonel Georg Bruchmüller and the Birth of Modern Artillery* (Westport, Conn.: Praeger, 1994). Meyer points out that the Germans did not delegate authority when centralized control was more appropriate, as was true in the case of Bruchmüller's artillery tactics.

26. Meyer, "Operational Art," chap. 6.

27. Ibid., 372-73.

28. That corps of staff officers eventually became known as the Truppengeneralstab or "General Staff with Troops."

29. The chain of command consists solely of the commanders at each level of an army's hierarchy. Under normal circumstances a staff officer has no command authority, that is, he cannot issue orders except in the name of the commander and with his permission.

30. Görlitz, *Generalstab,* 57; see also Craig, *Politics,* 63; White, *Enlightened Soldier,* 165.

31. See, e.g., Rosinski, *German Army,* 107.

32. The principle began to receive less attention after the First World War, as most officers achieved the same level of education and training. For more on its official demise, see chapter 3.

33. Bucholz, *Prussian War Planning,* 22-23, 72-77; Meyer, "Operational Art," 52-55; Detlef Bald, *Der deutsche Generalstab 1859-1939: Reform und Restauration in Ausbildung und Bildung* (Munich: Sozialwissenschaftliches Institut der Bundeswehr, 1977), 65-69. One should note that the trend toward technical specialization was common in all professional fields in this period.

34. Bucholz, *Prussian War Planning,* 77-83. See also his earlier work, *Hans Delbrück and the German Military Establishment: War Images in Conflict* (Iowa City: University of Iowa Press, 1985), esp. chaps. 2 and 3.

35. For the British experience, see Timothy Travers, *The Killing Ground: The British Army, the Western Front, and the Emergence of Modern Warfare, 1900-1918* (London: Allen & Unwin, 1987).

36. Moltke is quoted in Herwig, "Dynamics of Necessity," 88.

37. For more on the Schlieffen Plan, see Gerhard Ritter, *The Schlieffen Plan: Critique of a Myth* (New York: Praeger, 1958); Bucholz, *Prussian War Planning,* 270; Gunther Rothenberg, "Moltke, Schlieffen, and the Doctrine of Strategic Envelopment," in *Makers of Modern Strategy from Machiavelli to the Nuclear Age,* ed. Peter Paret (Princeton N.J.: Princeton University Press, 1986), 314. Michael Geyer has some interesting ideas on this and the broader topic of German strategy in his essay "German Strategy in the Age of Machine Warfare, 1914-1945," in Paret, *Makers of Modern Strategy,* 527-97, but the complexities of his argument and language will have most readers scratching their heads.

38. See Clausewitz, *On War,* bk. 1, chap. 1.

39. Volkmar Regling, "Grundzüge der Landkriegführung zur Zeit des Absolutismus und im 19. Jahrhundert," in *Handbuch zur deutschen Militärgeschichte: 1648-1939,* vol. 9, ed. Militärgeschichtliches Forschungsamt (Munich: Bernard & Graefe, 1979), 388-89; Murray, "Clausewitz," 268; Wallach, "Misperceptions," 228. See also Stig Förster, ed., *Moltke. Vom Kabinettskrieg zum Volkskrieg. Eine Werkeauswahl* (Bonn: Bouvier, 1992).

40. See Michael Howard, *The Franco-Prussian War: The German Invasion of France, 1870-1871* (New York: Dorset Press, 1961), chaps. 6-9, 11; also Craig, *Politics,* 195-215.

41. See Herwig, "Strategic Uncertainties," 242-43, and "Dynamics of Necessity," 87-88; Rothenberg, "Doctrine of Strategic Envelopment," 316.

42. This and the previous two quotes are from Paul Heider, "Der totale Krieg—seine Vorbereitung durch Reichswehr und Wehrmacht," in *Der Weg deutscher Eliten in den zweiten Weltkrieg,* ed. Ludwig Nestler (Berlin: Akademie, 1990), 43-44.

43. Manfred Messerschmidt, "Aussenpolitik und Kriegsvorbereitung," in *Das Deutsche Reich und der Zweite Weltkrieg,* ed. Militärgeschichtliches Forschungsamt (Stuttgart: Deutsche Verlags-Anstalt, 1979-90) (hereafter: DRZW), 1:549. See also Karl-Heinz Janssen, "Politische und militärische Zielvorstellungen der Wehrmachtführung," in *Die Wehrmacht: Mythos und Realität,* ed. Rolf-Dieter Müller and Hans-Erich Volkmann (Munich: Oldenbourg, 1999).

44. See Stig Förster, "Der deutsche Generalstab und die Illusion des kurzen Krieges, 1871-1914: Metakritik eines Mythos," *Militärgeschichtliche Mitteilungen* 54 (1995): 61-93; Helmut Otto, "Illusion und Fiasko: Der Blitzkriegsstrategie gegen Frankreich 1914," *Militärgeschichte* 28 (1989): 301-8.

45. Few historians have been able to resist quoting Ludendorff's remark about the 1918 offensive: "I object to the word 'operation.' We will punch a hole into [their line]. For the rest, we shall see. We also did it this way in Russia!" The quote is in Herwig, *First World War,* 400.

46. Heider, "Der totale Krieg," 40. On the operational mistakes, see Corum, *Roots of Blitzkrieg,* 2-5; tellingly, the Germans labeled these issues "strategic." See also, e.g., the memo "Notwendigkeit einer neuzeitlichen Wehrakademie," T2 III D Nr. 551/33, June 22, 1933 in BA-MA RH 2/1009, 101; this document ascribes the loss to the lack of a strong command structure. For assistance in deciphering German document citations, see the Appendix.

47. Klaus-Jürgen Müller, *Das Heer und Hitler: Armee und nationalsozialistisches Regime, 1933-1940* (Stuttgart: Deutsche Verlags-Anstalt, 1969), 17-18.

48. See also Hew Strachan, *European Armies and the Conduct of War* (London: Allen & Unwin, 1983), 160; Wilhelm Deist, *The Wehrmacht and German Rearmament* (London: Macmillan, 1981), 7–8.

49. Heider, "Der totale Krieg," 35, 38, 47, 48; Wilhelm Deist, "The Road to Ideological War: Germany, 1918–1945," in *The Making of Strategy,* 356–59; Klaus-Jürgen Müller, "Deutsche Militär-Elite in der Vorgeschichte des Zweiten Weltkrieges," in *Die deutschen Eliten und der Weg in den Zweiten Weltkrieg,* ed. Martin Broszat and Klaus Schwabe (Munich: C. H. Beck, 1989), 239; also Ludwig Beck, *Studien,* edited and with an introduction by Hans Speidel (Stuttgart: K. F. Koehler, 1955), 30, 72.

50. Geyer, "German Strategy," 561.

51. For an overview of these discussions within the German army, see Deist, "Ideological War," 361–69; Müller, "Militär-Elite," 227–28, 246–51; Dennis Showalter, "German Grand Strategy: A Contradiction in Terms?" *Militärgeschichtliche Mitteilungen* 48, no. 2 (1990): 86–87; Showalter, "Past and Future: The Military Crisis of the Weimar Republic," *War and Society* 14 (1996): 58; Michael Geyer, "The Dynamics of Military Revisionism in the Interwar Years: Military Politics Between Rearmament and Diplomacy," in *The German Military in the Age of Total War,* ed. Wilhelm Deist (Dover, N.H.: Berg Publishers, 1985), 107–9, 111; Messerschmidt, "German Military Effectiveness," 227–28; Hürter, *Groener,* 95–97.

52. Geyer, "German Strategy," 555–56; Borgert, "Grundzüge der Landkriegführung," 535–38; Corum, *Roots of Blitzkrieg,* 29–33.

53. Corum, *Roots of Blitzkrieg,* 262–66; Geyer, "German Strategy," 557–560; Müller, "Militär-Elite," 249.

54. Geyer, "German Strategy," 561–63; Müller, "Militär-Elite," 251; Wilhelm Deist, "Die Aufrüstung der Wehrmacht," in DRZW 1:531; Messerschmidt, "German Military Effectiveness," 228; Deist, *Wehrmacht and German Rearmament,* 12–14, 24.

55. Deist, "Ideological War," 359, 370; Geyer, "Revisionism," 109–10.

56. Müller, "Militär-Elite," 240.

57. Ibid., 239; Heider, "Der totale Krieg," 42–43, 46.

58. Messerschmidt, "German Military Effectiveness," 229; Müller, "Militär-Elite," 257–60; Geyer, "German Strategy," 564; Deist, *Wehrmacht and German Rearmament,* 26.

2. EXPANSION AND DEBATE

1. *Gleichschaltung* is often translated as "synchronization" or "coordination," but a more recent and literal translation is perhaps more enlightening: "a bringing or forcing into line." For more on the process, see Wolfram Wette, "Ideologien, Propaganda und Innenpolitik als Voraussetzungen der Kriegspolitik des dritten Reiches," in *Das Deutsche Reich und der Zweite Weltkrieg,* ed. Militärgeschichtliches Forschungsamt (Stuttgart: Deutsche Verlags-Anstalt, 1979–90) (hereafter: DRZW), 1:25–173.

2. Handwritten record of Major General Liebmann, in Thilo Vogelsang, "Neue Dokumente zur Geschichte der Reichswehr, 1930–1933," *Vierteljahrshefte für Zeitgeschichte* 2 (1954): 434–36. See also Wilhelm Deist, *The Wehrmacht and German Rearmament* (London: Macmillan, 1981), 26; Telford Taylor, *Sword and Swastika: Generals and Nazis in the Third Reich* (Chicago: Quadrangle Books, 1952), 79.

3. Harold Deutsch, *Hitler and His Generals: The Hidden Crisis, January–June 1938* (Minneapolis: University of Minnesota Press, 1974), 14.

4. Klaus-Jürgen Müller, *Armee und drittes Reich, 1933–1939: Darstellung und Dokumentation* (Paderborn: Schöningh, 1987), 31. Hitler had no say in Blomberg's selection.

5. Wilhelm Deist, "Die Aufrüstung der Wehrmacht," in DRZW 1:396; Deutsch, *Hitler and His Generals,* 8–10; Waldemar Erfurth, *Die Geschichte des deutschen Generalstabes von 1918 bis 1945,* 2d ed. (Göttingen: Musterschmidt, 1960), 162; Robert J. O'Neill, *The German Army and the Nazi Party, 1933–1939* (London: Cassell, 1966), 19.

6. Blomberg to the Gruppen- and Wehrkriesbefehlshaber (group and defense district commanders) on Feb. 3, 1933, in Vogelsang, "Neue Dokumente," 432.

7. I have chosen to use the term "General Staff" in several places where Truppenamt would have been technically correct, in order to emphasize the continuity within the organization. This corresponds to the practice of the time; the officers of the Reichswehr did not always bother with the cover name.

8. A sketch of Blomberg's career is found in O'Neill, *German Army and the Nazi Party,* 186. The source of his conflict with Groener lay in the winter war games of 1927–28 and 1928–29. These indicated that Germany could not defend itself against Poland or France, but Blomberg refused to accept that conclusion. He insisted that no great state could "tolerate military violation without military resistance." Such an attitude stood in stark contrast to Groener's rationality. See Michael Geyer, *Aufrüstung oder Sicherheit: Die Reichswehr in der Krise der Machtpolitik, 1924–1936* (Wiesbaden: Franz Steiner, 1980), 95–97, 191–94, 207–13; also Deist, "Aufrüstung," DRZW, 1:387.

9. O'Neill, *German Army and the Nazi Party,* 16–17.

10. Deist, "Aufrüstung," DRZW, 1:383. Actually Groener transferred the staff of the Political Department from the Truppenamt to the Defense Ministry, with the cooperation of the department chief, Kurt von Schleicher. In its new role the staff took on the name of Wehrmacht-Abteilung, or Armed Forces Branch; Schleicher expanded it and changed the name to Ministeramt in February 1929. See Gustav-Adolf Caspar and Herbert Schottelius, "Die Organisation des Heeres, 1933–1939," in *Handbuch zur deutschen Militärgeschichte, 1648–1939,* ed. Militärgeschichtliches Forschungsamt (Munich: Bernard & Graefe, 1978), 7:319; Erfurth, *Geschichte,* 90–119.

11. Deutsch, *Hitler and His Generals,* 9; Taylor, *Sword and Swastika,* 78; Klaus-Jürgen Müller, *Das Heer und Hitler: Armee und nationalsozialistisches Regime, 1933–1940* (Stuttgart: Deutsche Verlags-Anstalt, 1969), 52–53.

12. Wilhelm Deist, "The Road to Ideological War: Germany, 1918–1945," in *The Making of Strategy: Rulers, States and War,* ed. Williamson Murray, MacGregor Knox, and Alvin Bernstein (New York: Cambridge University Press, 1994), 379.

13. Moriz von Faber du Faur, *Macht und Ohnmacht: Erinnerungen eines alten Offiziers* (Stuttgart: Hans E. Günther, 1953), 159. Faber du Faur attended the briefing in which Blomberg made the remark to Geyr von Schweppenburg, the military attaché to London. On Blomberg's intentions in general, see Deist, "Aufrüstung," DRZW, 1:528–29.

14. Deist, "Aufrüstung," DRZW, 1:397–98; the passage is reproduced in English in *Wehrmacht and German Rearmament,* 22–23. Hitler approved Germany's withdrawal from the conference and the League of Nations only in October 1933, because French proposals before the former would have led to real disarmament.

15. Michael Geyer, "German Strategy in the Age of Machine Warfare, 1940-1945," in *Makers of Modern Strategy from Machiavelli to the Nuclear Age,* ed. Peter Paret (Princeton, N.J.: Princeton University Press, 1986), 565.

16. O'Neill, *German Army and the Nazi Party,* 24-29; Müller, *Armee und drittes Reich,* 33, 34; Deutsch, *Hitler and His Generals,* 25-29; Taylor, *Sword and Swastika,* 78. Fritsch's ambivalence was not enough to keep Goebbels from describing him at the time as "completely loyal"; see Hans-Erich Volkmann, "Von Blomberg zu Keitel: Die Wehrmachtführung und die Demontage des Rechtsstaates," in *Die Wehrmacht: Mythos und Realität,* ed. Rolf-Dieter Müller and Hans-Erich Volkmann (Munich: Oldenbourg, 1999), 48.

17. For some of the various views of Beck, see Wolfgang Foerster, *Generaloberst Ludwig Beck: Sein Kampf gegen den Krieg. Ausnachgelassenen Papieren des Generalstabschefs* (Munich: Isar, 1953); Klaus-Jürgen Müller, *General Ludwig Beck: Studien und Dokumente zur politisch-militärischen Vorstellungswelt und Tätigkeit des Generalstabschefs des deutschen Heeres, 1933-1938* (Boppard: Harald Boldt, 1980); Peter Hoffmann, "Generaloberst Ludwig Becks militärpolitisches Denken," *Historische Zeitschrift* 234 (1982): 101-21; and Hoffmann, "Ludwig Beck: Loyalty and Resistance," *Central European History* 14 (1981): 332-50. Foerster was a colleague of Beck's and presents him in a very positive light; his sources are not reliable. Müller has made the most extensive scholarly examination of Beck's tenure as chief of the General Staff. Hoffmann takes particular issue with parts of Müller's analytical framework and conclusions. A full, scholarly biography of Beck is still lacking.

18. O'Neill, *German Army and the Nazi Party,* 29. On *Truppenführung,* see chapter 1.

19. See Klaus-Jürgen Müller, "Clausewitz, Ludendorff and Beck: Some Remarks on Clausewitz' Influence on German Military Thinking in the 1930s and 1940s," *Journal of Strategic Studies* 9 (1986): 243-44; Geyer, *Aufrüstung oder Sicherheit,* 431-32.

20. Heinz-Ludger Borgert, "Grundzüge der Landkriegführung von Schlieffen bis Guderian," in *Handbuch zur deutschen Militärgeschichte: 1648-1939,* ed. Militärgeschichtliches Forschungsamt (Munich: Bernard & Graefe, 1979) 9:570-71; Geyer, "German Strategy," 567-68.

21. Borgert, "Grundzüge der Landkriegführung," 569. Although Beck's original goals for rearmament were defensive in nature, that represented a "first step" only; see "Denkschrift General Becks über eine Verbesserung der Angriffskraft des Heeres vom 30. Dezember 1935," in Müller, *Armee und drittes Reich,* 295.

22. Deist, "Aufrüstung," DRZW, 1:408.

23. See "Stellungnahme des Chefs des Truppenamtes, Generalleutnant Beck, zu einem Vorschlag des Allgemeinen Heeresamtes (AHA) über den Heeresaufbau, vom 20. Mai 1934," in Müller, *Armee und drittes Reich,* which lays out Beck's objections to the proposed expansion.

24. Deist, "Aufrüstung," DRZW, 1:413-15.

25. Klaus-Jürgen Müller, "Deutsche Militär-Elite in der Vorgeschichte des Zweiten Weltkrieges," in *Die deutschen Eliten und der Weg in den Zweiten Weltkrieg,* ed. Martin Broszat and Klaus Schwabe (Munich, C. H. Beck, 1989), 261-66; Deist, *Wehrmacht and German Rearmament,* 36-38; and Deist, "Aufrüstung," DRZW, 1:409-16. Deist also points out the political motives behind rapid rearmament: the army was preparing for conflict with the SA.

26. See Kurt Schützle, "Au sujet de l'organisation des organes suprêmes de la

Wehrmacht fasciste conformément à la théorie sur la guerre totale," *Revue Internationale d'Histoire Militaire* 47 (1980): 108, 111.

27. Deist, "Aufrüstung," DRZW, 1:500–501; Caspar and Schottelius, "Organisation des Heeres," 319–20; Burkhart Müller-Hillebrand, *Das Heer, 1933–1945: Entwicklung des organisatorischen Aufbaues* (Darmstadt: E. S. Mittler, 1954–69), 1:102–3.

28. Deutsch, *Hitler and His Generals,* 24; O'Neill, *German Army and the Nazi Party,* 19; Müller, *Heer und Hitler,* 161.

29. Müller, *Beck,* 105.

30. Chef T 2 Nr. 1218/33 g.Kdos., Den 7.12.1933, "Befugnisse der obersten politischen und militärischen Führung in Krieg und Frieden," Entwurf, in Bernfried von Beesten, *Untersuchungen zum System der militärischen Planung im Dritten Reich von 1933 bis zum Kriegsbeginn: Vorstellungen, Voraussetzungen, Beweggründe und Faktoren* (Münster: Lit-verlag, 1987), 640–45. The preceding quote is from the cover letter written by Lieutenant Colonel Georg Sodenstern, chief of the Army Organization Branch. There was already, in fact, a Reich Defense Council and, under it, a Working Committee. Beck had been chief of the latter since October 1933. See also Müller, *Beck,* 107–9. On Beck's motivations and on the studies that preceded this draft, see Müller, *Beck,* 61–64, 104–6; Deist, "Aufrüstung," DRZW, 1:501–2. See also Beesten, *Untersuchungen,* 195–96.

31. "Denkschrift des Chefs des Truppenamtes über die Organisation der obersten militärischen Führung (15.1.34)," in Müller, *Beck,* 345–49.

32. Deutsch, *Hitler and His Generals,* 24.

33. Müller-Hillebrand, *Heer,* 1:105; Müller, *Heer und Hitler,* 217 and n. 59; Müller, *Beck,* 115; Beesten, *Untersuchungen,* 192–93.

34. Deist, "Aufrüstung," DRZW, 1:502.

35. Ibid., 1:502, 505.

36. Erich von Manstein, *Aus einem Soldatenleben, 1887–1939* (Bonn: Athenäum, 1958), 291–92. Manstein was chief of the Operations Branch in the General Staff from July 1, 1935, to October 1, 1936, and then assistant chief of staff for operations until February 4, 1938. If Manstein's memory of the conversation is accurate, it must have taken place just before he left, because the War Ministry became the OKW (Oberkommando der Wehrmacht) by decree on February 4, 1938. The OKH was the Oberkommando des Heeres, the Army High Command, formerly the Army Directorate; the name change took place in 1935.

37. Deutsch, *Hitler and His Generals,* 12.

38. Taylor, *Sword and Swastika,* 65–66; O'Neill, *German Army and the Nazi Party,* 21. On the general issue of officer loyalty to National Socialism, see Volkmann, "Von Blomberg zu Keitel"; also Gerhard L. Weinberg, "Rollen- und Selbstverständnis des Offizierkorps der Wehrmacht im NS-Staat," in *Die Wehrmacht: Mythos und Realität,* ed. Rolf-Dieter Müller and Hans-Erich Volkmann (Munich: Oldenbourg, 1999).

39. On this issue see Müller, *Armee und drittes Reich,* 54; Deist, "Aufrüstung," DRZW, 1:515–16.

40. Michael Salewski, *Die deutsche Seekriegsleitung, 1935–1945* (Frankfurt am Main: Bernard & Graefe, 1970), 1:3.

41. Williamson Murray, *The Change in the European Balance of Power, 1938–1939: The Path to Ruin* (Princeton, N.J.: Princeton University Press, 1984), 28; Taylor, *Sword and Swastika,* 81; Deist, "Aufrüstung," DRZW, 1:500, 504, 508.

42. R. J. Overy, *Goering: The "Iron Man"* (London: Routledge & Kegan Paul, 1984), 11–15, 32–33; Williamson Murray, *Luftwaffe* (Baltimore: Nautical and Aviation Publishing Company of America, 1985), 6; Taylor, *Sword and Swastika,* 130–32; Deutsch, *Hitler and His Generals,* 34; Joachim Fest, *The Face of the Third Reich: Portraits of the Nazi Leadership* (New York: Pantheon, 1970), 71–82. Blomberg did support the creation of an Air Ministry; see Volkmann, "Von Blomberg zu Keitel," 51.

43. Alan Bullock, *Hitler and Stalin: Parallel Lives* (New York: Vintage Books, 1993), 333; Fest, *Face of the Third Reich,* 136–48.

44. For more on the Röhm purge, see Müller, *Armee und drittes Reich,* 62–68; Bullock, *Hitler and Stalin,* 334–41; and Deutsch, *Hitler and His Generals,* 13–19.

45. Müller, *Armee und drittes Reich,* 69.

46. Deist, "Aufrüstung," DRZW, 1:514–17.

47. Quoted in O'Neill, *German Army and the Nazi Party,* 55. For more on the oath, see Deutsch, *Hitler and His Generals,* 19–22. Albert Seaton argues convincingly that Blomberg and Reichenau would never have made a move of such consequence without discussing it with Hitler beforehand; see *The German Army, 1933–45* (London: Weidenfeld & Nicolson, 1982), 51–52. See also Müller, *Armee und drittes Reich,* 69–70.

48. Hoffmann, "Loyalty and Resistance," 335.

49. The quote and the assertion regarding Reichenau's intentions are both from Deutsch, *Hitler and His Generals,* 22.

50. After the war the surviving German generals made much of this oath and the obligation that it supposedly put them under to serve the regime loyally. Gerhard Weinberg has placed such statements in their proper perspective by pointing out that many generals quite happily broke their oath to the Weimar Republic and later went on to perjure themselves at the Nuremberg trials; see *A World at Arms: A Global History of World War II* (New York: Cambridge University Press, 1994), 481–82. The real significance of the oath lies in the fact that most officers took it willingly and obeyed to the bitter end, by their own choice.

51. E. M. Robertson, *Hitler's Pre-War Policy and Military Plans, 1933–1939* (New York: Citadel Press, 1967), 56.

52. Wiegand Schmidt-Richberg, *Die Generalstäbe in Deutschland, 1871–1945: Aufgaben in der Armee und Stellung im Staate* (Stuttgart: Deutsche Verlags-Anstalt, 1962), 73–74; Müller-Hillebrand, *Heer,* 1:26–27, 106, 180; the changes became effective June 1, 1935. See also Deist, "Aufrüstung," DRZW, 1:516–18.

53. Rearmament planning was, of course, a highly complex process; space limitations preclude a thorough treatment here. See Deist, *Wehrmacht and German Rearmament,* chaps. 3–5; and Deist, "Aufrüstung," DRZW, 1:415–46; Murray, *Change in the European Balance,* 4–27; Müller, "Militär-Elite," 266–69; Hans-Erich Volkmann, "Die NS-Wirtschaft in Vorbereitung de Krieges," DRZW, 1:177–368; Berenice A. Carroll, *Design for Total War: Arms and Economics in the Third Reich* (The Hague: Mouton, 1968), chaps. 6–8; Overy, *Goering;* Geyer, *Aufrüstung oder Sicherheit.*

54. Murray, *Change in the European Balance,* 22–23.

55. Deist, "Aufrüstung," DRZW, 1:421.

56. Deist, *Wehrmacht and German Rearmament,* 46.

57. Müller, "Militär-Elite," 267; Deist, *Wehrmacht and German Rearmament,* 40.

58. BA-MA RW 4/v. 841: Aufbau des Offizierskorps unter besonderer Berücksich-

tigung des Bekenntnisses der Bewerber zum nationalsozialistischen Staat. Der Reichs-kriegsminister und Oberbefehlshaber der Wehrmacht, Nr.1390/35 geh. L. II d. Berlin, den 22.Juli 1935.

59. Jürgen Förster, "Vom Führerheer der Republik zur nationalsozialistischen Volksarmee," in *Deutschland in Europa. Kontinuität und Bruch. Gedenkschrift für Andreas Hillgruber,* ed. Jost Dülffer, Bernd Martin, and Günter Wollstein (Frankfurt am Main: Propyläen, 1990), 314.

60. Erfurth, *Geschichte,* 165-68, 197-98; Gordon Craig, *The Politics of the Prussian Army, 1640-1945* (New York: Oxford University Press, 1956) 481-84; Förster, "Volksarmee," 315-16; Deist, "Aufrüstung," DRZW, 1:421.

61. O'Neill, *German Army and the Nazi Party,* 92-93; Deist, "Aufrüstung," DRZW, 1:434-36; Deist, *Wehrmacht and German Rearmament,* 46-49; Müller, "Militär-Elite," 267-68. Murray points out that, given the seriousness of Germany's economic problems, a more coherent planning structure would not have helped. There was really no way in which the Germans could have significantly increased arms production over and above the level they achieved. See *Change in the European Balance,* 12-15, 23.

62. Müller, "Militär-Elite," 270; Deist, *Wehrmacht and German Rearmament,* 46; Deist, "Aufrüstung," DRZW, 1:418.

63. Deist explains that this move did not surprise the army, which Hitler had informed several weeks earlier. Nor did the army's leadership have any intention of pulling back if the French intervened. See "Aufrüstung," DRZW, 1:424-26. See also Robertson, *Hitler's Pre-War Policy,* 66-81.

64. Hitler calculated the level of support carefully, with an eye to prolonging the war rather than helping the Nationalists win quickly. See Gerhard Weinberg, *The Foreign Policy of Hitler's Germany: Diplomatic Revolution in Europe, 1933-36* (Chicago: University of Chicago Press, 1983), 297-98; Murray, *Change in the European Balance,* 129-33. German engagement in Spain, which included the use of military units from October-November 1936 on, also had an important effect on Germany's position in Europe: German-Italian relations improved, and the contrary interests of democratic and fascist states emerged more concretely. See Messerschmidt, "Aussenpolitik und Kriegsvorbereitung," DRZW, 1:608-11.

65. The order is reproduced in Müller, *Beck,* 438 n. 2.

66. Müller, *Beck,* 118-19 and documents 28 and 29: "Schreiben Becks an den Chef der Heeresleitung mit Ankündigung seines Rücktritts für den Fall konkreter Kriegsvorbereitungen gegen Österreich [*sic*] vom 3.5.1935" and "Stellungnahme Becks zu einer Weisung des Reichskriegsministers über operative Planungen gegen die Tschechoslowakei (Unternehmen "Schulung")(o.D.)," 438-44.

67. Müller, *Beck,* 119; Deist, "Aufrüstung," DRZW, 1:505-6. On Beck's and Fritsch's attitude toward Hitler's goals, see also Karl-Heinz Janssen and Fritz Tobias, *Der Sturz der Generäle: Hitler und die Blomberg-Fritsch-Krise, 1938* (Munich: Beck, 1994), 13-20.

68. Geyer, "German Strategy," 569-70.

69. Ibid., 569; Müller, "Militär-Elite," 271; Deist, *Wehrmacht and German Rearmament,* 49.

70. For more on this issue, see Müller, "Militär-Elite," 272-76.

71. Müller, *Beck,* 438 n 2.

72. The first memo is "Der Reichskriegsminister und Oberbefehlshaber der Wehrmacht. W.A. Nr.1571/35 geh. L I a, 24.8.1935, *Betr.:* Unterrichtung des W.A., *Bezug:* Nr. 90/34 g.K. W II b v. 31.1.34, Ziffer 3 und W.A. Nr.1399/34 g.K. L I a v.17.10.34," in BA-MA RH 2/134, 48; the second memo is "Der Reichskriegsminister und Oberbefehlshaber der Wehrmacht, W.A.Nr.1571/35 [*sic*] geh.L Ia, *Betr.:* Unterrichtung des W.A., *Bezug:* W.A. Nr.1571/35 geh.L Ia v. 24.8.35," in BA-MA RH 2/134, 24.

73. Seaton, *German Army,* 77; Erfurth, *Geschichte,* 194.

74. Caspar and Schottelius, "Organisation des Heeres," 322-24; Müller-Hillebrand, *Heer,* 1:105-80; Schwedler told the story of Beck's request to Dr. Georg Meyer of the Militärgeschichtliches Forschungsamt after the war.

75. Caspar and Schottelius, "Organisation des Heeres," 324-25; Deist, "Aufrüstung," DRZW, 1:506.

76. See Hansgeorg Model, *Der deutsche Generalstabsoffizier: Seine Auswahl und Ausbildung in Reichswehr, Wehrmacht und Bundeswehr* (Frankfurt am Main: Bernard & Graefe, 1968), 105-7; Horst Boog, *Die deutsche Luftwaffenführung 1935-1945: Führungsprobleme—Spitzengliederung—Generalstabsausbildung* (Stuttgart: Deutsche Verlags-Anstalt, 1982), 406-7, 448-49; James S. Corum, *The Luftwaffe: Creating the Operational Air War, 1918-1940* (Lawrence: University Press of Kansas, 1997), 253-54; Taylor, *Sword and Swastika,* 104, 106, 202 n; Erfurth, *Geschichte,* 195.

77. Müller, *Beck,* 120, and document 36, "Denkschrift Becks über die Stellung und Befügnisse der Heeresführung im Kriegsfall," 466-69; see also Erfurth, *Geschichte,* 192.

78. Müller, *Beck,* 121-22. Admiral Raeder, the commander in chief of the navy, also received a promotion and ministerial rank.

79. Deutsch, *Hitler and His Generals,* 56-57; Keitel papers, BA-MA N 54, 4:31; Walter Görlitz, ed., *The Memoirs of Field Marshal Keitel,* translated by David Irving (New York: Stein & Day, 1966), 36; Taylor, *Sword and Swastika,* 140-41.

80. The memo in its entirety is in Walter Görlitz, ed., *Generalfeldmarschall Keitel: Verbrecher oder Offizier? Erinnerungen, Briefe, Dokumente des Chefs OKW* (Göttingen: Musterschmidt-Verlag, 1961), 123-42. An English translation is found in Donald Detwiler, ed., Charles B. Burdick and Jürgen Rohwer, assoc. eds., *World War II German Military Studies: A Collection of 213 Special Reports on the Second World War Prepared by Former Officers of the Wehrmacht for the United States Army* (hereafter: GMS) (New York: Garland Publishing, 1979), 5: annex 1a. See also Müller, *Beck,* 124-25. Manstein claimed to have been the author of the memorandum; see *Aus einem Soldatenleben,* 289-90. The ideas in the memo were hardly new, however; Manstein must have worked from earlier documents.

81. Blomberg's answer is appended to the end of Fritsch's memo. See Görlitz, *Generalfeldmarschall Keitel,* 142; GMS 5: annex 1a, 31.

82. Deutsch, *Hitler and His Generals,* 57.

83. Deist, "Aufrüstung," DRZW, 1:507; Manstein, *Aus einem Soldatenleben,* 292.

84. Amtliches Tagebuch vom Chef des Wehrmachtführungsstabes, Abt. Landesverteidigung, Oberst Jodl, für die Zeit vom 4.1.1937-24.8.1939, in BA-MA RW 4/31, entries for Jan. 7 and 27, Feb. 2, Apr. 28-30, May 14, and July 15, 1937; Keitel papers, 4:47. The Keitel papers indicate that he actually carried out the reorganization at this point, but that was not the case; see chapter 3. Keitel wrote his account in his cell at Nuremberg, and his memory for dates is not reliable.

3. CONVERGING TRENDS

1. On the meeting itself, see Williamson Murray, *The Change in the European Balance of Power, 1938-1939: The Path to Ruin* (Princeton, N.J.: Princeton University Press, 1984), 135-37; Manfred Messerschmidt, "Aussenpolitik und Kriegsvorbereitung," in *Das Deutsche Reich und der Zweite Weltkrieg*, ed. Militärgeschichtliches Forschungsamt (Stuttgart: Deutsche Verlags-Anstalt, 1979-90) (hereafter: DRZW), 1:623-25; Klaus-Jürgen Müller, *General Ludwig Beck: Studien und Dokumente zur politisch-militärischen Vorstellungswelt und Tätigkeit des Generalstabschefs des deutschen Heeres 1933-1938* (Boppard: Harald Boldt, 1980), 249-53; Harold Deutsch, *Hitler and His Generals: The Hidden Crisis, January-June 1938* (Minneapolis: University of Minnesota Press, 1974), 59-69; Karl-Heinz Janssen and Fritz Tobias, *Der Sturz der Generäle: Hitler und die Blomberg-Fritsch-Krise 1938* (Munich: Beck, 1994), 9-12; Telford Taylor, *Munich: The Price of Peace* (Garden City, N.Y.: Doubleday, 1979), 299-302. Murray's work is especially useful for its synthesis of economic with political and strategic factors. The so-called Hossbach Memorandum can be found in Friedrich Hossbach, *Zwischen Wehrmacht und Hitler 1934-1938* (Wolfenbüttel: Wolfenbütteler Verlagsanstalt, 1949), 207-17. The following account is drawn primarily from that document. An English version can be found in *Documents on German Foreign Policy, 1918-1945* (Washington, D.C.: U.S. Government Printing Office, 1949-66). For a critical appraisal of the document and Hossbach's use of it, see Jonathan Wright and Paul Stafford, "Hitler, Britain and the Hossbach Memorandum," *Militärgeschichtliche Mitteilungen* 2 (1987): 77-123.

2. See Murray, *Change in the European Balance*, 135-36.

3. See Janssen and Tobias, *Der Sturz der Generäle*, 13-20.

4. Deutsch, *Hitler and His Generals*, 71, 74-75. No record of the meeting exists. The evidence about it came from Hossbach and Neurath after the war, when both men had an interest in appearing in the most positive light possible. On the other hand, there is no evidence that contradicts their claims either.

5. Bemerkungen Becks zur Niederschrift des Obersts i.G. Hossbach über eine Besprechung in der Reichskanzlei am 05.11.1937 vom 12.11.1937, in Müller, *Beck*, 498-501. See also Wolfgang Foerster, *Generaloberst Ludwig Beck. Sein Kampf gegen den Krieg. Aus nachgelassenen Papieren des Generalstabschefs* (Munich: Isar, 1953), 80-82.

6. Peter Hoffmann, "Generaloberst Ludwig Becks militärpolitisches Denken," *Historische Zeitschrift* 234 (1982): 115; Müller, *Beck*, 266; and Müller, *Armee und drittes Reich 1933-1939. Darstellung und Dokumentation* (Paderborn: Schöningh, 1987), 305.

7. Wilhelm Deist, *The Wehrmacht and German Rearmament* (London: Macmillan, 1981), 98; Deist, "Die Aufrüstung der Wehrmacht," DRZW 1:523; Klaus-Jürgen Müller, "Deutsche Militär-Elite in der Vorgeschichte des Zweiten Weltkrieges," in *Die deutschen Eliten und der Weg in den Zweiten Weltkrieg*, ed. Martin Broszat and Klaus Schwabe (Munich: C. H. Beck, 1989), 276; Manfred Messerschmidt, "German Military Effectiveness Between 1919 and 1939," in *Military Effectiveness*, ed. Allan R. Millett and Williamson Murray, vol. 2, *The Interwar Period* (Boston: Unwin Hyman, 1990), 236.

8. Most historians believe that Hitler was looking for an excuse to fire Blomberg and Fritsch. See Wilhelm Deist, "The Road to Ideological War: Germany, 1918-1945," in *The Making of Strategy: Rulers, States and War*, ed. Williamson Murray, MacGregor Knox, and Alvin Bernstein (New York: Cambridge University Press,

1994), 379; Murray, *Change in the European Balance,* 138; Murray, "Net Assessment in Nazi Germany in the 1930s," in *Calculations: Net Assessment and the Coming of World War II,* ed. Williamson Murray and Allan R. Millett (New York: Free Press, 1992), 73; and especially Deutsch, *Hitler and His Generals,* 75-76. For an opposing viewpoint, see Janssen and Tobias, *Der Sturz der Generäle,* 9, 20-21. Their arguments have some merit but are not completely convincing.

9. Janssen and Tobias, *Der Sturz der Generäle,* 15; Robert J. O'Neill, *The German Army and the Nazi Party, 1933-1939* (London: Cassell, 1966), 128-30; Deutsch, *Hitler and His Generals,* 40-41.

10. Accounts differ as to when the idea occurred to Göring. Janssen and Tobias maintain that he had no such ambition until Blomberg was on the way out; see *Der Sturz der Generäle,* 48. Most others have described Göring's ambition, or at least his jealousy, as long-standing; see Alan Bullock, *Hitler and Stalin: Parallel Lives* (New York: Vintage Books, 1993), 555; Telford Taylor, *Sword and Swastika: Generals and Nazis in the Third Reich* (Chicago: Quadrangle Books, 1952), 131; Taylor, *Munich,* 313-14; Deutsch, *Hitler and His Generals,* 34.

11. Deist, "Aufrüstung," DRZW, 1:516-17; Deutsch, *Hitler and His Generals,* 40; Taylor, *Munich,* 314.

12. The best sources on the Blomberg-Fritsch affair are Janssen and Tobias, *Der Sturz der Generäle,* and Harold Deutsch, *Hitler and His Generals.* The affair is important enough that every history of the period deals with it. See especially: Müller, *Das Heer und Hitler: Armee und nationalsozialistisches Regime 1933-1940* (Stuttgart: Deutsche Verlags-Anstalt, 1969), 255-99; Bullock, *Hitler and Stalin,* 554-55; Taylor, *Sword and Swastika,* 147-61; and Taylor, *Munich,* 315-27.

The exact roles of the principal actors in the Blomberg affair remain unclear. Göring knew early on that Frau Blomberg had "a certain past"—Blomberg told him some time before the wedding—and he controlled the police forces that could have told him more, but the extent of his foreknowledge is not ascertainable. The information was certainly a shock to Hitler and the other army officers. Bullock writes that Fritsch told Hitler to fire Blomberg, but he presents no evidence; see *Hitler and Stalin,* 555. Janssen and Tobias present the idea as Hitler's, with later encouragement from the army; see *Der Sturz der Generäle,* 51-58. Deutsch barely touches on the army's attitude at all, but the officer corps' sense of outrage was real.

13. Information on these meetings comes primarily from the records of Blomberg's interrogation by the Americans on September 23, 1945; see Deutsch, *Hitler and His Generals,* 116-19; Janssen and Tobias, *Der Sturz der Generäle,* 126-27.

14. Walter Görlitz, ed., *The Memoirs of Field Marshal Keitel,* trans. David Irving (New York: Stein & Day, 1966), 47-49.

15. Peter Bor, *Gespräche mit Halder* (Wiesbaden: Limes, 1950), 115-16.

16. The quote is from Görlitz, *Memoirs of Keitel,* 29; on his nickname, see Helmuth Greiner, "OKW, World War II" (MS #C-065b), 9, in *World War II German Military Studies: A Collection of 213 Special Reports on the Second World War Prepared by Former Officers of the Wehrmacht for the United States Army,* ed. Donald Detwiler, assoc. ed. Charles B. Burdick and Jürgen Rohwer (New York: Garland, 1979) (hereafter: GMS), vol. 7.

17. Görlitz, *Memoirs of Keitel,* 48; see also Deutsch, *Hitler and His Generals,* 218-20; Janssen and Tobias, *Der Sturz der Generäle,* 200.

18. Amtliches Tagebuch vom Chef des Wehrmachtführungsstabes, Abt. Landesverteidigung, Oberst Jodl, für die Zeit vom 4.1.1937-24.8.1939 (hereafter: Jodl diary), in BA-MA RW 4/31, 97: Jan. 28, 1938. The "current command organization" in the third condition undoubtedly referred to the centralized Wehrmacht command that Keitel envisioned, since he and Hitler developed the conditions together. See Müller, *Heer und Hitler,* 264 n 46.

19. The circumstances remain a source of contention. Most authors describe Brauchitsch in wholly negative terms. See, e.g., Deutsch, *Hitler and His Generals,* 222-27; Christian Hartmann, *Halder: Generalstabschef Hitlers 1938-1942* (Paderborn: Schöningh, 1991), 88-89; Taylor, *Sword and Swastika,* 167; Taylor, *Munich,* 322-23; O'Neill, *German Army and the Nazi Party,* 146-47. For an alternative view, see Janssen and Tobias, *Der Sturz der Generäle,* 197-228. Janssen and Tobias maintain that Brauchitsch settled his divorce himself and that he took the command in order to protect the army, that is, to keep Reichenau from taking command. See also Peter Hoffmann, review of *Das Komplott oder Die Entmachtung der Generale. Blomberg- und Fritsch-Krise. Hitlers Weg zum Krieg,* by Harold C. Deutsch, *Militärgeschichtliche Mitteilungen* 20 (1976): 198-99.

20. Hartmann, *Halder,* 87-89.

21. Jodl diary, 95: Jan. 27, 1938.

22. Deutsch, *Hitler and His Generals,* 132; Deist, "Aufrüstung," DRZW, 1:508.

23. Müller, *Beck,* 130; Jodl diary, 96: Jan. 28, 1938.

24. Reproduced in Waldemar Erfurth, *Die Geschichte des deutschen Generalstabes von 1918 bis 1945,* 2d ed. (Göttingen: Musterschmidt, 1960), 207.

25. Deutsch, *Hitler and His Generals,* 263-65.

26. Keitel related a story in his memoirs that highlights his nature. On March 11 he received calls from a number of senior officers, including Brauchitsch, who urged him to appeal to Hitler to call off the operation. Keitel later returned their calls and told them that the Führer had refused—when in fact Keitel had never spoken with him at all. Keitel later wrote that Hitler's "verdict on the Army's leadership would have been devastating, a disillusionment I wanted to spare both parties." Görlitz, *Memoirs of Keitel,* 58-59.

27. On the annexation of Austria and its effect on the Fritsch crisis, see Janssen and Tobias, *Der Sturz der Generäle,* 8, 149; Murray, *Change in the European Balance,* 141-49; Messerschmidt, "Aussenpolitik und Kriegsvorbereitung," DRZW, 1:635-38; Deutsch, *Hitler and His Generals,* 338-39; Bullock, *Hitler and Stalin,* 557-62.

28. Deutsch, *Hitler and His Generals,* 265.

29. Ibid., 261-62; Janssen and Tobias, *Der Sturz der Generäle,* 149-52; Murray, *Change in the European Balance,* 138-39; Nicolaus von Below, *Als Hitlers Adjutant 1937-45* (Mainz: v.Hase & Koehler, 1980), 74. There is some disagreement over the motives behind the events. Deutsch and Murray present the widespread view that Hitler was purging the officer corps of opponents. In some cases, such as Schwedler's, that was true, but Janssen and Tobias argue convincingly that most of the officers concerned had no problems with the Führer or the Party. Certainly, that was the case with Manstein, who, like others in the group, had a successful career after this point.

30. Burkhart Müller-Hillebrand, *Das Heer, 1933-1945: Entwicklung des organisatorischen Aufbaues* (Darmstadt: E. S. Mittler, 1954-69), 1:111; Albert Seaton, *The*

German Army, 1933–45 (London: Weidenfeld and Nicolson, 1982), 86, 100; Taylor, *Sword and Swastika,* 106; Deutsch, *Hitler and His Generals,* 131.

31. Janssen and Tobias, *Der Sturz der Generäle,* 137; Below, *Als Hitlers Adjutant,* 71; Deutsch, *Hitler and His Generals,* 274–75; on Schmundt's nickname: General a.D. Johann Adolf Graf von Kielmansegg, interview by the author, Bad Krozingen, Germany, April 29, 1996. "His Master's Voice" was the slogan of the RCA Victor record company; the nickname thus implied that Schmundt lacked any independent opinions.

32. Hartmann, *Halder,* 79; Müller, *Beck,* 131–32; Deist, "Aufrüstung," DRZW, 1:508; Jodl diary, 110–11: Mar. 5, 1938.

33. Müller, *Beck,* 133.

34. Ibid., 133; Brauchitsch memo in GMS, 5: annex 1b.

35. Keitel memo in GMS, 5: annex 1c, 4.

36. Deist "Aufrüstung," DRZW, 1:508–9; Keitel memo in GMS, 5: annex 1c. See also Müller, *Beck,* 135.

37. Müller, *Beck,* 133, 135; Deist, "Aufrüstung," DRZW, 1:509.

38. The most detailed examination of the growing crisis with Czechoslovakia is in Taylor, *Munich;* see esp. chapters 16 and 25.

39. Görlitz, *Memoirs of Keitel,* 62–63. See also Müller, *Heer und Hitler,* 300–301. Taylor (*Munich,* 387, 389) says that Hitler ordered that the OKH not be informed of the plan.

40. Müller, *Heer und Hitler,* 301–5; Müller, *Beck,* 136.

41. On the so-called May crisis, see Taylor, *Munich,* 390–95; Murray, *Change in the European Balance,* 172–73.

42. Stellungnahme zu den Ausführungen Hitlers vom 28.05.1938 über die politischen und militärischen Voraussetzungen einer Aktion gegen die Tschechoslowakei vom 29.05.1938, in Müller, *Beck,* 521–28; the quote is from 528. On Beck's resistance, see also Murray, *Change in the European Balance,* 174–80; Murray, "Net Assessment," 75–81; Taylor, *Munich,* 680–84; Hoffmann, "Becks Denken," 119–20; Foerster, *Beck,* 97–146.

43. Erfurth, *Geschichte,* 211; Taylor, *Munich,* 681.

44. Der Oberste Befehlshaber der Wehrmacht Nr. 932/38, 30.5.38: Ausführungsbestimmungen zu dem Erlass vom 4.2.1938 über die Führung der Wehrmacht, in BA-MA RW 3/4. See also Müller, *Beck,* 140; and Deist, "Aufrüstung," DRZW, 1:509.

45. Denkschrift für den Oberbefehlshaber des Heeres über die Voraussetzungen und Erfolgsaussichten einer kriegerischen Aktion gegen die Tschechoslowakei aus Anlass einer Weisung des Oberbefehlshabers der Wehrmacht vom 03.06.1938, in Müller, *Beck,* 528–37; on both memos, see also 137–39.

46. Müller, *Beck,* 304–11, and the memos and briefing notes of July 16 and 19, 542–56; Müller, "Militär-Elite," 282; Deist, "Aufrüstung," DRZW, 1:518–19; Erfurth, *Geschichte,* 211–13; Peter Hoffmann, "Ludwig Beck: Loyalty and Resistance," *Central European History* 14 (1981): 347.

47. Letter from Manstein to Beck, dated July 21, 1938, in BA-MA N 28/3 (Beck papers).

48. See also Murray, *Change in the European Balance,* 180–81.

49. Erfurth, *Geschichte,* 214; Müller, Beck, 135. See also Gerhard Engel, *Heeresadjutant bei Hitler; 1938–1943: Aufzeichnungen des Majors Engel,* ed. Hildegard von Kotze (Stuttgart: Deutsche Verlags-Anstalt, 1974), 19: diary entry for March 28, 1938.

50. Murray, *Change in the European Balance,* 183; Hoffmann, "Loyalty and Resistance," 348.

51. Erfurth, *Geschichte,* 215; Seaton, *German Army,* 107-8.

52. Erfurth, *Geschichte,* 215-16.

53. The following is drawn primarily from Hartmann, *Halder,* esp. 67-77. See also Christian Hartmann and Sergij Slutsch, "Franz Halder und die Kriegsvorbereitungen im Frühjahr 1939: Eine Ansprache des Generalstabschefs des Heeres," *Vierteljahrshefte für Zeitgeschichte* 2 (1997): esp. 478.

54. Bor, *Gespräche mit Halder,* 86.

55. On the planned coup of 1938, the effect of the Munich Agreement, and especially Halder's participation, see Peter Hoffmann, *The History of the German Resistance, 1933-1945,* trans. Richard Barry (Cambridge, Mass.: MIT Press, 1977), 81-102; Hartmann, *Halder,* 99-116; Müller, "Militär-Elite," 284.

56. Hartmann, *Halder,* 105-6; Görlitz, *Memoirs of Keitel,* 67-69. Murray describes the planning process in detail; see *Change in the European Balance,* 217-63, on this incident esp. 225-29; Murray points out that Hitler's plan did have definite advantages over the one the army proposed.

57. Quoted in O'Neill, *German Army and the Nazi Party,* 67-68. Information on the officer purge of October 1938 is in Hartmann, *Halder,* 117; Müller, *Heer und Hitler,* 381; and Seaton, *German Army,* 110.

58. Murray, *Change in the European Balance,* 264-94; Hartmann, *Halder,* 122-23.

59. "Keitel Memorandum," in GMS 5: annex 1c, 7.

60. Keitel set up the staff organization in February 1938 as he had planned it the previous autumn; the order to do so was Oberkommando der Wehrmacht 169/38 WP, 7.2.1938, Betr: Organisation des Oberkommandos der Wehrmacht, in Müller, *Heer und Hitler,* 641; see also Müller, *Beck,* 131; Gustav-Adolf Caspar and Herbert Schottelius, "Die Organisation des Heeres 1933-1939," in *Handbuch zur deutschen Militärgeschichte 1648-1939,* ed. Militärgeschichtliches Forschungsamt (Munich: Bernard & Graefe, 1978), 7:323, 329; Deist, "Aufrüstung," DRZW, 1:508; Rudolf Absolon, *Die Wehrmacht im Dritten Reich. Aufbau, Gliederung, Recht, Verwaltung* (Boppard: Harald Boldt, 1969-95), 4:161-69; Fritz Frhr. von Siegler, *Die höheren Dienststellen der deutschen Wehrmacht 1933-1945* (Munich: Institut für Zeitgeschichte, 1953), 7-8; August Winter and others, "The German Armed Forces High Command, OKW (Oberkommando der Wehrmacht): A Critical Historical Study of Its Development, Organization, Missions and Functioning from 1938 to 1945" (MS #T-101), vol. II, in GMS vol. 4. The pagination of T-101 in GMS is complex. The main document is contained in vol. 4 of the *Studies,* with further related documents in vol. 5. Within the main document are "volumes," and in some cases "chapters" of volumes, that are separately paginated.

61. Gerhard Buck, "Der Wehrmachtführungsstab im Oberkommando der Wehrmacht," in *Jahresbibliographie 1973,* Bibliothek für Zeitgeschichte (Munich: Bernard & Graefe, 1973), 408-9. Viebahn was Beck's candidate, another vain attempt to gain influence.

62. Helmuth Greiner, *Die Oberste Wehrmachtführung 1939-1943* (Wiesbaden: Limes, 1951), 11.

63. Burkhart Müller-Hillebrand, "The Organizational Problems of the German High Command and Their Solutions: 1939-1945" (MS #P-041f, 1953), 11, 15, in *The*

German Army High Command, 1939-1945 (Arlington, Va.: University Publications of America, n.d., microfilm) (hereafter GAHC). Documents in GAHC are separately paginated; there are no master page numbers for the collection.

64. Heinz von Gyldenfeldt, "Army High Commander and Adjutant Division" (MS #P-041c, 1952), 1, 5, in GAHC; Wiegand Schmidt-Richberg, *Die Generalstäbe in Deutschland 1871-1945: Aufgaben in der Armee und Stellung im Staate* (Stuttgart: Deutsche Verlags-Anstalt, 1962), 78.

65. Burkhart Müller-Hillebrand, "The German Army High Command" (MS #P-041a, 1952?), 7, in GAHC.

66. Gyldenfeldt, "Army High Commander," 2.

67. "Dienstanweisungen für den Chef des Generalstabes des Heeres im Frieden sowie Friedensgliederung des Generalstabes des Heeres ab 1.7.1935," BA-MA RH 2/195, 30; Caspar and Schottelius, "Organisation des Heeres," 332; Schmidt-Richberg, *Die Generalstäbe,* 79.

68. "Dienstanweisung für den Chef des Generalstabes"; Gyldenfeldt, "Army High Commander," 2, 21. The abbreviation "I.A." should not be confused with "Ia," the designation for an operations officer.

69. For a description of the changes in the General Staff between 1935 and 1938, see Absolon, *Wehrmacht,* 4:178; Müller-Hillebrand, *Heer,* 111-12; Erfurth, *Geschichte,* 184.

70. Franz Halder, "The Chief of the Army General Staff" (MS #P-041d, 1952), 2, in GAHC; Alfred Zerbel, "Organization of the Army Quartermaster" (MS #P-041b, 1952), 2, in GAHC; Gyldenfeldt, "Army Commander," 23-24.

71. Up until the outbreak of the war, the branches were known by their numbers rather than their functional areas.

72. Hans von Greiffenberg, "Operations Branch of the Army General Staff" (MS #P-041e, 1952), 2-5, in GAHC. The following overview of the responsibilities of the different branches is drawn from Erfurth, *Geschichte,* 185-88.

73. Burkhart Müller-Hillebrand, "Schematische Darstellung der obersten Führung des deutschen Heeres 1938 bis Kriegsende mit Erläuterungen über organisatorische Beziehungen, Aufgaben und Verantwortlichkeiten der einzelnen Dienststellen des OKH im Laufe der Jahre 1938-1945" (MS #P-041a, unpublished), 28; Erfurth, *Geschichte,* 184; Günther Blumentritt and Alfred Zerbel, "Top-Level Agencies of the Army General Staff: The Chiefs of Operations, Training, and Organization" (MS #P-041d, 1952?), 1, in GAHC; Halder, "Chief," 2, 3.

74. Deist, "Aufrüstung," DRZW, 1:507.

75. Deutsch, *Hitler and His Generals,* 259.

76. Walter Görlitz, *Der deutsche Generalstab: Geschichte und Gestalt 1657-1945* (Frankfurt am Main Verlag der Frankfurter Hefte, 1950), 457.

77. Heinz Guderian, "General Critique of MSS #P-041a-P-041hh and a Report on the June 1944-March 1945 Period" (MS #P-041jj), 4, in GAHC.

78. Of 22,600 active officers at the end of 1938, only about one-seventh had been in the officer corps before 1933. Jürgen Förster, "Vom Führerheer der Republik zur nationalsozialistischen Volksarmee," in *Deutschland in Europa. Kontinuität und Bruch. Gedenkschrift für Andreas Hillgruber,* ed. Jost Dülffer, Bernd Martin, and Günter Wollstein (Frankfurt am Main: Propyläen, 1990), 315.

79. Bor, *Gespräche mit Halder,* 126.

80. Reinhard Stumpf, *Die Wehrmacht-Elite. Rang- und Herkunftstruktur der deutschen Generale und Admirale 1933-1945* (Boppard: Harald Boldt, 1982), 321; Seaton, *German Army,* 86; Erfurth, *Geschichte,* 210.

81. Germany, Heer, Heeresdienstvorschrift 92 (HDv 92), *Handbuch für den Generalstabsdienst im Kriege, Teil I, II, abgeschlossen am 1.8.1939* (Berlin: der Reichsdruckerei, 1939), 2.

82. See Hartmann, *Halder,* 118; Müller, *Heer und Hitler,* 381-82 and n. 13; Erfurth, *Geschichte,* 226.

83. Both Görlitz (*Generalstab,* 318) and Ulrich de Maizière (interview with the author, May 25, 1996) insist that the principle was dropped at the end of the First World War, but the process was not that quick or simple. There was an extensive discussion on the issue within the General Staff during Beck's tenure and another after Halder took over. See Erfurth, *Geschichte,* 225-26; Friedrich Hossbach, "Verantwortlichkeit der Generalstabsoffiziere in der deutschen Armee," in *Allgemeine Schweizerische Militärzeitschrift* 118 (1952): 222; Rolf Elble, *Führungsdenken, Stabsarbeit. Entwicklung und Ausblick—ein Versuch* (Darmstadt: Wehr und Wissen Verlagsgesellschaft, 1967), 93-94.

84. Hartmann, *Halder,* 119.

85. Winter and others, "Armed Forces High Command," 3: chapter B, 11, 15-16.

86. See Keitel's opening testimony, April 3, 1946, in International Military Tribunal, *Trial of the Major War Criminals Before the International Military Tribunal, Nuremberg, 14 November 1945-1 October 1946* (Nuremberg: International Military Tribunal, 1947), 10:473. Such testimony must be treated with extreme care, since Keitel obviously had an interest in minimizing his role, but in this case there are many pieces of anecdotal evidence that substantiate the claim. See also Buck, "Wehrmachtführungsstab," 407; Bernfried von Beesten, *Untersuchungen zum System der militärischen Planung im Dritten Reich von 1933 bis zum Kriegsbeginn: Vorstellungen, Voraussetzungen, Beweggründe und Faktoren* (Münster: Lit-Verlag, 1987), 198-99; Murray, "Net Assessment," 69-70.

87. Winter and others, "Armed Forces High Command," 3: chap. B, 9. See also Warlimont, *Im Hauptquartier der deutschen Wehrmacht 1939-1945: Grundlagen, Formen, Gestalten* (Frankfurt am Main: Bernard & Graefe, 1962), 35-36; Erfurth, *Geschichte,* 186.

4. THE ONSET OF WAR AND THE INITIAL VICTORIES

1. See Gerhard Weinberg, *A World at Arms: A Global History of World War II* (New York: Cambridge University Press, 1994), 28-34; Horst Rohde, "Hitlers erste 'Blitzkrieg' und seine Auswirkungen auf Nordosteuropa," in *Das Deutsche Reich und der Zweite Weltkrieg,* ed. Militärgeschichtliches Forschungsamt (Stuttgart: Deutsche Verlags-Anstalt, 1979-90) (hereafter: DRZW), 2:79-82; Williamson Murray, *The Change in the European Balance of Power, 1938-1939: The Path to Ruin* (Princeton, N.J.: Princeton University Press, 1984), 292-94.

2. Hitler's memorandum to Brauchitsch is in Paul R. Sweet and others, *Akten zur deutschen auswärtigen Politik 1918-1945* (Baden-Baden: Imprimerie Nationale, 1956) (hereafter ADAP), 6:98-99. An English version of this collection is available

as *Documents on German Foreign Policy, 1918–1945*, but it actually covers only the years through 1941.

3. Christian Hartmann, *Halder: Generalstabschef Hitlers 1938–1942* (Paderborn: Schöningh, 1991), 122–23; Walter Warlimont, *Im Hauptquartier der deutschen Wehrmacht 1939–1945: Grundlagen, Formen, Gestalten* (Frankfurt am Main: Bernard & Graefe, 1962), 34.

4. Rohde, "Hitlers erster 'Blitzkrieg,'" DRZW, 2:92; Warlimont, *Hauptquartier,* 34–35; Helmuth Greiner, *Die Oberste Wehrmachtführung 1939–1943* (Wiesbaden: Limes, 1951), 30–31.

5. ADAP 6:187–88.

6. Ibid., 6:154; see also Nuernberg Military Tribunals, *Trials of War Criminals Before the Nuernberg Military Tribunals Under Control Council Law No. 10, Nuernberg, October 1946–April 1949* (Washington, D.C.: U.S. Government Printing Office, 1949–53) (hereafter *Trials of the (minor) War Criminals*), 10:683–84; August Winter and others, "The Progress of Preparations for 'Case White'" (MS T-101 Annex 8), 5, in *World War II German Military Studies: A Collection of 213 Special Reports on the Second World War Prepared by Former Officers of the Wehrmacht for the United States Army,* ed. Donald Detwiler, assoc. ed. Charles B. Burdick and Jürgen Rohwer (New York: Garland, 1979) (hereafter: GMS), vol. 5.

7. See Christian Hartmann and Sergij Slutsch, "Franz Halder und die Kriegsvorbereitungen im Frühjahr 1939: Eine Ansprache des Generalstabschefs des Heeres," *Vierteljahrshefte für Zeitgeschichte* 2 (1997): 467–95; the quote is on 483. As the article points out, Halder's attitude stands in stark contrast to his testimony at his postwar trial, when he claimed that the army entered the campaign against its will.

8. Rohde, "Hitlers erster 'Blitzkrieg,'" DRZW, 2:93. Albert Seaton, *The German Army, 1933–45* (London: Weidenfeld & Nicolson, 1982), 114, cites Greiner (*Oberste Wehrmachtführung,* 53) as saying that Hitler made a change in 3d Army's mission. Waldemar Erfurth, *Die Geschichte des deutschen Generalstabes von 1918 bis 1945,* 2d ed. (Göttingen: Musterschmidt, 1960), 222, says the same thing, but gives no source. Franz Halder, "Der Komplex OKH-OKW," in the Halder papers, BA-MA N 220/95, 20, says that the only change Hitler made was to the plan of attack at Dirschau. Rohde mentions none of this; in any case, the Führer's role was certainly minor.

9. Rohde, "Hitlers erster 'Blitzkrieg,'" DRZW, 2:93; Hartmann, *Halder,* 123, 127–28.

10. Warlimont, *Hauptquartier,* 35–36, 39; Halder, "Komplex," 14–15; The directive of April 3 assigned the task of preparing the timetable to the OKW: see ADAP, 6:154.

11. Weinberg, *A World at Arms,* 34–42, for background; also Bernd Stegemann, "Politik und Kriegführung in der ersten Phase der deutschen Initiative," DRZW, 2:15–16.

12. See, e.g., 2.Abteilung Nr.1098/37 g.Kdos. III C., 1.7.37, *Betr.:* Gliederung des Gen St d H im Mob.Fall ab Herbst 1938. Besprechung am 25.6.37, in BA-MA RH 2/1063, 144. This is a record of a meeting at which the chief of the General Staff met with the chiefs of the Central, Troop Training, and Organization Branches. Among other things, they agreed upon the two-tiered headquarters structure that is described later.

13. See, e.g., Generalstab des Heeres, 2.Abt. (III C), Nr.1879/37 g.Kdos., *Betr.:* Kriegsspitzengliederung (Heer), 20.1.38, in BA-MA RH 2/1063, 178; this is a memo from the Second Branch to the other branches, asking for their input to the latest draft

mobilization plan. See also Burkhart Müller-Hillebrand, *Das Heer, 1933-1945: Entwicklung des organisatorischen Aufbaues* (Darmstadt: E. S. Mittler, 1954-69), 1:56.

14. Except as noted, the information for this section on the OKH mobilization comes from Müller-Hillebrand, *Heer,* 1:115-25; see also Hartmann, *Halder,* 94-95; and Erfurth, *Geschichte,* 229-31.

15. Burkhart Müller-Hillebrand, "Schematische Darstellung der obersten Führung des deutschen Heeres 1938 bis Kriegsende mit Erläuterungen über organisatorische Beziehungen, Aufgaben und Verantwortlichkeiten der einzelnen Dienststellen des OKH im Laufe der Jahre 1938-1945" (MS #P-041a, unpublished), 37; and Burkhart Müller-Hillebrand, "The German Army High Command" (MS #P-041a, 1952?), 18, in *The German Army High Command 1938-1945* (Arlington, Va.: University Publications of America, n.d. Microfilm) (hereafter: GAHC); Heinz von Gyldenfeldt, "Army High Commander and Adjutant Division" (MS #P-041c, 1952), 3-4, in GAHC; Seaton, *German Army,* 103; Alfred Zerbel, "Organization of the Army Quartermaster" (MS #P-041b, 1952), 2, in GAHC.

16. Müller-Hillebrand, "Army High Command," 32.

17. Günther Blumentritt and Alfred Zerbel, "Top-Level Agencies of the Army General Staff: The Chiefs of Operations, Training, and Organization" (MS #P-041d, 1952?), 2, 6, 11-12, 13, in GAHC.

18. Hans von Greiffenberg, "Operations Branch of the Army General Staff" (MS #P-041e, 1952), 1, in GAHC. The branches replaced their numerical with functional designations upon the outbreak of war.

19. Greiffenberg, "Operations Branch," 5-6, 18.

20. See Alan Bullock, *Hitler and Stalin: Parallel Lives* (New York: Vintage Books, 1993), 643-44; quote is on page 643. Gerhard Engel, in "Effect of the Composition and Movement of Hitler's Field Headquarters on the Conduct of the War" (MS #T-101 Annex 16), 3, in GMS, vol. 5, notes the propaganda motive as well as Hitler's desire to control the campaign directly. That second motive seems doubtful, however, given the size of his headquarters and his actions during the campaign.

21. For more information on the Führer's train and other headquarters arrangements, see Peter Hoffmann, *Hitler's Personal Security* (Cambridge, Mass.: MIT Press, 1979).

22. Franz Josef Schott, "Der Wehrmachtführungsstab im Führerhauptquartier 1939—1945" (Ph.D. diss., University of Bonn, 1980), 17, 39, 40.

23. Greiner, *Oberste Wehrmachtführung,* 8-9; Schott, "Wehrmachtführungsstab," 40.

24. Walter Görlitz, ed., *The Memoirs of Field Marshal Keitel,* trans. David Irving (New York: Stein & Day, 1966), 92; Bullock, *Hitler and Stalin,* 644.

25. Percy Ernst Schramm, ed., *Kriegstagebuch des Oberkommandos der Wehrmacht (Wehrmachtführungsstab)* (Munich: Manfred Pawlak, 1982) (hereafter OKW KTB), 1:174E-75E. Rohde, "Hitlers erster 'Blitzkrieg,'" describes the campaign in detail, 111-32, but does not mention any intervention by Hitler in operational matters. Keitel indicates, however, that Hitler intervened on several occasions; see Görlitz, *Memoirs of Keitel,* 94. Also, Halder's war diary shows one such action; see Franz Halder, *Kriegstagebuch: Tägliche Aufzeichnungen des Chefs des Generalstabes des Heeres 1939-1942,* ed. Arbeitskreis für Wehrforschung, Stuttgart (Stuttgart: Kohlhammer, 1962) (hereafter Halder KTB), 1:57 (Sept. 3, 1939).

26. Greiner, *Oberste Wehrmachtführung,* 13-14; Görlitz, *Memoirs of Keitel,* 94.

27. Greiner, *Oberste Wehrmachtführung,* 15; Warlimont, *Hauptquartier,* 47.

28. Halder, "Komplex," 21; Halder KTB, 1:30 (Aug. 25, 1939) (this entry notes Halder's warning to the OKW); Hartmann, *Halder,* 143; see also Bernhard von Lossberg, *Im Wehrmachtführungsstab: Bericht eines Generalstabsoffiziers* (Hamburg: Nölke, 1950), 20.

29. Halder KTB, 1:50–85 (Sept. 1–27, 1939). The entries include conferences and telephone conversations with staff officers in the OKH and the OKW, with senior commanders from all three services, and with foreign ministry representatives.

30. Rohde, "Hitlers erster 'Blitzkrieg,'" DRZW, 2:104–10, contains an excellent overview of the Polish plans. See also Robert M. Kennedy, *The German Campaign in Poland, 1939* (Washington, D.C.: Department of the Army, 1956). Nicholas Bethell, *The War That Hitler Won: September 1939* (London: Allen Lane The Penguin Press, 1972), contains a detailed account of the military and diplomatic moves by the Poles and western Allies.

31. Rohde, "Hitlers erster 'Blitzkrieg,'" DRZW, 2:118.

32. On Allied actions and their effects from September 1939 and May 1940, see Murray, *Change in the European Balance,* 326–34, 347–51.

33. Rohde, "Hitlers erster 'Blitzkrieg,'" DRZW, 2:115; Kennedy, *Campaign in Poland,* 92–93. One must bear in mind that neither Bock nor the OKH knew at this point of the Soviets' plans to invade.

34. *Das deutsche Reich und der Zweite Weltkrieg* has excellent maps of all the campaigns. For an even more detailed view of the Polish campaign, see Klaus-Jürgen Thies, ed., *Der Polenfeldzug: Ein Lageatlas der Operationsabteilung des Generalstabes des Heeres; neu gezeichnet nach den Unterlagen im Bundesarchiv/ Militärarchiv* (Osnabrück: Biblio Verlag, 1989). This contains the daily situation maps that the Operations Branch of the General Staff drew up. Atlases for the other campaigns are also available; the series title is *Der Zweite Weltkrieg im Kartenbild.*

35. Rohde, "Hitlers erster 'Blitzkrieg,'" 123–24; Kennedy, *Campaign in Poland,* 101–2.

36. Rohde, "Hitlers erster 'Blitzkrieg,'" DRZW, 2:126–29.

37. Halder KTB, 1:80 (Sept. 20, 1939).

38. Ibid., 1:70 (Sept. 10, 1939).

39. The most complete source on the planning for the invasion of France is Hans-Adolf Jacobsen, *Fall Gelb: Der Kampf um den deutschen Operationsplan zur Westoffensive 1940* (Wiesbaden: Franz Steiner Verlag, 1957). This source must be used with care, however; like most early works, it tends to view the army leadership a bit too sympathetically. See also Hans Umbreit, "Die Kampf um die Vormachtstellung in Westeuropa," DRZW, vol. 2; Telford Taylor, *The March of Conquest: The German Victories in Western Europe, 1940* (New York: Simon & Schuster, 1958); and Robert Allan Doughty, *The Breaking Point: Sedan and the Fall of France, 1940* (Hamden, Conn.: Archon Books, 1990).

40. On the first word to reach Halder, see Halder KTB, 1:84 (Sept. 25, 1939). On the September 27 meeting, see Umbreit, "Kampf," 238; Weinberg, *A World at Arms,* 108. Detailed notes on the meeting are in the Halder KTB, 1:86–90, but one must treat them with caution: Halder added them to his diary after 1950. See also OKW KTB 1:951, which contains a record of the meeting prepared for the war diary but then removed by Warlimont's order.

41. Notes from the conference are in the Halder KTB, 1:101–3; the directive (dated

October 9) is published in Walther Hubatsch, ed., *Hitlers Weisungen für die Krieg-führung 1939–1945: Dokumente des Oberkommandos der Wehrmacht* (Frankfurt am Main: Bernard & Graefe, 1962), 32–33. See also Taylor, *March of Conquest,* 43, 44.

42. Murray, *Change in the European Balance,* 326–33.

43. The Halder KTB, 1:70 (Sept. 10, 1939) notes Halder's plans to reorganize the army for positional warfare. Jacobsen, *Fall Gelb,* 10, discusses the Stülpnagel study. Another mention can be found in the OKW KTB, 1:950, which shows the original war diary entry for September 25.

44. Halder KTB, 1:93 (Sept. 29, 1939). See also Umbreit, "Kampf," DRZW, 2:239; Doughty, *Breaking Point,* 21.This is a good indication of how little faith many of the Germans still had in their "Blitzkrieg" tactics. In fact, all sides overestimated the effectiveness of the French army in 1940. It was large and well equipped, but its doctrine was hopelessly out of date. See Robert Allan Doughty, *The Seeds of Disaster: The Development of French Army Doctrine, 1919–1939* (Hamden, Conn.: Archon Books, 1985); and Eugenia C. Kiesling, *Arming Against Hitler: France and the Limits of Military Planning* (Lawrence: University Press of Kansas, 1996).

45. Umbreit, "Kampf," DRZW, 2:244. See also Görlitz, *Memoirs of Keitel,* 101–2; Keitel was present at the meeting. A record of the meeting also became part of the OKW war diary; see OKW KTB 1:951–52.

46. Halder KTB, 1:101–3 (Oct. 10, 1939). See also, e.g., Halder's notes of the conference on January 20, 1940, ibid., 1:165–67.

47. The directives are in Hubatch, *Weisungen,* 34–46; on Hitler's distrust of Brauchitsch, see the Keitel papers, BA-MA N 54, 5:57. Hitler was incensed at the resistance the army put up over his plans to attack in 1939; see Jacobsen, *Fall Gelb,* 12–13.

48. Doughty, *Breaking Point,* 22; Jacobsen, *Fall Gelb,* 40; Taylor, *March of Conquest,* 164–67.

49. For Halder, Hitler's interference in the planning process came as a real blow. See Hartmann, *Halder,* 182.

50. Klaus A. Maier, "Die Sicherung der europäischen Nordflanke; Die deutsche Strategie," DRZW, 2:197.

51. Warlimont, *Hauptquartier,* 83.

52. Maier, "Sicherung," DRWZ, 2:197; Order on preparations for *Weserübung,* dated Jan. 27, 1940, in Office of United States Chief of Council for Prosecution of Axis Criminality, *Nazi Conspiracy and Aggression* (hereafter *Nazi Conspiracy*) (Washington, D.C.: U.S. Government Printing Office, 1946), 6:883; Jodl's diary entries for February 18 and 21, 1940, in *Nazi Conspiracy,* 4:385.

53. Hubatsch, *Weisungen,* 47–49.

54. August Winter and others, "The German Armed Forces High Command, OKW (Oberkommando der Wehrmacht): A Critical Historical Study of Its Development, Organization, Missions and Functioning from 1938 to 1945" (MS #T-101), 3: chap. B1a, 24–25, in GMS, vol. 4.

55. Seaton, *German Army,* 132; see also Maier, "Sicherung," DRZW, 2:197–201.

56. Warlimont, *Hauptquartier,* 89–90.

57. Ibid., 88–89.

58. Halder KTB, 1:204 (Feb. 21, 1940).

59. On the conduct of the campaign in Denmark and Norway, see Bernd Stegemann, "Das Unternehmen 'Weserübung,'" in DRZW, 2:212–25; Walther Hubatsch,

"Weserübung": Die deutsche Besetzung von Dänemark und Norwegen 1940 (Göttingen: Musterschmidt, 1960); Helmuth Greiner, "The Campaigns in Western and Northern Europe, 1940" (MS #C-065d), in GMS, vol. 7.

60. Lossberg, *Im Wehrmachtführungsstab,* 67–69; BA-MA RW 4/32: Tagebuch Jodl (WFA) vom 1.2.–26.5.1940, 35 (14.4.1940); other parts of Jodl's diary for this period are reproduced in Warlimont, *Hauptquartier,* 93–94.

61. Lossberg, *Im Wehrmachtführungsstab,* 69. For other examples of Hitler's nervousness, see Stegemann, "'Weserübung,'" DRZW, 2:219.

62. BA-MA RH 2/93: OKH, Gen St d H Op.Abt.(IVb), Nr. 20 065/40 g.Kdos., 6.4.40: Neugliederung der Operationsabteilung, Stand: 7.4.1940.

63. Warlimont, *Hauptquartier,* 55–56.

64. Ibid., 55; Winter and others, "Armed Forces High Command," 3: chap. B1a, 60; Engel, "Hitler's Field Headquarters," 2. Schott, "Wehrmachtführungsstab," 43, says that the reasons for the limits that Hitler placed on his staff remain unclear, but that he might have been negatively influenced by the size and unwieldiness of the kaiser's staff in the First World War. Probably the truth lies in Hitler's vision of himself as the *Feldherr,* combined with his lack of understanding of staff functions.

65. OKW KTB, 1:881–82. On October 16, 1939, the "Office Groups" within the OKW had been redesignated "Offices"; Rudolf Absolon, *Die Wehrmacht im Dritten: Reich. Aufbau, Gliederung, Recht, Verwaltung* (Boppard: Harald Boldt, 1969–95), 5:51.

66. Schott, "Wehrmachtführungsstab," 10, 40–42. Greiner, *Oberste Wehrmachtführung,* 11, puts the number of other ranks at fifty to seventy-five. See also the OKW KTB, 1:877–946, for the duties and organization of the different elements of the OKW at the start of the war. From this point forward the Field Echelon of the National Defense Branch will simply be referred to as the National Defense Branch.

67. Schott, "Wehrmachtführungsstab," 64.

68. See the OKW KTB, 1:158E, for the dates, times, and subjects of these meetings. Brauchitsch was in contact with Hitler by telephone, however, usually twice each day. See Halder, "Komplex," 28.

69. Görlitz, *Memoirs of Keitel,* 146; Warlimont, *Hauptquartier,* 58–59; Halder, "Komplex," 28.

70. Lossberg, *Im Wehrmachtführungsstab,* 22.

71. Warlimont, *Hauptquartier,* 60–62. One must approach Warlimont's account with some degree of caution on this issue; like many survivors, he tended to make himself look good at the expense of those officers who were killed during or after the war. Still, there is little direct evidence to contradict Warlimont's version, and Lossberg's confirmation bears weight, since he was Jodl's friend as well as Warlimont's subordinate. See also Greiner, *Oberste Wehrmachtführung,* 13. There is no good biography of Jodl. That by Bodo Scheurig (*Alfred Jodl. Gehorsam und Verhängnis. Biographie* [Berlin: Propyläen, 1991]) is perhaps the best, but one cannot consider it a thorough, objective analysis.

72. Winter and others, "Armed Forces High Command," 3: chap. B1a, 42–43; Helmuth Greiner, "OKW, World War II" (MS #C-065b), 8–9, in GMS, vol. 7; Görlitz, *Memoirs of Keitel,* 110–11; Schott, "Wehrmachtführungsstab," 56–57; OKW KTB, 1:138E–39E. The subjects of the briefings given to Jodl are gleaned from an examination of the OKW KTB up to spring 1941.

73. Winter and others, "Armed Forces High Command," 3: chap. B1a, 43; Schott,

"Wehrmachtführungsstab," 57. One should bear in mind, as Schott points out, that such requests are not unusual in military staff work.

74. Gerhard Engel, "Adolf Hitler as Supreme Commander of the Armed Forces" (MS #T101 Annex 15), 7, in GMS, vol. 5.

75. Warlimont, *Hauptquartier,* 65-66.

76. Halder KTB, 1:336 (June 6, 1940).

77. Ibid., 1:303 (May 18, 1940).

78. Hartmann, *Halder,* 191.

79. Umbreit, "Kampf," DRZW, 2:289.

80. Halder KTB, 1:302 (May 17, 1940).

81. Ibid., 1:302 (May 18, 1940).

82. For the generals' attempts at self-justification, see, e.g., Gerd von Rundstedt, "Bemerkungen zum 'Feldzug im Westen'" (MS #C-053, unpublished); Lossberg, *Im Wehrmachtführungsstab,* 79; Warlimont, *Hauptquartier,* 109-10.

83. Umbreit, "Kampf," DRZW, 2:289-90.

84. Ibid., 2:293-96; Taylor, *March of Conquest,* 256-63. Umbreit argues convincingly against the idea that Hitler wanted to offer the British an olive branch by letting their army get away, as Rundstedt suggested after the war.

85. See Halder KTB, 1:319 (May 25, 1940), and 1:326 (May 30, 1940).

86. See ibid., 1:319-35 (May 25-June 5, 1940).

5. NEW DIRECTIONS, NEW PROBLEMS

1. Keitel apparently came up with the appellation after the French offered terms; see Christian Hartmann, *Halder: Generalstabschef Hitlers 1938-1942* (Paderborn: Schöningh, 1991), 205 and n 13. In time some senior officers would twist the title into the derisory nickname "GroFaZ," for "Grösster Feldherr aller Zeiten."

2. See Andreas Hillgruber, *Hitlers Strategie: Politik und Kriegsführung 1940-41* (Frankfurt am Main: Bernard & Graefe, 1965), 43, 48-49, 144.

3. The full document, dated June 30, 1940, is in International Military Tribunal, *Trial of the Major War Criminals Before the International Military Tribunal, Nuremberg, 14 November 1945-1 October 1946* (Nuremberg: International Military Tribunal, 1947) (hereafter: *Trial of the Major War Criminals*), 28:301-3; see also Charles B. Burdick, *Germany's Military Strategy and Spain in World War II* (Syracuse, N.Y.: Syracuse University Press, 1968), 3, 17; Bernd Stegemann, "Politik und Kriegführung in der ersten Phase der deutschen Initiative," in *Das Deutsche Reich und der Zweite Weltkrieg,* ed. Militärgeschichtliches Forschungsamt (Stuttgart: Deutsche Verlags-Anstalt, 1979-90) (hereafter: DRZW), 2:29; Hans Umbreit, "Deutsche Pläne und Vorbereitungen für eine Landung in England," DRZW, 2:369; Bernhard von Lossberg, *Im Wehrmachtführungsstab: Bericht eines Generalstabsoffiziers* (Hamburg: Nölke, 1950), 86-88.

4. To give just a few examples: Hillgruber, *Hitlers Strategie;* Hillgruber, "Noch einmal: Hitlers Wendung gegen die Sowjetunion 1940," in *Geschichte in Wissenschaft und Unterricht* 33 (1982): 214-26; Gerhard Schreiber, "The Mediterranean in Hitler's Strategy in 1940: 'Programme' and Military Planning," in *The German Military in the Age of Total War,* ed.Wilhelm Deist (Dover, N.H.: Berg, 1985), 240-81; Stegemann, "Politik und Kriegführung," DRZW, 2:15-39; Stegemann, "Der Entschluss zum

Unternehmen Barbarossa. Strategie oder Ideologie?" in *Geschichte in Wissenschaft und Unterricht* 33 (1982): 205-13; Martin van Creveld, *Hitler's Strategy, 1940-1941: The Balkan Clue* (London: Cambridge University Press, 1973); Gerhard Weinberg, *A World at Arms: A Global History of World War II* (New York: Cambridge University Press, 1994), 179-86.

5. Umbreit, "Landung," DRZW, Z:369-70; Hillgruber, *Hitlers Strategie,* 163.

6. Hitler remarked on this danger to Halder and Brauchitsch on July 13; see Franz Halder, *Kriegstagebuch: Tägliche Aufzeichnungen des Chefs des Generalstabes des Heeres 1939-1942,* ed. Arbeitskreis für Wehrforschung, Stuttgart (Stuttgart: Kohlhammer, 1962) (hereafter: Halder KTB), 2:21.

7. See Hillgruber, *Hitlers Strategie,* 144-57.

8. Order OKW/WFA/L Nr. 33124/40 g.Kdos.Chefs., 2.7.1940, betr. Kriegführung gegen England, cited in Karl Klee, *Das Unternehmen "Seelöwe": Die geplante deutsche Landung in England 1940* (Göttingen: Musterschmidt 1958). Klee's work remains the best examination of the preparations for *Sea Lion.* A companion volume, *Dokumenten zum Unternehmen "Seelöwe,"* appeared in 1959.

9. OKW/WFA/L Nr. 33 160/40 g.Kdos. Chefsache, 16.7.1940, Weisung Nr. 16, in Walther Hubatsch, *Hitlers Weisungen für die Kriegführung 1939-1945: Dokumente des Oberkommandos der Wehrmacht* (Frankfurt am Main: Bernard & Graefe, 1962), 61-65.

10. See Burdick, *Spain,* 18, 21; also Creveld, in *Hitler's Strategy,* examines the peripheral strategy in detail, although he places too much emphasis on it.

11. See Halder KTB, 2:31 (July 22, 1940).

12. The best study of the preparations for an attack on Gibraltar is in Burdick, *Spain.*

13. Ernst Klink, "Die militärische Konzeption des Krieges gegen die Sowjetunion: 1. Die Landkriegführung," DRZW, 4:203.

14. Ibid., DRZW, 4:213-14; Halder KTB, 2:21 (July 13), 31-32 (July 22); Burdick, *Spain,* 18, 22-23; Hillgruber, *Hitlers Strategie,* 216-19. The military planning for the attack on the Soviet Union is a theme to which I will return in later chapters.

15. On this meeting, see the Halder KTB, 2:46-50; Gerhard Wagner, ed., *Lagevorträge des Oberbefehlshabers der Kriegsmarine vor Hitler 1939-1945* (Munich: J. F. Lehmanns, 1972), 126-28; also Burdick, *Spain,* 31-32; Schreiber, "The Mediterranean in Hitler's Strategy," 248; Klink, "Landkriegführung," DRZW, 4:215-16; Hillgruber, *Hitlers Strategie,* 171, 222-26. This meeting provides an excellent example of how historians have treated these events. No single author gives a complete account of it, although all of them say that it is significant. For the most part, each author concentrates only on those parts of the meeting that dealt with the operation that he believes was foremost in Hitler's mind.

16. Umbreit, "Landung," DRZW, 2:374.

17. See, e.g., Wagner, *Lagevorträge,* 136 (6.9.1940), 143 (26.9.1940).

18. Hans Umbreit, "Die Rückkehr zu einer indirekten Strategie gegen England," DRZW, 2:412-13; Paul Preston, *Franco: A Biography* (New York: Basic Books, 1994), esp. chap 15.

19. See Hillgruber, *Hitlers Strategie,* 237-42, 352-61; also Umbreit, "Rückkehr," DRZW, 2:412.

20. Umbreit, "Rückkehr," DRZW, 2:410. See also Charles B. Burdick, *Unternehmen Sonnenblume: Der Entschluss zum Afrika-Feldzug* (Neckargemünd: Kurt Kowinckel, 1972).

21. On the Italian offensive, see Gerhard Schreiber, "Die politische und militärische Entwicklung im Mittelmeerraum 1939/40," DRZW, 3:239-49; on the British riposte, see Bernd Stegemann, "Die italienisch-deutsche Kriegführung im Mittelmeer und in Afrika," DRZW, 3:591-98.

22. See Gerhard Schreiber, "Deutschland, Italien und Südosteuropa. Von der politischen und wirtschaftlichen Hegemonie zur militärischen Aggression," DRZW, 3:368-94. On the Italian efforts in North Africa and Greece, see MacGregor Knox, *Mussolini Unleashed, 1939-1941: Politics and Strategy in Fascist Italy's Last War* (New York: Cambridge University Press, 1982), esp. chap. 5.

23. The directive for *Marita* came out in December 1940, that for *Sunflower* and *Cyclamen* in January 1941; see Hubatsch, *Weisungen*, 79-81, 93-97. See also Detlef Vogel, "Das Eingreifen Deutschlands auf dem Balkan," DRZW, 3:417-41; Stegemann, "Kriegführung im Mittelmeer und in Afrika," DRZW, 3:599-600.

24. Schreiber, "The Mediterranean and Hitler's Strategy," 240-41, 245. See also Reinhard Stumpf, "Probleme der Logistik im Afrikafeldzug 1941-1943," in *Die Bedeutung der Logistik für die militärische Führung von der Antike bis in die neueste Zeit,* ed. Militärgeschichtliches Forschungsamt (Herford: E. S. Mittler & Sohn, 1986), 213.

25. Umbreit, "Rückkehr," DRZW, 2:411; Hillgruber, "Noch einmal," 216.

26. Jürgen Förster supports this interpretation; see "Hitlers Entscheidung für den Krieg gegen die Sowjetunion," DRZW, 4, esp. 14.

27. Klink, "Landkriegführung," DRZW, 4:235-36.

28. The most thorough and convincing analysis of the decision to attack in the east remains Hillgruber's *Hitlers Strategie.* Creveld *(Hitler's Strategy)* gives the peripheral strategy more credit than it deserves. Weinberg's brief analysis in *A World at Arms* goes in the other direction; it makes Hitler's "Program" sound too inflexible.

29. Halder KTB, 2:191.

30. Ibid., 2:194.

31. For an overview of the debate, see Klee, *"Seelöwe,"* 91-112.

32. Halder KTB, 2:26.

33. Williamson Murray, *Luftwaffe* (Baltimore, Md.: Nautical and Aviation Publishing Company of America, 1985), 46-47; Michael Salewski, *Die deutsche Seekriegsleitung 1935-1945* (Frankfurt am Main: Bernard & Graefe, 1970-75), 1:258-60.

34. The account that follows is drawn from Percy Ernst Schramm, ed., *Kriegstagebuch des Oberkommandos der Wehrmacht (Wehrmachtführungsstab)* (Munich: Bernard & Graefe, 1961-65; Manfred Pawlak, 1982) (hereafter: OKW KTB), 1:3-14 (Aug. 1-8, 1940); and from Klee, *"Seelöwe,"* except as noted.

35. See Halder KTB 2:55 (Aug. 5, 1940), "Seekriegsleitung schickt 2 Schreiben, . . ."

36. Ibid., 2:57 (Aug. 6, 1940).

37. For an overview of this trend and its effects, see Geoffrey P. Megargee, "Triumph of the Null: Structure and Conflict in the Command of German Land Forces, 1939-1945," *War in History* 4 (1997): 60-80.

38. OKW KTB, 1:134. See also Burkhart Müller-Hillebrand, *Das Heer, 1933-1945: Entwicklung des organisatorischen Aufbaues* (Darmstadt: E. S. Mittler, 1954-69), 2:59-60.

39. OKW KTB 1:326. The OKW also established an Armed Forces Commander (Wehrmachtbefehlshaber) in the Netherlands on May 18, 1940; see BA-MA RW 37/1: Stammtafeln des Stabes Kommando Wehrmachtbefehlshaber in den Niederlanden.

By March 1941 at the latest, the OKW was sending orders on coastal defense to this headquarters; see OKW Nr. 44349/41 gK.Chefs. WFSt/Abt.L (I Op), 26.3.41, in BA-MA RW 4/563, 11.

40. Based on an examination of the Halder KTB and of the daily reports of the Operations Branch of the General Staff from June 22 to December 6, 1941, in the OKW KTB, 2:490–796. The timing of the change is impossible to pin down. Most of the secondary sources, such as Albert Seaton, *The German Army, 1933–45* (London: Weidenfeld & Nicolson, 1982); Hartmann, *Halder;* Hans-Adolf Jacobsen (in the introduction to the OKW KTB) and Müller-Hillebrand, *Heer,* maintain that the OKW picked up all its theaters before the start of *Barbarossa.* Keitel also states this. Most other authors, including Warlimont, put the date later, and some documentary evidence seems to support them, but the case is not absolutely clear.

41. Walter Warlimont, *Im Hauptquartier der deutschen Wehrmacht 1939–1945: Grundlagen, Formen, Gestalten* (Frankfurt am Main: Bernard & Graefe, 1962), 157–58; OKW KTB, 1:362 (Mar. 18, 1941).

42. OKW/WFSt/Abt. L Nr. 33 406/40 g.K.Chefs., 13.12.1940, Weisung Nr. 20: Unternehmen Marita, in Hubatsch, *Weisungen,* 81–83; the quote is on page 82.

43. See OKW/WFSt/Abt.L (I Op) Nr. 44 379/41 g.K. Chefs., 27.3.41, Weisung Nr. 25, in ibid., 106–8.

44. OKW/WFSt/Abt.L Nr. 44395/41 g.K.Ch., 3.4.41, in ibid., 108–11; the quote is on page 109. Halder noted with regret that Hungarian troops would not be under German command; see his KTB, 2:342 (Apr. 3, 1941), "OQu IV teilt mit . . ."

45. OKW/WFSt/Abt.L (I Op-IV/Qu) Nr. 44 900/41 g.K. Chefs., 9.6.41, in Hubatsch, *Weisungen,* 122–25.

46. Vogel, "Eingreifen auf dem Balkan," DRZW, 3:488. See also Der Führer und Oberste Befehlshaber der Wehrmacht Nr. 44 581/41 g.Kdos. Chefs. WFSt/Abt. L (I Op), 25.4.41, Weisung Nr. 28 (Unternehmen Merkur), in Hubatsch, *Weisungen,* 115–16.

47. Halder KTB, 2:433 (May 28, 1941); August Winter and others, "The German Armed Forces High Command, OKW (Oberkommando der Wehrmacht): A Critical Historical Study of Its Development, Organization, Missions and Functioning from 1938 to 1945" (MS #T-101), in *World War II German Military Studies: A Collection of 213 Special Reports on the Second World War Prepared by Former Officers of the Wehrmacht for the United States Army,* ed. Donald Detwiler, assoc. ed. Charles B. Burdick and Jürgen Rohwer (New York: Garland, 1979) (hereafter: GMS), 3: chap. B1a, 28. The Germans' efforts were not helped by the fact that their plan was known to the British, down to the hour.

48. OKW/WFSt/Abt. L Nr. 44018/41 g.K. Chefs., 11.1.41, Weisung Nr. 22: Mithilfe deutscher Kräfte bei den Kämpfen im Mittelmeerraum; and OKW/WFSt/Abt.L (I Op) Nr. 44075/41 gK. Chefs., ?.2.41, Betr.: Verhalten deutscher Truppen auf italienischen Kriegsschauplätzen, in Hubatsch, *Weisungen,* 93–95, 99–100; OKW KTB, 1:321; Seaton, *German Army,* 154–55.

49. Halder KTB, 2:272 (Feb. 7, 1941); Seaton, *German Army,* 155.

50. Halder KTB, 2:272 (Feb. 7, 1941). Paulus had been OQu I since September 3, 1940; see Halder KTB, 2:90 (Sept. 6, 1940); also Walter Görlitz, ed., *Paulus and Stalingrad: A Life of Field-Marshal Friedrich Paulus with Notes, Correspondence and Documents from His Papers,* trans. Col. R. H. Stevens (New York: Citadel Press, 1963), 24.

51. Siegfried Westphal, *The German Army in the West* (London: Cassell, 1951), 144; Seaton, *German Army,* 197; Warlimont, *Hauptquartier,* 210.

52. Waldemar Erfurth, *Die Geschichte des deutschen Generalstabes von 1918 bis 1945,* 2d ed. (Göttingen: Musterschmidt, 1960), 253, 257–58. See also Siegfried Westphal, *Erinnerungen* (Mainz: v.Hase & Koehler, 1975), 117–90.

53. Oberkommando der Wehrmacht, WFSt/Abt. L (IV/Qu) Nr. 44125/41 g.K. Chefs., 13. März 1941, Richtlinien auf Sondergebieten zur Weisung Nr. 21 *(Barbarossa),* in Hubatsch, *Weisungen,* 88–91; see also OKW KTB, 1:341.

54. Hartmann, *Halder,* 242.

55. *Hauptquartier,* 228; see also Hartmann, *Halder,* 265–66.

56. Walter Görlitz, ed., *The Memoirs of Field Marshal Keitel,* trans. David Irving (New York: Stein & Day, 1966), 129, 141, 146; Winter and others, "Armed Forces High Command," 3: chap. B1a, 31–32; Helmuth Greiner, "OKW, World War II" (MS #C-065b), 8, in GMS, vol. 7.

57. Letter from Lossberg to Wilhelm-Ernst Paulus, Sept. 7, 1956, in Lossberg papers, BA-MA N 219, vol. 5.

58. Johann Adolf Graf von Kielmansegg, interview by Geoffrey P. Megargee, April 29, 1996, Bad Krozingen, Germany.

59. This is Warlimont's thesis; see *Hauptquartier,* 77.

60. In BA-MA RH 2/459: "Sonnenblume": Chefsachen and other records of the OpAbt, from Jan. 41 to March 42,' 24.

61. Halder KTB, 2:384 (April 28, 1941); the minutes of the meeting and the Teletype message announcing the decision (in favor of the army) are in National Archives and Records Administration, National Archives Collection of Captured German War Records Microfilmed at Alexandria, Va., Microfilm Publication (NAMP) T-77 (Records of Headquarters, German Armed Forces High Command), roll 1429, frame 842.

62. Ferdinand Prinz von der Leyen, *Rückblick zum Mauerwald: Vier Kriegsjahre im OKH* (Munich: Biederstein, 1965), 15.

63. OKW KTB, 1:15 (Aug. 8, 1940); emphasis in original.

64. Keitel papers, BA-MA N 54, 5:76. Keitel received a promotion on July 19, to field marshal. Other promotions included: Jodl to lieutenant general; Rundstedt, Bock, and Leeb (commanders of armies in the French campaign) to field marshal; Halder to general; and Göring to Reichs marshal, a rank that Hitler invented for the occasion.

65. Hartmann, *Halder,* 210. Unfortunately, there is no record of Halder's reaction.

66. On early German plans for an invasion of Yugoslavia, see Creveld, *Hitler's Strategy,* 145.

67. OKW KTB, 1:368 (27.3.1941); Hillgruber, *Hitlers Strategie,* Appendix 7, Hitler's itinerary from Sept. 1, 1939, to Dec. 12, 1941, 687; Halder KTB, 2:330–31.

68. Heusinger took over from Greiffenberg as chief of the Operations Branch on October 1, 1940. See Fritz Frhr. von Siegler, *Die höheren Dienststellen der deutschen Wehrmacht 1933–1945* (Munich: Institut für Zeitgeschichte, 1953), 12.

69. Halder KTB, 2:331–37 (Mar. 28–30, 1941).

70. Ibid., 2:331 (Mar. 28), 338–40 (Mar. 31–Apr. 2); OKW KTB, 1:369 (Mar. 28), 370 (Mar. 29), 371 (Mar. 31), 374 (Apr. 1); Hubatsch, *Weisungen,* 108–10.

71. Creveld, *Hitler's Strategy,* 145.

6. MILITARY INTELLIGENCE AND THE PLAN OF ATTACK IN THE EAST

1. With that said, the following caveat applies: the focus here is still upon strategic and operational decision making. An examination of the support functions within the high command can easily lead off into areas such as espionage, resource and manpower allocation, weapons procurement, scientific research, and civil-military relations, which are important in their own right but tangential to the purposes of this study.

2. Franz Halder, "Der Komplex OKH-OKW," in the Halder papers, BA-MA N 220/95, 36, 46–47.

3. Adolf Heusinger, interrogation by U.S. Army Intelligence, February 1, 1946, unpublished.

4. Heinz Guderian, *Erinnerungen eines Soldaten* (Heidelberg: Kurt Vowinckel, 1951), 128.

5. Franz Halder, *Kriegstagebuch: Tägliche Aufzeichnungen des Chefs des Generalstabes des Heeres 1939-1942,* ed. Arbeitskreis für Wehrforschung, Stuttgart (Stuttgart: Kohlhammer, 1962) (hereafter: Halder KTB), 2:46.

6. General a.D. Ulrich de Maizière, interview by the author, Bonn, Germany, May 25, 1996.

7. Walter Görlitz, ed., *Generalfeldmarschall Keitel: Verbrecher oder Offizier? Erinnerungen, Briefe, Dokumente des Chefs OKW* (Göttingen: Musterschmidt-Verlag, 1961), 242–45; Andreas Hillgruber, "Noch einmal: Hitlers Wendung gegen die Sowjetunion 1940," Geschichte in Wissenschaft und Unterricht 33 (1982): 223.

8. Halder KTB, 2:261 (Jan. 28, 1941).

9. Hillgruber, "Noch einmal," 220. Hitler made the remark to Keitel on June 25, 1940. See also Klaus Reinhardt, *Die Wende vor Moskau: Das Scheitern der Strategie Hitlers im Winter 1941/42* (Stuttgart: Deutsche Verlags-Anstalt, 1972), 21.

10. Halder KTB, 2:6. Speculation about Halder's motives remains just that. Ernst Klink, in "Die militärische Konzeption des Krieges gegen die Sowjetunion: 1. Die Landkriegführung," in *Das Deutsche Reich und der Zweite Weltkrieg,* ed. Militärgeschichtliches Forschungsamt (Stuttgart: Deutsche Verlags-Anstalt, 1979–90) (hereafter: DRZW), 4:207, says that both Halder and Greiffenberg started with the assumption that the defeat of Russia would remove Britain's last hope of victory. There is nothing in the KTB entry to support this conclusion, but Hitler had mentioned this idea to Brauchitsch over a week earlier. In any case, Halder's remarks are difficult to reconcile with the agreement he and Brauchitsch reached on July 30. The most plausible interpretation is that at this point (July 3) Halder was assuming that Britain would fall soon, *after* which Germany would turn on the Soviet Union. In any case, his discussion with Greiffenberg indicates that Halder did not shy away from the idea of a campaign against Russia. See Andreas Hillgruber, *Hitlers Strategie: Politik und Kriegsführung 1940-41* (Frankfurt am Main: Bernard & Graefe, 1965), 210–12.

11. See Klink, "Landkriegführung," 216.

12. *Erinnerungen,* 128. Guderian insists that he had his chief of staff bring his objections up to OKH, but there does not seem to be any record to substantiate this claim. Also, on several occasions Guderian expressed his low opinion of Soviet forces. See Gerhard Engel, *Heeresadjutant bei Hitler, 1938–1943: Aufzeichnungen des majors Engels,* ed. Hildegard von Kotze (Stuttgart: Deutsche Verlags-Anstalt, 1974), 86 (Aug. 10, 1940) and 87–88 (Sept. 15, 1940); also Andreas Hillgruber, "Das Russland-Bild der

führenden deutschen Militärs vor Beginn des Angriffs auf die Sowjetunion," in *Russland-Deutschland-Amerika. Russia-Germany-America. Festschrift für Fritz T. Epstein zum 80. Geburtstag,* ed. Alexander Fischer, Günter Moltmann, and Klaus Schwabe (Wiesbaden: Franz Steiner, 1978), 307.

13. The following overview is drawn from Klink, "Landkriegführung," DRZW, 4:207-37.

14. Walter Warlimont, *Im Hauptquartier der deutschen Wehrmacht 1939-1945: Grundlagen, Formen, Gestalten* (Frankfurt am Main: Bernard & Graefe, 1962), 126. Lossberg describes the occasion less dramatically; see *Im Wehrmachtführungsstab: Bericht eines Generalstabsoffiziers* (Hamburg: Nölke, 1950), 105.

15. Klink, "Landkriegführung," DRZW, 4:230-33.

16. Duty descriptions and organizational charts for the OKW's intelligence organs are in "Kriegsspitzengliederung des Oberkommandos der Wehrmacht, Heft 1, Ausgabe 1.3.1939," in Percy Ernst Schramm, ed., *Kriegstagebuch des Oberkommandos der Wehrmacht (Wehrmachtführungsstab)* (Munich: Manfred Pawlak, 1982) (hereafter: OKW KTB), 1:884-87, 901-2. See also David Kahn, *Hitler's Spies: German Military Intelligence in World War II* (New York: Macmillan, 1978), 47. Kahn's work is the most complete on the German intelligence apparatus, but the quality is spotty, and he analyzes only a few actual historical cases. For excellent supplemental analyses, see Michael Geyer, "National Socialist Germany: The Politics of Information," in *Knowing One's Enemies: Intelligence Assessment Before the Two World Wars,* ed. Ernest R. May (Princeton, N.J.: Princeton Universty Press, 1984), 310-46; and Hans-Heinrich Wilhelm, "Die Prognosen der Abteilung Fremde Heere Ost 1942-1945," in *Zwei Legenden aus dem Dritten Reich* (Stuttgart: Deutsche Verlags-Anstalt, 1974), 7-75.

17. Lauran Paine claims that this branch also maintained an extensive counterintelligence network, but unfortunately his work lacks citations. See *German Military Intelligence in World War II: The Abwehr* (New York: Stein & Day, 1984), 10-11.

18. The internal work plans for the Office of Foreign- and Counterintelligence, the Counterintelligence Branch I, and the Foreign Branch are in the "Kriegsspitzengliederung," in OKW KTB 1:916-21.

19. Unfortunately, the records do not reveal the reasons that the intelligence authorities chose one organizational scheme over another. We know only that the group leaders worked the structures out for their groups, under the supervision of the branch chiefs. The office chief, Canaris, probably signed off on the groups' schemes without making any changes, but he perhaps would have had a say in the organization of the branches and certainly approved the overall structure of the office.

20. Gerhard Matzky, Lothar Metz, and Kurt von Tippelskirch, "Army High Command. Organization and Working Methods of the Intelligence Division" (MS #P-041i), 71-72, 73-74, in *The German Army High Command, 1938-1945* (Arlington, Va.: University Publications of America, n.d. Microfilm) (hereafter: GAHC); Kahn, *Hitler's Spies,* 191-93, 373-79.

21. See, e.g., Halder KTB, 2:12 (July 5, 1940), which shows the two discussing tensions between Russia and Romania.

22. Based on an examination of ibid., 2:8-153.

23. See, e.g., Halder's meetings with Etzdorf on October 8 and 15, in which they discussed the conference that Hitler and Mussolini had at the Brenner Pass. Ibid., 2:129, 136.

24. Brief profiles of Tippelskirch and his successor, Colonel Gerhard Matzky, are

in Kahn, *Hitler's Spies,* 391–92. Matzky replaced Tippelskirch on January 5, 1941. Halder knew and liked both men.

25. Matzky and others, "Intelligence Division," GAHC, 6.

26. Günther Blumentritt, "Der 'Oberquartiermeister I' im O.K.H. Generalstab des Heeres" (MS #P-041d, chap. 2, unpublished), 4. The separate meetings between Tippelskirch and Halder show up in the latter's diary.

27. On the origins of these branches and an overview of their history up to 1941, see Kahn, *Hitler's Spies,* 418–23, 428.

28. Gliederung und Stellenbesetzung der Abteilung O.Qu. IV /Fremde Heere, BA-MA RH 2/1472, 27.

29. Matzky and others, "Intelligence Division," GAHC; see the chart on page 8.

30. Ibid., 5.

31. Ibid., 9–15; David Thomas, "Foreign Armies East and German Military Intelligence in Russia, 1941–45," *Journal of Contemporary History* 22 (1987): 262.

32. Reinhard Gehlen, *Der Dienst: Erinnerungen, 1942–1971* (Mainz-Wiesbaden: v.Hase & Koehler, 1971), 10.

33. As Kahn notes; see *Hitler's Spies,* 401. For the relevant sections of the manual, see Germany, Heer, Heeresdienstvorschrift 300/1, I.Teil (H.Dv. 300/1); *Truppenführung* (Berlin: E. S. Mittler & Sohn, 1936), 10–19.

34. Germany, Heer, Heeresdienstvorschrift 92 (H.Dv. 92), *Handbuch für den Generalstabsdienst im Kriege,* Teil I, II, abgeschlossen am 1.8.1939 (Berlin: der Reichsdruckerei, 1939), 18–20.

35. H.Dv. g. 89, *Feindnachrichtendienst,* March 1, 1941, 11–12, quoted in Kahn, *Hitler's Spies,* 400.

36. Kahn, *Hitler's Spies,* 400.

37. Gehlen, *Der Dienst,* 42–43; Matzky and others, "Intelligence Division," GAHC, 42.

38. Gliederung und Stellenbesetzung der Abteilung O.Qu. IV /Fremde Heere, BA-MA RH 2/1472, 6–10. One should note that all German staffs were small; this issue will be examined in more detail in the next chapter.

39. Gehlen, *Der Dienst,* 43. On tensions between General Staff and reserve officers, see Ferdinand Prinz von der Leyen, *Rückblick zum Mauerwald. Vier Kriegsjahre im OKH* (Munich: Biederstein, 1965), 21–22.

40. See Hillgruber, "Russland-Bild."

41. On this aspect see Jürgen Förster, "Hitlers Entscheidung für den Krieg gegen die Sowjetunion," DRZW, 4:23.

42. This image went back to the period after the Crimean War. See Hillgruber, "Russland-Bild," 296.

43. Halder KTB, 2:86 (Sept. 3, 1940).

44. Thomas, "Foreign Armies East," 275; Kahn, *Hitler's Spies,* 450–55.

45. Klink, "Landkriegführung," DRZW, 4:197; Wilhelm, "Prognosen," 13–14.

46. John Erickson, *The Soviet High Command: A Military-Political History, 1918–1941* (London: Macmillan, 1962), 506.

47. Halder KTB, 2:86 (Sept. 3, 1940).

48. Kahn, *Hitler's Spies,* 456.

49. Halder KTB, 2:29–30. This refutes Kahn's assertion that Germany's military leaders did not call in the intelligence services until after Hitler issued Directive No. 21 in December 1940. See *Hitler's Spies,* 445.

50. Halder KTB, 2:37 (July 26, 1940).

51. As Hillgruber points out; see "Russland-Bild," 303.

52. Klink, "Landkriegführung," DRZW, 4:219-23; Hillgruber, "Russland-Bild," 299-300.

53. Hillgruber, "Russland-Bild," 305.

54. See ibid., 305, 306; Klink, "Landkriegführung," DRZW, 4:198-200; Thomas, "Foreign Armies East," 275-77; Kahn, *Hitler's Spies,* 459.

55. Thomas, "Foreign Armies East," 277-78.

56. Kahn, *Hitler's Spies,* 457-59.

57. David Glantz, *Soviet Military Intelligence in War* (London: Frank Cass, 1990), 44. Glantz points out that the Soviets may have employed a *maskirovka,* a deception plan, designed to make the Germans believe that the Red Army was stronger along the border than it actually was, perhaps in the hope of deterring an attack.

58. Robert Cecil, *Hitler's Decision to Invade Russia* (London: Davis-Poynter, 1975), 121; Hillgruber, "Russland-Bild," 309.

59. Cecil, *Hitler's Decision to Invade Russia,* 121.

60. Klink, "Landkriegführung," DRZW, 4:220. See also Rolf-Dieter Müller, "Von der Wirtschaftsallianz zum kolonialen Ausbeutungskrieg," DRZW, 4:114.

61. Hillgruber, "Russland-Bild," 300; Klink, "Landkriegführung," DRZW, 4:225.

62. Klink, "Landkriegführung," DRZW, 4:300.

63. Ibid., 226-27.

64. Ibid., 228-29.

65. Ibid., 244; Halder KTB, 2:319 (Mar. 17, 1941). Klink implies that Foreign Armies East prepared the initial study for Hitler without Halder's knowledge, but that is highly unlikely.

66. See Geyer, "Politics of Information," 343.

7. LOGISTICS, PERSONNEL, AND *BARBAROSSA*

1. Erich von Manstein, *Verlorene Siege* (Bonn: Athenäum, 1955), 305-6.

2. Oberkommando der Wehrmacht 11 b 10 WFSt/Abt.L (II) 2750/40 geh., 4.11.40, in BA-MA RW 19/686, 19.

3. Percy Ernst Schramm, *Kriegstagebuch des Oberkommandos der Wehrmacht (Wehrmachtführungsstab)* (Manfred Pawlak, 1982) (hereafter: OKW KTB), 1:144, 146 (Nov. 1, 1940), 149 (November 4, 1940). See also Franz Josef Schott, "Der Wehrmachtführungsstab im Führerhauptquartier 1939-1945" (Ph.D. diss., University of Bonn, 1980), 78-80.

4. From this point forward, the "chief of army equipment and commander of the Replacement Army" will simply be called the Replacement Army commander.

5. Wagner took over as general quartermaster on October 1, 1940, from Lieutenant General Eugen Müller; prior to that date, Wagner was Müller's chief of staff. See Franz Halder, *Kriegstagebuch. Tägliche Aufzeichnungen des Chefs des Generalstabes des Heeres 1939-1942,* ed. Arbeitskreis für Wehrforschung, Stuttgart (Stuttgart: Kohlhammer, 1962) (hereafter: Halder KTB), 2:120.

6. Günther Blumentritt, "Der 'Oberquartiermeister I' im O.K.H. Generalstab des Heeres" (MS #P-041d, chap. 2, unpublished), 4.

7. Burkhart Müller-Hillebrand, "Schematische Darstellung der obersten Führung des deutschen Heeres 1938 bis Kriegsende mit Erläuterungen über organisatorische Beziehungen, Aufgaben und Verantwortlichkeiten der einzelnen Dienststellen des OKH im Laufe der Jahre 1938-1945" (MS #P-041a, unpublished), 33; Müller-Hillebrand, "Die organisatorischen Aufgaben der obersten Heeresführung von 1938 bis 45 und ihre Lösung" (MS #P-041f, unpublished), 7.

8. Blumentritt, "'Oberquartiermeister I,'" 6.

9. Rudolf Absolon, *Die Wehrmacht im Dritten Reich. Aufbau, Gliederung, Recht, Verwaltung* (Boppard: a.Rh.: Harald Boldt, 1969-95), 5:56-57.

10. August Winter and others, "The German Armed Forces High Command, OKW (Oberkommando der Wehrmacht): A Critical Historical Study of Its Development, Organization, Missions and Functioning from 1938 to 1945" (MS #T-101), in *World War II German Military Studies: A Collection of 213 Special Reports on the Second World War Prepared by Former Officers of the Wehrmacht for the United States Army,* ed. Donald Detwiler, assoc. ed. Charles B. Burdick and Jürgen Rohwer (New York: Garland, 1979) (hereafter: GMS), 3: chap. B1c, 13.

11. Ernst Klink, "Die militärische Konzeption des Krieges gegen die Sowjetunion: 1. Die Landkriegführung," in *Das Deutsche Reich und der Zweite Weltkrieg,* ed. Militärgeschichtliches Forschungsamt (Stuttgart: Deutsche Verlags-Anstalt, 1979-90) (hereafter: DRZW), 4:248.

12. On Wagner's nickname, see Ferdinand Prinz von der Leyen, *Rückblick zum Mauerwald: Vier Kriegsjahre im OKH* (Munich: Biederstein, 1965), 16.

13. A chart showing the organization of the General Quartermaster is DRZW, 4:250.

14. For more on the activities of the Army Supply Distribution Group, see Leyen, *Rückblick zum Mauerwald.*

15. Winter and others, "Armed Forces High Command," 3: chap. B1c, 13-15.

16. Peter Bor, *Gespräche mit Halder* (Wiesbaden: Limes, 1950), 85-86.

17. Johann Adolf Graf von Kielmansegg, interview by the author, June 14, 1996, Bad Krozingen, Germany.

18. Halder KTB, 2:176; Martin van Creveld, *Supplying War: Logistics from Wallenstein to Patton* (Cambridge: Cambridge Univiversity Press, 1980), 150.

19. Wilhelm von Rücker, "Die Vorbereitungen für den Feldzug gegen Russland," in *Der Generalquartier-meister. Briefe und Tagebuchaufzeichnungen des Generalquartiermeisters des Heeres, General der Artillerie Eduard Wagner,* ed. Elizabeth Wagner, (Munich: Günter Olzog, 1963), 313.

20. Creveld, *Supplying War,* 149-51.

21. Ibid., 151-54; Klink, "Landkriegführung," DRZW, 4:252-58; Rücker, "Vorbereitungen," 314-15.

22. Klink, "Landkriegführung," DRZW, 4:234-35.

23. Robert Cecil, *Hitler's Decision to Invade Russia* (London: Davis-Poynter, 1975), 128-29.

24. Heinz von Gyldenfeldt, "Die oberste Führung des deutschen Heeres (OKH) im Rahmen der Wehrmachtführung. a) Ob.d.H. mit Adjutantur" (MS #P-041c, unpublished), 32; Franz Halder, "Der Chef des Generalstabes des Heeres" (MS #P-041d, chapter 1, unpublished), 7-8.

25. Absolon, *Wehrmacht,* 5:49.

26. Halder KTB, 2:143. My use of the word "frocking" here—a translation of

"Charakter-Verleihung"—differs somewhat from the understanding common in our army today. Here it means that an officer who could not be promoted received the title and authority of the next higher position, without the pay or benefits. The "supernumerary officers" *(Ergänzungsoffiziere)* were officers who were unqualified for frontline service because they were too old, sick, or injured. On that last, see Müller-Hillebrand, "Darstellung," Übersichtsblatt II.

27. OKW KTB, 1:879, 899, 907.

28. Jürgen Förster, "Vom Führerheer der Republik zur nationalsozialistischen Volksarmee," in *Deutschland in Europa. Kontinuität und Bruch. Gedenkschrift für Andreas Hillgruber,* ed. Jost Dülffer, Bernd Martin, and Günter Wollstein (Frankfurt am Main: Propyläen, 1990), esp. 314.

29. Gerhard Papke, "Offizierkorps und Anciennität," in *Untersuchungen zur Geschichte des Offizierkorps. Anciennität und Beförderung nach Leistung,* ed. Militärgeschichtliches Forschungsamt (Stuttgart: Deutsche Verlags-Anstalt, 1962), 199, cited in Förster, "Volksarmee," 313.

30. For a thorough treatment of this phenomenon, see Norman J. W. Goda, "Black Marks: Hitler's Bribery of His Senior Officers During World War II," *Journal of Modern History,* forthcoming; see also Gerhard Weinberg, "Some Thoughts on World War II," *Journal of Military History* 56 (1992): 660–61; Olaf Groehler, "Die Güter der Generale: Dotationen im zweiten Weltkrieg," *Zeitschrift für Geschichtswissenschaft* 29(1971): 655–63.

31. "Dienstanweisung für den Chef des Generalstabes des Heeres im Frieden," May 31, 1935, in BA-MA RH 2/195, 31.

32. BA-MA RH 2/238: "Die personelle Entwicklung des GenStdH (1939–1942)," 3. This file contains Central Branch records on the numbers of General Staff officers and positions. See also Bernhard R. Kroener, "Die personellen Ressourcen des Dritten Reiches im Spannungsfeld zwischen Wehrmacht, Bürokratie und Kriegswirtschaft 1939–1942," DRZW, 5:736–39; Franz Halder, "Die Leitung des Generalstabes des Heeres" (MS #P-041d, chapter 7, unpublished), 8–10; Absolon, *Wehrmacht,* 5:78–79.

33. RH 2/238: "Personelle Entwicklung," 5; Halder, "Leitung," 8–10.

34. Halder, "Leitung," 10–11, 15.

35. Ibid., 13–15.

36. Ibid., 16–17.

37. OKH, GenStdH, Op.Abt. Nr. 1110/41 g.Kdos.(IV), 6.6.41, "Neugliederung der Op.Abt. mit Wirkung vom 1.6.1941," in BA-MA RH 2/1520, 186. This record also indicates that, as of this date, the army had not relinquished operational control in the "OKW theaters." Another group of officers handled Western Europe and the Balkans.

38. See David Kahn, *Hitler's Spies: German Military Intelligence in World War II* (New York: Macmillan, 1978), 404. Both Kielmansegg and de Maizière confirmed that the German army traditionally kept staffs small (in the interviews of June 14 and May 25, respectively). See also Blumentritt, "'Oberquartiermeister I,'" 14; Hans von Greiffenberg, "Die Operationsabteilung des O.K.H. (Generalstab des Heeres)" (MS #P-041e, unpublished), 1.

39. Absolon, *Wehrmacht,* 5:60–62; Müller-Hillebrand, "Darstellung," 24, 32. The Organization Branch also provided broad assessments of the army's fighting strength, in which it would assign each division to one of four categories: ready for all missions; ready, but only in a limited sense for strong attacks; ready for defense on main fronts

and for light attacks; suited for defense on quiet fronts. See Gen St d H, Org.Abt.(1.St.) Nr.267/39 g.Kdos., 13.12.1939: "Beurteilung des Kampfwertes der Divisionen Mitte Dezember 1939," in BA-MA RH 2/1520.

40. Klink, "Landkriegführung," DRZW, 4:260-67; van Creveld, *Supplying War,* 150. See also Kroener, "Personellen Ressourcen," 840-59.

41. Halder KTB, 2:422.

42. Klink, "Landkriegführung," DRZW, 4:269-70.

43. Germany, Heer, Heeresdienstvorschrift 300/1 (H.Dv. 300/1), I.Teil, *Truppenführung* (Berlin: E. S. Mittler & Sohn, 1936), 1. This is pure Clausewitz.

44. The best works are Earl F. Ziemke and Magna E. Bauer, *Moscow to Stalingrad: Decision in the East* (Washington, D.C.: U.S. Government Printing Office, 1987); John Erickson, *The Road to Stalingrad: Stalin's War with Germany,* vol. 1 (London: Weidenfeld and Nicolson, 1975); David Glantz and Jonathan M. House, *When Titans Clashed: How the Red Army Stopped Hitler* (Lawrence: University Press of Kansas, 1995); DRZW, vol. 4, *Der Angriff auf die Sowjetunion* (Stuttgart: Deutsche Verlags-Anstalt, 1983).

45. Walther Hubatsch, *Hitlers Weisungen für die Kriegführung 1939-1945: Dokumente des Oberkommandos der Wehrmacht* (Frankfurt am Main: Bernard & Graefe, 1962), 85-86; see also Klink, "Landkriegführung," DRZW, 4:238-39; Klaus Reinhardt, *Die Wende vor Moskau: Das Scheitern der Strategie Hitlers im Winter 1941/42* (Stuttgart: Deutsche Verlags-Anstalt, 1972), 17-18.

46. See Klink, "Landkriegführung," DRZW, 4:240-42.

47. Walter Warlimont, *Im Hauptquartier der deutschen Wehrmacht 1939-1945: Grundlagen, Formen, Gestalten* (Frankfurt am Main: Bernard & Graefe, 1962), 194-95.

48. Halder KTB, 3:38-39.

49. Oberquartiermeister I des Generalstabes des Heeres Nr. 430/41 g.Kdos. Chefs., 3.7.41: Vorbereitung der Operationen für die Zeit nach Barbarossa, in BA-MA RH 2/ 1520, 217.

50. Halder KTB, 3:107.

51. Lauran Paine, *German Military Intelligence in World War II: The Abwehr* (New York: Stein & Day, 1984), 152; Alan Clark, *Barbarossa: The Russian-German Conflict, 1941-45* (New York: William Morrow, 1965), 111. One General Staff officer described the *Abwehr's* contribution as *"Mist,"* which translates politely as "rubbish"; see David Thomas, "Foreign Armies East and German Military Intelligence in Russia, 1941-45," *Journal of Contemporary History* 22 (1987): 265.

52. Creveld, *Supplying War,* 155-59.

53. Landesverteidigung-Chef Nr. 441339/41 g.K.Ch., 6.8.1941: Kurzer strategischer Überblick über die Fortführung des Krieges nach dem Ostfeldzug, in BA-MA RM 7/ 258, 6.

54. Halder KTB, 3:170.

55. Based on the entry for June 25, 1941, OKW KTB, 1:409-410. Unfortunately, that is the last day in 1941 for which the actual diary exists (contrary to what the published table of contents indicates).

56. The record of this conversation is in the document appendix of the OKW KTB, 1:1035-36.

57. Halder KTB, 3:15.

58. Ibid., 3:25.

59. Ibid., 3:39.

60. Gyldenfeldt, "Ob.d.H.," 27–29. See also Klink, "Landkriegführung," DRZW, 4:248, on Halder's resistance to Brauchitsch's efforts to play a role in operations.

61. See Ziemke and Bauer, *Moscow to Stalingrad,* 33.

62. See OKW KTB, 1:1036–37, 1043–44, 1054–55; the last two are Armed Forces Command Staff studies on the situation on the eastern front, with arguments for a drive on Moscow.

63. Martin van Creveld maintains that, given the supply difficulties that Army Group Center was having in July, August, and September, the diversion to the south actually did not delay the advance on Moscow by more than one or two weeks at most; see *Supplying War,* 176.

64. Wagner, *Generalquartiermeister,* 207.

65. Ibid., 202 (letter of Sept. 29, 1941).

66. Ibid., 204.

67. OKW KTB, 1:1038–40. That amounted to an advance of over one thousand miles from the German position in southern Russia.

68. Ibid., 1:1072–73.

69. Wagner, *Generalquartiermeister,* 210.

70. Halder KTB, 3:283. Note that Hitler's own staff had come to this conclusion four months earlier.

71. On the Orsha conference and Halder's preparations for it, see Ziemke and Bauer, *Moscow to Stalingrad,* 43–46; Earl F. Ziemke, "Franz Halder at Orsha: The German General Staff Seeks a Consensus," *Military Affairs* 39, no. 4 (1975), 173–76; Reinhardt, *Wende,* 139–41.

72. Naturally. Halder KTB, 3:306 (Nov. 23, 1941); emphasis in the original. The notes are also in the Halder papers, BA-MA N 220/62, 166–70. The quotes from the Orsha conference that Ziemke and Bauer use in *Moscow to Stalingrad* indicate that Halder made virtually the same remarks on both occasions.

73. On Halder's expectations of good weather, see Reinhardt, *Wende,* 139–40; Bernhard von Lossberg, *Im Wehrmachtführungsstab. Bericht eines Generalstabsoffiziers* (Hamburg: Nölke, 1950), 138. On the plans for Moscow, see GenStdH OpAbt (IM) Nr. 1571/41 g.Kdos. Chefs., 12.10.41, in OKW KTB, 1:1070–71.

74. Ziemke and Bauer, *Moscow to Stalingrad,* 47–48.

75. Halder KTB, 3:286.

76. Organisationsabteilung (Ia) Nr. 731/41 g.Kdos. Chef-Sache!, 6.11.41, Beurteilung der Kampfkraft des Ostheeres, in OKW KTB 1:1074–75.

77. Creveld, *Supplying War,* 172–73.

78. Reinhardt, *Wende,* 126–27.

79. Otto Eckstein, "Maschinenschriftliche Aufzeichnung von Oberst a.D. Otto Eckstein über General E. Wagner, seine Arbeitsgebiet Quartiermeisterwesen und den Aufbau seiner Dienststelle," in BA-MA N 510/27 (Wagner papers), 19–20. This account also appears in Wagner, *Generalquartiermeister,* 289.

80. Halder KTB, 3:311.

81. Ziemke and Bauer, *Moscow to Stalingrad,* 50–68; Reinhardt, *Wende,* 202–13.

82. Halder KTB, 3:331.

83. See Norman J. W. Goda, *Tomorrow the World: Hitler, Northwest Africa, and the Path Toward America* (College Station: Texas A&M University Press, 1998).

84. Gerhard Weinberg, *A World at Arms: A Global History of World War II* (New York: Cambridge University Press, 1994), 250, 262; and Weinberg "Why Hitler Declared War on the United States," *MHQ: The Quarterly Journal of Military History* 4, no. 3 (1992): 18–23. A slightly revised and documented version of Weinberg's article is reprinted in his book *Germany, Hitler, and World War II: Essays in Modern German and World History* (New York: Cambridge University Press, 1995), 194–204, under the title "Pearl Harbor: The German Perspective." See also Enrico Syring, "Hitlers Kriegserklärung an Amerika vom 11. Dezember 1941," in *Der Zweite Weltkrieg: Analysen, Grundzüge, Forschungsbilanz,* ed. Wolfgang Michalka (Munich: Piper, 1989), 683–96.

85. Werner Jochmann, ed., *Adolf Hitler. Monologe im Führerhauptquartier 1941–1944. Die Aufzeichnungen Heinrich Heims* (Munich: A. Knaus, 1982), 101 (night of October 21–22, 1941).

86. Halder KTB, 3:136 (July 31, 1941).

87. Ibid., 3:332.

88. Leyen, *Rückblick zum Mauerwald,* 40. See also Hermann Balck, *Ordnung im Chaos: Erinnerungen 1893–1948,* Soldatenschicksale des 20. Jahrhunderts als Geschichtsquelle, Bd. 1 (Osnabrück: Biblio, Verlag, 1981), 347.

89. Halder KTB, 3:348.

90. There is some question as to whether Hitler forced Brauchitsch to resign, but the latter, in his own statement at Nuremberg, said that he asked to be relieved on December 7. See Walter Görlitz, ed., *Generalfeldmarschall Keitel: Verbrecher oder Offizier? Erinnerungen, Briefe, Dokumente des Chefs OKW* (Göttingen: Musterschmidt-Verlag, 1961), 287 n. 142; the quote is from that same page.

91. See Warlimont, *Hauptquartier,* 226.

92. Görlitz, *Generalfeldmarschall Keitel,* 317.

93. See Christian Hartmann, *Halder: Generalstabschef Hitlers 1938–1942* (Paderborn: Schöningh, 1991), 301–4; Müller-Hillebrand, "Darstellung," 20.

94. Hartmann, *Halder,* 305.

95. Burkhart Müller-Hillebrand, *Das Heer, 1933–1945: Entwicklung des organisatorischen Aufbaues* (Darmstadt: E. S. Mittler, 1954–69), 3:37.

96. Müller-Hillebrand, "Darstellung," 21; Arne W. Zoepf, *Wehrmacht zwischen Tradition und Ideologie: Der NS-Führungsoffizier im Zweiten Weltkrieg* (Frankfurt am Main: Lang, 1988), 45–46.

97. Gyldenfeldt, "Ob.d.H.," 46.

98. Görlitz, *Generalfeldmarschall Keitel,* 320.

99. Müller-Hillebrand, *Heer,* 3:37–40.

100. Ulrich de Maizière, *In der Pflicht: Lebensbericht eines deutschen Soldaten im 20. Jahrhundert* (Herford: E. S. Mittler & Sohn, 1989), 70.

101. See, e.g., R. H. S. Stolfi, *Hitler's Panzer's East: World War II Reinterpreted* (Norman: University of Oklahoma Press, 1991). This is one of those rare cases in which one can indeed judge a book by its cover; this one says, "But for one fateful decision, Germany could have won World War II in the summer of 1941."

102. Weinberg, *A World at Arms,* 281.

103. Ziemke and Bauer, *Moscow to Stalingrad,* 42.

8. THE SYSTEM AT WORK

1. This summary of the first phase of the Soviets' counteroffensive is drawn from Earl F. Ziemke and Magna E. Bauer, *Moscow to Stalingrad: Decision in the East* (Washington, D.C.: U.S. Government Printing Office, 1987), 65-80.

2. See Walther Hubatsch, *Hitlers Weisungen für die Kriegführung 1939-1945: Dokumente des Oberkommandos der Wehrmacht* (Frankfurt am Main: Bernard & Graefe, 1962), 171-74; and Percy Ernst Schramm, ed., *Kriegstagebuch des Oberkommandos der Wehrmacht (Wehrmachtführungsstab)* (Munich: Bernard & Graefe, 1961-65; Manfred Pawlak, 1982) (hereafter: OKW KTB), 1:1076-82.

3. Quoted in Ziemke and Bauer, *Moscow to Stalingrad,* 78.

4. OKH, GenStdH, Op.Abt. Nr. 1110/41 g.Kdos.(IV), 6.6.41: Neugliederung der Op.Abt. mit Wirkung vom 1.6.1941, in BA-MA RH 2/1520, 186-87. Heusinger received a promotion to brigadier general on December 1.

5. This account of the activities within the Operations Branch comes from Johann Adolf Graf von Kielmansegg, interviews by the author, April 29, 1996, Bad Krozingen, Germany; Hans von Greiffenberg, "Die Operationsabteilung des O.K.H. (Generalstab des Heeres)" (MS #P-041e, unpublished), 7.

6. Günther Blumentritt, "Der 'Oberquartiermeister I' im O.K.H. Generalstab des Heeres." (MS #P-041d, chap. 2, unpublished), 4; Kielmansegg interview, April 29, 1996; Franz Halder, "The Chief of the Army General Staff" (MS #P-041d, 1952), 10, in *The German Army High Command, 1938-1945* (Arlington, Va.: University Publications of America, n.d., microfilm) (hereafter: GAHC); Alfred Zerbel, "Organization of Army Quartermaster," (MS #P-041b) 1952, 2-3, in GAHC. If a branch chief could not attend for any reason, the assistant chief of staff for operations would brief him later. The list of attendees for this date is an educated guess, based upon the list of people who were usually at the briefing.

7. Heinz von Gyldenfeldt, "Die oberste Führung des deutschen Heeres (OKH) im Rahmen der Wehrmachtführung. a) Ob.d.H. mit Adjutantur" (MS #P-041c, unpublished), 41-42. Brauchitsch normally met with his principal advisers both before and after the morning General Staff meeting.

8. Army Group Center consisted of, from south to north, 2d Army, 2d Panzer Army, 4th Army, and 9th Army.

9. This overview of Halder's activities comes from Franz Halder, *Kriegstagebuch: Tägliche Aufzeichnungen des Chefs des Generalstabes des Heeres 1939-1942,* ed. Arbeitskreis für Wehrforschung, Stuttgart (Stuttgart: Kohlhammer, 1962), (hereafter: Halder KTB), 3:346-48 (Dec. 15, 1941). For the phone calls to the Army Groups Center and South chiefs of staff, see also BA-MA RH 19 II/122: Heeresgruppe Mitte KTB, 1.-31.12.41, (hereafter: HGr M KTB), 124; and RH 19 I/88: Heeresgruppe Süd KTB, 1.-31.12.41, (hereafter: HGr S KTB), 111-12. The commanders and principal staff officers in the army groups are in BA-MA RH 2/172, Kriegsstellenbesetzung OKW und OKH, 13 (status as of Nov. 1, 1941).

10. Halder KTB, 3:347; HGr M KTB, 124.

11. Halder KTB, 3:347; BA-MA RH 19 III/769, Heeresgruppe Nord KTB 1.-31.12.41 (hereafter: HGr N KTB), 88-94; Chef OKW/WFSt/L Nr. 442174/41 g.Kdos. Ch., 15.12.41, in BA-MA RH 2/1327, Chefsachen "Barbarossa," Sept. 41-Feb. 42, 90-91, also printed in OKW KTB 1:1083. The HGr N KTB indicates that Jodl's call

to Brennecke occurred at 7:02 P.M., but that makes little sense, since Keitel was on the phone to Leeb at that moment. Also, the order cited here records the time when Jodl called Brennecke as being 8:10 P.M.

12. HGr N KTB, 92–93; Halder KTB, 3:349; Wilhelm Ritter von Leeb, *Generalfeld-marschall Wilhelm Ritter von Leeb: Tagebuchaufzeichnungen und Lagebeurteilungen aus zwei Weltkriegen,* ed. Georg Meyer, (Stuttgart: Deutsche Verlags-Anstalt, 1976), 418.

13. Halder KTB, 3:348.

14. That is if he followed his normal routine; see Blumentritt, "'Oberquartiermeister I,'" 5.

15. Bernhard von Lossberg, *Im Wehrmachtführungsstab: Bericht eines Generalstabs-offiziers* (Hamburg: Nölke, 1950), 146–47. Lossberg does not specify the date on which this conversation occurred, and there are some indications in his book that it took place as much as a week earlier, but the night of December 15–16 is the only one that seems to match Hitler's schedule and the situation in the east.

16. Peter Hoffmann, *Hitler's Personal Security* (Cambridge, Mass.: MIT Press, 1979), 234. Hoffmann's book is an excellent source on the physical layout of "Wolfs-schanze" (including three maps of the compound and its environs) and on the security arrangements there.

17. Walter Görlitz, ed., *Generalfeldmarschall Keitel: Verbrecher oder Offizier? Erin-nerungen, Briefe, Dokumente des Chefs OKW* (Göttingen: Musterschmidt-Verlag, 1961), 265–66.

18. See Franz Josef Schott, "Der Wehrmachtführungsstab im Führerhauptquartier 1939–1945" (Ph.D. diss., University of Bonn, 1980), 44, 17; Hoffmann, *Security,* 226; Walter Warlimont, *Im Hauptquartier der deutschen Wehrmacht 1939–1945: Grund-lagen, Formen, Gestalten* (Frankfurt am Main: Bernard & Graefe, 1962), 191.

19. August Winter and others, "The German Armed Forces High Command, OKW (Oberkommando der Wehrmacht): A Critical Historical Study of Its Develop-ment, Organization, Missions and Functioning from 1938 to 1945" (MS #T-101), in *World War II German Military Studies: A Collection of 213 Special Reports on the Sec-ond World War Prepared by Former Officers of the Wehrmacht for the United States Army,* ed. Donald Detwiler, assoc. ed. Charles B. Burdick and Jürgen Rohwer (New York: Garland, 1979) (hereafter: GMS), 3: chap. B1a, 60.

20. Warlimont, *Hauptquartier,* 192.

21. Alan Bullock, *Hitler: A Study in Tyranny* (New York: Harper & Row, 1962), 719.

22. Warlimont, *Hauptquartier,* 190.

23. Schott, "Wehrmachtführungsstab," 52–54.

24. Leeb, *Leeb,* 418 (Dec. 16, 1941), 419 (Dec. 17; on this date Leeb recorded the previous day's events in detail); HGr M KTB, 98.

25. Der Führer und Oberbefehlshaber der Wehrmacht Nr. 442182/41 g.K.Chefs. WFSt/Abt.L(I Op), 16.12.41, in BA-MA RW 4/677. The version that the OKH sent on to Army Group Center is in BA-MA RH 2/1327, 92–94, and OKW KTB, 1:1083; in that order, the Operations Branch excerpted the paragraphs from the original that pertained to the army group, including a portion of Army Group South's mission that the two headquarters needed to coordinate.

26. Heinz Guderian, *Erinnerungen eines Soldaten* (Heidelberg: Kurt Vowinckel, 1951), 238.

27. On the use of liaison officers, see Winter and others, "Armed Forces High Command," 3: chap. B1a, 57; Warlimont, *Hauptquartier,* 107.

28. HGr M KTB, 129. 3d and 4th Panzer Groups were under 9th and 4th Armies, respectively.

29. HGr M KTB, 138. Ziemke and Bauer are off by a day in the arrival of this order; see *Moscow to Stalingrad,* 82.

30. Order Nr. 442182/41, as in note 25.

31. HGr M KTB, 129–32. According to Nicolaus von Below, then Hitler's Luftwaffe adjutant, Hitler decided on this night to take command of the army. See *Als Hitlers Adjutant 1937–45* (Mainz: v.Hase & Koehler, 1980), 298.

32. Winter and others, "Armed Forces High Command," 3: chap. B1a, 32, 42; Helmuth Greiner, "OKW, World War II" (MS #C-065b), in GMS, vol. 7; Görlitz, *Generalfeldmarschall Keitel,* 269. On the general form of Hitler's briefings, see chapter 4.

33. Halder KTB, 3:350 (Dec. 16, 1941). Halder and the others might not have been surprised by this order, which the OKW sent to the OKH at 11:00 P.M.; there might have been just enough time for them to go over it before they left for the "Wolfsschanze."

34. HGr M KTB, 132–33. By this point Schmundt had presumably also told Hitler of Guderian's remarks.

35. Hoffmann, *Security,* 234.

36. Ferdinand Prinz von der Leyen, *Rückblick zum Mauerwald. Vier Kriegsjahre im OKH* (Munich: Biederstein, 1965), 17.

37. BA-MA N 124/17: Aussage C. Kühlein v.23.4.1948, quoted in Christian Hartmann, *Halder: Generalstabschef Hitlers 1938–1942* (Paderborn: Schöningh, 1991), 69.

38. Hartmann, *Halder,* 70.

39. Kielmansegg interview, June 14, 1996.

40. Ibid.

41. Warlimont, *Hauptquartier,* 190.

42. Ibid., 104.

43. See Lossberg, *Im Wehrmachtführungsstab,* 122–26; OKW KTB, 1:140E; Below, *Als Hitlers Adjutant,* 282–83.

44. Leyen, *Rückblick zum Mauerwald,* 22–23. The German army was also the only force that came close to subordinating rank to task. One could find lieutenant colonels working under majors, for example. The colonel in such a case is *"nachgeordnet"* rather than *"unterstellt";* that is, attached for a special task rather than truly subordinate. Still, such a working relationship was unheard of in other armies.

45. OKW/WFSt/Abt.L (I Op) Nr. 442164/41 gK. Chefs. B., 15.12.41, in BA-MA RW 4/521, 7; this order is also reproduced in Hubatsch, Weisungen, 175.

46. Chef OKW/WFSt/L Nr. 442174/41 g.Kdos. Ch., 15.12.1941; see note 11.

47. Generalstab des Heeres/Ausb.Abt.(Ia)/Nr. 3122/41 g, 15.12.41, in BA-MA RH 2/428, 113.

48. The note from Heusinger to Paulus and the latter's reply (typed on the same sheet) are in BA-MA RH 2/428, 111.

49. Op IIa Nr. 38195/41 g.Kdos. to HGr D, info BdE/AHA, 16.12.41, in BA-MA RH 2/538, 55.

50. Op IIa to HGrn D & N, 16.12.41, in BA-MA RH 2/538, 53. Note that although a subgroup drafted and sent this message, Heusinger signed it; in this way he stayed up to date on the staff's activities and outside developments.

51. See BA-MA RH 2/531, 70, for the charts kept by Op.Abt. IIa for the period December 15-17, 1941.

52. Halder KTB, 3:349 (December 16).

53. Order Nr. 442182/41; see note 25.

54. Halder KTB, 3:351 (December 17).

55. Ibid., 3:351. At this point the two also discussed the need to replace Bock because of his declining health.

56. Ibid., 3:351.

57. On Heusinger's and Gercke's activities, see ibid., 3:352.

58. HGr M KTB, 138. Unfortunately, the records do not indicate how the OKH and Army Group Center resolved this disagreement.

59. For an overview of the first few days of phase two of the Soviets' counteroffensive, which would begin on this day, see Ziemke and Bauer, *Moscow to Stalingrad,* 88-97.

60. HGr N KTB, 106; Halder KTB, 3:353.

61. HGr M KTB, 139; Halder KTB, 3:354. The change in command would be effective at midday on December 19.

62. Halder KTB, 3:353-54.

63. HGr S KTB, 127. A corps is, technically speaking, simply a headquarters, with some supporting specialist troops, to which two or more divisions are assigned.

64. Ibid., 127-28, 131-32.

65. Oberkommando des Heeres/Gen St d H/Op.Abt.(III) Nr. 1068/41 g.Kdos., 6.6.1941, *Betr.:* Meldungen an OKH, in BA-MA RH 2/459, 94-101.

66. Note that there was no time difference between the OKH and the front; that is, 08:00 at the OKH was 08:00 at each army group headquarters.

67. BA-MA RM 7/271: 1. Skl KTB Teil D 1: Lageberichte "Kriegsmarine" an OKW (Bd. 6) 21.7.-31.12.41 and RM 7/772: 1. Skl KTB Teil D 8 g: Lage Kriegsmarine 1941 für GenStdH Fremde Heere Ost, Bd. 5 (1.11.-31.12.1941). The sources do not reveal why the navy's report to the army went to Foreign Armies East.

68. BA-MA RH 2/479: Lagenberichte der Operationsabteilung, Bd 9 (1.-31.12.41). Unfortunately, this log does not show intentions or orders; it is simply a chronicle of events.

69. BA-MA RH 2/734: Lageorientierung Ostfront sowie Beitrag Heer zum Wehrmachtbericht, Bd 1: 23.6.-26.12.41. See also Erich Murawski, "Die amtliche deutsche Kriegsberichterstattung im zweiten Weltkriege," in *Publizistik* 7 (1962): 158-64; and also by Murawski, *Der deutsche Wehrmachtbericht 1939-1945. Ein Beitrag zur Untersuchung der geistigen Kriegführung. Mit einer Dokumentation der Wehrmachtberichte vom 1.7.1944 bis zum 9.5.1945* (Boppard: Harald Boldt, 1962).

70. BA-MA RH 2/614: Lageorientierungen Nordafrika der Operationsabteilung GenStdH (II b).

71. See also, e.g., OKH/GenStdH/O Qu IV/Abt Fremde Heere Ost III, "Meldungen zur Lage in Pazifischen Raum" (daily reports) in BA-MA RH 2/1246: Lage Pazifik und ostasiatischer Raum.- Lagemeldungen, -berichte, "Überblicke," sowie "Notizen," Dez 1941—März 1945.

72. BA-MA RH 2/1498: Lageberichte West Nr.483-578, Juni-Dez. 1941.

73. BA-MA RH 2/1973: Wesentliche Merkmale der Feindlage (Ostfront) 9.12.41-31.1.42.

74. BA-MA RH 2/2094: Stärke und Verteilung der sowjetischen Landstreitkräfte—

Tägliche Berechnungen des Feindkräfteeinsatzes an der deutschen Ostfront, Bd.3: 1.12.41–31.3.42.

75. BA-MA RH 2/1613: Das Gesamtheer des Britischen Reiches. Verwendungsfähige Verbände, 1941–44.

76. BA-MA RH 2/1251a/b: Die japanische Wehrmacht, 1941–44, 76.

77. Der Wehrmachtbefehlshaber in den Niederlanden Ic/WPr Nr.52555/41 geh., 16.12.41, Lagebericht für die Woche vom 8.–14.12.41, in BA-MA RW 37/22: Wöchentliche Lageberichte des Wehrmachtbefehlshabers in den Niederlanden, Januar–Dezember 1941, 245.

78. BA-MA RH 2/428: Ops Abt. Chefsachen for late 1941–early 1942, 193. See also Schott, "Wehrmachtführungsstab," 107–8.

79. Halder KTB, 3:354.

80. Ibid., 3:355.

81. Peter Bor, *Gespräche mit Halder* (Wiesbaden: Limes, 1950), 214. The words may not be accurate; as far as we know, Halder did not write them down until after the war. However, the spirit of the quote is accurate, as Hitler's subsequent actions would prove.

82. Halder KTB, 3:354.

83. Ibid., 3:354–55.

84. BA-MA RH 19 I/258, Anlagen zum KTB HGr Süd, 179.

85. See BA-MA RH 19 III/772: Grundlegende Befehle und Weisungen, 27.4.40–17.4.42.

86. Halder KTB, 3:355.

87. Brauchitsch's status is the topic of a conversation between Heusinger and Gyldenfeldt, as portrayed in Heusinger's book *Befehl im Widerstreit: Schicksalsstunden der deutschen Armee 1923-1945* (Tübingen: Rainer Wunderlich, 1950), 151–53. Unfortunately, the reliability of the account is impossible to determine; Heusinger deliberately made the accounts in this book vague, and he has no supporting material; he wanted to portray the tone of events, which of course means that we get his version of them.

88. Warlimont, *Hauptquartier,* 232; Görlitz, *Generalfeldmarschall Keitel,* 269. Halder's briefing notes for this day are in his personal papers; see BA-MA N 220/58, Tägliche Aufzeichnungen als Chef des GenStdH, insbesondere zu den täglichen Lagebesprechungen, zu Besprechungen innerhalb des OKH und zu Fergesprächen; Kommentierte Ausgabe der Historical Division, bearbeitet von Franz Halder und Alfred Philippi, Band 1: Dez 1941 (hereafter: "Halder Notes"). When used in conjunction with the Halder KTB, this source provides a more complete picture of Halder's activities, although for the period December 15–19 there are no notes beyond what the KTB contains.

89. Warlimont, *Hauptquartier,* 233; OKW KTB, 1:138–39E; Kielmansegg interview, April 29, 1996.

90. Warlimont, *Hauptquartier,* 233.

91. Halder KTB, 3:356–59.

92. On this issue, see OKW KTB, 1:144–51E.

93. See, e.g., the *Führerbefehl* that Hitler sent via the OKW's Armed Forces Command Staff to the OKH on December 24, 1941, in OKW KTB, 1:1086; the Operations Branch then sent it on to Army Group Center.

94. See OKW/WFSt/ Abt.L(I Op.) Nr. 442217/41 g.K.Chefs., 21.12.1941, in BA-MA RW 4/578, 176; the text of the document is also printed in OKW KTB, 1:1085-86, without the distribution list. Specifically, the memorandum was a product of the Army Operations Group in the National Defense Branch of the Armed Forces Command Staff. In addition to the Operations Branch, the memo also went to the war diary section, the Luftwaffe Operations Group and the Quartermaster Group, all in the National Defense Branch.

95. Halder KTB, 3:356. The following account of the discussions regarding Army Group Center is drawn from the Halder KTB, the Halder Notes, and the HGr M KTB for this date.

96. Guderian gives a long account of this meeting; see *Erinnerungen,* 240-43. His use of direct quotes is highly questionable, but there is little doubt that this was a stormy confrontation. See also Görlitz, *Generalfeldmarschall Keitel,* 291-92.

97. Halder KTB, 3:361.

98. HGr M KTB, 165.

99. Halder KTB, 3:362. Kluge actually gave the order to hold; see Halder Notes for this date.

100. Ibid., 3:362.

101. Leyen, *Rückblick zum Mauerwald,* 47.

102. On this issue, see OKW KTB, 1:169-70E; Walter Warlimont, "Commentary on T-101" (MS #T-101 K1), 97, in GMS, vol. 6; Winter and others, "Armed Forces High Command," 3: chap. B1a, 47-49; Franz Halder, "Der Komplex OKH-OKW," in the Halder papers, BA-MA N 220/95, 60.

103. HGr M KTB, 172: telephone conversation at 11:00 P.M.

104. See Bullock, *Hitler,* 403-5.

105. Germany, Heer, Heeresdienstvorschrift 92 (H.Dv. 92), *Handbuch für den Generalstabsdienst im Kriege,* Teil I, II, abgeschlossen am 1.8.1939 (Berlin: der Reichsdruckerei, 1939), approved by Halder on August 1, 1939, 14.

106. As a comparison, think of Patton appealing to Roosevelt over some decision that Eisenhower had made. The comparison might seem ridiculous, since the two command systems were so different—but that is exactly the point.

107. Elizabeth Wagner, ed., *Der Generalquartiermeister. Briefe und Tagebuchaufzeichnungen des Generalquartiermeisters des Heeres, General der Artillerie Eduard Wagner* (Munich: Günter Olzog, 1963), 202; emphasis added.

108. Ibid., 205.

109. Geoffrey Parker, *The Grand Strategy of Philip II* (New Haven, Conn.: Yale University Press, 1998).

110. The issue of staff size is one that calls for a comparative study; at this point none exists.

9. THE LAST GRASP

1. WFSt/L (I K Op) Nr. 44 2173/41 g.K.Chefs., 14.12.41: Überblick über die Bedeutung des Kriegseintritts der U.S.A und Japans, in BA-MA RM 7/258. This assessment was primarily the navy's product; the draft studies from which it originated are also in the file. See also Bernd Wegner, "Hitlers Strategie zwischen Pearl Harbor und

Stalingrad," in *Das Deutsche Reich und der Zweite Weltkrieg,* ed. Militärgeschichtliches Forschungsamt (Stuttgart: Deutsche Verlags-Anstalt, 1979-90) (hereafter: DRZW), 6:101-5.

2. As Wegner points out; see "Strategie," DRZW, 6:105 n 39.

3. On Hitler's thinking, see Wegner, "Strategie," DRZW, 6:107-14; also Earl F. Ziemke and Magna E. Bauer, *Moscow to Stalingrad: Decision in the East* (Washington, D.C.: U.S. Government Printing Office, 1987), 283-86; Gerhard Weinberg, *A World at Arms: A Global History of World War II* (New York: Cambridge University Press, 1994), 408-10.

4. Franz Halder, *Kriegstagebuch. Tägliche Aufzeichnungen des Chefs des Generalstabes des Heeres 1939-1942,* ed. Arbeitskreis für Wehrforschung, Stuttgart (Stuttgart: Kohlhammer, 1962) (hereafter: Halder KTB), 3:371-72 (Jan. 2, 1942).

5. Quoted in Ziemke and Bauer, *Moscow to Stalingrad,* 148.

6. Der Chef des Generalstabes des Heeres Nr.10/42 g.Kdos. Chefs., 17.1.42, Betr.: Beurteilung der Feindlage, in BA-MA RH 2/2582, 46.

7. Oberkommando der Wehrmacht WZ(I) Nr. 4768/41 geh, WFSt (Org.) Nr. 3870/41 geh, 14.12.41, in BA-MA RW 4/459, 2. See also BA-MA NOKW 168, Aussage WARLIMONTs vor dem Internationalen Militärgerichtshof vom Oktober 1946, 4.

8. Buttlar-Brandenfels replaced Lossberg on January 1, 1942, at Hitler's insistence; apparently, the Führer did not like the latter's attitude. See Bernhard von Lossberg, *Im Wehrmachtführungsstab: Bericht eines Generalstabsoffiziers* (Hamburg: Nölke, 1950), 149; Walter Warlimont, *Im Hauptquartier der deutschen Wehrmacht 1939-1945: Grundlagen, Formen, Gestalten* (Frankfurt am Main: Bernard & Graefe, 1962), 231.

9. Warlimont, *Hauptquartier,* 229-31; NOKW 168, 3-4; see also Franz Josef Schott, "Der Wehrmachtführungsstab im Führerhauptquartier 1939-1945" (Ph.D. diss., University of Bonn, 1980), 65-67.

10. A slightly more substantive change took place in the autumn, when the Command Staff added a Group Ic (*Feindlage:* Enemy Situation) to gather and evaluate intelligence. With one chief and two or three other officers, however, it represented no great change in German intelligence assessment capabilities. See Schott, "Wehrmachtführungsstab," 77.

11. OKW Az 11 b WZ (I) 17637/41, 8.12.41, Betr.: Schriftverkehr mit den dem OKW nachgeordneten Dienststellen, in BA-MA RW 19/521, 21.

12. Chef OKW Az. B 13 geh 4840/41 WZ (I), 31.12.41, Betr.: Dienstverkehr OKH-OKW, in BA-MA RH 2/156, 29.

13. W F St Az.: 14 a 10 WFSt/Org (I) Nr.: 165/42 geh., 15.4.1942, *Betr.:* Befehls- und Kommandogewalt des Chefs des Oberkommandos der Wehrmacht, in BA-MA RW 19/687, 86-87.

14. BA-MA RH 2/821: KTB GenStdH/Organisationsabteilung, Bd. 3: 1.1.-31.7.1942, 173.

15. Der Chef des Oberkommandos der Wehrmacht Nr.1662/42 geh WFSt/Org (I), 14.5.1942, in BA-MA RW 19/687, 96.

16. Bernd Wegner, "Der Krieg gegen die Sowjetunion 1942/43," in DRZW 6:778-79. For a detailed examination of German losses through the winter crisis of 1941-42, see Bernhard R. Kroener, "Die personellen Ressourcen des Dritten Reiches im Spannungsfeld zwischen Wehrmacht, Bürokratie und Kriegswirtschaft 1939-1942," in DRZW 5, esp. 877-88.

17. Wegner, "Krieg 1942/43," DRZW, 6:786–88. The figure for artillery includes antitank and antiaircraft pieces.

18. Williamson Murray, *Luftwaffe* (Baltimore, Md.: Nautical and Aviation Publishing Company of America, 1985), 101.

19. Halder KTB, 3:401 n 1.

20. See Wegner, "Krieg 1942/43," DRZW, 6:774–77.

21. Halder KTB, 3:422.

22. See Reinhard Gehlen, *Der Dienst: Erinnerungen, 1942–1971* (Mainz-Wiesbaden: v.Hase & Koehler, 1971), esp. 17.

23. Gehlen, *Der Dienst,* 42.

24. Ibid., 55–56; see also Wegner, "Krieg 1942/43," DRZW, 6:798.

25. Foreign Armies East submitted an estimate of personnel resources on March 23, and the OKW's Military Economy and Armaments Office submitted an estimate of the USSR's industrial potential on March 31. For the details on these documents and their influence, see Wegner, "Krieg 1942/43," DRZW, 6:798–815.

26. See OKW Nr. 00 956/42 g.Kdos.WFSt/Op., 17.3.42, in BA-MA RM 7/259, 143.

27. Percy Ernst Schramm, ed., *Kriegstagebuch des Oberkommandos der Wehrmacht (Wehrmachtführungsstab)* (Munich: Manfred Pawlak, 1982) (hereafter: OKW KTB), 2:314. Hitler first saw the OKW study on April 7; see Wegner, "Krieg 1942/43," DRZW, 6:804.

28. Based on an examination of the Halder KTB from March 23 through April 10.

29. See Tägliche Aufzeichnungen als Chef des GenStdH, insbesondere zu den täglichen Lagebesprechungen, zu Besprechungen innerhalb des OKH und zu Ferngesprächen; Kommentierte Ausgabe der Historical Division, bearbeitet von Franz Halder und Alfred Philippi, Band 1: Dez 1941 (hereafter: "Halder Notes"), in BA-MA N 220/58, 97–110, notes for Dec. 24, 1941.

30. Bock took command of Army Group South on January 19, after Reichenau suffered a stroke.

31. Halder KTB, 3:420–21.

32. Der Führer und Oberste Befehlshaber der Wehrmacht OKW/WFSt Nr. 55616/42 g.K. Chefs., 5.4.1942, Weisung 41, in Walther Hubatsch, *Hitlers Weisungen für die Kriegführung 1939–1945: Dokumente des Oberkommandos der Wehrmacht* (Frankfurt am Main: Bernard & Graefe, 1962), 183–88; the quote is on 184.

33. OKW KTB, 2:316 (April 5, 1942). Actually, the Armed Forces Command Staff's war diary for 1942 is missing; this portion of the published work consists of the war diary of the OKW's Military History Branch.

34. For a discussion of the plan, including maps, see Ziemke and Bauer, *Moscow to Stalingrad,* 286–90; also Wegner, "Krieg 1942/43," DRZW, 6:761–62, and map opposite 773; also Manfred Kehrig, *Stalingrad: Analyse und Dokumentation einer Schlacht* (Stuttgart: Deutsche Verlags-Anstalt, 1974).

35. Hubatsch, *Weisungen,* 187.

36. Actually the operation now went by the name of *Braunschweig* because on June 19 a staff officer had, against all orders, carried a set of attack plans with him on a light plane that strayed across the front and landed in Soviet-held territory. Fortunately for the Germans, Stalin decided the plans were a plant and disregarded them; he expected a German offensive against Moscow. Naturally, the incident added to Hitler's fixation on security.

37. As early as July 9, he issued a document in which he predicted that Britain faced the choice of either invading the Continent or losing the USSR as a political and military factor. See OKW/WFSt Nr. 551213/42 g.Kdos. Chefs., in the Müller-Hillebrand papers, BA-MA N 553/56.

38. The Germans split Army Group South into Army Groups A and B on July 9. See Hubatsch, *Weisungen,* 196–200, for Directive No. 45.

39. Halder KTB, 3:489.

40. Ibid., 3:475.

41. Ibid., 3:493–94.

42. Compare Aufzeichnungen Greiner zum 8. September 1942, in OKW KTB 2:696, and Erläuterungen des Generals Warlimont zu den Aufzeichnungen Greiners, in OKW KTB 2:697. See also Ziemke and Bauer, *Moscow to Stalingrad,* 377; Nicolaus von Below, *Als Hitlers Adjutant 1937–45* (Mainz: v.Hase & Koehler, 1980), 315.

43. See Christian Hartmann, *Halder: Generalstabschef Hitlers 1938–1942* (Paderborn: Schöningh, 1991), 333.

44. Walter Görlitz, ed., *Generalfeldmarschall Keitel: Verbrecher oder Offizier? Erinnerungen, Briefe, Dokumente des Chefs OKW* (Göttingen: Musterschmidt-Verlag, 1961), 305–6. Unfortunately, a Party official, acting against Hitler's wishes, ordered the resulting treasure trove of historical material burned at the end of the war. Of approximately 103,000 pages of transcripts, only a fraction survived. They are published in Helmut Heiber, ed., *Hitlers Lagebesprechungen: Die Protokollfragmente seiner militärischen Konferenzen 1942–1945* (Stuttgart: Deutsche Verlags-Anstalt, 1962). An abridged edition appeared in 1964.

45. Halder KTB, 3:519.

46. From July 16 to November 1, 1942, Hitler worked out of a field headquarters compound slightly north of Vinnitsa in the Ukraine.

47. See Görlitz, *Generalfeldmarschall Keitel,* 165.

48. See Hartmann, *Halder,* 328–29.

49. This is the incident as Christian Hartmann relates it; see ibid., 331. Adolf Heusinger witnessed this exchange and put it into his book *Befehl im Widerstreit: Schicksalsstunden der deutschen Armee 1923–1945* (Tübingen: Rainer Wunderlich, 1950), 200–201, but he changed Hitler's last comment because he did not want to publicize the fact that Halder had never received a wound in combat. Hitler's final comment therefore comes from the account of Major Gerhard Engel, *Heeresadjutant bei Hitler, 1938–1943: Aufzeichnungen des Majors Engel,* ed. Hildegard von Kotze (Stuttgart: Deutsche Verlags-Anstalt, 1974), 125, entry dated Sept. 4, 1942.

50. Johann Adolf Graf von Kielmansegg, interview with the author, April 29, 1996, Bad Krozingen, Germany.

51. Halder KTB, 3:519. See also OKW KTB, 2:704–5 (Aufzeichnungen Greiners zum 9. September 1942).

52. Halder KTB, 3:524.

53. Ibid., 3:528; Görlitz, *Generalfeldmarschall Keitel,* 309. For Hitler's later assessment of Halder, see Engel, *Heeresadjutant,* 131 (Oct. 19, 1942).

54. Kielmansegg interview, April 29, 1996; unfortunately, Kielmansegg did not note Halder's exact words. For the order that sent Halder into the Führerreserve and put General Zeitzler in his place, see BA-MA RH 2/157, 48.

55. Quoted in Hartmann, *Halder,* 335–36.

56. Ibid., 336.

57. Letter of Aug. 6, 1951, to Günther Blumentritt, in the Halder papers, BA-MA N 220/8. Halder continued: "Naturally a German soldier cannot give such an answer to a foreigner, however, without putting that man-eating German militarism on trial again."

58. For a contrary view, according to which Halder engineered his own dismissal because he did not believe the war could be won, see Wegner, "Krieg 1942/43," DRZW, 6:954-56.

59. Albert Seaton, *The German Army, 1933-45* (London: Weidenfeld & Nicolson, 1982), 193. Schmundt received a promotion to brigadier general on January 1, 1942, with an effective date of December 1, 1941.

60. Görlitz, *Generalfeldmarschall Keitel,* 308-9; Warlimont, *Hauptquartier,* 271.

61. Halder noted Blumentritt's departure and its purpose in his diary. See Halder KTB, 3:524. Blumentritt had taken over as assistant chief of staff for operations in January 1942, when Paulus took command of 6th Army for Operation *Blue.*

62. This from Zeitzler's own account; see the Zeitzler papers, BA-MA N 63/18.

63. Kielmansegg provided this information and the description that follows of Zeitzler's initial meeting with the General Staff officers in "Mauerwald." Interview of April 29, 1996.

64. BA-MA RH 2/157, 50; emphasis in original.

65. See, e.g., Moriz von Faber du Faur, *Macht und Ohnmacht. Erinnerungen eines alten Offiziers* (Stuttgart: Hans E. Günther, 1953), 165.

66. See Ulrich de Maizière, *In der Pflicht: Lebensbericht eines deutschen Soldaten im 20. Jahrhundert* (Bonn: E. S. Mittler & Sohn, 1989), 79-80. Both General a.D. de Maizière and General a.D. Kielmansegg provided valuable background information on Zeitzler, in interviews on May 25 and April 29, 1996, respectively.

67. The orders for these changes, which took place on October 13 (OQu I) and 15 (OQu IV) and November 10 (OQu V), are in BA-MA RH 2/157, 123-29.

68. Walter Görlitz, *Der deutsche Generalstab: Geschichte und Gestalt 1657-1945* (Frankfurt am Main: Verlag der Frankfurter Hefte, 1950), 596. Unfortunately, Görlitz offers no evidence to substantiate this claim.

69. Waldemar Erfurth, *Die Geschichte des deutschen Generalstabes von 1918 bis 1945,* 2d ed. (Göttingen: Musterschmidt, 1960), 233; Zeitzler papers, BA-MA N 63/99, 78. See also Kurt Zeitzler, "German Army High Command. General Critique of MSS #P-041a–P-041ll and a Report on the September 1942–June 1944 Period" (MS #P-041ii), 30, in *The German Army High Command, 1938-1945* (Arlington, Va.: University Publications of America, n.d. Microfilm) (hereafter: GAHC); this is the English translation of volume 99 of his papers.

70. Erfurth, *Geschichte,* 233.

71. See Gerhard Matzky, Lothar Metz, and Kurt von Tippelskirch, "Army High Command. Organization and Working Methods of the Intelligence Division" (MS #P-041i), 52-55, in GAHC. Given the Germans' track record in this sphere, the loss might not have been that great.

72. OKH, Der Chef d Gen St d H, Org. Abt. (II), Nr.9900/42 geh., 8.10.42, Grundlegender Befehl Nr. 1 (Hebung der Gefechtsstärke), in BA-MA RH 2/2919, 5. Heusinger stated after the war that Hitler ordered the cuts; this in an interrogation by the Military Intelligence Service Center, United States Forces European Theater, on February 5, 1946.

73. Der Chef d Gen St d H, Az. 12 G Z (I3), Nr. 3753/42 geh., 14.10.42, *Bezug:* O.K.H. Der Chef des Gen St d H / Org.Abt. (II), Nr. 9900/42 geh. vom 8.10.42., *Betr.:* Verringerung der Iststärken, in BA-MA RH 2/2919, 16.

74. Führer Order of October 1, 1942, in BA-MA RH 2/2919, 3.

75. Dermot Bradley and Richard Schulze-Kossens, eds., *Tätigkeitsbericht des Chefs des Heerespersonalamtes General der Infanterie Rudolf Schmundt, 1.10.1942–29.10.1944* (Osnabrück: Biblio, 1984), 1–2. In order to relieve himself of some of the work involved in holding down both positions, Schmundt created the post of deputy chief of the Army Personnel Office and appointed Brigadier General Wilhelm Burgdorf to fill it. See also Burkhart Müller-Hillebrand, "Schematische Darstellung der obersten Führung des deutschen Heeres 1938 bis Kriegsende mit Erläuterungen über organisatorische Beziehungen, Aufgaben und Verantwortlichkeiten der einzelnen Dienststellen des OKH im Laufe der Jahre 1938–1945" (MS #P-041a, unpublished), 25.

76. BA-MA RH 2/157 contains a series of documents that provide some insight into this issue, 59–66, 101–110. They culminate in a memorandum in which Schmundt and Zeitzler agree on their respective powers and responsibilities.

77. Oberkommando des Heeres Az. 12 / P A / Gen St d H / G Z (I1) Nr. 4310/42 geh., 14.11.1942, in BA-MA RH 2/471b, 79–80. See also Müller-Hillebrand, "Darstellung," 24; Bradley and Schulze-Kossens, *Schmundt,* 6–7.

78. Bradley and Schulze-Kossens, *Schmundt,* 2–4. Of the officers in service at the beginning of October 1942, about one in seven was a Regular officer, while the rest were reservists.

79. Ibid., 4–5. See also Reinhard Stumpf, *Die Wehrmacht-Elite. Rang- und Herkunftstruktur der deutschen Generale und Admirale 1933–1945* (Boppard: Harald Boldt, 1982), 322–28; and Jürgen Förster, "Vom Führerheer der Republik zur nationalsozialistischen Volksarmee," in *Deutschland in Europa. Kontinuität und Bruch. Gedenkschrift für Andreas Hillgruber,* ed. Jost Dülffer, Bernd Martin, and Günter Wollstein (Frankfurt am Main: Propyläen, 1990), 317–18.

80. Bradley and Schulze-Kossens, *Schmundt,* 8 (Oct. 9, 1942); Stumpf, *Wehrmacht-Elite,* 329. Hitler even discussed the changes in one of his increasingly rare speeches; see Max Domarus, *Hitler: Reden und Proklamationen 1932–1945* (Würzburg: Schmidt, Neustadt a.d. Aisch, 1962–63), 2:1922. Part of the reasoning behind the decision was the simple fact that there were not enough secondary school graduates to meet the demand for officers.

81. Bradley and Schulze-Kossens, *Schmundt,* 6.

82. Ibid., 25; Stumpf, *Wehrmacht-Elite,* 328–29.

83. Stumpf, *Wehrmacht-Elite,* 328.

84. Rudolf Absolon, *Die Wehrmacht im Dritten Reich. Aufbau, Gliederung, Recht, Verwaltung* (Boppard: Harald Boldt, 1969–95), 6:505.

85. Stumpf, *Wehrmacht-Elite,* 329; Bradley and Schulze-Kossens, *Schmundt,* 16.

86. Förster, "Volksarmee," 318.

87. Stumpf, *Wehrmacht-Elite,* 330–31.

88. Ferdinand Prinz von der Leyen, *Rückblick zum Mauerwald: Vier Kriegsjahre im OKH* (Munich: Biederstein, 1965), 23.

89. Leyen, *Rückblick zum Mauerwald,* 78–79.

90. See ibid., 80–81.

91. Görlitz, *Generalfeldmarschall Keitel,* 309.

92. Zeitzler papers, BA-MA N 63/18, 49–50.

93. Zeitzler papers, BA-MA N 63/15, 66; Zeitzler, "Critique," in GAHC, 47–48.

94. Warlimont, *Hauptquartier,* 272–73. See also OKW KTB 2:795 (Erläuterungen des Generals Warlimont zu den Aufzeichnungen Greiners, 5. Okt. 1942).

95. Keitel stated that this happened "frequently" (Görlitz, *Generalfeldmarschall Keitel,* 309). See also Warlimont, *Hauptquartier,* 273; Aufzeichnungen Greiners für den Zeitraum 10. bis 13. Oktober 1942, in OKW KTB, 2:814.

96. Actually, this development was not as sudden as Greiner, Warlimont, and Keitel make it seem. For instance, in the evening briefing on December 1, 1942, Jodl and Hitler discussed the situation in south Russia in some depth. Unfortunately, too few stenographic records exist to support a thorough analysis.

97. Hans von Greiffenberg, "Die Operationsabteilung des O.K.H. (Generalstab des Heeres)" (MS #P-041e, unpublished), 9, and tables 4 and 5; see also, e.g., Halder KTB 3:416, Besprechung mit Gen. Buhle (March 18, 1942).

98. Based on an examination of Hubatsch, *Weisungen.*

99. The change is visible in the directives in Hubatsch for this time period. See also, e.g., Der Führer/OKH—Gen St d H—Op Abt (I) Nr. 420817/42 g.Kdos.Chefs., H.Qu.OKH, 14.Oktober 1942: *Operationsbefehl Nr. 1,* in BA-MA RH 2/470, 40.

100. *Operationsbefehl Nr. 1,* as above, in BA-MA RH 2/470, 40. See also Ziemke and Bauer, *Moscow to Stalingrad,* 450–51.

101. OKH/Chef d GenStdH/Op Abt (I) Nr.420858/42 g.Kdos.Chefs., H.Qu.OKH, 23.10.42: *1. Ergänzung zum Operationsbefehl Nr. 1,* in BA-MA RH 2/470, 51.

102. On German intelligence failures at this juncture, see Hans-Heinrich Wilhelm, "Die Prognosen der Abteilung Fremde Heere Ost 1942–1945," in *Zwei Legenden aus dem Dritten Reich* (Stuttgart: Deutsche Verlags-Anstalt, 1974), 47–48; also David Glantz, *Soviet Military Deception in the Second World War* (London: Frank Cass, 1989), 108–19.

103. Maizière, *In der Pflicht,* 80–81. See also BA-MA RH 2/824: KTB GenStdH/ Org.Abt., Bd 4: 1.8.-31.12.42, 85.

104. Engel, *Heeresadjutant,* 132 (Oct. 22, 1942).

10. A COMMAND DIVIDED AGAINST ITSELF

1. Quoted in Ernst Klink, *Das Gesetz des Handelns: Die Operation "Zitadelle" 1943* (Stuttgart: Deutsche Verlags-Anstalt, 1966), 32.

2. This was one of the many areas in which the Allied ability to read German signals traffic was crucial. For an overview of this aspect of the war, see Gerhard Weinberg, *A World at Arms: A Global History of World War II* (New York: Cambridge University Press, 1994), 554–57.

3. For the text of this document plus an analysis, see Jürgen Förster, "Strategische Überlegungen des Wehrmachtführungsstabes für das Jahr 1943," in *Militärgeschichtliche Mitteilungen* 13/1(1973); 95–107.

4. The study is also interesting in that it addressed the east at all. This was Jodl's last attempt to have a say in the fundamentals of strategy there.

5. Dr. Bernd Wegner offered this concise evaluation ("must" versus "how") at the Militärgeschichtliches Forschungsamt's (MGFA) international academic conference

"Die Wehrmacht: Selbstverständnis, Professionalität, Verantwortlichkeit," Potsdam, Germany, Sept. 8-11, 1997. See also his article, "Defensive ohne Strategie: Die Wehrmacht und das Jahr 1943," in *Die Wehrmacht: Mythos und Realität,* im Auftrag des Militärgeschtlichen Forschungsamtes, ed. Rolf-Dieter Müller and Hans-Erich Volkmann (Munich: Oldenbourg, 1999), 199.

6. This from the Organization Branch's statistical summaries. See Percy Ernst Schramm, ed., *Kriegstagebuch des Oberkommandos der Wehrmacht (Wehrmachtführungsstab)* (Munich: Manfred Pawlak, 1982) (hereafter: OKW KTB), 2:95. See also Ruediger Overmans, *Deutsche militärische Verluste im Zweiten Weltkrieg* (Munich: Oldenbourg, 1999).

7. OKW KTB, 3:130-33.

8. For a detailed examination of the planning and conduct of *Citadel,* see Klink, *Gesetz.* Some of Klink's broader conclusions are questionable; in general he tends to lay too much of the blame at Hitler's feet and credits the generals with too much talent and willingness to resist the Führer. For a more concise, English account, see Earl F. Ziemke, *Stalingrad to Berlin: The German Defeat in the East* (Washington, D.C.: U.S. Army Center of Military History, 1987), 124-39.

9. This is the version contained in Klink, *Gesetz,* 58. Figuring out who really wanted to do what is difficult. Albert Seaton, *The German Army, 1933-45* (London: Weidenfeld & Nicolson, 1982), 204, says that Zeitzler favored the attack, while Jodl and Guderian wanted forces for the west, but he offers no evidence. Heinz Guderian, if his memoir is credible, did not want any major attack in 1943; see *Erinnerungen eines Soldaten* (Heidelberg: Kurt Vowinckel, 1951), 270. Hitler had recalled Guderian to be the inspector general of armored troops; see below.

10. OKH/GenStdH/OpAbt Nr. 430 163/43 g.Kdos./Chefs., 13.3.43, in Klink, *Gesetz,* 277-78.

11. Ziemke, *Stalingrad to Berlin,* 131-32.

12. OKW KTB, 3:77 (Jan. 27, 1943).

13. Ibid., 3:140-41 (Feb. 18, 1943).

14. On the Italian request, see Dermot Bradley and Richard Schulze-Kossens, eds., *Tätigkeitsbericht des Chefs des Heerespersonalamtes General der Infanterie Rudolf Schmundt, 1.10.1942-29.10.1944* (Osnabrück: Biblio, 1984), 47 (Feb. 22, 1943).

15. OKW/WFSt/Op Nr. 661055/43 gKdos—Chefsache, 12.5.1943, in OKW KTB, 3:1429.

16. Ibid., 3:763-64 (July 9, 1943).

17. Oberkommando des Heeres GenStdH/Org.Abt.(I) Nr. 1002/43 g.K.Chefs., 6.2.1943, Betr.: Personal- und Materialplanung des Heeres 1943, in ibid., 3:1415-17.

18. Ibid., 3:165 (Feb. 27, 1943).

19. Bradley and Schulze-Kossens, *Schmundt,* 47 (Feb. 28, 1943). Guderian conveniently passes over such remarks in his memoir; see *Erinnerungen,* 260-64.

20. Louis P. Lochner, ed., *The Goebbels Diaries* (New York: Eagle Books, 1948), 474.

21. Dienstanweisung für den Generalinspektor der Panzertruppen, appendix to Burkhart Müller-Hillebrand, "Schematische Darstellung der obersten Führung des deutschen Heeres 1938 bis Kriegsende mit Erläuterungen über organisatorische Beziehungen, Aufgaben und Verantwortlichkeiten der einzelnen Dienststellen des OKH im Laufe der Jahre 1938-1945" (MS #P-041a, unpublished). The only armored forces left out of Guderian's sphere were the assault guns, which remained under the artillery.

22. Guderian, *Erinnerungen,* 266-67. Some authors have been inclined to take Guderian at his word; see, e.g., Matthew Cooper, *The German Army, 1933-1945: Its Political and Military Failure* (Chelsea, Mich.: Scarborough House, 1990), 454.

23. See Burkhart Müller-Hillebrand, "The German Army High Command" (MS #P-041a) 1952(?), in *The German Army High Command 1938-1945* (Arlington, Va.: University Publications of America, n.d. Microfilm) (hereafter: GAHC). By definition, Guderian's role usurped part of the Organization Branch's, where Müller-Hillebrand had been chief.

24. See Seaton, *German Army,* 203.

25. Memo dated Sept. 3, 1943, in BA-MA RH 2/831: Anlagen zum KTB Org.Abt., Bd. VI 1: 31.8.-15.9.43.

26. See Walter Warlimont, *Im Hauptquartier der deutschen Wehrmacht 1939-1945. Grundlagen, Formen, Gestalten* (Frankfurt am Main: Bernard & Graefe, 1962), 347-48; also Hitler's midday briefing of July 25, discussed below, in Helmut Heiber, ed., *Hitlers Lagebesprechungen: Die Protokollfragmente seiner militärischen Konferenzen 1942-1945* (Stuttgart: Deutsche Verlags-Anstalt, 1962), 299-302. Bullock (*Hitler and Stalin,* 792) also mentions that Hitler had made preparations to pull units out of the east if necessary, but he provides no citations; see *Hitler and Stalin: Parallel Lives* (New York: Vintage Books, 1993), 792. Warlimont claims that Zeitzler deliberately withheld information on the location and status of the units upon which the OKW was counting, but there is no corroboration for that claim.

27. For an excellent overview of the Italian campaign, see Dominick Graham and Shelford Bidwell, *Tug of War: The Battle for Italy, 1943-1945* (New York: St. Martin's Press, 1986).

28. Dönitz took over for Raeder as commander in chief of the navy in January 1943.

29. Hans-Heinrich Wilhelm, "Die Prognosen der Abteilung Fremde Heere Ost 1942-1945," in *Zwei Legenden aus dem Dritten Reich* (Stuttgart: Deutsche Verlags-Anstalt, 1974), 53-54.

30. Ibid., 54.

31. OKW KTB, 3:759-60 (July 8, 1943).

32. Heiber, *Lagebesprechungen,* 299-302.

33. Ibid., 373 (July 26, 1943). In this instance Zeitzler clearly supported Hitler against Kluge, even though that meant the loss of units to the OKW.

34. On Schmundt's discussion with Fromm, see Bradley and Schulze-Kossens, *Schmundt,* 88 (Aug. 17, 1943); on the General Staff's order, see OKW KTB, 3:987 (Aug. 22, 1943).

35. See Zeitzler's papers: BA-MA N 63/15, 67-68 and N 63/99, 82; also Adolf Heusinger, interview by U.S. Army Intelligence, February 1, 1946; Burkhart Müller-Hillebrand, *Das Heer, 1933-1945: Entwicklung des organisatorischen Aufbaues* (Darmstadt: E. S. Mittler, 1954-69), 3:157. Kielmansegg confirmed that the debates also went on at the staff level; interview by the author, June 14, 1996, Bad Krozingen, Germany.

36. OKW KTB, 3:1091 (Sept. 11, 1943).

37. Bradley and Schulze-Kossens, *Schmundt,* 97-98 (Sept. 27, 1943).

38. Der Chef des Wehrmachtführungsstabes im Oberkommando der Wehrmacht Nr.662214/43 g.K.Chefs. OKW/WFSt/Op (H), 14.9.43, in BA-MA RM 7/260, 321.

39. OKW KTB, 3:1043, 1131-35, 1168-70, 1209.

40. Ibid., 3:1212 (Oct. 21), 1219-20 (Oct. 25), 1223-24 (Oct. 27).

41. Walther Hubatsch, *Hitlers Weisungen für die Kriegführung 1939-1945: Dokumente des Oberkommandos der Wehrmacht* (Frankfurt am Main:: Bernard & Graefe, 1962), 233-37.

42. See BA-MA RH 2/828: KTB GenStdH/Org.Abt., Bd VII: 1.10.-31.12.43, 43 (Nov. 6), 61 (Nov. 18).

43. See OKW KTB 3:1314-15 (Nov. 27, 1943): also Bradley and Schulze-Kossens, *Schmundt,* 115-16.

44. There was a pervasive prejudice against support troops in the German army, as Dr. Bernhard Kroener pointed out on September 10, 1997, in his remarks at the MG-FA's conference in Potsdam.

45. See Bradley and Schulze-Kossens, *Schmundt,* 116; and Ziemke, *Stalingrad to Berlin,* 215. On the so-called *Feldjägerbataillonen,* see also OKW KTB 3:1342 (Dec. 7, 1943).

46. See Ziemke, *Stalingrad to Berlin,* 214-15.

47. KH, Der Chef des GenStdH, Op.Abt./Org.Abt./Gen.Qu. Nr. II/2150/43 g.Kdos., 5.12.1943, in BA-MA RH 2/940, 101-6. See also the supplementary orders: Oberkommando des Heeres GenStdH/Org.Abt. Nr. II/23247/43 geh., 13.12.1943 (BA-MA RH 2/940, 137-38); and Oberkommando des Heeres GenStdH/Org.Abt. Nr. II/31139/44 geh., 14.2.1944 (BA-MA RH 2/940, 140-42).

48. OKH, Der Chef des GenStdH, Der Generalinspekteur der Panzertruppen Nr. 2861/43 geh., 7.12.1943, in BA-MA RH 2/940, 172-74.

49. Halder papers, BA-MA N 220/58: Tägliche Aufzeichnungen als Chef des GenStdH, insbesondere zu den täglichen Lagebesprechungen, zu Besprechungen innerhalb des OKH und zu Ferngesprächen, Dez. 1941, (hereafter: Halder Notes), 111-12. A further note, which might have been added after the war, says that this was to counteract the increasingly obvious practice of falsifying reports in order to forestall further ridiculous orders from Hitler.

50. OKH, Der Chef des Generalstabes des Heeres, Op.Abt. (I) Nr. 11 609/42 geh., 7.11.42: Grundlegender Befehl Nr.6 (Op Abt) (Aufrichtigkeit und Anständigkeit der Führung), in BA-MA RH 2/940, 38; emphasis in original.

51. See Jodl's statement in International Military Tribunal, *Trial of the Major War Criminals Before the International Military Tribunal, Nuremberg, 14 November 1945-1 October 1946* (Nuremberg: International Military Tribunal, 1947), 15:297-98; also chapter 4.

52. Warlimont, *Hauptquartier,* 106-7; August Winter and others, "The German Armed Forces High Command, OKW (Oberkommando der Wehrmacht): A Critical Historical Study of Its Development, Organization, Missions and Functioning from 1938 to 1945" (MS #T-101), in *World War II German Military Studies: A collection of 213 Special Reports on the Second World War Prepared by Former Officers of the Wehrmacht for the United States Army,* ed. Donald Detwiler, assoc. ed. Charles B. Burdick and Jürgen Rohwer (New York: Garland, 1979) (hereafter: GMS), 3: chap. B1a, 56.

53. Jürgen Förster maintains that this practice became more, not less, common from 1943 on. See "The Dynamics of *Volksgemeinschaft:* The Effectiveness of the German Military Establishment in the Second World War," in *Military Effectiveness,* ed. Allan R. Millett and Williamson Murray, vol. 3, *The Second World War* (Boston: Unwin Hyman, 1990), 201. This seems unlikely, given the propensity of senior German commanders to report any deviation from orders on the part of their subordinates.

54. OKW KTB, 3:239 (March 24, 1943).

55. On this issue, see Wilhelm, "Prognosen," 21–26. As Wilhelm points out, historians must treat all reports, especially those from the last years of the war, with skepticism.

56. OKW KTB, 1:1156. The courier in question disobeyed explicit, standing orders not to carry secret materials aboard an aircraft. See Telford Taylor, *The March of Conquest: The German Victories in Western Europe, 1940* (New York: Simon & Schuster, 1958), 61.

57. Zeitzler papers, BA-MA N 63/15, 48 and N 63/99, 103.

58. OKW KTB, 4:113.

59. By the middle of 1943, Hitler's health was clearly suffering from the strain. He was experiencing severe headaches, a tremor in his arm, a balky leg, stomach cramps, insomnia, and bouts of depression. Dr. Morell, his personal physician, took to giving him hormones and a patent medicine that contained strychnine and atropine. See Bullock, *Hitler and Stalin,* 797–98. Ellen Gibbels argues convincingly that Hitler had Parkinson's disease, but that it probably did not affect his decisions to any significant degree; nor did his medications. See "Hitlers Nervenkrankheit: Eine neurologisch-psychiatrische Studie," *Vierteljahrshefte für Zeitgeschichte* 42 (1994): 155–220.

60. Nicolaus von Below, *Als Hitlers Adjutant 1937–45* (Mainz: v.Hase & Koehler, 1980), 329 (Feb. 6, 1943).

61. Walter Görlitz, ed., *Generalfeldmarschall Keitel: Verbrecher oder Offizier? Erinnerungen, Briefe, Dokumente des Chefs OKW* (Göttingen: Musterschmidt-Verlag, 1961), 318, 321–22; Zeitzler papers, BA-MA N 63/15, 67–69. Such efforts would continue in 1944, and the generals were very critical of Hitler for not accepting the proposed changes. What they failed to explain then or later was how a new command structure would allow them to win the war.

62. Organisationsabteilung Nr. II/12872/43 g.Kdos., 8.10.43, Betr.: Stellung des Chef des Generalstabes des Heeres in der Spitzengliederung der Wehrmacht und Gliederung des Generalstabes des Heeres, in Item OKW/2236, National Archives Microfilm Publication (NAMP) T77, Roll 786, frame 5514286; see also BA-MA RH 2/828: KTB GenStdH/Org.Abt., Bd VII: 1.10.–31.12.43, 11 (8.10.1943). The study is the first official, written acknowledgment we have of the structural problem in the high command.

63. Rudolf Absolon, *Die Wehrmacht im Dritten Reich: Aufbau, Gliederung, Recht, Verwaltung* (Boppard: Harald Boldt, 1969–95), 6:189; Gerhard Buck, "Der Wehrmachtführungsstab im Oberkommando der Wehrmacht," in *Jahresbibliographie 1973,* ed. Bibliothek für Zeitgeschichte (Munich: Bernard & Graefe, 1973), 413. The OKW war diary shows that the Command Staff was also still tracking events in the east, if only very broadly.

64. See Hubatsch, *Weisungen,* 240.

65. See OKW KTB 3:1223.

66. Ibid., 3:826 (July 24, 1943); BA-MA RW 4/10: Stellenbesetzung im WFSt., Stand 25.8.1943.

67. Unterlagen für einen Vortrag des Gen.-Obersten Jodl, des Chefs WFStab, vor den Reichs- und Gauleitern über die militärische Lage (Munich, 7 November 1943), in OKW KTB 4:1534–62. See also Hans-Adolf Jacobsen, *Deutsche Kriegführung 1939–1945: Ein Überblick mit 2 Skizzen u. 1 Spitzengliederung* (Hannover: Hannoversche Druck- und Verlagsgesellschaft, 1961), 55–56.

68. OKW KTB 4:1537.

69. Ibid., 4:1560.

70. Ibid., 4:1562.

71. Heiber, *Lagebesprechungen,* 440–41, 444.

72. Hitler explained his plans on several other occasions as well. See Weinberg, *A World at Arms,* 665. See also Michael Salewski, "Die Abwehr der Invasion als Schlüssel zum 'Endsieg'?" in *Die Wehrmacht: Mythos und Realität,* ed. Rolf-Dieter Müller and Hans-Erich Volkmann (Munich: Oldenbourg, 1999).

73. Bradley and Schulze-Kossens, *Schmundt,* 100 (Oct. 10, 1943), and 101 (Oct. 12, 1943).

74. Ibid., 55 (Mar. 29, 1943).

75. Ibid., 96 (Sept. 12, 1943).

76. Ibid., 111–12 (Nov. 10, 1943), 115 (Nov. 20, 1943). At about this time several field marshals—Rundstedt, Kleist, Rommel, Busch, Manstein, and Weichs—presented Hitler with a declaration of their loyalty, in order to try to counteract the effect of the propaganda that the German officers in Russian captivity were generating. The declaration was Schmundt's idea. See ibid., 129–30, 131, 134.

77. Arne W. Zoepf, *Wehrmacht zwischen Tradition und Ideologie: Der NS-Führungsoffizier im Zweiten Weltkrieg* (Frankfurt am Main: Lang, 1988), 48–52.

78. Zoepf, *NS-Führungsoffizier,* 74–81. See also Jürgen Förster, "Vom Führerheer der Republik zur nationalsozialistischen Volksarmee," in *Deutschland in Europa: Kontinuität und Bruch. Gedenkschrift für Andreas Hillgruber,* ed. Jost Dülffer, Bernd Martin, and Günter Wollstein (Frankfurt am Main: Propyläen, 1990), 322.

79. Absolon, *Wehrmacht,* 6:193; Zoepf, *NS-Führungsoffizier,* 104–5.

80. Taken from Schörner's first decree, quoted in Müller-Hillebrand, *Heer,* 3:160.

81. Zoepf, *NS-Führungsoffizier,* 99. Zoepf's work is unclear concerning the effectiveness and popularity of the program. For the most part he indicates that it was neither, but other sources show that political indoctrination was widespread and influential. See Russell A. Hart, "Learning Lessons: Military Adaptation and Innovation in the American, British, Canadian, and German Armies During the 1944 Normandy Campaign" (Ph.D. diss., Ohio State University, 1997), 344–45.

82. Gehlen and Foreign Armies East made a series of long-range predictions before and during the Soviet offensive, none of which proved correct. See Wilhelm, "Prognosen," 56–59.

83. The change in army group designations took effect at the same time as the change in command. Army Group North Ukraine had been Army Group South; Army Group South Ukraine had been Army Group A.

84. Weinberg, *A World at Arms,* 617; Williamson Murray, *Luftwaffe* (Baltimore, Md.: Nautical and Aviation Publishing Company of America, 1985), 176–82, 214–18.

85. See Der Führer, Oberkommando des Heeres, Gen.St.d.H./Op. Abt.(I) Nr. 2434/44 g.Kdos., 8.3.1944, Führerbefehl Nr. 11 (Kommandanten der festen Plätze und Kampfkommandanten), in Hubatsch, *Weisungen,* 243–50.

86. In early May the bad feelings between Guderian and Zeitzler came to a head when the former made some remarks that the latter deemed critical of the General Staff. Efforts to mediate between the two men failed. Zeitzler complained to Hitler and offered to resign if the Führer had any doubts about the General Staff's loyalty, but Hitler put him off.

87. Heiber, *Lagebesprechungen,* 449.

88. OKW KTB, 4:107-9.

89. Ibid., 4:112-15; see also Ziemke, *Stalingrad to Berlin,* 309-10. The charts that the Armed Forces Command Staff prepared to support Jodl's briefing are in BA-MA RW 4/845: Zustand der Divisionen auf den OKW-Kriegsschauplätzen, Stand: 1.4.-1.7.44. They went direct to the General Staff's Operations and Organization Branches, among others.

90. See Hart, "Learning Lessons," 351. Also Dieter Ose, *Entscheidung im Westen, 1944: Der Oberbefehlshaber West und die Abwehr der alliierten Invasion* (Stuttgart: Deutsche Verlags-Anstalt, 1982). On the intelligence failure, see David Kahn, *Hitler's Spies: German Military Intelligence in World War II* (New York: Macmillan, 1978), 479.

91. Wilhelm, "Prognosen," 60. Even five days after the Soviets opened their attack, Foreign Armies East expected the "main" attack farther south. See also David Glantz, *Soviet Military Deception in the Second World War* (London: Frank Cass, 1989), 348-58, 360-79.

92. Fernschreiben des Gen.-Feldm.s Rommel, des OB der Heeresgr. B, an Hitler über die Lage an der Invasionsfront in der Normandie (15. Juli), in OKW KTB, 4:1572-73.

93. Besprechung des Führers mit Gen.-Lt. Westphal (ab 9. September Chef des Gen.-Stabs des OB West) und Gen.-Lt. Krebs (ab 5. September Chef des Gen.-Stabs der Heeresgruppe B) in der "Wolfsschanze" (Ostpreussen), in OKW KTB, 4:1633-35; the quote is on 1634.

11. COLLAPSE

1. Quoted in Alan Bullock, *Hitler and Stalin: Parallel Lives* (New York: Vintage Books, 1993), 837; pages 833-41 of this work contain an overview of the bomb plot. For a full examination of the resistance movement and the July 20 coup attempt, see Peter Hoffmann, *The History of the German Resistance, 1933-1945,* trans. Richard Barry (Cambridge, Mass.: MIT Press, 1977). This work also examines the trial process, but it does not provide information on the effect within the high command.

2. Dermot Bradley and Richard Schulze-Kossens, eds., *Tätigkeitsbericht des Chefs des Heerespersonalamtes General der Infanterie Rudolf Schmundt, 1.10.1942-29.10.1944* (Osnabrück: Biblio, 1984), 160 (July 18, 1944); also Burkhart Müller-Hillebrand, *Das Heer, 1933-1945: Entwicklung des organisatorischen Aufbaues* (Darmstadt: E. S. Mittler, 1954-69), 3:192. On Zeitzler's resignation attempt, see Earl F. Ziemke, *Stalingrad to Berlin: The German Defeat in the East* (Washington, D.C.: U.S. Army Center of Military History, 1987), 329.

3. Rudolf Absolon, *Die Wehrmacht im Dritten Reich. Aufbau, Gliederung, Recht, Verwaltung* (Boppard: Harald Boldt, 1969-95), 6:196.

4. See Ziemke, *Stalingrad to Berlin,* 335. The temporary nature of Guderian's position shows up in the fact that Hitler did not name him chief of the General Staff but only tasked him to manage the affairs of that office; see Bradley and Schulze-Kossens, *Schmundt,* 169 (July 20, 1944); and Absolon, *Wehrmacht,* 6:196. The fact that Hitler denied Guderian the title itself also demonstrates the importance of titles within the German command hierarchy.

5. Heinz Guderian, *Erinnerungen eines Soldaten* (Heidelberg: Kurt Vowinckel, 1951), 307.

6. For an examination of Guderian's role and that of the other military leaders in this last phase of the war, see Heinrich Schwendemann, "Strategie der Selbstvernichtung: Die Wehrmachtführung im 'Endkampf' um das 'Dritte Reich,'" in *Die Wehrmacht: Mythos und Realität,* im Auftrag des Militärgeschichtlichen Forschungsamtes, ed. Rolf-Dieter Müller and Hans-Erich Volkmann (Munich: Oldenbourg, 1999), 224–44.

7. Bradley and Schulze-Kossens, *Schmundt,* 186–87 (Aug. 2, 1944). The "court of honor" passed judgment on each suspect "without a hearing, without formal evidence, without a finding, merely on the basis of the *Gestapo*'s report on the results of their investigations": Hoffmann, *Resistance,* 525.

8. Guderian, *Erinnerungen,* 315.

9. Telex dated Aug. 24, 1944, "An alle Generalstabsoffiziere des Heeres," in BA-MA RH 19 II/203, 128–29. The officers who heard this order in person in the Headquarters OKH had to lay their weapons aside beforehand; see Müller-Hillebrand, *Heer,* 3:192.

10. Dienstanweisung für den NS-Führungsoffizier beim Chef des Generalstabes des Heeres, 23.8.1944, in BA-MA RH 19 II/203, 141–42.

11. See Hoffmann, *Resistance,* 524–34. Arrest did not always mean conviction; the Gestapo released Kielmansegg, among others, for lack of evidence.

12. Ferdinand Prinz von der Leyen, *Rückblick zum Mauerwald: Vier Kriegsjahre im OKH* (Munich: Biederstein, 1965), 156.

13. See Siegfried Westphal, *Erinnerungen* (Mainz: v.Hase & Koehler, 1975), 265.

14. BA-MA RL 2 I/21: General der Fl. Kreipe, Chef des Generalstabes, 1.8.–28.10.44 (Persönliches Tagebuch, Fotokopie mit Anlagen), 5.

15. Müller-Hillebrand, *Heer,* 3:192. See also BA-MA RH 7/30, which contains lists of the officers who were executed, committed suicide, or were placed under arrest after July 20.

16. The reorganization became effective on September 1, 1944. Burkhart Müller-Hillebrand, "Schematische Darstellung der obersten Führung des deutschen Heeres 1938 bis Kriegsende mit Erläuterungen über organisatorische Beziehungen, Aufgaben und Verantwortlichkeiten der einzelnen Dienststellen des OKH im Laufe der Jahre 1938–1945" (MS #P-041a, unpublished), Übersichtsblatt III/2. Guderian claims (*Erinnerungen,* 310) that the reorganization was his idea (the quote is his), while Kielmansegg maintains that it was Heusinger's, and that Wenck implemented it; interview by the author, April 29, 1996.

17. Kielmansegg interview, April 29, 1996; see also Bradley and Schulze-Kossens, *Schmundt,* 189 (Aug. 4, 1944).

18. Helmut Heiber, ed., *Hitlers Lagebesprechungen: Die Protokollfragmente seiner militärischen Konferenzen 1942–1945* (Stuttgart: Deutsche Verlags-Anstalt, 1962), 584–609.

19. See Heiber, *Lagebesprechungen,* 593 n 1.

20. Kluge took over from Rundstedt on July 6. The latter's removal may have had something to do with an incident on July 1, after a German attack against the British position at Caen had failed. When Rundstedt reported the defeat to Keitel, the latter asked helplessly, "What shall we do? What shall we do?" Rundstedt replied, "Make peace, you fools. What else can you do?" Richard Brett-Smith, *Hitler's Generals*

(London: Osprey, 1976), 35. This was the third of four times that Hitler would relieve Rundstedt.

21. Heiber, *Lagebesprechungen,* 620.

22. Except as noted, the following overview of the planning process for the 1944 Ardennes offensive comes from Hermann Jung, *Die Ardennenoffensive 1944/45: Ein Beispiel für die Kriegführung Hitlers* (Göttingen: Musterschmidt, 1971), 101-41.

23. Guderian, *Erinnerungen,* 334.

24. On this meeting, which took place on September 16, see also the Kreipe war diary (BA-MA RL 2 I/21), 21. Rundstedt took over as commander in chief west again on September 5 from Model, who had succeeded Kluge on August 18.

25. The lack of fuel was already so serious that Hitler had issued an order on August 25, stating that anyone who "negligently or deliberately uses fuel for any purpose that is not decisive for the war will be treated as a saboteur"; see BA-MA RW 4/458, 2.

26. Model commanded Army Group B, which would execute the attack. Siegfried Westphal, then Rundstedt's chief of staff, describes the meeting in his memoir, although he gives the date as October 24; Westphal, *Erinnerungen,* 290-94.

27. Heiber, *Lagebesprechungen,* 721.

28. Stabsbefehl Nr.20, 24.12.44, BA-MA RW 4/458, 62.

29. Guderian concluded by asking that the Hungarians curtail civilian evacuations on the railroads so that German military shipments could get through. OKH/GenStdH/Op Abt (I/S) Nr. 13739/44 g.Kdos., 31.12.44, in BA-MA RH 2/317, 204.

30. Bullock, *Hitler and Stalin,* 858.

31. Captain Gerhard Boldt, quoted in ibid., 874.

32. Ulrich de Maizière, *In der Pflicht: Lebensbericht eines deutschen Soldaten im 20. Jahrhundert* (Herford: E. S. Mittler & Sohn, 1989), 104-5. An examination of the last surviving briefing transcript, that for March 23, seems to corroborate de Maizière's impression. See Heiber, *Lagebesprechungen,* 922-46.

33. See Bullock, *Hitler and Stalin,* 880.

34. See the order of March 19, "Zerstörungsmassnamen im Reichsgebiet," in Walther Hubatsch, *Hitlers Weisungen für die Kriegführung 1939-1945: Dokumente des Oberkommandos der Wehrmacht* (Frankfurt am Main: Bernard & Graefe, 1962), 303.

35. Heiber, *Lagebesprechungen,* 587.

36. Ibid., 588.

37. Twenty-three people joined him for the midday briefing on January 27, for example; ibid., 820.

38. Der Führer/Chef OKW/Heeresstab (I) Nr. 1835/44, 15.7.1944, quoted in Jung, *Ardennenoffensive,* 11.

39. On the transfer of power to the SS, see Absolon, *Wehrmacht,* 6:200; Müller-Hillebrand, *Heer,* 3:166-67; Albert Seaton, *The German Army, 1933-45* (London: Weidenfeld & Nicolson, 1982), 233. Schmundt was seriously wounded in the bomb blast; he died on October 1. His replacement was Major General Wilhelm Burgdorf, who, if anything, outshone his late superior in devotion to the Nazi cause.

40. Absolon, *Wehrmacht,* 6:592; Jung, *Ardennenoffensive,* 13.

41. Jung, *Ardennenoffensive,* 12. Himmler even tried to create an SS air force in the autumn of 1944, but he failed in the face of opposition from Göring.

42. OKW/WFSt/Op.(H)/Qu Nr. 00 11325/44 g.K., 19.9.44, in BA-MA RL 2 II/10.

43. Absolon, *Wehrmacht,* 6:225.

44. Jung, *Ardennenoffensive*, 12.

45. Telex: Chef des Generalstabes des Heeres Nr. 4177/44 g.Kdos., 23.11.44, in BA-MA RL 2 II/10: Kriegführung alle Fronten/Verteidigung Reich (Wehrmacht) (Befehle WFSt., Genst. d.H.), 1944–45.

46. Der Führer, Hauptquartier, den 25.11.44, in Hubatsch, *Weisungen*, 298–99.

47. Jung, *Ardennenoffensive*, 14.

48. BA-MA RW 4/571: Führerbefehl betr. volle und unverzügliche Berichterstattung, 19.1.45. The order is also in Hubatsch, *Weisungen*, 300.

49. See Schwendemann, "Strategie der Selbstvernichtung," 234–35.

50. Bradley and Schulze-Kossens, *Schmundt*, 174.

51. Arne W. Zoepf, *Wehrmacht zwischen Tradition und Ideologie: Der NS-Führungsoffizier im Zweiten Weltkrieg* (Frankfurt am Main: Lang, 1988), 254.

52. Ibid., 256; Absolon, *Wehrmacht*, 6:512–13. The law became effective on October 1.

53. Quoted in Schwendemann, "Strategie der Selbstvernichtung," 228.

54. OKW/WFSt/Op (H) Südost Nr. 0014139/44 g.Kdos., 1.12.44, in BA-MA RH 2/317, 10.

55. Befehl des Chefs OKW betr. Vorbereitungen für die Verteidigung des Reichs, 19.7.44, in Hubatsch, *Weisungen*, 260–64.

56. Vorbereitungen für die Verteidigung des Reiches, 24.7.44, in ibid., 255–60.

57. OKH/GenStdH/Op Abt/Abt Lds Bef Nr. 60/45 g.Kdos., 10.1.45, in BA-MA RL 2 II/10.

58. OKH/GenStdH/Op Abt/Abt Lds Bef (röm 1) Nr. 1 139/45 g.Kdos, 27.1.45, in BA-MA RL 2 II/10.

59. Guderian, *Erinnerungen*, 346–50; also Jodl's diary, in BA-MA RW 4/33, 72: "Guderian calls at 19:20 and asks urgently that everything be thrown to the east."

60. Guderian, *Erinnerungen*, 347.

61. Ibid., 348–49.

62. Heiber, *Lagebesprechungen*, 752–53 (Dec. 28, 1944).

63. Guderian, *Erinnerungen*, 374–75. Maizière witnessed this argument; see *In der Pflicht*, 103–04.

64. Quoted in Schwendemann, "Strategie der Selbstvernichtung," 225.

65. Guderian, *Erinnerungen*, 389.

66. Ziemke, *Stalingrad to Berlin*, 465.

67. See Guderian, *Erinnerungen*, 359–60.

68. Fritz Frhr. von Siegler, *Die höheren Dienststellen der deutschen Wehrmacht 1933–1945* (Munich: Institut für Zeitgeschichte, 1953), 12. Siegler shows Ulrich de Maizière as the chief of the Operations Branch after April 10, 1945, but de Maizière maintains that he never assumed that post officially; interview by the author, May 25, 1996.

69. See Maizière, *In der Pflicht*, 100–102; interview of May 25, 1996. Both Maizière and Kielmansegg went on to hold senior positions in the Bundeswehr, the postwar German defense forces.

70. Leyen, *Rückblick zum Mauerwald*, 177.

71. Maizière, *In der Pflicht*, 102–3.

72. See BA-MA RH 2/318–25: Operations Abteilung KTB and annexes for 1945.

73. Maizière, *In der Pflicht*, 81.

74. Der Chef des Generalstabes des Heeres Az. NSFO No. 750/44 geh., dtd 30.12.44,

Betr.: NS-Führung und politisch-weltanschauliche Schulung im H.Qu.OKH, in BA-MA RH 2/1985, 3.

75. Quoted in Jung, *Ardennenoffensive,* 21.

76. See Bullock, *Hitler and Stalin,* 883-84.

77. Oberkommando der Wehrmacht WFSt/Op./Qu 2 Nr. 02147/45 g., 11.4.45, in BA-MA RM 7/850, 54.

78. Der Führer OKW/WFSt/OpNr.88813/45 Gkdos Chefs., 15.4.45, in BA-MA RM 7/850, 124. The order is also in Hubatsch, *Weisungen,* 308-10.

79. Gerhard Buck, "Der Wehrmachtführungsstab im Oberkommando der Wehrmacht," in *Jahresbibliographie 1973,* Bibliothek für Zeitgeschichte (Munich: Bernard & Graefe, 1973), 414; Absolon, *Wehrmacht,* 6:188. See also the war diaries of the two staffs, in Percy Ernst Schramm, ed., *Kriegstagebuch des Oberkommandos der Wehrmacht (Wehrmachtführungsstab)* (Manfred Pawlak, 1982) (hereafter: OKW KTB), 4:1436-507.

80. Winter had replaced Warlimont in that position on November 8, 1944, after the latter began suffering delayed effects of the July 20 bomb blast.

81. Der Führer Nr. 88 875/45 g.Kdos.Chefs., 24.4.45, in BA-MA RW 44 I/33, 168.

82. Hitler confirmed the new structure on April 26; see OKW/WFSt/Op/Qu Nr. 003857/45 g.Kdos., 26.4.45, in BA-MA RW 4 I/33, 155.

83. See WFSt/Org. Nr.88777/45 g.K.Chefs., F.H.Qu., den 7.April 1945, in BA-MA RW 4/490.

84. On the battle, see Tony Le Tissier, *The Battle of Berlin, 1945* (London: Jonathan Cape, 1988).

85. Walter Görlitz, ed., *Generalfeldmarschall Keitel: Verbrecher oder Offizier? Erinnerungen, Briefe, Dokumente des Chefs OKW* (Göttingen: Musterschmidt-Verlag, 1961), 354-56.

86. The story of Hitler's last days is fascinating reading, if of little value for this study. See H. R. Trevor-Roper, *The Last Days of Hitler* (New York: Macmillan, 1947); Ada Petrova and Peter Watson, *The Death of Hitler: The Full Story with New Evidence from Secret Russian Archives* (New York: W. W. Norton, 1995); and Bullock, *Hitler and Stalin,* 881-87.

87. Gerhard Weinberg, *A World at Arms: A Global History of World War II* (New York: Cambridge University Press, 1994), 826.

88. See the orders from Jodl, OKW/WFSt/Op. Nr.003005/45 g.Kdos., 4.5.45, in BA-MA RW 4 I/33, 37.

89. See OKW/WFSt/Org Abt (H) Nr. 5808/45 g.K., 1.5.45, in BA-MA RW 44 I/58. This provides details on the formation of the "Command Group (Army)" from elements of the Army General Staff and the Armed Forces Command Staff.

90. See Buck, "Wehrmachtführungsstab," 414.

91. See OKW Chefgruppe/Org Abt (H) Nr. 5813/45, 10.5.45: *Befehl zur Neugliederung des Oberkommandos der Wehrmacht,* in BA-MA RW 44 I/59.

Bibliography

UNPUBLISHED PRIMARY SOURCES

Interviews

Kielmansegg, Johann Adolf Graf von. Interviews by Geoffrey P. Megargee, April 29 and June 14, 1996, Bad Krozingen, Germany.
de Maizière, Ulrich. Interview by Geoffrey P. Megargee, May 25, 1996, Bonn, Germany.

Personal Papers in the Bundesarchiv-Militärarchiv Freiburg

N 252   Blumentritt, Günter
N 118   Engel, Gerhard
N 220   Halder, Franz
N 24   Hossbach, Friedrich
N 54   Keitel, Wilhelm
N 626   Kielmansegg, Johann Adolf Graf v.
N 219   Lossberg, Bernhard v.
N 510   Wagner, Eduard
N 654   Winter, August
N 63   Zeitzler, Kurt

(For reasons of space, the list of records from the Bundesarchiv-Militärarchiv Freiburg has been deleted. The full list may be found in Geoffrey P. Megargee, "Triumph of the Null: The War Within the German High Command, 1933–1945," Ph.D. diss., Ohio State University, 1998.)

UNPUBLISHED STUDIES IN THE NATIONAL ARCHIVES, WASHINGTON, D.C.

Blumentritt, Günther. "Der 'Oberquartiermeister I' im O.K.H. Generalstab des Heeres." MS #P-041d, chap. 2.

Greiffenberg, Hans von. "Die Operationsabteilung des O.K.H. (Generalstab des Heeres)" MS #P-041e.

Guderian, Heinz. "Stellungnahme zu der Ausarbeitung: 'Die Oberste Führung des deutschen Heeres (OKH) im Rahmen der Wehrmachtführung.'" MS #P-041jj.

Gyldenfeldt, Heinz von. "Die oberste Führung des deutschen Heeres (OKH) im Rahmen der Wehrmachtführung. a) Ob.d.H. mit Adjutantur." MS #P-041c.

Halder, Franz. "Der Chef des Generalstabes des Heeres." MS #P-041d, chapter 1.

―――. "Die Leitung des Generalstabes des Heeres." MS #P-041d, chapter 7.

Heusinger, Adolf. Interview by U.S. Army Intelligence, February 1, 1946.

Müller-Hillebrand, Burkhart. "Die organisatorischen Aufgaben der obersten Heeresführung von 1938 bis 45 und ihre Lösung." MS #P-041f.

―――. "Schematische Darstellung der obersten Führung des deutschen Heeres 1938 bis Kriegsende mit Erläuterungen über organisatorische Beziehungen, Aufgaben und Verantwortlichkeiten der einzelnen Dienststellen des OKH im Laufe der Jahre 1938-1945." MS #P-041a.

PUBLISHED PRIMARY SOURCES

Balck, Hermann. *Ordnung im Chaos: Erinnerungen 1893-1948.* Soldatenschicksale des 20. Jahrhunderts als Geschichtsquelle, Bd. 1. Osnabrück: Biblio, 1981.

Beck, Ludwig. *Studien.* Edited and with an introduction by Hans Speidel. Stuttgart: K. F. Koehler, 1955.

Below, Nicolaus von. *Als Hitlers Adjutant 1937-45.* Mainz: v.Hase & Koehler, 1980.

Bradley, Dermot, and Richard Schulze-Kossens, eds. *Tätigkeitsbericht des Chefs des Heerespersonalamtes General der Infanterie Rudolf Schmundt, 1.10.1942-29.10.1944.* Osnabrück: Biblio, 1984.

Clausewitz, Carl von. *On War.* Indexed edition. Edited and translated by Michael Howard and Peter Paret. Princeton, N.J.: Princeton University Press, 1984.

Detwiler, Donald, ed. Charles B. Burdick and Jürgen Rohwer, assoc. eds. *World War II German Military Studies: A Collection of 213 Special Reports on the Second World War Prepared by Former Officers of the Wehrmacht for the United States Army.* New York: Garland, 1979.

Domarus, Max. *Hitler: Reden und Proklamationen 1932-1945.* 2 vols. Würzburg: Schmidt, Neustadt a.d. Aisch, 1962-63.

Dreetz, Dieter. "Denkschrift der deutschen Obersten Heeresleitung vom 17. September 1919 über die Reichswehr und deren Rolle bei der Schaffung einer imperialistischen deutschen Grossmacht." *Militärgeschichte* 21 (1982): 595-608.

Engel, Gerhard. *Heeresadjutant bei Hitler, 1938-1943: Aufzeichnungen des Majors Engel.* Edited by Hildegard von Kotze. Stuttgart: Deutsche Verlags-Anstalt, 1974.

Faber du Faur, Moriz von. *Macht und Ohnmacht: Erinnerungen eines alten Offiziers.* Stuttgart: Hans E. Günther, 1953.

Förster, Stig, ed. *Moltke. Vom Kabinettskrieg zum Volkskrieg. Eine Werkeauswahl.* Bonn: Bouvier, 1992.

Gehlen, Reinhard. *Der Dienst. Erinnerungen, 1942–1971.* Mainz-Wiesbaden: v.Hase & Koehler, 1971.

The German Army High Command, 1938–1945. Arlington, Va.: University Publications of America, n.d. Microfilm.

Germany. Auswärtiges Amt. *Akten zur deutschen auswärtigen Politik 1918–1945.* Series D, 1937–1945. Baden-Baden, Imprimerie Nationale, later P. Keppler, 1950–. English translation: *Documents on German Foreign Policy, 1918–1945.* Washington, D. C.: U.S. Government Printing Office, 1957–.

Germany. Heer. Heeresdienstvorschrift 92 (H.Dv. 92). *Handbuch für den Generalstabsdienst im Kriege.* Teil I, II, abgeschlossen am 1.8.1939. Berlin: der Reichsdruckerei, 1939.

———. Heeresdienstvorschrift 291 (H.Dv. 291). *Bestimmungen über Aufstellung und Vorlage der Beurteilungen der Offiziere des Heeres (Beurteilungsbestimmungen) vom 11.5.36.* Revised edition, Berlin: der Reichsdruckerei, 1942.

———. Heeresdienstvorschrift 300/1, I.Teil (H.Dv. 300/1). *Truppenführung.* Berlin: E. S. Mittler & Sohn, 1936.

———. Merkblatt 14/2: *Zusammendruck von grundsätzlichen Verfügungen für die Bearbeitung der Offizierpersonalien vom 1.7.1944.*

Gessler, Otto. *Reichswehrpolitik in der Weimarer Zeit.* Stuttgart: Deutsche Verlags-Anstalt, 1958.

Görlitz, Walter, ed. *Generalfeldmarschall Keitel: Verbrecher oder Offizier? Erinnerungen, Briefe, Dokumente des Chefs OKW.* Göttingen: Musterschmidt-Verlag, 1961. English translation: *The Memoirs of Field Marshal Keitel.* Translated by David Irving. New York: Stein & Day, 1966.

———. *"Ich stehe hier auf Befehl!" Lebensweg des Generalfeldmarschalls Friedrich Paulus. Mit den Aufzeichnungen aus dem Nachlass, Briefen und Dokumenten.* Frankfurt am Main: Bernard & Graefe, 1960. English translation: *Paulus and Stalingrad: A Life of Field-Marshal Friedrich Paulus with Notes, Correspondence and Documents from His Papers.* Translated by Colonel R. H. Stevens. New York: Citadel Press, 1963.

Groener, Wilhelm. *Lebenserinnerungen: Jugend-Generalstab-Weltkrieg.* Edited by Friedrich Frhr. Hiller von Gaertringen. Göttingen: Vandenhoeck & Ruprecht, 1957.

Groscurth, Helmut. *Tagebücher eines Abwehroffiziers 1938–1940.* Edited by Helmut Krausnick and Harold C. Deutsch. Stuttgart: Deutsche Verlags-Anstalt, 1970.

Guderian, Heinz. *Erinnerungen eines Soldaten.* Heidelberg: Kurt Vowinckel, 1951. English translation: *Panzer Leader.* Translated by Constantine Fitzgibbon. New York: Dutton, 1952. Reprint, New York: Da Capo Press, 1996.

Halder, Franz. *Kriegstagebuch: Tägliche Aufzeichnungen des Chefs des Generalstabes des Heeres 1939–1942.* Edited by Arbeitskreis für Wehrforschung, Stuttgart. 3 vols. Stuttgart: Kohlhammer, 1962.

Hassell, Ulrich von. *Die Hassell-Tagebücher 1938–1944. Aufzeichnungen vom Andern Deutschland. Nach der Handschrift revidierte und erweiterte Ausgabe.* Edited by Frhr. Hiller von Gaertringen. Berlin: Siedler, 1988.

Heiber, Helmut, ed. *Hitlers Lagebesprechungen: Die Protokollfragmente seiner militärischen Konferenzen 1942–1945.* Stuttgart: Deutsche Verlags-Anstalt, 1962.

Heusinger, Adolf. *Befehl im Widerstreit: Schicksalsstunden der deutschen Armee 1923–1945.* Tübingen: Rainer Wunderlich, 1950.

Hossbach, Friedrich. *Zwischen Wehrmacht und Hitler 1934–1938.* Wolfenbüttel: Wolfenbütteler Verlagsanstalt, 1949.

Hubatsch, Walther. *Hitlers Weisungen für die Kriegführung 1939–1945: Dokumente des Oberkommandos der Wehrmacht.* Frankfurt am Main: Bernard & Graefe, 1962.

International Military Tribunal. *Trial of the Major War Criminals Before the International Military Tribunal, Nuremberg, 14 November 1945–1 October 1946.* 42 vols. Nuremberg: International Military Tribunal, 1947.

Jochmann, Werner, ed. *Adolf Hitler. Monologe im Führerhauptquartier 1941–1944. Die Aufzeichnungen Heinrich Heims.* Munich: A. Knaus, 1982.

Kielmansegg, Johann Adolf Graf von. "Bemerkungen eines Zeitzeugen zu den Schlachten von Char'kov und Kursk aus der Sicht des damaligen Generalstabsoffiziers Ia in der Operationsabteilung des Generalstabs des Heeres." In *Gezeitenwechsel im Zweiten Weltkrieg? Die Schlachten von Char'kov und Kursk im Frühjahr und Sommer 1943 in operativer Anlage, Verlauf und politischer Bedeutung,* edited by Roland Foerster, 137–48. Hamburg: Verlag E. S. Mittler & Sohn, 1996.

Koller, K. *Der letzte Monat. Tagebuchaufzeichnungen des ehemaligen Chefs des Generalstabes der deutschen Luftwaffe vom 14. April bis zum 27. Mai 1945.* Mannheim: Wohlgemuth, 1949.

Leeb, Wilhelm Ritter von. *Generalfeldmarschall Wilhelm Ritter von Leeb. Tagebuchaufzeichnungen u. Lagebeurteilungen aus zwei Weltkriegen.* Edited by Georg Meyer. Stuttgart: Deutsche Verlags-Anstalt, 1976.

Leyen, Ferdinand Prinz von der. *Rückblick zum Mauerwald: Vier Kriegsjahre im OKH.* Munich: Biederstein, 1965.

Lochner, Louis P., ed. *The Goebbels Diaries.* New York: Eagle Books, 1948.

Lossberg, Bernhard von. *Im Wehrmachtführungsstab: Bericht eines Generalstabsoffiziers.* Hamburg: Nölke, 1950.

Maizière, Ulrich de. *In der Pflicht. Lebensbericht eines deutschen Soldaten im 20. Jahrhundert.* Herford: E. S. Mittler & Sohn, 1989.

Manstein, Erich von. *Aus einem Soldatenleben 1887–1939.* Bonn: Athenäum, 1958.

———. *Verlorene Siege.* Bonn: Athenäum, 1955. English translation: *Lost Victories.* Edited and translated by Anthony G. Powell. Novato, Calif.: Presidio Press, 1982.

Meier-Welcker, Hans. *Aufzeichnungen eines Generalstabsoffiziers 1939–1942.* Hrsg. v. Militärgeschichtliches Forschungsamt. Einzelschriften zur militärischen Geschichte des Zweiten Weltkrieges, Bd. 26. Freiburg im Breisgau: Rombach, 1982.

National Archives and Records Administration. National Archives Collection of Captured German War Records Microfilmed at Alexandria, Va. Microfilm Publications T-77 (Records of Headquarters, German Armed Forces High Command) and T-78 (Records of Headquarters, German Army High Command).

Nuernberg Military Tribunals. *Trials of War Criminals Before the Nuernberg Military Tribunals Under Control Council Law No. 10, Nuernberg, October 1946–April 1949.* 15 vols. Washington, D.C.: U.S. Government Printing Office, 1949–53.

Office of the United States Chief of Council for Prosecution of Axis Criminality. *Nazi Conspiracy and Aggression.* Washington, D.C.: U.S. Government Printing Office, 1946.

Schramm, Percy Ernst, ed. *Kriegstagebuch des Oberkommandos der Wehrmacht (Wehrmachtführungsstab)*. 4 vols. Munich: Pawlak, 1982.

Thies, Klaus-Jürgen, ed. *Der Zweite Weltkrieg im Kartenbild*. 4 vols. to date. Osnabrück: Biblio Verlag, 1989–.

Vogelsang, Thilo. "Neue Dokumente zur Geschichte der Reichswehr 1930–1933." *Vierteljahrshefte für Zeitgeschichte* 2 (1954): 397–436.

Wagner, Elizabeth, ed. *Der Generalquartiermeister: Briefe und Tagebuchaufzeichnungen des Generalquartiermeisters des Heeres, General der Artillerie Eduard Wagner*. Munich: Günter Olzog, 1963.

Wagner, Gerhard, ed. *Lagevorträge des Oberbefehlshabers der Kriegsmarine vor Hitler 1939–1945*. Munich: J. F. Lehmanns, 1972.

Warlimont, Walter. *Im Hauptquartier der deutschen Wehrmacht 1939–1945: Grundlagen, Formen, Gestalten*. Frankfurt am Main: Bernard & Graefe, 1962. English translation: *Inside Hitler's Headquarters 1939–45*. Translated by R. H. Barry. New York: Praeger, 1964.

Westphal, Siegfried. *Erinnerungen*. Mainz: v.Hase & Koehler, 1975.

SECONDARY WORKS

Absolon, Rudolf. "Das Offizierkorps des deutschen Heeres 1935–1945." In *Das Deutsche Offizierkorps 1860–1960*, edited by Hans Hubert Hofmann, 247–68. Boppard: Harald Boldt, 1980.

———. *Die Wehrmacht im Dritten Reich: Aufbau, Gliederung, Recht, Verwaltung*. Bd. I–VI. Boppard: Harald Boldt, 1969–95.

Bald, Detlef. *Der deutsche Generalstab 1859–1939: Reform und Restauration in Ausbildung und Bildung*. Munich: Sozialwissenschaftliches Institut der Bundeswehr, 1977.

Barnett, Correlli, ed. *Hitler's Generals*. New York: Grove Weidenfeld, 1989.

Beesten, Bernfried von. *Untersuchungen zum System der militärischen Planung im Dritten Reich von 1933 bis zum Kriegsbeginn: Vorstellungen, Voraussetzungen, Beweggründe und Faktoren*. Münster: Lit-Verlag, 1987.

Bethell, Nicholas. *The War Hitler Won: September 1939*. London: Allen Lane The Penguin Press, 1972.

Beyerchen, Alan. "Clausewitz, Nonlinearity, and the Unpredictability of War." *International Security* 17, no. 3 (1992–93), 59–90.

Boog, Horst. *Die deutsche Luftwaffenführung 1935–1945: Führungsprobleme— Spitzengliederung—Generalstabsausbildung*. Stuttgart: Deutsche Verlags-Anstalt, 1982.

Bor, Peter. *Gespräche mit Halder*. Wiesbaden: Limes, 1950.

Borgert, Heinz-Ludger. "Grundzüge der Landkriegführung von Schlieffen bis Guderian." In *Handbuch zur deutschen Militärgeschichte: 1648–1939*, edited by Militärgeschichtliches Forschungsamt, vol. 9, 427–585. Munich: Bernard & Graefe, 1979.

Bradley, Dermot, Karl-Friedrich Hildebrand, and Markus Rövekamp. *Die Generale des Heeres 1921–1945*. 4 vols. to date. Osnabrück: Biblio, 1993–.

Brett-Smith, Richard. *Hitler's Generals*. London: Osprey, 1976.

Bucholz, Arden. *Hans Delbrück and the German Military Establishment: War Images in Conflict.* Iowa City: University of Iowa Press, 1985.

———. *Moltke, Schlieffen and Prussian War Planning.* New York: Berg, 1991.

Buck, Gerhard. "Der Wehrmachtführungsstab im Oberkommando der Wehrmacht." In *Jahresbibliographie 1973*, Bibliothek für Zeitgeschichte, 407–54. Munich: Bernard & Graefe, 1973.

———. *Das Führerhauptquartier 1939–1945: Zeitgeschichte im Bild.* Leoni a. Starnberger See: Druffel, 1977?

Bullock, Alan. *Hitler: A Study in Tyranny.* New York: Harper & Row, 1962.

———. *Hitler and Stalin: Parallel Lives.* New York: Vintage Books, 1993.

Burdick, Charles B. "German Military Planning for the War in the West, 1935–1940." Ph.D. diss., Stanford University, 1955.

———. *Germany's Military Strategy and Spain in World War II.* Syracuse, N.Y.: Syracuse University Press, 1968.

———. *Unternehmen Sonnenblume: Der Entschluss zum Afrika-Feldzug.* Neckargemünd: Kurt Kowinckel, 1972.

Burk, Kurt. "Planungen und Massnahmen der Reichswehr zur Sicherung der deutschen Ostgrenzen." *Militärgeschichtliche Mitteilungen* 48, no. 2 (1990): 41–64.

Carroll, Berenice A. *Design for Total War: Arms and Economics in the Third Reich.* The Hague, Paris: Mouton, 1968.

Caspar, Gustav-Adolf, and Herbert Schottelius. "Die Organisation des Heeres 1933–1939." In *Handbuch zur deutschen Militärgeschichte 1648–1939*, edited by Militärgeschichtliches Forschungsamt, vol. 7, 299–399. Munich: Bernard & Graefe, 1978.

Cecil, Robert. *Hitler's Decision to Invade Russia.* London: Davis-Poynter, 1975.

Clark, Alan. *Barbarossa: The Russian-German Conflict, 1941–45.* New York: William Morrow, 1965.

Cooper, Matthew. *The German Army 1933–1945: Its Political and Military Failure.* Chelsea, Mich.: Scarborough House, 1990.

Corum, James S. *The Luftwaffe: Creating the Operational Air War, 1918–1940.* Lawrence: University Press of Kansas, 1997.

———. *The Roots of Blitzkrieg: Hans von Seeckt and German Military Reform.* Lawrence: University Press of Kansas, 1992.

Craig, Gordon. *The Politics of the Prussian Army, 1640–1945.* New York: Oxford University Press, 1956.

Creveld, Martin van. *Hitler's Strategy, 1940–1941: The Balkan Clue.* London: Cambridge University Press, 1973.

———. *Supplying War: Logistics from Wallenstein to Patton.* Cambridge: Cambridge University Press, 1977, 1980.

Deist, Wilhelm. *Militär, Staat und Gesellschaft. Studien zur preussisch-deutschen Militärgeschichte.* Munich: Oldenbourg, 1991.

———. "The Road to Ideological War: Germany, 1918–1945." In *The Making of Strategy. Rulers, States and War*, edited by Williamson Murray, MacGregor Knox, and Alvin Bernstein, 352–92. New York: Cambridge University Press, 1994.

———. *The Wehrmacht and German Rearmament.* London: Macmillan, 1981.

———. "Zur Geschichte des preussischen Offizierkorps 1888–1918." In *Das Deutsche*

Offizierkorps 1860-1960, edited by Hans Hubert Hofmann, 39-57. Boppard: Harald Boldt, 1980.

Demeter, Karl. *Das deutsche Offizierkorps in Gesellschaft und Staat 1650-1945.* Frankfurt am Main: Bernard & Graefe, 1962. English translation: *The German Officer-Corps in Society and State, 1650-1945.* 2d ed. Translated by Angus Malcolm. New York: Praeger, 1965.

Deutsch, Harold. *Hitler and His Generals: The Hidden Crisis, January-June 1938.* Minneapolis: University of Minnesota Press, 1974.

———. "Military Planning and National Policy: German Overtures to Two World Wars." The Harmon Memorial Lectures in Military History, No. 27. U.S. Air Force Academy, 1984.

Doughty, Robert Allan. *The Breaking Point: Sedan and the Fall of France, 1940.* Hamden, Conn.: Archon Books, 1990.

———. *The Seeds of Disaster: The Development of French Army Doctrine, 1919-1939.* Hamden, Conn.: Archon Books, 1985.

Dülffer, Jost. "Überlegungen von Kriegsmarine und Heer zur Wehrmacht-spitzengliederung und zur Führung der Wehrmacht im Krieg im Februar-März 1938." In *Militärgeschichtliche Mitteilungen* 9 (1971), 145-71.

Dupuy, Trevor N. *A Genius for War: The German Army and General Staff, 1807-1945.* Englewood Cliffs, N.J.: Prentice-Hall, 1977.

Elble, Rolf. *Führungsdenken, Stabsarbeit. Entwicklung und Ausblick—ein Versuch.* Darmstadt: Wehr und Wissen Verlagsgesellschaft, 1967.

Erfurth, Waldemar. *Die Geschichte des deutschen Generalstabes von 1918 bis 1945.* 2d ed. Göttingen: Musterschmidt, 1960.

Erickson, John. *The Road to Berlin: Stalin's War with Germany,* vol. 2. London: Weidenfeld & Nicolson, 1983.

———. *The Road to Stalingrad: Stalin's War with Germany.* vol. 1. London: Weidenfeld and Nicolson, 1975.

———. *The Soviet High Command: A Military-Political History, 1918-1941.* London: Macmillan, 1962.

Fest, Joachim. *The Face of the Third Reich: Portraits of the Nazi Leadership.* New York: Pantheon, 1970.

Fischer, Fritz. *Germany's Aims in the First World War.* New York: W. W. Norton, 1967.

Foerster, Wolfgang. *Generaloberst Ludwig Beck. Sein Kampf gegen den Krieg. Aus nachgelassenen Papieren des Generalstabschefs.* Munich: Isar, 1953.

Förster, Gerhard, Heinz Helmert, Helmut Otto, and Helmut Schnitter. *Der preussisch-deutsche Generalstab, 1640-1965: Zu seiner politischen Rolle in der Geschichte.* Berlin: Dietz, 1966.

Förster, Jürgen. "The Dynamics of *Volksgemeinschaft:* The Effectiveness of the German Military Establishment in the Second World War." In *Military Effectiveness,* edited by Allan R. Millett and Williamson Murray. Vol. 3, *The Second World War,* 180-220. Boston: Unwin Hyman, 1988, 1990.

———. "Strategische Überlegungen des Wehrmachtführungsstabes für das Jahr 1943." In *Militärgeschichtliche Mitteilungen* 13/1(1973): 95-107.

———. "Vom Führerheer der Republik zur nationalsozialistischen Volksarmee." In *Deutschland in Europa. Kontinuität und Bruch. Gedenkschrift für Andreas Hill-*

gruber, edited by Jost Dülffer, Bernd Martin, and Günter Wollstein, 311–28. Frankfurt am Main: Propyläen, 1990.

Förster, Stig. "Der deutsche Generalstab und die Illusion des kurzen Krieges, 1871–1914: Metakritik eines Mythos." *Militärgeschichtliche Mitteilungen* 54 (1995): 61–93.

Fraser, David. *Knight's Cross: A Life of Field Marshal Erwin Rommel.* New York: HarperCollins, 1993.

The German General Staff Corps. Washington, D.C.: Adjutant General's Office, 1946.

Geyer, Michael. *Aufrüstung oder Sicherheit: Die Reichswehr in der Krise der Machtpolitik 1924–1936.* Wiesbaden: Franz Steiner, 1980.

———. "The Dynamics of Military Revisionism in the Interwar Years: Military Politics Between Rearmament and Diplomacy." In *The German Military in the Age of Total War,* edited by Wilhelm Deist, 100–151. Dover, N.H.: Berg Publishers, 1985.

———. "German Strategy in the Age of Machine Warfare, 1914–1945." In *Makers of Modern Strategy from Machiavelli to the Nuclear Age,* edited by Peter Paret, 527–97. Princeton, N.J.: Princeton University Press, 1986.

———. "National Socialist Germany: The Politics of Information." In *Knowing One's Enemies: Intelligence Assessment Before the Two World Wars,* edited by Ernest R. May, 310–46. Princeton, N.J.: Princeton University Press, 1984.

Gibbels, Ellen. "Hitlers Nervenkrankheit: Eine neurologisch-psychiatrische Studie." *Vierteljahrshefte für Zeitgeschichte* 42 (1994): 155–220.

Glantz, David. *Soviet Military Deception in the Second World War.* London: Frank Cass, 1989.

———. *Soviet Military Intelligence in War.* London: Frank Cass, 1990.

Glantz, David, and Jonathan M. House. *When Titans Clashed: How the Red Army Stopped Hitler.* Lawrence: University Press of Kansas, 1995.

Goda, Norman J. W. "Black Marks: Hitler's Bribery of His Senior Officers." Paper presented at the German Studies Association Annual Meeting 1997. Publication pending.

———. *Tomorrow the World: Hitler, Northwest Africa, and the Path Toward America.* College Station: Texas A&M University Press, 1998.

Görlitz, Walter. *Der deutsche Generalstab: Geschichte und Gestalt 1657–1945.* Frankfurt am Main: Verlag der Frankfurter Hefte, 1950. English translation: *History of the German General Staff, 1657–1945.* Translated by Brian Battershaw. New York: Praeger, 1953.

Graham, Dominick, and Shelford Bidwell. *Tug of War: The Battle for Italy, 1943–1945.* New York: St. Martin's Press, 1986.

Greiner, Helmuth. *Die Oberste Wehrmachtführung 1939–1943.* Wiesbaden: Limes, 1951.

Groehler, Olaf. "Die Güter der Generale: Dotationen im zweiten Weltkrieg." *Zeitschrift für Geschichtswissenschaft* 29 (1971): 655–63.

Hart, Russell A. "Feeding Mars: The Role of Logistics in the German Defeat in Normandy, 1944." *War in History* 3 (1996): 418–35.

———. "Learning Lessons: Military Adaptation and Innovation in the American, British, Canadian, and German Armies During the 1944 Normandy Campaign." Ph.D. diss., Ohio State University, 1997.

Hartmann, Christian. *Halder: Generalstabschef Hitlers 1938–1942.* Paderborn: Schöningh, 1991.

Hartmann, Christian, and Sergij Slutsch. "Franz Halder und die Kriegsvorbereitungen im Frühjahr 1939. Eine Ansprache des Generalstabschefs des Heeres." *Vierteljahrshefte für Zeitgeschichte* 2 (1997): 467–95.

Heider, Paul. "Der totale Krieg—seine Vorbereitung durch Reichswehr und Wehrmacht." In *Der Weg deutscher Eliten in den zweiten Weltkrieg,* edited by Ludwig Nestler, 35–80. Berlin: Akademie, 1990.

Herwig, Holger H. "The Dynamics of Necessity: German Military Policy During the First World War." In *Military Effectiveness,* edited by Allan R. Millett and Williamson Murray. Vol. 1, *The First World War,* 80–115. Boston: Unwin Hyman, 1989.

———. *The First World War: Germany and Austria-Hungary, 1914–1918.* New York: Arnold, 1997.

———. "Strategic Uncertainties of a Nation-State: Prussia-Germany, 1871–1918." In *The Making of Strategy: Rulers, States and War,* edited by Williamson Murray, MacGregor Knox, and Alvin Bernstein, 242–77. New York: Cambridge University Press, 1994.

Hillgruber, Andreas. *Hitlers Strategie: Politik und Kriegsführung 1940–41.* Frankfurt am Main: Bernard & Graefe, 1965.

———. "Das Kriegsjahr 1942, ein militärpolitisch-operativer Überblick aus dem Blickwinkel der deutschen Obersten Führung." In *Kriegstagebuch des Oberkommandos der Wehrmacht (Wehrmachtführungsstab),* vol. 2, edited by Percy Ernst Schramm and Andreas Hillgruber, 3–177. Munich: Manfred Pawlak, 1982.

———. "Noch einmal: Hitlers Wendung gegen die Sowjetunion 1940." *Geschichte in Wissenschaft und Unterricht* 33 (1982): 214–26.

———. "Das Russland-Bild der führenden deutschen Militärs vor Beginn des Angriffs auf die Sowjetunion." In *Russland-Deutschland-Amerika. Russia-Germany-America. Festschrift für Fritz T. Epstein zum 80. Geburtstag,* edited by Alexander Fischer, Günter Moltmann, and Klaus Schwabe, 296–310. Wiesbaden: Franz Steiner, 1978.

Hittle, J. D. *The Military Staff: Its History and Development.* Harrisburg, Pa.: Military Service Publishing Co., 1949.

Hoffmann, Peter. "Generaloberst Ludwig Becks militärpolitisches Denken." *Historische Zeitschrift* 234 (1982): 101–21.

———. *The History of the German Resistance, 1933–1945.* Translated by Richard Barry. Cambridge, Mass.: MIT Press, 1977.

———. *Hitler's Personal Security.* Cambridge, Mass.: MIT Press, 1979.

———. "Ludwig Beck: Loyalty and Resistance." *Central European History* 14 (1981): 332–50.

———. Review of *Das Komplott oder Die Entmachtung der Generale. Blomberg- und Fritsch-Krise. Hitlers Weg zum Krieg,* by Harold C. Deutsch. In *Militärgeschichtliche Mitteilungen* 20 (1976): 196–201.

Holborn, Hajo. "The Prusso-German School: Moltke and the Rise of the German General Staff." In *Makers of Modern Strategy from Machiavelli to the Nuclear Age,* edited by Peter Paret, 281–95. Princeton N.J.: Princeton University Press, 1986.

Hossbach, Friedrich. "Verantwortlichkeit der Generalstabsoffiziere in der deutschen Armee." *Allgemeine Schweizerische Militärzeitschrift* 118 (1952): 220–225.

Howard, Michael. *The Franco-Prussian War: The German Invasion of France, 1870–1871.* New York: Dorset Press, 1961.

———. *Studies in War and Peace.* New York: Viking Press, 1971.

Hubatsch, Walther. *"Weserübung": Die deutsche Besetzung von Dänemark und Norwegen 1940.* Göttingen: Musterschmidt, 1960.

Hürten, Heinz. "Das Offizierkorps des Reichsheeres." In *Das Deutsche Offizierkorps 1860–1960,* edited by Hans Hubert Hofmann, 231–45. Boppard: Harald Boldt, 1980.

Hürter, Johannes. *Wilhelm Groener: Reichswehrminister am Ende der Weimarer Republik (1928–1932).* Munich: Oldenbourg, 1993.

Jacobsen, Hans-Adolf. *Deutsche Kriegsführung 1939–1945: Ein Überblick mit 2 Skizzen u. 1 Spitzengliederung.* Hannover: Hannoversche Druck- und Verlagsgesellschaft, 1961.

———. *Fall Gelb. Der Kampf um den deutschen Operationsplan zur Westoffensive 1940.* Wiesbaden: Franz Steiner, 1957.

Janssen, Karl-Heinz, and Fritz Tobias. *Der Sturz der Generäle: Hitler und die Blomberg-Fritsch-Krise 1938.* Munich: Beck, 1994.

Jodl, Luise. *Jenseits des Endes: Leben und Sterben des Generaloberst Alfred Jodl.* Vienna: Molden, 1976.

Jung, Hermann. *Die Ardennenoffensive 1944/45: Ein Beispiel für die Kriegführung Hitlers.* Göttingen: Musterschmidt, 1971.

Junker, Detlef. "Hitler's Perception of Franklin D. Roosevelt and the United States of America." *Amerikastudien/American Studies* 38 (1993): 25–36.

Kahn, David. *Hitler's Spies: German Military Intelligence in World War II.* New York: Macmillan, 1978.

Kehrig, Manfred. *Stalingrad: Analyse und Dokumentation einer Schlacht.* Stuttgart: Deutsche Verlags-Anstalt, 1974.

Kennedy, Robert M. *The German Campaign in Poland, 1939.* Washington, D.C.: Department of the Army, 1956.

Kessel, Eberhard. *Moltke.* Stuttgart: K. F. Koehler, 1957.

Kiesling, Eugenia C. *Arming Against Hitler: France and the Limits of Military Planning.* Lawrence: University Press of Kansas, 1996.

Kissel, Hans. *Der Deutsche Volkssturm 1944/45: Eine territoriale Miliz im Rahmen der Landesverteidigung.* Frankfurt am Main: E. S. Mittler & Sohn, 1962.

Kitchen, Martin. *The German Officer Corps, 1890–1914.* Oxford: Clarendon Press, 1968.

———. *A Military History of Germany from the Eighteenth Century to the Present Day.* Bloomington: Indiana University Press, 1975.

———. *The Silent Dictatorship: The Politics of the German High Command Under Hindenburg and Ludendorff, 1916–1918.* New York: Croom Helm, 1976.

Klee, Karl. *Das Unternehmen "Seelöwe": Die geplante deutsche Landung in England 1940.* Göttingen: Musterschmidt, 1958.

———. *Dokumenten zum Unternehmen Seelöwe.* Göttingen: Musterschmidt, 1959.

Klink, Ernst. *Das Gesetz des Handelns: Die Operation "Zitadelle" 1943.* Stuttgart: Deutsche Verlags-Anstalt, 1966.

———. "The Organization of the German Military High Command in World War II." *Revue Internationale d'Histoire Militaire* 47 (1980): 129–57.

Knox, MacGregor. *Mussolini Unleashed, 1939–1941: Politics and Strategy in Fascist Italy's Last War.* New York: Cambridge University Press, 1982.

Kroener, Bernhard R. "Auf dem Weg zu einer 'nationalsozialistischen Volksarmee.' Die soziale Öffnung des Heeresoffizierkorps im Zweiten Weltkrieg." In *Von Stalingrad bis Währungsreform. Zur Sozialgeschichte des Umbruchs in Deutschland,* edited by Martin Broszat, 651–82. Munich: Oldenbourg, 1988.

Le Tissier, Tony. *The Battle of Berlin, 1945.* London: Jonathan Cape, 1988.

Liddell Hart, Sir Basil Henry. *The Other Side of the Hill. Germany's Generals: Their Rise and Fall, with Their Own Account of Military Events, 1939–1945.* London: Cassell, 1973.

Lupfer, Timothy T. *The Dynamics of Doctrine: The Changes in German Tactical Doctrine During the First World War.* Leavenworth Papers No. 4. Fort Leavenworth, Kans.: Combat Studies Institute, 1981.

Magenheimer, Heinz. "Das Gesetz des Schwergewichts: Zur strategischen Lage Deutschlands im Frühjahr 1944." *Wehrwissenschaftliche Rundschau* 31 (1981): 18–25.

Megargee, Geoffrey P. "Triumph of the Null: Structure and Conflict in the Command of German Land Forces, 1939–1945." *War in History* 4 (1997): 60–80.

Meier-Welcker, Hans. *Seeckt.* Frankfurt am Main: Bernard & Graefe, 1967.

Meinck, Gerhard. *Hitler und die deutsche Aufrüstung 1933–1937.* Wiesbaden: Franz Steiner, 1959.

Messerschmidt, Manfred. "German Military Effectiveness Between 1919 and 1939." In *Military Effectiveness,* edited by Allan R. Millett and Williamson Murray. Vol. 2, *The Interwar Period,* 218–55. Boston: Unwin Hyman, 1990.

———. "Die politische Geschichte der preussisch-deutschen Armee." Vol. 4 of *Handbuch zur deutschen Militärgeschichte 1648–1939,* edited by Militärgeschichtliches Forschungsamt. Munich: Bernard & Graefe, 1975.

———. *Die Wehrmacht im NS-Staat: Zeit der Indoktrination.* Hamburg: R. v. Decker, 1969.

———. "The Wehrmacht and the Volksgemeinschaft." Translated by Anthony Wells. *Journal of Contemporary History* 18 (1983): 719–44.

Meyer, Bradley J. "Operational Art and the German Command System in World War I." Ph.D. diss., Ohio State University, 1988.

Michalka, Wolfgang, ed. *Der Zweite Weltkrieg: Analysen, Grundzüge, Forschungsbilanz. Im Auftrag des Militärgeschichtlichen Forschungsamtes.* Munich: Piper, 1989.

Militärgeschichtliches Forschungsamt, ed. *Das Deutsche Reich und der Zweite Weltkrieg.* 6 volumes to date. Stuttgart: Deutsche Verlags-Anstalt, 1979–90. English translation: *Germany and the Second World War.* Translated by P. S. Falla, Dean S. McMurry, Ewald Osers, and Louise Willmot. 4 volumes to date. New York: Oxford University Press, 1990–99.

Millett, Allan R., Williamson Murray, and Kenneth H. Watman. "The Effectiveness of Military Organizations." In *Military Effectiveness,* edited by Allan R. Millett and Williamson Murray. Vol. 1, *The First World War,* 1–30. Boston: Unwin Hyman, 1988, 1989.

Model, Hansgeorg. *Der deutsche Generalstabsoffizier: Seine Auswahl und Ausbildung in Reichswehr, Wehrmacht und Bundeswehr.* Frankfurt am Main: Bernard & Graefe, 1968.

Müller, Klaus-Jürgen. *Armee, Politik und Gesellschaft in Deutschland 1933–1945: Studien zum Verhältnis von Armee und NS-System.* Paderborn: Schöningh, 1979.

———. *Armee und drittes Reich 1933–1939: Darstellung und Dokumentation.* Paderborn: Schöningh, 1987.

———. "Clausewitz, Ludendorff and Beck: Some Remarks on Clausewitz' Influence on German Military Thinking in the 1930s and 1940s." *Journal of Strategic Studies* 9 (1986): 240–66.

———. "Deutsche Militär-Elite in der Vorgeschichte des Zweiten Weltkrieges." In *Die deutschen Eliten und der Weg in den Zweiten Weltkrieg,* edited by Martin Broszat and Klaus Schwabe, 226–90. Munich: C. H. Beck, 1989.

———. *General Ludwig Beck: Studien und Dokumente zur politisch-militärischen Vorstellungswelt und Tätigkeit des Generalstabschefs des deutschen Heeres 1933–1938.* Boppard: Harald Boldt, 1980.

———. *Das Heer und Hitler: Armee und nationalsozialistisches Regime 1933–1940.* Stuttgart: Deutsche Verlags-Anstalt, 1969.

Müller, Rolf-Dieter, and Gerd R. Ueberschär. *Hitler's War in the East, 1941–1945: A Critical Assessment.* Translation of texts by Bruce D. Little. Providence, R.I.: Berghahn Books, 1997.

Müller, Rolf-Dieter, and Hans-Erich Volkmann, eds. *Die Wehrmacht: Mythos und Realität.* Im Auftrag des Militärgeschichtlichen Forschungsamtes. Munich: Oldenbourg, 1999.

Müller-Hillebrand, Burkhart. *Das Heer, 1933–1945: Entwicklung des organisatorischen Aufbaues.* 3 vols. Darmstadt: E. S. Mittler, 1954–69.

Murawski, Erich. "Die amtliche deutsche Kriegsberichterstattung im zweiten Weltkriege." *Publizistik* 7 (1962): 158–64.

———. *Der deutsche Wehrmachtbericht 1939–1945. Ein Beitrag zur Untersuchung der geistigen Kriegführung. Mit einer Dokumentation der Wehrmachtberichte vom 1.7.1944 bis zum 9.5.1945.* Boppard: Harald Boldt, 1962.

Murray, Williamson. *The Change in the European Balance of Power, 1938–1939: The Path to Ruin.* Princeton, N.J.: Princeton University Press, 1984.

———. "Clausewitz: Some Thoughts on What the Germans Got Right." *Journal of Strategic Studies* 9 (1986): 267–86. Also reprinted in *Clausewitz and Modern Strategy,* edited by Michael I. Handel, 267–86. Totowa, N.J.: Frank Cass, 1986.

———. "The German Response to Victory in Poland: A Case Study in Professionalism." *Armed Forces and Society* 7 (1981): 285–98.

———. *Luftwaffe.* Baltimore, Md.: Nautical and Aviation Publishing Company of America, 1985.

———. "Net Assessment in Nazi Germany in the 1930s." In *Calculations: Net Assessment and the Coming of World War II,* edited by Williamson Murray and Allan R. Millett, 60–96. New York: Free Press, 1992.

O'Neill, Robert J. *The German Army and the Nazi Party, 1933–1939.* London: Cassell, 1966.

Ose, Dieter. *Entscheidung im Westen, 1944: Der Oberbefehlshaber West und die Abwehr der alliierten Invasion.* Stuttgart: Deutsche Verlags-Anstalt, 1982.

Otto, Helmut. "Illusion und Fiasko: Der Blitzkriegsstrategie gegen Frankreich 1914." *Militärgeschichte* 28 (1989): 301–8.

Overmans, Ruediger. *Deutsche militärische Verluste im Zweiten Weltkrieg.* Munich: Oldenbourg, 1999.

Overy, R. J. *Goering: The "Iron Man."* London: Routledge & Kegan Paul, 1984.

Paine, Lauran. *German Military Intelligence in World War II: The Abwehr.* New York: Stein & Day, 1984.

Parker, Geoffrey. *The Grand Strategy of Philip II.* New Haven, Conn.: Yale University Press, 1998.

Petrova, Ada, and Peter Watson. *The Death of Hitler: The Full Story with New Evidence from Secret Russian Archives.* New York: W. W. Norton, 1995.

Pinson, Koppel S. *Modern Germany: Its History and Civilization.* 2d ed. New York: Macmillan, 1966: Reprint, Prospect Heights, Ill.: Waveland Press, 1989.

Preston, Paul. *Franco: A Biography.* New York: Basic Books, 1994.

Raudzens, George. "Blitzkrieg Ambiguities: Doubtful Usage of a Famous Word." *War and Society* 7 (1989): 77–94.

Regling, Volkmar. "Grundzüge der Landkriegführung zur Zeit des Absolutismus und im 19. Jahrhundert." In *Handbuch zur deutschen Militärgeschichte: 1648-1939,* edited by Militärgeschichtliches Forschungsamt, vol. 9, 11–425. Munich: Bernard & Graefe, 1979.

Reinhardt, Klaus. *Die Wende vor Moskau: Das Scheitern der Strategie Hitlers im Winter 1941/42.* Stuttgart: Deutsche Verlags-Anstalt, 1972. English translation: *Moscow—The Turning Point: The Failure of Hitler's Strategy in the Winter of 1942-42.* Translated by Karl B. Keenan. Providence, R.I.: Berg, 1992.

Ritter, Gerhard. *The Schlieffen Plan: Critique of a Myth.* New York: Praeger, 1958.

———. *The Sword and the Scepter: The Problem of Militarism in Germany.* Translated by Heinz Norden. 4 vols. Coral Gables, Fla.: University of Miami Press, 1969.

Robertson, E. M. *Hitler's Pre-War Policy and Military Plans, 1933-1939.* New York: Citadel Press, 1967.

Rosinski, Herbert. *The German Army.* Edited and with an introduction by Gordon A. Craig. New York: Praeger, 1966.

Rothenberg, Gunther E. *The Art of Warfare in the Age of Napoleon.* Bloomington: University of Indiana Press, 1978.

———. "Moltke, Schlieffen, and the Doctrine of Strategic Envelopment." In *Makers of Modern Strategy from Machiavelli to the Nuclear Age,* edited by Peter Paret, 296–325. Princeton N.J.: Princeton University Press, 1986.

Salewski, Michael. *Die deutsche Seekriegsleitung 1935-1945.* 3 vols. Frankfurt am Main: München: Bernard & Graefe, 1970–75.

Samuels, Martin. *Command or Control? Command, Training and Tactics in the British and German Armies, 1888-1918.* London: Frank Cass, 1995.

Scheurig, Bodo. *Alfred Jodl. Gehorsam und Verhängnis. Biographie.* Berlin: Propyläen, 1991.

Schmidt-Richberg, Wiegand. *Die Generalstäbe in Deutschland 1871-1945: Aufgaben in der Armee und Stellung im Staate.* Stuttgart: Deutsche Verlags-Anstalt, 1962.

Schott, Franz Josef. "Der Wehrmachtführungsstab im Führerhauptquartier 1939-1945." Ph.D. diss., University of Bonn, 1980.

Schreiber, Gerhard. "The Mediterranean in Hitler's Strategy in 1940. 'Programme' and Military Planning." In *The German Military in the Age of Total War,* edited by Wilhelm Deist, 240–81. Dover, N.H.: Berg, 1985.

Schützle, Kurt. "Au sujet de l'organisation des organes suprêmes de la Wehrmacht fasciste conformément à la theorie sur la guerre totale." *Revue Internationale d'Histoire Militaire* 47 (1980): 107–28.

Seaton, Albert. *The German Army, 1933–45.* London: Weidenfeld & Nicolson, 1982.

Shanahan, William O. *Prussian Military Reforms, 1786–1813.* New York: Columbia University Press, 1945.

Showalter, Dennis. "The Eastern Front and German Military Planning, 1871–1914: Some Observations." *East European Quarterly* 15 (1981): 163–80.

———. "German Grand Strategy: A Contradiction in Terms?" *Militärgeschichtliche Mitteilungen* 48 (1990): 65–102.

———. "Past and Future: The Military Crisis of the Weimar Republic." *War and Society* 14 (1996): 49–72.

Siegler, Fritz Frhr. von. *Die höheren Dienststellen der deutschen Wehrmacht 1933–1945.* Munich: Institut für Zeitgeschichte, 1953.

Spires, David N. *Image and Reality: The Making of the German Officer, 1921–1933.* Westport, Conn.: Greenwood Press, 1984.

Stamps, T. Dodson, and Vincent J. Esposito. *A Military History of World War II (Atlas).* West Point, N.Y.: Department of Military Art and Engineering, United States Military Academy, 1956.

Stegemann, Bernd. "Der Entschluss zum Unternehmen Barbarossa. Strategie oder Ideologie?" *Geschichte in Wissenschaft und Unterricht* 33 (1982): 205–13.

Stolfi, R. H. S. *Hitler's Panzers East: World War II Reinterpreted.* Norman: University of Oklahoma Press, 1991.

Strachan, Hew. *European Armies and the Conduct of War.* London: Allen & Unwin, 1983.

Stumpf, Reinhard. "Probleme der Logistik im Afrikafeldzug 1941–1943." In *Die Bedeutung der Logistik für die militärische Führung von der Antike bis in die neueste Zeit,* edited by Militärgeschichtliches Forschungsamt. Herford: E. S. Mittler & Sohn, 1986.

———. *Die Wehrmacht-Elite: Rang- und Herkunftstruktur der deutschen Generale und Admirale 1933–1945.* Boppard: Harald Boldt, 1982.

Syring, Enrico. "Hitler's Kriegserklärung an Amerika vom 11. Dezember 1941." In *Der Zweite Weltrieg: Analysen, Grundzüge, Forschungsbilanz,* ed. Wolfgang Michalka, 683–96. Munich: Piper, 1989.

Taylor, Telford. *The March of Conquest: The German Victories in Western Europe, 1940.* New York: Simon & Schuster, 1958.

———. *Munich: The Price of Peace.* Garden City, N.Y.: Doubleday, 1979.

———. *Sword and Swastika: Generals and Nazis in the Third Reich.* Chicago: Quadrangle Books, 1952.

Thomas, David. "Foreign Armies East and German Military Intelligence in Russia, 1941–45." *Journal of Contemporary History* 22 (1987): 261–302.

Travers, Timothy. *The Killing Ground: The British Army, the Western Front, and the Emergence of Modern Warfare, 1900–1918.* London: Allen & Unwin, 1987.

Trevor-Roper, H. R. *The Last Days of Hitler.* New York: Macmillan, 1947.

Walde, Karl J. *Guderian.* Frankfurt am Main: Berlin, Wien: Ullstein, 1976.

Wallach, Jehuda L. *The Dogma of the Battle of Annihilation: The Theories of Clausewitz and Schlieffen and Their Impact on the German Conduct of Two World Wars.* Westport, Conn.: Greenwood Press, 1986.

———. "Misperceptions of Clausewitz' *On War* by the German Military." *Journal of Strategic Studies* 9 (1986): 213–39.

Weinberg, Gerhard. *The Foreign Policy of Hitler's Germany: Diplomatic Revolution in Europe, 1933–36.* Chicago: University of Chicago Press, 1983.

———. "German Plans for Victory, 1944–45." *Central European History* 26 (1993): 215–28.

———. *Germany, Hitler, and World War II: Essays in Modern German and World History.* New York: Cambridge University Press, 1995.

———. "Some Thoughts on World War II." *Journal of Military History* 56 (1992): 659–68.

———. "Why Hitler Declared War on the United States." *MHQ: The Quarterly Journal of Military History* 4, no. 3 (1992): 8–17.

———. *A World at Arms: A Global History of World War II.* New York: Cambridge University Press, 1994.

Westphal, Siegfried. *The German Army in the West.* London: Cassell & Co., 1951.

White, Charles Edward. *The Enlightened Soldier: Scharnhorst and the Militärische Gesellschaft in Berlin, 1801–1805.* New York: Praeger, 1989.

Wilhelm, Hans-Heinrich, ed. "Hitlers Ansprache vor Generalen und Offiziere am 26. Mai 1944." *Militärgeschichtliche Mitteilungen* 20 (1976): 123–70.

———. "Die Prognosen der Abteilung Fremde Heere Ost 1942–1945." In *Zwei Legenden aus dem Dritten Reich,* 7–75. Stuttgart: Deutsche Verlags-Anstalt, 1974.

Wilt, Alan F. *War from the Top: German and British Military Decision-making During World War II.* London: Tauris, 1990.

Wright, Jonathan, and Paul Stafford. "Hitler, Britain and the Hossbach Memorandum." *Militärgeschichtliche Mitteilungen* 2 (1987): 77–123.

Zabecki, David T. *Steel Wind: Colonel Georg Bruchmüller and the Birth of Modern Artillery.* Westport, Conn.: Praeger, 1994.

Ziemke, Earl F. "Franz Halder at Orsha: The German General Staff Seeks a Consensus." *Military Affairs* 39 (1975): 173–76.

———. *Stalingrad to Berlin: The German Defeat in the East.* Washington, D.C.: U.S. Army Center of Military History, 1987.

Ziemke, Earl F., and Magna E. Bauer. *Moscow to Stalingrad: Decision in the East.* Washington, D.C.: U.S. Government Printing Office, 1987.

Zoepf, Arne W. *Wehrmacht zwischen Tradition und Ideologie. Der NS-Führungsoffizier im Zweiten Weltkrieg.* Frankfurt am Main: Lang, 1988.

SPECIALIST BIBLIOGRAPHICAL WORKS

Buck, Gerhard. "Das Führerhauptquartier: Seine Darstellung in der deutschen Literatur." *Jahresbibliographie der Bibliothek für Zeitgeschichte* 38 (1966): 549–66.

Hubatsch, Walther. "Das Kriegstagebuch als Geschichtsquelle." *Wehrwissenschaftliche Rundschau,* 15 (1965) 615–23.

Jacobsen, Hans-Adolf. "Das 'Halder-Tagebuch' als historische Quelle." In *Festschrift Percy Ernst Schramm zu seinum siebzigsten Geburtstag von Schülern und Freunden zugeeignet.* Edited by Peter Classen. Wiesbaden: Franz Steiner, 1961, 251ff.

Showalter, Dennis. *German Military History, 1648–1982: A Critical Bibliography.* New York: Garland, 1984.

Index